FOUNDATIONS
OF EDUCATION

A Social View

FOUNDATIONS
OF EDUCATION
A Social View

edited by
ALBERT W. VOGEL
JOHN T. ZEPPER
DAVID L. BACHELOR

Albuquerque
UNIVERSITY OF NEW MEXICO PRESS

Contents

General Introduction

This anthology began as many anthologies began—out of a need. And like all anthologists, we thought our anthology would be different.

It is intended for a first course for prospective teachers. All colleges or departments of education have such a course, and ours had grown larger and larger over the years. And, as the students pointed out from time to time, irrelevant. The faculty of the Department of Educational Foundations decided to do something about it. Changing the size of the classes was not a difficult job. We had been using our graduate students ineffectively as discussion group leaders—in spite of their experience or training. We changed our scheduling arrangements so that each of the graduate students could teach one or two sections of Foundations of Education under supervision. All of the instructors participated during the first semester in an Internship course which was responsible for all the details of classroom management. The new program also included tutoring in the local public schools or with the Career Opportunities Programs on campus by the students taking the introductory course.

Finding a relevant text was another matter. There are several kinds of books designed for courses at this level. We examined "introductory" texts but felt they were usually too generalized and often trivial. These books too often have the word "introduction" in the text and try to say *everything* about education—except, in many cases, the truth. Our students sensed the gap between their own experience and the idealized world of the book. A second kind of book also proved unsatisfactory. That was the One Man—One Philosophy book that set out the ideas of some distinguished educators. Unhappily, this kind of book too often describes things the way they are in the head of the author rather than the way they are in the world. For several years we used George Kneller's *Foundations of Education,* an excellent book in many ways, but too general from our point of view. Other anthologies seemed to suffer from the same defect. They covered too much, were uneven, and tried to meet the demands of every course offered anywhere in the country.

We determined that our collection of readings could do more by doing less. We asked the instructors of each of the sections to go to the library and bring back readings they thought they needed and could not find in the available textbooks. The instructors who assisted in collecting those readings were Dale M. Johnson, Rose A. Wallace, and Thomas R. Lopez, Jr. Others who contributed articles were John T. Abrahamson, Karen Belgrade, G. P. Duquette, Douglas A. Franklin, Gloria E. Griffin, Stanley K. Lester, Michael T. Long, and William Vineyard.

After they had compiled the stack of essays, articles, book chapters, etc., we sorted the materials into categories. Five categories leaped up at us immediately: Classrooms and Schools, Teachers, Pupils and Families, Community, Programs of Reform. There were some miscellaneous pieces left over, and we decided to leave them out. The first four categories seemed to us to come together as a unit describing a portion of the sociology of education—the portion our instructors and their students felt was most important in a first course in education. The fifth category seemed to fill our need for something hopeful, pointing in the direction of possible ways teachers might participate in social reform through education. We underscore the word *participate*. We find that even the most optimistic undergraduates no longer feel that education can solve all of the world's problems by itself.

Our insistence that we do more by doing less caused us to leave out things others might have included. We do not deal with curriculum, professionalism, or research. Nor do we deal with foreign school systems or psychology and learning theory, although the materials provide ample opportunity for an individual instructor to go off on those tangents if he wishes. But with only a limited amount of time at our disposal, we will be satisfied if our students understand the school as a social system—its strengths and weaknesses. There is plenty of time for the other matters in a good, well-thought-out program of teacher preparation.

Our most important need, however, was for realistic and relevant multicultural materials. Many of the anthologies we examined had a chapter on "Mexican-Americans," "Blacks," "Puerto Ricans," or others, but they were not integrated into the other parts of the book. We wanted ours to be organic. This approach we hope will give our prospective teachers a more realistic sense of the cultural mix which constitutes the American classroom.

We had originally intended our anthology to be local. If one accepts even part of the notion that America is a pluralistic society consisting of numerous minority, ethnic, social, or regional groups, it would be pointless to try to cover them all. In fact, our investigations of other anthologies showed us that all too often the anthologists' efforts to become global had forced them to spread themselves too thin. For the most part, our materials are either general in the sense that they have meaning throughout the country, or local in that they tend to be drawn from the Southwestern part of the United States. But looking back on our compilation, we're not so sure that our book is as regional as it seems. The principles that should emerge with the help of a skillful instructor are applicable throughout the country.

America is a great country not because it is one people, but because it is many people. And it is the sense of cultural complexity and diversity that needs to be preserved. Any instructor who needs this book, or who cannot add to it from his own scholarship, is a failure. The book is aimed at the *student,* to give him a sense of the complex social nature of America and its schools. We are not able to offer final solutions to cultural problems, but we can take a step forward toward understanding. Almost forty years ago Willard Waller described the school, and teachers, in a manner that is still appropriate.

> The belief is abroad that young people ought to be trained to think the world a little more beautiful and much more just than it is, as they ought to think men more honest and women more virtuous than they are. . . . There are other ideals which are nearly out of print, because people do not believe in them any more. Though most adults have left such ideals behind, they are not willing to discard them finally. The school must keep them alive. The school must serve as a museum of virtue. [1]

We believe that the hanging onto antique virtues in schools and colleges is the proximate starting point for understanding the unrest and rebellion in schools, the radicalism on campuses, the strong relationship between minority group membership and school failure. Only when this relationship is grasped and the "museum of virtue" function of schools is repudiated can the schools become more pertinent to the fearful stresses our society now faces. What we hope to have some hand in training is a generation of teachers who are free of the sentimental illusions about education which have characterized professional education for too long. What we want are relevant, hard-nosed educators who see the school as a social phenomenon, desperately in need of reform, desperately in need of new ideas, desperately in need of people who will be strong enough to use those new ideas. Education needs people who will see first of all that the school is an institution that possesses all of the faults and the blindnesses of the society around it and of the human candition.

The short introductions which begin the five parts of this book are unsigned because in many ways—although not entirely—they represent the views of the editors together. The introduction to Part IV also had the help of Thomas R. Lopez, Jr.

Albert W. Vogel
John Thomas Zepper
David L. Bachelor
Department of Educational Foundations
University of New Mexico
Albuquerque, New Mexico

NOTES: GENERAL INTRODUCTION

1. Willard Waller, *Sociology of Teaching* (New York: Russell and Russell, 1961—first published in 1932), pp. 33-34.

Part 1

CLASSROOMS AND SCHOOLS

Introduction

To describe American classrooms and schools in any detail would require more space than we can afford here. Part of the difficulty lies in their ambiguity. Broadly speaking, American schoolrooms all look alike. True, there have been a few innovations in recent years, such as sliding walls, but beyond that they haven't changed much in the past hundred years or so. They still smell of chalk, and they still have a desk at one end, behind or upon which the teacher sometimes sits. Under the windows there may be a row of cabinets in the more modern schools. Nowadays the desk-chair units probably aren't bolted to the floor, but the illusion of freedom is just that, an illusion. It would surprise millions of students if we described the desk-chair units as anything but torture racks. If it is an art room there may be a sink (too small), and then again there may not be. The art room might also contain additional cabinets for art supplies: i.e., construction paper, scissors, glue, watercolors, and poster board. In many art classes, making posters for athletic events is an important part of the art program. The band may have a band room, or then again it may practice in the "all-purpose room" between the body odors of the physical education class and the cooking odors of lunch (surprisingly good, in fact, considering the cost, facilities, and training of the lunchroom staff.) Every so often the faculty will have a meeting in the "all-purpose room" and they will sit listening to the principal tell them things they already know or aren't interested in. The information communicated from principal to teacher probably concerns matters of routine maintenance (the mimeograph machine is broken again, wash your own cups in the lounge) that could have been duplicated and sent around, but the principal has learned that no one reads his memos unless they happen to be writing a satirical novel. The P.E. instructor, who comes to the meeting in his sweatshirt ("Property of Something-or-Other Athletic Department") and wash pants—a special dispensation—falls asleep halfway through the meeting. He sells real estate on the weekends and studies school administration during the summer. If it is a high school, the faculty dress by subject: tweed and longish hair for English and the social studies; bow ties for the science teachers on the assumption that four-in-hands get into chemicals or burnt in Bunsen burners. The principal wears a dark suit and black shoes. The white socks are a holdover from his days as a coach. The principal worries a great deal about the skirt length of his junior female faculty and (if it is a high school) the effect of such short

3

skirts upon the students. If it is an elementary school with a high percentage of young women teachers, he worries about the skirts also, but for reasons deep in the recesses of his mind. He watches younger male faculty for signs of beginning sideburns, mustaches, or beards. He wears his own hair short and has since his days in the service. Many of the young women on the faculty are thinking about marriage. But their minds wander over the whole spectrum of human thought. At social gatherings they talk about the school, and on weekends, driving by, they feel the impulse to go in.

The students know nothing of this. There are traditions, of course: Mr. So-and-So is "queer," Miss So-and-So and Miss So-and-So have been good friends for years. A certain biology teacher, now in her fifties and recently taken to wearing exaggerated makeup, is rumored to have had an affair with the captain of the football team twenty years ago. There are stories about a wild NEA convention and something the principal did, but the details have not survived intact. But for the most part the students have difficulty ascribing human characteristics to their teachers and feel embarrassed surprise when they meet them in public places.

The PTA will meet in the "all-purpose room" later in the week.

A good school is a quiet school. The rooms are well ventilated and the shades properly adjusted. In the afternoon the shades should draw a straight line from window to window on the street side. In a good school, students do not go to the restroom without a pass. They do not litter the school grounds. They show respect for their teachers and do not throw milk boxes at lunchtime. In a good high school they do not riot at basketball games although there is every reason to hate the opponents. A good school develops good sportsmanship on the field and off.

In a good classroom assignments are turned in on time, neatly. Report cards are returned, signed, on the day designated. All rules of the teacher, whether pertaining to academics or discipline, are obeyed or grades suffer. Occasionally the good must suffer along with the bad for some major infraction of discipline. The material in the text is covered in the time allotted. One does not cheat on tests, discuss pregnancy (real or imagined), curse, drop acid, have sexual fantasies, or worry about war.

In a good school, students do not have drunken parents, are not poor, and do not have special problems because they are Black, Brown, Red, Yellow, talk funny, talk a different language, or limp. Everyone gets equal treatment and those who apply themselves will go a long way. Education is a good investment. Children are our most important national resource.

There are variations, of course. And perhaps less ambiguity than we thought at the beginning of this essay. Teaching is teaching, the same one place as another; students are individuals, but all about the same after all. People are people after all. Just cover the material in the course outline. . . .

I

Illusions and Disillusions in American Education*

THEODORE BRAMELD

I

The volatile state of education today is illustrated by articles recently featured
on the covers of two mass-circulation magazines: "Angry Teachers—Why They
Will Strike 300 Times This School Year" and "Students Against the World."

These feature stories are unprecedented. Neither could hardly have been
imagined a year or two ago. Each symbolizes the phenomenal unrest that has
begun to permeate educational events. They signalize a movement that has already succeeded in penetrating and, in some respects, even shattering the whole
facade of beliefs, processes, and structures that have hitherto seemed impervious
to if not oblivious of inadequacies in the vast institution of modern education.

I use the term "facade" deliberately because, to an extraordinary extent,
education in America (in many other parts of the world as well) is now demonstrating itself to be an increasingly artificial if not obsolete enterprise—artificial
and obsolete in the sense that it distorts, conceals, and avoids many of the most
fundamental perplexities and compulsions of our age. I should like accordingly
to present a series of what may be termed great "illusions" and "disillusions" of
contemporary education. By the former I mean, of course, the fallacies and
shibboleths that remain only too apparent. By the latter I imply, however, more
than a negative connotation: Disillusionment is often the forerunner of reawak-
ening and renewal. It is largely in this sense that I speak of "disillusion."

One cannot, of course, list all that might be included in such a series. Moreover, with the aim of succinctness, I am compelled invariably to oversimplify.
Nevertheless, my examples should serve to establish the contention that education is today being forged as a double-edged sword. With one edge, it proves a
novel capability to cut through more and more of the facade; in this sense it
plays the indispensable role of exposing its own obsolescences. With the other
edge, it enables us to consider how this capability may be channeled toward
more impelling alternatives—toward reconstructed beliefs, processes, structures,
and most crucially toward new and urgent goals that are the fruits of its own
disillusions.

*Copyright 1968 by Phi Delta Kappa. Reprinted by permission of the publisher from *Phi Delta Kappan*, December 1968, pp. 202-06.

II

Here, then are ten of our illusions.

1. Education's primary task has always been and must always be to perpetuate the customs, attitudes, practices, and institutions that prevail from generation to generation. This still-dominant characteristic, although not always explicitly rationalized, is maintained not only by many educators but by remarkably large quotas of psychologists, sociologists, and anthropologists. Terms familiar in this context may include "adjustment," "socialization," "enculturation," and "transmission."

2. It follows from No. 1 that the primary task of teaching is to assure such perpetuation, thereby qualifying each successive generation for induction into and approval by adult society. This task is exemplified in modern America by the heavy emphasis placed upon preparatory curricula of the secondary school, and thus upon the kinds of training that enable the young to climb the social and economic ladder by admission to higher institutions of education, preferably those of such prestigious standing as virtually to assure acceptance by the more affluent sections of that society.

3. Conversely, the primary task of learning is to respond to the task of teaching noted in No. 2. Today, this capacity is being refined and accelerated by the new technology—particularly by the multimillion-dollar complexes of what is often referred to as the "educational hardware" industry. With its proliferation of automatized gadgetry, the learner can be increasingly "prepared" in highly systematized conveyer-belt teaching factories, hitherto known as schools.

4. Largely because of the assumptions embodied in Nos. 1, 2, and 3, educational institutions have been effectively organized and controlled chiefly by means of hierarchical structures of authority centering in school boards and boards of trustees, and through these in their appointed representatives: college presidents, deans, superintendents of schools, principals, and lesser echelons who determine policies and implement them in the practices of learning and teaching. Students are expected to recognize and accept such authority, since it provides, after all, the legitimate basis on which they are admitted in the first place.

5. From No. 4 it follows that the proper role of the teaching profession is to perform the duties established under the same hierarchical system. Such duties, being professional, cannot justify any behavior on the part of teachers, and still less so of college professors, who besmirch their status by "unprofessional" conduct that disturbs in any notable way the sanctions of "professional" conduct already ordained by the directors of this system.

6. From No. 4, also, it follows that the obligation of students is to perceive and respect the established criteria of knowledge and wisdom that those in authority have approved by the virtue of their academic appointees. After all, are not students in schools and colleges to learn from superiors assigned to teach them? This rhetorical question applies to the higher learning. But it applies even

more completely to the lower levels where immaturity and inexperience can only be guided by those who are qualified because they are mature and experienced.

7. From No. 6 we may infer that the responsibility of education, being primarily that of continuous transmission of such cultural behavior as habits, attitudes, and wisdom, centers in those *kinds* of learning that are most universally acceptable and most useful to society. These have differed at different times, of course, but today they are characterized above all in the demands of an age of industrial technology. Hence the curriculum, especially of the primary school, is weighted with the teaching of proper rules of social acceptance and necessary skills such as reading and writing, whereas that of the secondary school is weighted with such subject matters as mathematics and science to assure manpower for our burgeoning technology.

8. By the same token, characteristics of the curriculum that do not lend themselves directly to this supreme imperative tend, justifiably, to be relegated to second, third, or fourth strata of importance. The musical and graphic arts in the primary and secondary schools are one example. Another is the social studies, where American history alone is oftener than not considered the one academic essential to cultural perpetuity but where other dimensions of cultural experience, because they are more liable to controversial interpretation and therefore to public criticism, are best treated mildly if at all. I refer, of course, to such dimensions as the major political strife of capitalism and communism, to class conflicts, to sexual and religious issues, to civilizations of the East or Africa, and to complex dilemmas of international polity versus national sovereignty. Sometimes, to be sure, they may be treated with care. By and large, nevertheless, they are not; and it is only another illusion to pretend that they are.

9. Education, like virtue, is a wonderful achievement, and almost everybody believes in it. But this is not to say that to believe in it should require the nation to provide financial support for this institution anything like that of certain other institutions—above all, the military. Teachers and students should be grateful that the amount of expenditure is presently by far the highest in our history. Coupled with this gratitude should be another, especially among Americans, that no federal authority supervises education. Just as most of the money is provided by local or at most state taxation, so too does educational authority remain rightly decentralized.

10. The same tradition is, of course, extended to the control of education on an international scale. Despite the magnificent efforts of UNESCO, we must remember that this is not an international educational authority. It is a vehicle for nations who may or may not wish to cooperate with it. Nationalism remains the ultimate educational authority, just as it does for political authority in the United Nations as a whole.

III

Now an extraordinary fact of today is, I believe, that not a single one of these ten attitudes, policies, or practices (not including others here neglected) can withstand searching scrutiny. Some, perhaps, are less glaringly suspect than others. But all are beginning to waver, and some are threatened even now with virtual disintegration.

One point by way of anticipation. The reader will already have observed that none of these illusions is to be characterized as *totally* illusory. Let us then generously term them "half-illusions." Like half-truths, however, half-illusions are extremely treacherous. We have learned only too painfully from current political rhetoric that half-truths often prove to be more insidious than total falsehoods. It is these as much as total illusions that now compel us to view our selected series of ten as, more exactly, disillusions.

1. The underlying and usually unstated belief that education is an instrument of social and cultural transmission is an excellent case in point. Of course, education does provide indispensable cultural continuity. (This function is just as indispensable to so-called nonliterate cultures that often have no formal educational systems at all.)

The distortion derives from steadily growing evidence that the learning-teaching process, inclusively defined, is rarely if ever reducible to mere transmission. Anthropological research (not always sufficiently noted, to be sure, by anthropologists themselves) demonstrates that all cultures undergo degrees of modification by virtue of the obvious fact that they are never static. More or less constantly, therefore, their members confront degrees of novelty if only because the evolutionary process is itelf always novel—a generalization demonstrated sometimes dramatically but oftener modestly in their struggles to combat and control their inanimate and animate environments. Anyone, for example, who has watched perhaps the most primitive culture on earth today (the Australian aborigines) is struck by the fantastic ingenuity with which they search out and discover food, invent their own tools, and in many ways demonstrate abilities and skills suitable to their arduous needs. How more truly, then, do complex and sophisticated cultures prove their own genius for originality, discovery, and inventiveness.

The point I wish to make penetrates still more deeply into the whole psychology of learning and teaching than is commonly assumed. It takes issue with the behaviorist assumptions that have recently obsessed so many psychological practitioners under the influence of B. F. Skinner and his coterie of followers. And it equally undergirds a major quality of the nature of human power. Surely, however, to belabor further the creative capabilities latent if not always overt in human experience is itself redundant. One may only recall the amazing achievements that abound in the arts—in painting, the dance, sculpture, music, architecture, and others—through millennia of history and across all continents.

A great deal more could be said about our first illusion (as it could for those to follow). Yet even the sparse remarks already offered would be wholly superfluous were we not so often still befuddled by the metacultural assumption of education regarded so predominantly as a "reinforcing" or "socializing" process.

2. The view to be repudiated here is that education, especially for the increasing middle classes of America, France, Japan, and other countries, must be designed primarily to assure the young, and even more their parents, that they should go to college and that in order to do so they must therefore meet the admissions standards established *by* the colleges.

Lively criticism has been generated also against this complacent view. Not only are some of us beginning to question why the typical high school curriculum should so often be tailor-made for the conventional college-bound student, but more seriously we may question whether the curriculum is a defensible one even for him. To a shocking extent both the high school and college curricula of today are the same in overall structure as they were 30 or even more years ago—an "egg-crate" of courses with little if any significant relation either to each other or to the central streams of life around them. All, or mostly all, are still bound on the contrary by the all-too-familiar rubrics of English, mathematics, science, social studies, and foreign language, plus a smattering of peripheral subjects.

3. Until our second illusion is dissipated, the illusion that worthwhile learning can be successfully automated is unlikely to be challenged either. To put the point differently, as long as ambitious, competitive grade-seeking motivations remain as paramount as they are now, school and college hierarchies will respond eagerly to the already high-pressure promotion campaigns of General Electric, Westinghouse, and other huge corporations in open collaboration with the "software industry" of book publishing. But the focal question is whether the kind of efficient, stimulus-response learning induced by this technology can actually produce "educated" people. Disillusionment lies in the greater likelihood, given a free rein, that it will produce excellently conditioned human beings but neither autonomous nor creative ones. *Walden Two, 1984,* and *Brave New World* are only too ominous alternatives.

4. The plausibility of radical challenge to automatization and computerization in education remains remote, in turn, as long as our fourth illusion carries its own heavy burden of influence—namely, that the best organization of education is to be found in models of business, with directors and managers properly in command, and with the rest of the personnel of education largely subject to their orders. The line-staff structure of education, as it is often called, thus becomes by far the most prevailing one. It is also a major source of current student and faculty revolt. Behind this revolt, I submit, is an awakening if still semiconscious realization that the analogy with business models is blatantly false—rather, that education should be conceived as an institution designed not to reinforce efficiency or comparable virtues of the prevailing power structure but rather to encourage critical-mindedness, distinctiveness, "dissentual knowl-

edge," and participation by both students and faculties in every segment of educational life and on every level.

5. I have mentioned faculties here, and thus we return to the illusion of conventional teacher and professional subservience to educational control. It would be difficult to find better samples of exposure to this illusion than a widely quoted statement by Mrs. Ruth Trigg, former president of the Department of Classroom Teachers of the National Education Association:

"I maintain that a teacher who finds himself in a situation where conditions are such that good education is an impossibility, having exhausted every other means of improving those conditions with no success, should walk out. I further maintain that this teacher shows more dedication to his profession than does the teacher who stays on the job, perpetuating mediocrity. Perhaps the child's education will be interrupted for a week or a month, but what is one week or one month when measured against years of education, all less than adequate? If the teacher's militancy leads to improved conditions of learning, the child's opportunities are enhanced for a lifetime."

Here surely is a remarkable reputation of encrusted mores of the teaching profession. Yet it is only a more general statement of another even more pointed one by David Selden, an official spokesman for the labor-affiliated American Federation of Teachers:

"I think the best thing that can happen to this country is a nation-wide teachers' strike to bring about the vast improvement in schools that we need."

If one recalls events in several cities during the past year in the light of what Mrs. Trigg and Mr. Selden have said, he will agree that illusion No. 5 may be on the verge of collapse. And if he underscores such a likelihood with the record of teachers' organizations in several other countries, he must perceive this phenomenon even more clearly. In Japan, for example, Nikkyoso, the national Teachers' Union, is not only the largest union in the entire country but one of the most militant, most politically minded opponents of the economic, social, and educational establishment.

6. Closely related to the intensifying militancy of teacher power is, of course, that of students. Here again I can no better pinpoint the fallacy at issue than by a quotation, this time from Professor Alaine Touraine of the University of Paris:

"The student revolt is not merely a crisis of the adaptation of the universities to the modern society, nor is it only a revolt of youth against tradition. Rather, it signals the birth of new conflicts, the first act in the drama of putting the new, computerized industrial state on trial. But it is within the universities that its future lies, because it is there that learning takes place. The student movement is no longer the *avant-garde* of a peasant or worker movement, but the *avant-garde* of itself." What this means, of course, is that increasing minorities of students all the way from Rome, Madrid, and Paris to Rio de Janeiro, Mexico City, and

Tokyo are also defying the creaky apparatus both of learning-teaching and of time-exhausted curricula.

The student upheaval invites a further point of far-reaching relevance. I think that profound, if also subtle and intricate, connections are traceable between student unrest and black unrest. Both kinds already overlap, of course—witness the Columbia University struggles or, before that, the courageous lunch-counter student sit-ins. But whether the alignment is tenuous or not, its roots spread deep into the malaise hinted at by Professor Touraine—a malaise typified by such widely recognized symptoms as alienation with all their accompaniments of guilt, frustration, hatred, and (in the existentialist sense) meaninglessness.

This is surely not to say that the student and the black share *identical* travails. But they do often share *common* ones. The average black is the victim of white racism, as the Commission on Civil Disorders so impressively demonstrated. The average student is the victim of outmoded policies and programs which may just as ubiquitously if often more covertly generate negativism and skepticism toward education and its supporting triple structure of the industrial, political, and military. The students' and, to some extent, teachers' uprisings that have now become chronic herald a deep-seated want of self and social fulfillment quite as urgent as do the blacks' uprisings herald theirs.

The comparison may be carried further. Just as militant organizations such as the Students for a Democratic Society are inclined to reject the more classic sociopolitical theories of radical change, and along with them the dominance of the entrenched generation, so the black power movement has rejected a good deal of older liberal doctrines characterized by integration and equality of opportunity.

May I venture a personal note? Twenty years ago I, too, was much persuaded by these doctrines. As a staff member of both the Bureau for Intercultural Education and later the Center for Human Relations Studies (New York University), I accordingly tried to the best of my ability to contribute to such well-meaning integrative ventures. But today I am convinced that they have largely failed. Instead, I am inclined to sympathize far more strongly with such Negro leaders as I have recently come to know in the Roxbury ghetto of Boston—all of whom, from the most militant to the more moderate, regard black power as the clarion call of their programs. Moreover, after having read only recently one of the most deeply moving and enlightening books I have ever had the privilege of reading—*The Autobiography of Malcolm X*—I hope that I am now somewhat better prepared to identify with the mood of both blacks and students than I could have been earlier.

At the same time, let me seriously question whether the frequently defiant and disillusioning posture of student activism is any more a mature or decisive answer than is black nationalism a mature or decisive answer of our Negro citizens. Both movements are manifestations of anguish, of strength, of courage, of self-respect and group-identity. But both need to be superseded by a more clearly affirmative and powerful set of democratic strategies and goals. To recall an old concept from Hegel, student power and black power are both in a stage of "antithesis" against the older "thesis" of traditional patterns. But both should strive to reach much further than this, just as Malcolm X had himself begun to strive further toward "synthesis" during the last months of his young and tragic life.

7 and 8. These two illusions may be combined, because both confront the need for what I may call "the disillusioned curriculum"—the overemphasis, on the one hand, of the technological and the underemphasis, on the other, of the esthetic, moral, social, and humanistic. In both cases, the fallacy centers in what is anticipated in previous comments upon the revolt of the younger generation, white and black alike. Its correction lies in thorough rebuilding of prevailing curricula of the public schools and colleges—a rebuilding already inherent in sweeping demands for maximum satisfaction of human needs and wants, and of great aspirations that hitherto have only in small measure been recognized or gratified.

Here again difficult questions confront us, for on paper there are almost as many curricula as there are curriculum planners. Yet the crucial question remains clear enough: *whether learning and teaching both as process and in substantive quality can cope directly, constantly, penetratingly, with the central character of human life itself.* Plenty of evidence points to the answer; indeed, some schools all the way from Summerhill in England to Tamagawa Gakuen in Japan are already proving that this kind of energizing and transformative adventure is both practicable and vastly exciting.

Of course, the curriculum envisaged here does not minimize necessary transmissive skills such as reading. What it does demonstrate, as John Dewey so brilliantly wrote in one of his more neglected and least remembered books, is that "interest and effort" in education are reciprocal, not antagonistic, propensities of human learning. To promote this kind of reciprocity is never, to be sure, easy—certainly not when, by the time typical students reach high school, they have often become so miseducated and hence so unmotivated both by the egg-crate curriculum and by ordained requirements of learning that one should be astonished to find how comparatively small the dropout rate actually is.

The disillusioned and therefore innovated curriculum is, by contrast, geared at every stage to the very real experience of learners—and no matter of what age. Consequently, it means that something like half of all the school program occurs, not in the formal classroom at all, but in the local, regional, national, and ultimately international community. It means that teachers are effectively trained anthropologically and sociologically as well as psychologically, and hence that both they and students engage in continuous, expertly directed involvement all the way from nearby ghetto life to fairly distant foreign cultures. It means that the surrounding natural and social environment is constantly utilized as a boundless resource of learning. Finally, and as a result, it means a freshly designed model of the "community school"—not the caricature we now often hear about but one which provides wide, busy, two-way avenues equally traveled in both directions by learners on the adult level and by children of nursery school age upward.

9. This illusion, you recall, is the hoary one of the alleged evils of economic support and federal control of education. Notwithstanding the expanding political iniquities of the Vietnam cutback, we have already pretty well exploded the myth of local and state financial adequacy for education. But we have hardly begun to think through a political philosophy sufficiently updated to realize not only that enormously strengthened federal support is necessary but that so are carefully formulated practices of federal authority necessary as well.

Thus the relevant issue is not in the least whether we can or should artificially dichotomize federal support and control. Rather, that issue is whether such control is or could be democratically and authentically expressive of the largest possible majority of people. Here, of course, power becomes central once more. Behind it is the question of whether we can still construct a nation with the locus of power genuinely centered in that majority. I do not myself believe that we shall be able to do so until and unless the present network of concentrated industrial, political, and military power is superseded by patterns of modern democratic socialization mandated by and geared to the maximum needs of the citizenry as a whole. Simultaneously, "decentralization" of control counterbalanced with federal control becomes a concomitant principle—not at all for the sake of new forms of authority that could be just as disillusioning as the old, but for the sake of cooperatively developed community plans and tasks by means of which parents, students, and teachers engage in open unrestricted dialogue and arrive as patiently as possible at tenable, functioning, and self-correcting guides of operation.

But these samples of controversial contention themselves precisely illustrate the meaning of a modernized and revitalized curriculum—a curriculum focusing on the pressing, concrete problems of mankind and subjected to the most searching, unmitigated questions and criticisms that can be raised in the adventure of teaching and learning.

10. The illusion of nationalism, as exemplified by the truncated programs of UNESCO, is another example of much the same sort of archaism mentioned just above.

Thus far in this agenda we have, however, paid far less attention to power as ends than to power as means. It is hoped, even so, that power as ends is at least implicit in what has been said about means—in, for example, the as yet only partially, crudely articulated goals of student power and black power.

Nevertheless, a desperate demand arises in education for much more *explicit* attention to these goals—above all, to the goal of a realizable international order. Here is a theme demanding more patient, more probing diagnosis and prognosis than does any other single problem endemic to our time.

The pity is that, to an alarming extent, the means and ends of a viable community of nations remain neglected by most education. One hears, to be sure, occasional lip service to the United Nations. But what in actuality is required is vastly more than this: It is that the problems and expectations of mankind as a whole should become nothing less than the pervading theme of *every* curriculum, beginning in its own terms of maturation at the kindergarten level and extending all the way to the college and adult levels. Here surely is a captivating theme—one compelling us to utilize and to discover all that we can know about the earth's resources, about population control, about the dangers and promises of technology, about the deep-seated conflicts that pervade political-economic struggles, and certainly about the similar as well as dissimilar value patterns of cross-cultural ethnic and racial clusterings. It is a theme that can galvanize and provide direction as no patchwork remedies of the curriculum can possibly provide; that can replace the emptiness and sterility of much of the present program; that can arouse the younger generation (in partnership with the older) to seek and express its own significance and purpose; and finally that can strive for the establishment of a UNESCO with authority to construct a planetary, democratically directed program of education.

Like all the preceding nine illusions that I have outlined, the disillusion of nationalism is not to be interpreted, therefore, in a merely negative sense. The corollary of this disillusion can be the positive and universal affirmation of an earthwide humanity—of life-vitalizing goals that could and should transcend our long overworked illusions.

I should like to reinforce these concluding comments with a passage from another recent book (*The City of Man,* by W. Warren Wagar), which I warmly recommend for its encompassing relevance. Here is a magnificent epitomization of what a curriculum could mean to all our children and to all our citizens:

"Whoever enlists in the cause of man in this age will find no time for nostalgia. We are the link between the traditional civilizations of a well-remembered past and the emergent world civilization. We stand between. If we break under the strain, there will be no future. All posterity is in our keeping. Such a task against such towering odds joins man to man and weaves meaning into the vast fabric of confusion. It can be the difference between the life and death of the soul."

2

"Hey, Man, You Our Principal?"*

LUVERN L. CUNNINGHAM

This is a report. It is as objective as I can make it. The remarks that follow are based on a few days' experience as principal of an inner-city junior high school—a problem-saturated place.

I want it known that although what I say here is critical, it is not intended to be critical of any person or group of persons. But it is an indictment of us all—educators and laymen, critics and the criticized.

The notion of an exchange cropped up out of the woodwork. Someone had an idea that this would be a good thing to do. The big-city people agreed and we agreed and so we were off and running. We didn't have the luxury of much advanced planning time. Had we had a chance to contemplate the event in Columbus (in the peace and quiet and solitude of the ivory tower) we could have lost our courage and copped out on the whole deal. We didn't have that time, so we did appear at our respective schools at the appointed hour, Monday, May 5. On that fateful morning (like little kids going to kindergarten) we picked up our pencil boxes and marched off to the school house.

I arrived at about 7:45 a.m. I had read about the city's riots in 1966 and I knew it was here that they had started. I was aware too that this was a junior high that had been having its share of trouble. I knew that the faculty had walked out in January in protest of school conditions. Most of the faculty stayed away for two days, saying that this school was an unfit place in which to carry on professional activity.

My first several minutes as the new helmsman were exciting, to say the least. I walked in through the front door and introduced myself to the regular principal's secretary. She was most cordial and smiled knowingly. I think she chuckled to herself, thinking that this guy is really in for an education. If those were her feelings she was quite right.

I walked into the office and was about to set my briefcase down. I looked up and there must have been 20 faces, most of them black, all around. And others were coming through the office door. Some were students, some were faculty members with students in tow, others were clerks who wanted me to make some monumental decisions about events of the day.

*Copyright 1969 by Phi Delta Kappa. Reprinted by permission of the publisher from *Phi Delta Kappan*, November 1969, pp. 123-27.

They weren't even in line. They were all just kind of standing around there competing for attention. And to make life more exciting a little black fellow with a flat hat and a cane about two feet long came up to me. He whipped that cane around on his arm and stuck it in my stomach and said, "Hey, man, you our principal?" I began thinking longingly of Columbus and said, "Well, no, I'm not. But I'm here for a week and I am going to be taking his place." I was backpeddling and trying to think of some answer that would make sense to this eighth grade student.

A number of youngsters who were crowding around were just curious; others had problems. One was a girl who had recently been released from a correctional institution and was under court order to come back to school. She was there for an appointment, but she didn't want to come back to this or any other school. She was openly hostile, asking harshly that she not be made to come back. I had no file. I didn't have any background on this young lady. I was unprepared to make a decision. So instead of displaying administrative genius, I said, "Would you sit down over there and I'll talk to you later." She sat—head down, sullen, oblivious to the confusion surrounding us. It was an hour before I got back to her problem.

There was tragedy and comedy. A teacher who was obviously disturbed about something had a very attractive sixteen-year-old girl by the hand. She came in and said, "I understand you're the new principal, Mr. Cunningham. Look at that skirt. Look at that mini-skirt. It's entirely too short. Just look at that thing. I think we ought to send her home. Aren't you going to send her home?"

She turned to the girl and said, "Is your mother home?" The girl said "No." "When will she be home?" "Well, she'll be home about 6:15 tonight."

The teacher turned to me and said, "We can't send her home." Then she marched the girl over in front of me, rolled that brief skirt up several inches and said, "Look at that, it's got a hem in it. It's got a hem in it that long. We ought to be able to take that hem out. Let's go back to the classroom." I didn't have a chance to say a word.

In the meantime other kids were still clustered around. They had their own brand of problems so I said, "Would you go and wait outside the office please and come in one at a time?" They kept coming in with their questions, some that I could answer, most that I could not.

When the first bell rang and the students had to go to their homerooms, faces disappeared, the corridors cleared a bit, and there was an atmosphere of temporary calm. I was able to sit down and try to get my bearings. It was an inauspicious beginning, to say the least.

Let me comment a bit about Lester Butler. Lester was assigned to the principal's office. His responsibility was to be available during free periods for phone calls, delivery of messages, and any other tasks that might appropriately be handled by an eager, intelligent seventh-grader. After quiet had been established in the office on that first day he gave me a quick tour of the building. He took me to the obvious places like the library, the auditorium, the gymnasium, and special classrooms, but he also pointed out the nooks and crannies, the special recesses, the hideaways of the old structure. With his special brand of radar he was able to track me down and bring messages to me during the week when I was about the building. We became unusually fine friends.

This junior high school building is old. The oldest part was built sixty-five years ago. It has had two additions. Despite its age the building has been refurbished from time to time; it was painted and the windows were in. It's not particularly unattractive from the inside, but as a structure to house education it's a nightmare of inefficiency. Traffic patterns are unbelievable. You have to go upstairs to get downstairs. You go upstairs across a kind of plateau and down the other side to reach another part of the building. The arrangements for science and home economics facilities, as well as classrooms housing other particular specialized aspects of the curriculum, do not accommodate decent traffic patterns. When the bell sounds and classes pass it is a wild place. It's wild in between times, too, for that matter.

The absentee rate is very high. Of the nearly 1,800 enrolled, between 350 and 400 were absent every day. Where they were no one really knows. There was no apparent relationship between my presence and the absentee rate; that's the way it is every day. During my first day a counselor took me in his car and just crisscrossed the neighborhood. He wanted to point out the housing, the neighborhood, the fact that the streets were crowded with humanity just milling around. It was a warm week, the first week in May. People were outside. Kids of all ages were all over. There appeared to be as many youngsters on the street as there were in the elementary school and junior and senior highs.

Ironically, everybody shows up during the lunch period. The lunches are partly financed with federal funds and the youngsters are admitted to the lunchroom by ticket. Kids who are truant get into the building (despite door guards) and into the cafeteria. They have something to eat and then melt into the community.

The building is a sea of motion—people are moving about all the time. Adults (teachers, teaching assistants, observers, student teachers, door guards, other people who get in through the doors despite the guards) and students are in the halls all the time. Some of the students have passes to go somewhere given by somebody, but most students are just there. Those who don't have passes have excuses. As a newcomer seeing all of this motion, what should I have done? Should I have gotten tough? Should I have tried to shout them back to class? Should I have threatened such and such? Or should I have turned my head and let them go on about their own purposes? I turned my head.

When I was in my office students would come in with all sorts of questions, grievances, or requests for excuses. Apparently the pattern in the building is that if you can't get a hearing for your complaint anywhere else you end up in the principal's office. I had a steady flow of customers.

The school has eighty-five teachers. There is a high absence rate each day among teachers too. They fail to show up for many reasons. The teacher absentee numbers (while I was there) would range from eleven to fourteen per day. If you have a faculty of eighty-five and fourteen teachers fail to show (and you don't get substitutes), you have to make some kind of ad hoc arrangements quickly to handle the crises. Each day three to five substitutes would appear and they would be assigned quickly to cover classes. But they were not enough. Furthermore, there was little relation between the substitutes' teaching fields and their assignments. The first priority is to put live people in classes to maintain some semblance of order.

The youngsters, as I said, were in motion. I had the feeling that I was walking on a live volcano. Classes were often noisy and rowdy. Fights and squabbles broke out frequently. Fights between girls occurred about five to one more often than fights among boys. But the fights among the girls were often over boys. The adult population was on pins and needles from the time the building opened in the morning until school was out at 3:30 in the afternoon. Everyone hoped to make it through the day without large-scale violence.

The day is organized around eight periods. Students have a number of free periods, during which time they are assigned to study halls. Some go to a large auditorium; others go to classrooms with teachers assigned to study hall duty there. Large numbers congregate in the cafeteria on the ground floor for "study." The cafeteria accommodates around 300 youngsters. Teachers are reluctant to supervise the cafeteria study halls. When they do it is with fear and trembling. The place is noisy. Kids move around despite the efforts of several teachers to keep them seated. They shoot craps. Some play other games. There is bickering and fighting. Kids pick up chairs and fling them across the room at one another. It's dirty and hot.

The whole building is hot, because the custodians cannot shut off the heat. It is the only way to provide hot water for the lunch program. So they keep the stokers going to have hot water for the federally subsidized lunches. Everybody complains about it: the principal, the assistant principals, the teachers, the students, and the PTA.

The lunchroom study halls are unbearable. The undermanned custodial staff is unable to keep the table tops clean; a slimy film covers them. They are neither attractive for eating nor for study purposes. Because of the danger of intruders coming in off the streets, the major cafeteria emergency exit has been nailed shut. Teachers asked the principal to have the custodians do this. The custodians refused because of fire regulations. In desperation the principal himself nailed it shut. Each day he lives in fear that a fire will break out and students will be trapped. Large numbers might not get out through the narrow passageways that serve as entrances and exits. Thus a measure taken to protect the teachers could lead to another type of disaster.

We called the police only once during my stay. It was different at another junior high school where my colleague Lew Hess served as principal. At night following his first day a fire bomb was thrown through his office window. It was a dud and didn't go off. On his last day three fire bombs were thrown inside the building and they did go off. The police and fire department had to be summoned each time.

On the second day, in a classroom study hall right across from my office, a young boy was late. His name was Willy Denton. He was about a minute and a half tardy and his excuse was that he had been next door signing up for a special program of summer employment. The study hall supervisor had obviously had a hectic morning. As Willy entered the room a few words were exchanged. The supervisor grabbed Willy, put a hammerlock around his neck, kind of choked him, and wrestled him out into the corridor. The noise attracted other kids. Immediately there were about forty students as well as door guards right around the teacher and Willy. Willy got free for a moment but the supervisor caught him again, this time grabbing him by the shoulders. He shook him against the lockers and that was like whomping a big bass drum. The sound reverberated around that part of the building and more people came. The supervisor got a fresh hammerlock on Willy, dragged him over to my office, threw him in and across to the other side, and said, "Take charge."

I suppose that I turned whiter in that sea of black, but I took charge. I closed the door and asked Willy to sit down. All of a sudden another teacher opened the door about six inches and shouted, "Willy's got a good head on his shoulders," slammed the door, and left.

It was about 12 noon. The period had just started. There were nearly thirty-five minutes until Willy was to go to another class. So Willy and I just talked. I didn't think that lining him up for swats would make much difference. He was livid. If he had been white he would have been purple. He was furious, and so we just sat and talked.

We talked about what he liked and what he disliked. I asked him if he had worked last summer, since he was going to be employed this coming summer. He said that he had. I asked where and he said, "I worked in a church." And he added, "You know I teach Sunday School." I asked how old his class members were and he said, "Well they're about the same age as I am." "How many do you have?" "About fifteen, and sometimes I teach on Saturdays too." "Do you like to teach?" He said, "Well, it's okay. But boy those first Sundays my stomach just kind of turned around and I didn't know what I was doing. But it's better now. Like last Sunday, did you hear about that plane that was shot down in Korea? You know, we just talked about that. I sat down and we talked about that."

It was clear that Willy loved what he was doing in Sunday School. He liked math too and he planned to go to high school. But he was so angry at that study hall supervisor. He trembled for several minutes; he just couldn't get control. We talked through the balance of the hour till the bell rang. I sent him on to his next class sans swats.

The PTA leaders came in to meet with me on Wednesday. They shared their definitions of the school's problems. I held a faculty meeting on Thursday. And I was amazed at the similarity between faculty and parent sentiments on the issues facing the school.

The teachers, by and large, are a very dedicated lot. Many of them are young; some of them are coming out of MAT programs. Despite their youth they, like the rest of the faculty, are tired, disheartened, even despondent. But they don't want to fail.

One of the teachers was shot ten days before I arrived on the scene. He missed his lunch break and went across the street to get a coke and a bag of potato chips. Coming back he was held up on the street and shot with a pellet gun. He came back into the building, walked into the principal's office, with his hand pressed against his side. Blood was spewing between his fingers and he said, "I'm shot, I'm shot, I'm shot." The principal called an ambulance and got him to the hospital. But he was back teaching while I was there, with the pellet still in him. He hadn't had time to have it taken out. He was going to the hospital that weekend to have the bullet removed.

I tried to visit classes and meet teachers. As I became known around the building, it was rather like walking down the hall and being attacked by aard-varks. Teachers would come out, grab me by the arm, pull me back into the teachers' lounge or their classrooms, and say, "Let me tell it like it is here." Every one of them had deep feelings for the school and for the kids, but an inability to define the specific changes that would make a difference. Their intense desire to solve the school's problems mixed with overwhelming despair is one of the powerful impressions that remains with me as a consequence of those days.

In many ways it is an overmotivated but underprepared staff. As one young fellow who came in March said, "This is an overpeopled and understaffed school. We've gots lots of special people running around under federal grants doing their particular thing. But they don't fit into any kind of mosaic that has meaning for solving the problems of the school."

Many teachers have the too-little-and-too-late kind of feeling. No one is apologetic about it. There is no sense of humiliation about being assigned to the school. But most of them want to get out because they feel that it is an absolutely hopeless situation, that they can't afford to spend whatever psychic energy they have in fighting a losing battle. Even though they are emotionally committed to the place they still want to leave. So the turnover rate is high. Some youngsters had had several different teachers in some of their classes since the beginning of the year.

After the early chaos of my first morning I was able to visit a class being taught by a Peace Corps returnee. She was a young woman with an MAT degree. She had two adults with her in the room assisting with the youngsters. And it was pandemonium. She was trying to teach social studies. She was obviously searching desperately to locate something that might motivate or have some interest for fifteen seventh-graders. Her Peace Corps assignment had been in Africa, so she was showing slides of how people construct thatched cottages there. It was something she knew about first-hand—she had been on the scene But the kids tuned her out. They were making funny remarks and fighting.

One of the other adults in that room was a young man, a practice teacher who had arrived that morning. He had already been slugged twice by students before my 11 a.m. visit. I talked with him later in the week trying to find out whether he was going to give up or stick around. I had to admire his tenacity. He was going to stay; he wasn't going to be licked by that set of events.

During the lunch hour a group of seventh-grade teachers who were cooperating in a transitional program (transitional from the sixth grade into junior high) were meeting for a planning session. I was invited to sit in. The young Peace Corps returnee came in with a tear-stained face. She just couldn't manage her situation. She didn't know what to do. She had to go back and face those classes that afternoon and the next day and the next. She had been advised by the principal and by others to turn in her chips and move to another school. But she just wouldn't do it. She had been fighting it since September, facing failure all year long, but she just would not give up. Others like her were having similar experiences.

The curriculum at this junior high is archaic, outmoded, irrelevant, and unimportant in the minds of the kids who are there. The faculty has agreed for the most part that this is true. But no one is able to design a pattern of change which will remedy or act upon all of the deficiencies that are so prominent in the program of studies. Because of the way the building is constructed (room sizes, locations, and the like) they are locked into an eight-period day. There just are not enough classrooms to handle a six-period organization. Furthermore, there is ambiguity about who is responsible for curriculum reform. Everyone wants change but no one knows how to achieve it.

They were administering the Stanford Achievement Test the week I was there. Large numbers of kids couldn't read it. Many couldn't even read the name of the test. Some of them would mark all of the alternative responses; some wouldn't mark any; some would just casually draw pictures on the test; some would stare;

others would raise their hands and ask for help from those who were monitoring the testing.

A few teachers raised the question with me, "Why test?" It is a good question. Or why use that kind of testing for youngsters in a junior high school like this one? Apparently standardized testing is a systemwide requirement which may have had historical significance and is continued merely because no one has considered not doing it.

As I have said, most of the teachers' energy goes into control. I found few classrooms where I could say with any confidence that there was excitement relative to learning. The only place where I saw interest and motivation and product was in home economics, which enrolls both boys and girls. In other areas interest and motivation appeared to be near zero. It seems to me that the traditional school "subjects" have to be very carefully analyzed in terms of some relevancy criterion.

We toss that word around a great deal—relevance. It's in everybody's language. It has reached cliche status more rapidly than most similar words in our professional jargon. Nevertheless, there is some meaning there.

When I ask myself what would be relevant to the young people at this school I reach an impasse very quickly. It is hard to know what is relevant. Certainly it ties to motivation. If we were insightful enough to know what the prominent motivations are among such young people, then maybe we could organize a program of studies in keeping with interest areas. The program might look quite unlike the traditional subject-centered arrangement in these schools.

I mentioned earlier the "leakage" of the building, both inside out and outside in. The staff walkout in January, 1969, took place because the school was an unsafe place in which to teach. The Board of Education responded by putting door guards on the doors. The measure was to protect teachers and students from a range of intruder types. It was also to control students coming in and going out during the day. The guards have helped a bit in keeping invaders out of the building, but this move hasn't solved the pupil "leakage" problem. An outsider (or an insider for that matter) will cause a disturbance at one of the doors. Door guards come quickly from their posts to help out, leaving their own stations unattended. Other kids will then open the unprotected doors and run out or run in, whichever suits their fancy.

Administrators and teachers resort to corporal punishment. The chief vehicle for control is the swat system. The teachers worked out a scheme to improve control following the January walkout. Teachers volunteer to help with discipline in the "gym balcony," a little area overlooking the gymnasium. During free periods kids who have misbehaved, for whatever reason, are brought there. They queue up, outside, both boys and girls, waiting to be swatted. Teachers take their turns up there in the gym balcony. Similar disciplinary lineups occur outside of the office doors of the three assistant principals, who have paddles or razor straps hanging from their belts. If they need to use them in the corridors they do.

Disciplinary cases are brought first to their door. If they or the principal are too busy, in juvenile court or at home with a case of nerves or whatever it might be, then the students go to the gym balcony to get their swats. Afterward they go back to class or study hall or library or get out of the building.

I didn't administer corporal punishment. I don't know whether I was psychologically capable of it. I don't think I could have forced myself. Teachers on a few occasions brought students to my office. One teacher just threw them in, saying "Take charge" and leaving.

There doesn't seem to be any intrinsic motivation, any way of appealing to the interests of pupils to stay and learn. So everyone (adults and students) adjusts to the corporal punishment routine. No one likes it; no one wants it. Teachers hate it; the principals hate it. But they have no other alternative. They have not been able to discover any better control measure.

And now about death. There is an astonishing callousness about death among the students here. One of them had been killed a few days earlier. He was shot in a car wash down the street. I have mentioned the shooting of the teacher; fortunately that did not end in death. There were other shoot-outs in the neighborhood ending in fatalities. Lester Butler, on my last day, sought an excuse to attend a funeral. I asked for particulars. He said, "It's for my friend's father. He was killed a week ago. He was shot right outside the school. I want to attend the funeral. I'll come right back after it's over." I wrote the excuse.

Lester described the event without emotion, with placidness, with matter-of-factness. Death is a part of life here. Life is filled with its own brand of violence. Its violence is routine. It is not necessarily racial. It is grounded in hate which feeds upon itself. It is cancerous and spreads and spreads and spreads.

The cancer of hate is latent within the student body. You sense its presence and the prospect for its release at any moment. You do not know when it will burst forth and cascade around you. It is everywhere; it is nowhere. Lester sensed that the school was a powder keg. He would even try to describe it to me in his own way.

In many ways life at this junior high is a charade. People go about the business of routine schooling. Teachers laugh and smile. They walk through the corridors ignoring the rowdiness. They try at times, halfheartedly, to establish a bit of order. The administrative staff takes the problem more seriously; they shout and cajole and urge and plead. The counselors do their thing. They talk with students. They describe worlds of glitter and gold. The students squirm and stare and ignore. The counselors' cubicles, tucked away here and there, are temporary refuges from the storm.

I was impressed with the door guards. They try. They understand the charade. Many of them have played the game for a lifetime. They represent well the male image. They are for the most part young, strong, handsome. They are on the side of the angels. That is, they try to support the purposes of the school. They work closely with teachers and administrative officials. They do their job. It involves keeping hoodlums off the street out of the building, avoiding physical encounters but not turning away from them. There is no training for their positions. They must exercise amazing discretion every minute of the day. Most of them have little formal education. But they have established a bond with the professional staff that is harmonious and marked by mutual respect. Each day I issued up a silent prayer of thanks that they were there.

What to do about this school? And other similar junior highs in other places? An archaic building, a largely uncaring community, an irrelevant program of studies, a student population that is out of hand, an underprepared, overpressured staff, a sympathetic but essentially frustrated central administration, a city that wishes such schools would go away. A proposal from the staff and administrators was to burn the school down. Destroy it. Get the symbol out of the neighborhood. This was more than a half-serious proposal.

Short of that, what can be done? This question haunted me during my stay. What could be done? Only a few feeble proposals occurred to me.

I would argue for complete building-level autonomy. The principal and faculty should run the show without concern for other places. They should be allowed to organize the program of studies without adherence to district-wide curriculum guides and the like. The principal should be free to select his own faculty without reference to certification. He should look for talented people anywhere and everywhere. They could be found across the street or across the nation. The principal should build his own budget and make internal allocations in terms of the faculty and staff's definition of need.

More radically, I would ask that the principal be given complete control over time. That is, he should be able to open and close the school at will. If in his judgment events are getting out of hand, he should have the power—indeed be expected—to close the school down for a day, a week, or a month. During the time the building is closed, all of the adults in the school, in cooperation with students and community leaders, should focus on the problems that are overwhelming them. They should develop a problem-solving ethos. They should include genuine and substantial neighborhood participation. They should zero in on questions one by one, work them through and seek solutions. The state, the city, and the central school administration should support but not interfere. What is required in schools like these is a set of solutions. There is no justification for keeping the building open simply to observe the state code.

The staff should be kept on during the summer. Give them an air-conditioned retreat; allow them to plan for the year ahead. Work on the program of studies, work on motivation, work on community linkage, work on patterns of staffing, work on everything.

It occurred to me that it might be wise for the boys and girls to be separated

—have boys' schools and girls' schools. There are some research data to support this recommendation. I remembered a study in Illinois that I directed a few years ago. There we tried to discover the impact of segregated learning on achievement. We examined a small district where youngsters were feeding into one junior high school out of white schools, black schools, and integrated schools. We were interested in such factors as pupil alienation, attitudes toward schooling, and achievement in the traditional subject fields. We discovered some significant differences, but the overwhelming difference was how boys responded to the learning environments in contrast with how girls responded. The boys were getting the short end of the stick on most things.

Systems should depress the emphasis on attendance. I would even support abandoning compulsory education for this part of the city. Emphasize programs of interest and attractiveness; de-emphasize regimentation. Much of the faculty's energy goes into keeping kids in school. And once in school, keeping them in class. Why fight it? Jettison the pressure toward control. Enroll students on the basis of interest only. Such policies violate the rich American tradition of education for everyone, but why carry on the charade? Why?

Again I want it understood that I came away from this school with profound admiration and respect for the regular principal, the three assistant principals, the several counselors, the many teachers, and the many special staff members, as well as the central administration. And I came away with respect for the students. The adults in the building are struggling feverishly. They are dedicated. They are in their own way in love with the school. But they are shell-shocked, exhausted, and desperate. They need help but they are not sure what kind of help. And I am not sure. I have advanced a few notions but they need careful scrutiny and considerable elaboration.

It is clear that we have no experts in this sort of urban education anywhere. The most expert may be those professionals who are there every day engaging in the fray. But they are reaching out, and it is for this reason that some kind of liaison with universities and other sources of ideas is critical. Refined, umbilical relationships need to be developed. We are just scratching the surface at Ohio State. No one has *the* answer. Anyone who thinks he has is a fool. At best there are only partial answers—pieces of a larger mosaic that could at some point in the future fit together in a more productive fashion than today's mosaic.

There are many schools in America like the one I have described. We don't want to admit it but there are. And all of us who bear professional credentials must carry that cross.

Such educational institutions are an indictment of presidents and senators; of justices and teachers; of governors and legislators. It is ludicrous the way we behave. Our pathetic politicians wailing and wringing their hands, spouting platitudes and diatribes. They advance shallow excuses. They say that bold acts will not find favor with unnamed constituencies. And we educators stand impotent, frightened, disheveled in the face of such tragedy.

3

The Anachronistic Practices of American Education as Perpetrated by an Unenlightened Citizenry and Misguided Pedagogues Against the Inmates of the Public Schools*

HAROLD W. SOBEL

At a time when our society has been described as sick and young people are advised to "turn on, tune in, and drop out," it would be rather surprising if our educational institutions, which have historically mirrored the society, were spared their share of criticism. The critics of society at large are radical in that they call for a fundamental restructuring of our political and value systems. So too with the new breed of educational critics. When Paul Goodman wrote *Compulsory Mis-Education,* his condemnation was total:

> At present, in most states, for 10 to 13 years every young person is obliged to sit the better part of his day in a room almost always too crowded, facing front, doing lessons predetermined by a distant administration . . . that have no relation to his own intellectual, social, or animal interests. . . . The overcrowding precludes individuality or spontaneity, reduces the young to ciphers and the teacher to a martinet.[1]

Some would label this statement gross exaggeration or half-truth. They would point proudly to the record of our scientific and technological progress, our exalted affluence, and our high rate of literacy and credit the schools with making these societal desiderata possible. When defenders of the status quo admit that some educational problems exist, they hasten to add that the remedy lies in a curriculum innovation here or an additional expenditure of funds there. They do not see anything fundamentally wrong with the way we have gone about schoolkeeping lo these many years.

The writers whose work this article attempts to summarize contend that the problems we face are basic, are built into the system, and are not amenable to simplistic solutions. Their hope is that those responsible for educational policy will see fit to restructure the schools. If we are to pass through this winter of our discent, we need to abandon the conventional wisdom. We need the courage to choose alternatives which call for tidal waves of change.

FULL-SCALE MODELS

One way to appraise the schools is in terms of models. Frederick McDonald claims that our schools follow a mass production model. This means that

> certain kinds of units are to be produced on a systematic and regular basis. In order to produce these units, resources are concentrated in strategic locations. . . . A school assembles 600 or more children in one very restrictive physical location. Such an arrangement facilitates the processing of these children, because the resources necessary to educate them are concentrated in these areas also.[2]

This analogy to a factory also includes the notion of specialization of labor. Teachers are trained according to the age of students they plan to instruct and, in the case of junior and senior high school teachers, by subject matter specialty as well. In school, students are grouped into manageable units called classes and are exposed to a largely standardized curriculum. They are subjected to uniform examinations in the earliest grades to assess their intelligence or achievement and, later, to nation-wide tests which determine their suitability for college.

The factory model was not designed by diabolical men intent upon stultifying learning. It was, rather, the creation of clever social engineers whose goal was the efficient processing of masses of young people. The only problem with it is that "Underlying the whole system of administrative organization . . . is a concept of uniformity in children. Such a concept, despite all disclaimers, presupposes a commonality or similarity among children which simply does not exist and could never exist."[3]

Joseph C. Grannis, formerly of the Harvard Graduate School of Education, points out that in the factory school students generally work on identical material at a uniform pace. "Much of the work," he writes, "is assign and recite, and the pattern of dialogue is often rote teaching. . . . Thus the students in the factory school learn to think in terms of crude standardization of products, effort, and reward. . . ."[4] Grannis also discusses a corporation school, found most often in the suburbs and characterized by team teaching and nongraded patterns. With features such as the careful grouping of students and teachers, the use of expensive equipment (computers, teaching machines, tape recorders, and headsets), and the institutionalization of change and innovation, this seems like an eminently desirable model. However, serious drawbacks do exist. For one thing, there are rigid time constraints which may preclude a group's persevering in rewarding activity or discontinuing something it dislikes. More important is the loss of feeling relationships among students and between teachers and students. The faults of the corporation school are similar to those of the large and impersonal business organization. The millenium has not been reached when a wealthy suburban community transforms its schools from the factory to the corporation model.

Like Goodman, Grannis believes that initiation into society's institutions is a prerequisite for understanding them. He recommends that youth be much more actively involved in political affairs, that work-study programs be developed promoting active interchange between students and business and industry, and that adults other than teachers participate directly in the education of the young. Grannis is not very sanguine about how educators will respond to the problems he raises. "A number of observers have concluded that the schools are too wedded to the nation's system of economic and social selection, in ways that the schools do not even know, to take seriously the goals of personal and social integration."[5] It is sad to think that the job schools may be doing best is screening out future candidates for employment as clerks or corporation executives.

From the mass-production model, which the vast majority of schools follow, stem the myriad problems which beset American education. These include trying to individualize instruction, arriving at a sane policy on grading and promotion, escaping the four walls of the schoolhouse and exposing children to the wider world of reality outside, and "disciplining" children to sit quietly and learn in what is clearly an unnatural environment. It is disgust with the factory model which has led Goodman to suggest that, for a few classes, we might dispense with the school building "and use the city itself as the school—its streets, cafeterias, stores, movies, museums, parks, and factories."[6] Other visionary possibilities include using appropriate unlicensed adults as teachers, making class attendance voluntary, decentralizing units by creating storefront schools, and experimenting with nongrading by age. These notions strike fear into the hearts of establishment pedagogues whose power, position, and pecuniary interest are linked to the factory model. This, however, is no argument for the retention of archaic practices. And since factories are more famous for the production of pickles than for the education of free men, it is high time we looked around for a new model.

LESS INCLUSIVE MODELS

Less comprehensive in scope than the models cited above is the school-as-prison paradigm. In a brilliantly satirical article, Herbert Gans describes the speculations of archeologists, circa 3,000 A.D., who have excavated a 20th century school building. Hypothesizing as to its use, he writes, "Some team members believe the building was a prison, the series of uniform rooms housing groups of prisoners, each overseen by a guard." Another group of archeologists contends that the building was a school, but the author rejects this thesis on the following grounds:

It is simply inconceivable to me . . . that the Early Atomic Age would have used special educational institutions which segregated, physically and socially, this alert and vital age group from everyday life of the community. Surely the culture was sophisticated enough to know that Man learns best by doing and problem solving in an ongoing enterprise, that the 13-17 age group is much too energetic to spend its days cooped up in training rooms, and that youngsters of any age learn best from each other, and not from an elder. . . . [7]

Ah to see ourselves as others see us! The idea that schools resemble prisons comes from another source—a study funded by the Carnegie Corporation of New York and headed by *Fortune* magazine editor Charles Silberman. In terms remarkably like those used to describe penal institutions, Silberman said, "The public schools are quite literally destructive of human beings. . . . I think they are the most grim, joyless places on the face of the earth. They are needlessly authoritarian and repressive. . . ."[8] Negative characterizations such as this lead one to ask, "Why can't schools be more like carnivals than concentration camps?" "Is there anything inherent in the teaching-learning process which necessitates its being such a serious enterprise?" Or more simply, "Can't schools be fun?"

Still another way of viewing the school is in terms of the pupil-teacher, or as Jerry Farber, formerly of UCLA, would have it, the slave-master relationship. His controversial article, "The Student as Nigger," deals with roles, and the claim is made that students are analogous to pre-Civil War blacks. He cites the "separate and unequal" dining and lavatory facilities which exist in most schools; the fact that students are expected to "know their place" in all social relationships with faculty; and the total disfranchisement of students in matters affecting their academic lives. It is this last-mentioned condition which has given rise to much of the student unrest on college campuses across the country. Farber argues that students live in an "academic Lowndes County," that they are "allowed to have a toy government run for the most part by Uncle Toms and concerned principally with trivia. The faculty and administrators decide what courses will be offered; the students get to choose their own homecoming queen.[9] Not all students are as passive as Farber would have us believe—witness Berkeley, Columbia, San Francisco, and Wisconsin. In fact, one is led to speculate that if significant changes in university governance do come about, it will be because of student prodding rather than administrative enlightenment. This is not to condone all recent student activity but to point out the heretofore unexercised power which resides amongst students.

CRITICISMS WITHOUT MODELS

The remainder of this article deals with general criticism not easily identifiable with any particular model. A forthcoming book by Noyes and McAndrew indicates that students are as disillusioned by the educational process as are the professional critics. In their nationwide survey, the authors found that the vast majority of students see the school as a "system" which they must beat, or as an impersonal "machine" which they get fed into at the age of five and which spews them forth at eighteen. Students believe that the purpose of the elementary school is to prepare kids for high school, which in turn prepares kids for college. None of this, of course, has anything to do with the adult conception so piously stated that schooling prepares young people to live full and meaningful lives. Noyes and McAndrew hold that

> As presently organized, the inescapable truth is that our schools seldom promote and frequently deny the objectives we, as a nation, espouse. Rather than being assisted and encouraged to develop their own individuality, our children are locked into a regimented system that attempts to stamp them all into the same mold. The student is filled with facts and figures which only accidentally and infrequently have anything whatsoever to do with the problems and conflicts of modern life or his own inner concerns.[10]

The best that can be said for our schools is that they train for public service. The student with a high grade point average in college usually finds a good job waiting upon graduation. "And then," in the words of Professor Michael Wreszin, "with a little luck there come . . . the kiddies, a house in the suburbs— what Zorba the Greek called the 'full catastrophe.' "[11]

Peter Marin, writing about youth in the context of our culture, provides still another incisive analysis. He views the schools as a Victorian institution, suspicious of life itself, and the natural enemy of children.

> They manipulate them through the repression of energies; they isolate them and close off most parts of the community; they categorically refuse to make use of the individual's private experience. The direction of all these tendencies is toward a cultural schizophrenia in which the student is forced to choose between his own relation to reality and the one demanded by the institution.[12]

Marin contends that most proposed changes are mere palliatives. Curriculum revisions, teaching machines, smaller classes are stop-gap measures designed to resuscitate an institution already in its death throes. And one cannot look to teachers for answers because this group, by and large, is committed to ideas they have never clearly understood. This is evidenced by their questions: "What will children do if they're not in school?" "How will they learn?" The assumption that learning occurs only, or even best, in schools is a rather presumptuous one. Marin points out that mass schooling is a recent innovation.

> In most cultures the passage from childhood to maturity occurs because of social necessity, the need for responsible adults, and is marked by clear changes in role. Children in the past seem to have learned the ways of the community or tribe through constant contact with interchange with adults, and it was taken for granted that the young learned continually through their place close to the heart of the community.[13]

As alternatives to current practice, Marin forsees the possibility of dropping the compulsory schooling age to fourteen or less, having children live away from home and with peers, discovering jobs in the community which youth can take and which will provide minimal income and a sense of independence and responsibility. In short, adults must stop fabricating artificial environments for children and stop denying them individual volition. For those to whom the schoolhouse is a sacred temple of learning, it is suggested that more knowledge exists outside its walls than within. Or as Marshall McLuhan has stated, "The child knows that in going to school he's in a sense interrupting his education."

CONCLUSIONS

The picture of the schools painted above is bleak indeed. It is sad that words like *repressive, irrelevant, impersonal, destructive, joyless, obsolete,* and *authoritarian* are deemed appropriate in describing present-day schools. But if truth is the beginning of wisdom, then the worst enemies of education may not be those who find fault but those who stand in the way of change. If the models of the factory, the prison, and the slave-master relationship seem harsh, then let us relegate the practices which gave rise to them to the trash heap of history. As Harold Howe II said in one of his speeches while U.S. Commissioner of Education, "The story of survival is the story of creatures who adapted to changes in their environment. . . . The dodo had no control over his lack of ability to survive. School boards do."

3. NOTES

1. Paul Goodman, *Compulsory Mis-Education* (New York: Vintage Books, 1962), p. 56.
2. Frederick J. McDonald, "Beyond the Schoolhouse," *The Urban Review,* November 1968, p. 10.
3. *Ibid.,* p. 11.
4. Joseph C. Grannis, "The School as a Model of Society," *Harvard Graduate School of Education Bulletin,* Fall 1967, p. 18.
5. *Ibid.,* p. 26
6. Goodman, *op. cit.,* p. 32.
7. Herbert Gans, "Report from the Center for Urban Archaeology," *The Urban Review,* November 1968, p. 16.
8. Charles E. Silberman, quoted in Israel Shenker, "Schools Assailed in Carnegie Study," *The New York Times,* January 26, 1969, p. 48.
9. Jerry Farber, "The Student as Nigger," *This Magazine Is About Schools,* Winter 1968, p. 109.
10. Kathryn Johnston Noyes and Gordon L. McAndrew, "Is This What Schools Are For?" *Saturday Review,* December 21, 1968, p. 65.
11. Michael Wreszin, Freshman Convocation Address, Queens College, September 4, 1968.
12. Peter Marin, "The Open Truth and Fiery Vehemence of Youth," *The Center Magazine,* a publication of the Center for the Study of Democratic Institutions, January 1969, p. 65.
13. *Ibid.,* p. 67.

4

Cultural Pluralism: Its Implications for Education*

THOMAS C. HOGG and MARLIN R. McCOMB

Cultural pluralism has been a dominant feature in man's very recent history; and, yet, there has been a general failure to consider its meaning and to examine its implications for American culture in general and the field of education in particular. The persistence of antecedent cultural traditions and successive migrations of vast numbers of people accounts, in very large measure, for the present cultural pluralism existing in the United States and specific settings therein.

The processes of cultural survival and migration contribute to a diverse and conflictive sociocultural condition to which all institutions, including schools, must adapt. Today, the very spatial and social mobility of populations, both in terms of their urban concentration around the city core and their subsequent flight and extension to the city's more rural environs, has created many new problems for the schools and the educational process.

AMERICAN CULTURAL PLURALISM AND EDUCATION

As a society, America has come to enshrine education with the idealism, hope, and missionary qualities that characterize other American systems and the value system as a whole (Curti, 1960). Equally, and typically, there is a growing recognition that the professions of idealism do *not* match the practices of reality for *many,* including children, in our society.

America's educational system has long been held up as a model, free and open to children from all social and economic levels, all religous and cultural backgrounds. Also, the educational system has been pointed to with pride by those who see it as an enculturation mechanism whereby such diverse backgrounds would be changed so that individuals might be made culturally capable and able to function in American society and would be offered through education an invaluable means for self-realization and social mobility. Looking beyond the enculturation, social mobility and self-realization processes, the school has been pictured as a force for social change—a source of innovation and a laboratory for bold experimentation (cf. Cremin, 1961).

In fact, however, the end product of the educational process has now been recognized by educators and public alike to be something less for those children who came from different cultural backgrounds (Hickerson, 1966; *Report of the National Commission on Civil Disorders,* 1968; Clark, 1965; and Conant, 1964). For the poor black, Indian, Puerto Rican, Mexican-American, or white child, the American educational process has been inadequate, and it has systematically devaluated and attempted to destroy their cultural uniqueness. This educational inadequacy has been assaulted through massive public expenditures to accelerate the process of "better" education, but in its train has also come cultural devaluation.

Deviations from the posited cultural norm have been labeled as manifestations of "cultural deprivation or [of being] disadvantaged" in the educational world (cf. Riessman, 1962). Exemplars of such diversity in America have been poked at, probed, and diagnosed *ad infinitum* by a bewildered educational profession, utilizing a string of euphemisms that change as the problems they fail to conceptualize remain. For too long the educational profession has been content to place the blame on the culturally different for failing to be compatible with and malleable to the school environment. Perhaps even more important is the implication that the culturally different offer an appearance, in poverty and lifeway, of what America should not be—culturally heterogeneous and socially disintegrated.

Such cultural examples are seen as being different, but it has been held that they can and should be made the same, that they, too, can become a part of the American mainstream and melting pot. How to bring this state into being was the difficult question that plagued past American educators, and it continues to vex us in our time.

The fundamental premises of assimilationist approaches to education have seldom been seriously questioned, even though many of the sources of our past and present assimilation dilemmas appear to stem from two fundamental fallacies about the American social and cultural situation. First, is the notion that there is occurring and has occurred a proper melting-pot effect in assimilating the culturally different; and second, is the notion that American society *should be,* and therefore *is,* a homogeneous cultural system. It is becoming more apparent in other cultures around the world that there exists a wide range of pluralistic structures and cultures (Hogg, 1965; Mitchell, 1960; P. M. Hauser, 1961). The same appears to hold for the United States, a culture often held to be a prime example of the "melting pot" thesis. Even here, contrary to many existing beliefs, assimilation has been more myth than fact (Kiser, 1949). It appears that only now, after we have come to recognize cultural diversity within other nations of the world, not only in Africa (Mayer, 1962) and Asia (Burling, 1965), but in Europe as well, have we dared to apply realistic frameworks to the American cultural milieu.

Indeed, pluralism in America stems from earliest colonial days (Crevecoeur, 1962), appears again in the debates and compromises surrounding the Constitution, and is associated with the cultural separatist features of the Westward Movement. It also looms large in the causes of the Civil War, multiplies due to urban-industrialism, European immigration, and internal migrations by Afro-Americans, accelerates during World War I, the Depression, and World War II as mobile Americans discover new cultures at home and abroad.

In more recent years, the demand for "Black Power," "Red Power," and other additional evidences of a new cultural awareness on the part of many American cultural categories are becoming more manifest for all Americans to see (cf. Carmichael and Hamilton, 1967; and Steiner, 1968). Many of these manifestations are part and parcel of the urban crisis, the context for which is cultural pluralism and social nonarticulation. Similarly, even now we are slowly coming to recognize, contrary to the ideas expressed in literature but a decade or two ago, that the small towns of rural America are not, and probably never were, as homogeneous as we thought (cf. Vidich and Bensman, 1960).

Our own recent researches in Sweet Home, Oregon, for example, have revealed the survivals of antecedent traditions as well as a situation of cultural conflict for small and rural settings. Nestled as it is in the foothills of the Cascade Mountains of western Oregon, Sweet Home has served as the base for bands of hunting and gathering Indians, early settlers seeking escape from religious discrimination, robust loggers or "timber beasts" exploiting the forest by brawn and individual ability, the modern logging and milling industries, and now, water reservoirs promising recreation and new abundance. This local setting has gone through a series of adaptive stages as new immigrants and new modes of subsistence, both carrying distinctive forms of human organization and world view, have replaced the old. Though largely superseded, early stages of Euro-American cultural adaptation continue to be manifest in Sweet Home, not only in terms of values and norms, but also in terms of behavioral patterns.

We have found that the multiple orientations of townsmen toward schools and government are more, much more than a stubborn adherence to conservatism. Their views constitute values which have served well in other cultural challenges, values to which others, those lacking that experience and socialized in still other idioms of thought, behavior, and things, cannot relate. It is in this persisting conflict situation that institutions try to maintain themselves, and yet it is also the type-situation which most severely threatens the existence of institutions, particularly those designed to accomplish basic social processes like education.

In Sweet Home, as in America more generally, the fundamental question appears to be, education for what? To what value system, to what form of cultural adaptation does an educational system structure itself when no clear trends of cultural substitution are apparent, when many cultures are manifest, and when a setting still possesses an ecology which permits a number of technical, social, and ideological choices? More critically, can our schools survive the game of cultural roulette? Which tradition is to be given educational legitimacy? Which bearers of what culture are to be ignored and therefore destroyed?

Cultural pluralism and its attendant conflicts in America are increasing under the impact of industry; pluralism plus conflict appear to be part of the new quality of industrial, social, and cultural life. Thus, a condition which in eras only recently past was viewed as a strain in the social system now appears to be the system. The new adaptation is not a matter of choosing one of many cultures, it is to succeed with many cultures.

CULTURAL ADAPTATIONS FOR EDUCATION

It is our view, then, that the school in the American setting, and the educational process more generally, must adapt to cultural conditions. Given the existence of varying cultural traditions, and assuming that a setting's institutions are formal and enduring manifestations of local culture, then the school and the educational process must formally adjust to extant pluralism, if they are to retain their institutional character. Moreover, not only must education itself adapt to cultural pluralism, it must educate the young for cultural pluralism. This latter task necessarily involves revision of not only educational technology and organization, but the ideology as well.

In this process of change the following considerations must be given due weight. First, in cultural terms, the school must provide each student with a set of relevant cultural experiences so that successful and meaningful cultural adaptations might be made. In accomplishing this task, it must work within and tolerate multiple ranges of interaction and ideology, providing reasons for expression of and respect for distinctive behaviors and thoughts. Basic to the task is the necessity for the school to go through the process of a fundamental redefinition and redirection of assumptions presently made about our society, the purpose of the school, and the school's organization and external relationships in culturally pluralistic settings.

Failing this, the school is encouraging the range of social problems afflicting all culturally different youth—dropping out of school, unemployment, deteriorated self-image, hostility toward authority, and withdrawal from social involvement. Moreover, by a failure to recognize cultural pluralism, the school discourages innovation and syncretism of conflictive cultural elements, thereby increasing conflict and public apathy. What education has done *to* the American Indian, it is also doing to those of a different culture not recognized through skin color and tongue.

Second, in educational terms, through a premise of individual "cultural worth" the school must establish means for cultural expression in the widest variety of school contexts—classrooms, assemblies, clubs, and curricula. This could mean a revision of curriculum including redirection of language and other art programs as well as technical *expression* (rather than training) programs, an expansion of the technical concept beyond training simply for placement in economic technology. Such means as these require special training and recruitment of teachers and administrators and their sensitization to cultural pluralism. In order to ensure its community future, the school must maintain constant contact with community members in family and organizational contexts. This means cooperation with and study of other private and public agencies. Through consciously sought "cultural feedback" the school must restructure its organization and activities and attempt to become a center of community interaction.

Finally, the school must go beyond just becoming a reflection of cultural diversity. It must participate in, and prepare youth for, a culturally pluralistic life and society; and such an educational strategy must become a major and clearly articulated set of goals in the educational process. The extent to which these challenges can be met in culturally pluralistic settings depends ultimately upon the extent to which the school is sensitized to cultural differences within the setting. So long as cultural pluralism is a factor, the school's role must be to educate itself.

4. NOTES

Robbins Burling, *Hill Farms and Padi Fields* (Englewood Cliffs, Prentice-Hall, 1965).

Stokely Carmichael and Charles V. Hamilton, *Black Power: The Politics of Liberation in America* (New York: Vintage Books, 1967).

Kennth Clark, *Dark Ghetto* (New York: Harper & Row, 1965).

Lloyd R. Collins, "Cultural Position of the Kalapuya in the Pacific Northwest" (M.S. Anthropology thesis, University of Oregon, June 1951).

James B. Conant, *Slums and Suburbs* (New York: New American Library of World Literature, 1964).

Lawrence Cremin, *The Transformation of the School* (New York, Knopf, 1961).

Michel-Guillaume de Crevecoeur, "What Is an American?" in Henry Steele Commager (ed.), *America in Perspective* (New York: Mentor Books, 1961).

Merle Curti, *The Social Ideas of American Educators* (New York: Pageant, 1960).

Nathan Glazer and Daniel P. Moynihan, *Beyond the Melting Pot* (Cambridge: M.I.T. Press, 1963).

Milton Gordon, *Assimilation in American Life* (New York: Oxford University Press, 1964).

Philip M. Hauser, *Urbanization in Latin America* (New York: Columbia University Press, 1961).

Nathaniel Hickerson, *Education for Alienation* (Englewood Cliffs: Prentice-Hall, 1966).

Thomas C. Hogg, "Urban Immigrants and Associations in Sub-Saharan Africa" (Ph.D. dissertation, University of Oregon: Ann Arbor University Microfilm Service, 1965).

Horace Kallen, *Cultural Pluralism and the American Idea* (Philadelphia: University of Pennsylvania Press, 1956).

Clyde V. Kiser, "Cultural Pluralism," *The Annals of the American Academy of Political and Social Science* 262 (March 1949), 117-30.

Philip Mayer, "The Study of Multi-Tribalism," introduction to A. A. Dubb (ed.), *The Multi-tribal Society* (Lusaka: Rhodes-Livingstone, 1962).

J. Clyde Mitchell, *Tribalism and the Plural Society* (London: Oxford University Press, 1960).

Report of the National Advisory Commission on Civil Disorders (New York: Bantam Books, 1968).

Frank Riessman, *The Culturally Deprived Child* (New York: Harper & Row, 1962).

Stan Steiner, *The New Indians* (New York: Harper & Row, 1968).

Arthur J. Vidich and Joseph Bensman, *Small Town in Mass Society* (Garden City, Anchor Books, 1960).

5

Docility, or Giving Teacher What She Wants*

JULES HENRY

This essay deals with one aspect of American character, the process whereby urban middle-class children in elementary school acquire the habit of giving their teachers the answers expected of them. Though it could hardly be said that I deal exhaustively with this matter, what I do discuss, using suggestions largely from psychoanalysis and communications theory, is the signaling process whereby children and teacher come to understand each other or, better, to pseudo-understand each other within the limited framework of certain school-room situations.

I think it will be readily understood that such a study has intercultural significance and interesting biosocial implications. The smooth operation of human interaction, or "transaction," if one prefers the Dewey and Bentley décor, requires that in any culture much of the give and take of life be reduced to a conventional, parsimonious system of quickly decipherable messages and appropriate responses. These messages, however, are different in different cultures, because the give and take of life is different in different cultures. At a simple level, for example, a Pilagá Indian paints his face red when he is looking for a sexual affair with a woman, whereas were an American man to paint his face red, the significance of this to other Americans would be quite different. Behaviors that have been variously called signal, cue, and sign are as characteristic of the animal world as they are of the human, and in both groups tend to be highly specific both with respect to themselves (signs, signals, cues) and with respect to the behavior they release in those for whom they are intended. Since, furthermore, each culture tends to standardize these, it would seem that any study of such behaviors, or rather behavior systems, in humans in any culture would throw light on two problems: (1) What the signal-response system is; and (2) How humans learn the system.

Since in humans the mastery of a signal-response system often involves the emotional life, and since in this paper on docility I am dealing with urban American middle-class children, it will readily be seen that a study of the manner in which they learn the signal-response system called docility carries us toward an understanding of the character of these children.

When we say a human being is docile we mean that, without the use of external force, he performs relatively few acts as a function of personal choice as compared with the number of acts he performs as a function of the will of others. In a very real sense, we mean that he behaves mostly as others wish him to. In our culture this is thought undesirable, for nobody is supposed to like docile people. On the other hand, every culture must develop in its members forms of behavior that approximate docility; otherwise it could not conduct its business. Without obedience to traffic signals transportation in a large American city would be a mess. This is a dilemma of our culture: to be able to keep the streets uncluttered with automotive wrecks, and to fill our armies with fighting men who will obey orders, while at the same time we teach our citizens not to be docile.

It is to be supposed that, although the basic processes as outlined are universal, every culture has its own way of creating the mechanism of docility. It will be the purpose of the rest of this paper to examine the accomplishment of docility in some American middle-class schoolrooms. The study was carried out by several of my graduate students and me. Names of persons and places are withheld in order to give maximum protection to all concerned.

In the following examples I shall be concerned only with demonstrating that aspect of docility which has to do with the teacher's getting from the children the answers she wants; and I rely almost entirely on verbal behavior, for without cameras it is impossible to record nonverbal signals. The first example is from the second grade.

1

The children have been shown movies of birds. The first film ended with a picture of a baby bluebird.

Teacher: Did the last bird ever look like he would be blue?
The children did not seem to understand the slant of the question and answered somewhat hesitantly: Yes.
Teacher: I think he looked more like a robin, didn't he?
Children, in chorus: Yes.

In this example one suspects that teacher's intonation on the word "ever" did not come through as a clear signal, for it did not create enough doubt in the children's minds to bring the right answer, "No." The teacher discovered that her signal had not been clear enough for these seven-year-olds, so she made it crystal clear the second time, and got the "right" response. Its correctness is demonstrated by the unanimity of the children's response and the teacher's acceptance of it. Here the desire of the teacher, that the children shall acknowledge that a bird looks like a robin, is simple, and the children, after one false try, find the correct response.

In the next example we see the relation of signal to cultural values and context.

2a

A fourth grade art lesson. Teacher holds up a picture.

Teacher: Isn't Bobby getting a nice effect of moss and trees?
Ecstatic Oh's and Ah's from the children. . . .

2b

The art lesson is now over.

Teacher: How many enjoyed this?
Many hands go up.
Teacher: How many learned something?
Quite a number of hands come down.
Teacher: How many will do better next time?
Many hands go up.

Here the shifts in response are interesting. The word "nice" triggers a vigorously docile response, as does the word "enjoy." "Learned something," however, for a reason that is not quite clear, fails to produce the desired unanimity. On the other hand, the shibboleth, "better next time" gets the same response as "enjoyed." We see then that the precise triggering signal is related to important cultural values, and that the value-signal must be released in proper context. One suspects that the children's resistance to saying they had learned something occurred because "learned something" appeared out of context. On the other hand, it would be incorrect to describe these children as perfectly docile.

The next example is from the same fourth grade classroom:

3

The children have just finished reading the story "The Sun, Moon, and Stars Clock."

Teacher: What was the highest point of interest—the climax?
The children tell what they think it is. Teacher is aiming to get from them what she thinks it is, but the children give everything else but. At last Bobby says: When they capture the thieves.
Teacher: How many agree with Bobby?
Hands, hands, hands.

In this example the observer was not able to record all the verbal signals, for they came too fast. However, it is clear that hunting occurred, while the children waited for the teacher to give the clear signal, which was "(I) agree with Bobby."

In all the examples given thus far, the desired answer could be indicated rather clearly by the teacher, for the required response was relatively unambiguous. Even so, there was some trouble in obtaining most of the answers. In the example that follows, however, the entire situation becomes exceedingly ambiguous because emotional factors in the children make proper interpretation of teacher's signals difficult. The central issue is that teacher and children are seen to have requirements that are complementary on one level, because teacher wants the children to accept her point of view, and they want to be accepted by her; but these requirements are not complementary on a different level, because the children's emotional organization is different from the teacher's. Hence exact complementarity is never achieved, but rather a pseudo-complementarity, which enables teacher and pupils to extricate themselves from a difficult situation. The example comes from a fifth grade schoolroom:

4

This is a lesson on "healthy thoughts" for which the children have a special book that depicts specific conflictful events among children. There are appropriate illustrations and text, and the teacher is supposed to discuss each incident with the children in order to help them understand how to handle their emotions.

One of the illustrations is of two boys, one of whom is griping because his brother has been given something he wants for himself—a football, I think. The other is saying his brother couldn't help being given it—they'll both play with it.

(Observer is saying that this sibling pair is illustrated by three boys: (1) The one who has received the ball. (2) The one who is imagined to react with displeasure. (3) The one who is imagined to react benignly and philosophically, by saying: My brother couldn't help being given the football; we'll use it together.)

Teacher: Do you believe it's easier to deal with your thoughts if you own up to them, Betty?

Betty: Yes it is, if you're not cross and angry.

Teacher: Have you any experience like this in the book, Alice?

Alice tells how her brother was given a watch and she envied him and wanted one too, but her mother said she wasn't to have one until she was fifteen, but now she has one anyway.

Teacher: How could you have helped—could you have changed your thinking? How could you have handled it? What could you do with mean feelings?

Alice seems stymied; she hems and haws.

Teacher: What did Susie (a character in the book) do?

Alice: She talked to her mother.

Teacher: If you talk to someone, you often feel that 'It was foolish of me to feel that way. . . . '

Tommy: He says he had an experience like that. His cousin was given a bike, and he envied it. But he wasn't ugly about it. He asked if he might ride it, and his cousin let him, and then I got one myself; and I wasn't mean or ugly or jealous.

Here the process of signal development is intricate, and children and teacher do not quite manage to arrive at a mutually intelligible complex of signals and behavior. The stage is set by the presentation of a common but culturally un-acceptable situation: A child is pictured as envious of the good luck of his sibling. Since American culture cannot accept two of its commonest traits, sib-ling rivalry and envy, the children are asked by teacher to acknowledge that they are "bad," and to accept specific ways of dealing with these emotions. The children are thus asked to fly in the face of their own feelings, and, since this is impossible, the little pigeons never quite get home. This is because teacher and pupil wants are not complementary.

It will have been observed that at first Alice does well, for by docilely admit-ting that it is good to own up to evil, she correctly interprets the teacher's wish to hear her say that the ancient ritual of confession is still good for the soul; and she continues docile behavior by giving a story of her own envy. However, eventually she muffs the signal, for she says she was gratified anyway; she did get a watch. And the reason Alice muffs the signal is that her own impulses dom-inate over the signals coming in from the teacher. Teacher, however, does not reject Alice's *story* but tries, rather, to get Alice to say she could have "handled" her thoughts by "owning up" to them and talking them over with someone. Alice, however, stops dead because she *cannot* understand the teacher. Mean-while Tommy has picked up the signal, only to be misled by it, just as Alice was. By this time, however, the matter has become more complex: Tommy thinks that because teacher did not reject Alice's story it is "correct." Teacher's appar-ent acceptance of Alice's story then becomes Tommy's signal; therefore, he duplicates Alice's story almost exactly, except that a bike is substituted for a watch. Like Alice he is not "mean" or "ugly" or "jealous," not because he "dealt with" his thoughts in the culturally approved-but-impossible manner, but because he too got what he wanted. So far, the only part of the message that is getting through to the children from the teacher is that it is uncomfortable—not wrong—to be jealous, etc. Thus the emotions of the children filter out an impor-tant part of the message from the teacher.

We may summarize the hypotheses up to this point as follows: (1) By virtue of their visible goal-correcting behavior the pupils are trying hard to be docile with respect to the teacher. (2) They hunt for signals and try to direct their behavior accordingly. (3) The signals occur in a matrix of cultural value and immediate circumstance. (4) This fact at times makes interpretation and conversion into action difficult. (5) A basis in mutual understanding is sought, but not quite realized at times. (6) The children's internal signals sometimes conflict with external ones and thus "jam the receiver." (7) Both children and teacher want something. At present we may say that the children want acceptance by the teacher, and teacher wants acceptance by the children. (8) However, it is clear, because of the mix-up that may occur in interpreting signals, as in the lesson on healthy thoughts, that the desires of teacher and pupil are sometimes not quite complementary. (9) Teacher must avoid too many frustrating (painful) failures like that of Alice, otherwise lessons will break down.

As we proceed with this lesson, we shall see how teacher and pupils strive to "get on the same wave length," a condition never quite reached because of the different levels of organization of teacher and pupil and the unawareness of this fact on the part of the teacher.

Two boys, the "dialogue team," now come to the front of the class and dramatize the football incident.

Teacher, to the class: Which boy do you think handled the problem in a better way?
Rupert: Billy did, because he didn't get angry. . . . It was better to play together than to do nothing with the football.
Teacher: That's a good answer, Rupert. Has anything similar happened to you, Joan?
Joan can think of nothing.
(Observer notes: I do not approve of this business in action, though I have not yet thought it through. But I was intermittently uncomfortable, disapproving, and rebellious at the time.)
Sylvester: I had an experience. My brother got a hat with his initials on it because he belongs to a fraternity, and I wanted one like it and couldn't have one and his was too big for me to wear, and it ended up that I asked him if he could get me some letters with my initials, and he did.
Betty: My girl-friend got a bike that was a 26-inch, and mine was only 24, and I asked my sister what I should do. Then my girl-friend came over and was real nice about it, and let me ride it.
Teacher approves of this and says: Didn't it end up that they both had fun without unhappiness? (Observer notes: Constant questioning of class, with expectation of affirmative answers: that wasn't this the right way, the best way, etc., to do it?)

Here we note that the teacher herself has gone astray, for on the one hand her aim is to get instances from the children in which they themselves have been yielding and capable of resolving their own jealousy, etc., while on the other hand, in the instance given by Betty, it was not Betty who yielded, but her friend. The child immediately following Betty imitated her since Betty had been praised by the teacher:

Matilde: My girl-friend got a 26-inch bike and mine was only 24, but she only let me ride it once a month. But for my birthday my mother's getting me a new one, probably (proudly) a "28." (Many children rush in with the information that "28" doesn't exist.) Matilde replies that she'll probably have to raise the seat then, for she's too big for a "26."

This instance suggests more clearly, perhaps, than the others another possible factor in making the stories of the children end always with their getting what they want: the children may be afraid to lose face with their peers by acknowledging they did not get something they wanted.

As we go on with this lesson, we shall see how the children's need for substitute gratification and their inability to accept frustration prevent them from picking up the teacher's message. As we continue, we shall see how, in spite of the teacher's driving insistence on her point, the children continue to inject their conflicts into the lesson, while at the same time they gropingly try to find a way to gratify the teacher. *They* cannot give the right answers because of their conflicts; teacher cannot handle their conflicts because she cannot perceive them. The lesson goes on:

Teacher: I notice that some of you are only happy when you get your own way. (Observer noticed too, horrified.) You're not thinking this through, and I want you to. Think of an experience when you didn't get what you want. Think it through. (Observer wonders: Are the children volunteering because of expectations, making desperate efforts to meet the expectation even though they do not quite understand it?)

Charlie: His ma was going to the movies and he wanted to go with her, and she wouldn't let him, and she went off to the movies, and he was mad, but then he went outside and there were some kids playing baseball, so he played baseball.

Teacher: But suppose you hadn't gotten to play baseball? You would have felt hurt because you didn't get what you wanted. We can't help feeling hurt when we are disappointed. What could you have done? How could you have handled it? (Observer notes: Teacher is not getting what she wants, but I am not sure the kids can understand. Is this a function of immaturity, or of spoiling by parents? Seems to me the continued effort to extract an idea they have not encompassed may be resulting in reinforcement of the one they *have* got—that you eventually get the watch, or the bicycle, or whatever.)

Charlie: So I can't go to the movies; so I can't play baseball; so I'll do something around the house.

Teacher: Now you're beginning to think! It takes courage to take disappointments. (Turning to the class) What did we learn? The helpful way. . . .

Class: is the healthy way!

Thus the lesson reaches this point on a note of triumphant docility, but of pseudo-complementarity. If the teacher had been able to perceive the underlying factors that made it impossible for these children to accept delayed gratification or total momentary frustration, and had handled *that* problem instead of doggedly sticking to a text that required a stereotyped answer, she would have come closer to the children and would not have had to back out of the situation by extracting a parrot-like chorusing. The teacher had to get a "right" answer, and the children ended up giving her one, since that is what they are in school for. Thus on one level teacher and pupils were complementary, but on another they were widely divergent. This is the characteristic condition of the American middle-class schoolroom.

If we review all the verbal messages sent by the teacher, we will see how hard she has worked to get the answer she wants; how she has corrected and "improved" her signaling in response to the eager feedback from the children:

1. Do you believe it's easier to deal with your thoughts if you own up to them, Betty?
2. Have you any experience like this in the book, Alice?
3. What could you do with mean feelings?
4. What did Susie (in the book) do?
5. (Rupert says that Billy, the character in the book, handled the problem in the better way because he did not get angry.) That's a good answer, Rupert.
6. (Betty tells how nice her girl-friend was, letting her ride her bike.) Teacher approves of this and says. Didn't it end up that they both had fun without unhappiness?
7. I notice that some of you are happy only when you get your own way.
8. What could you have done (when you did not get your own way)?
9. Now you're beginning to think. It takes courage to take disappointments. What did we learn? The helpful way . . . and the class responds, is the healthy way.

DISCUSSION AND CONCLUSIONS

This paper has been an effort to describe the mental docility of middle-class American children *in their schoolrooms.* It says nothing about the home or the play groups. The analysis shows how children are taught to find the answer the teacher wants, and to give it to her. That they sometimes fail is beside the point, because their trying so hard is itself evidence of docility; and an understanding of the reasons for failure helps us to see why communication breaks down and pseudo-understanding takes its place. When communication breaks down it is often because complementarity between sender (teacher) and receivers (pupils) is not exact; and it is not exact because teacher and pupils are at different levels of emotional organization.

We may now ask: Why are these children, whose phantasies our unpublished research has found to contain so many hostile and anxious elements, so docile in the classroom? Whey do they struggle so hard to gratify the teacher and try in so many ways, as our protocols show, to bring themselves to the teacher's attention?

We might, of course, start with the idea of the teacher as a parent-figure and the children as siblings competing for teacher's favor. We could refer to the unresolved dependency needs of children of this age, which makes them seek support in the teacher, who then manipulates this seeking and the children's sibling rivalry in order, as our unpublished research suggests, to pit the children against each other. Other important factors, however, that appear in middle-class schoolrooms ought to be taken into consideration. For example, our research shows the children's tendency to destructively criticize each other and the teacher's repeated reinforcement of this tendency. We have taken note, in our research, of the anxiety in the children as illustrated in the stories they tell and observed that these very stories are subjected to carping criticism by other children, the consequence of which would be anything but an alleviation of that anxiety. Hence the schoolroom is a place in which the child's underlying anxiety may be heightened. In an effort to alleviate this he seeks approval of the teacher, by giving right answers and by doing what teacher wants him to do under most circumstances. Finally, we cannot omit the teacher's need to be gratified by the attention-hungry behavior of the children.

A word is necessary about these classrooms as middle-class. The novel *Blackboard Jungle,* by Evan Hunt, describes schoolroom behavior of lower-class children. There we see them solidly against the teacher, as representative of the middle class. But in the classes we have observed we see the children against each other, with the teacher abetting the process. Thus, as the teacher in middle-class schools directs the hostility of the children toward one another (particularly in the form of criticism), and away from herself, she reinforces the competitive dynamics within the middle class itself. The teacher in the lower-class schools, on the other hand, appears to become the organizing stimulus for behavior that integrates the lower class, as the children unite in expressing their hostility to the teacher.

In conclusion, it should be pointed out that the mental docility (or near docility) achieved in these middle-class schoolrooms is a peculiar middle-class kind of docility. It is not based on authoritarian control backed by fear of corporal punishment, but rather on fear of loss of love. More precisely, it rests on the need to bask in the sun of the teacher's acceptance. It is not fear of scolding or of physical pain that makes these children docile, but rather fear of finding oneself outside the warmth of the inner circle of teacher's sheltering acceptance. This kind of docility can be more lethal than the other, for it does not breed rebellion and independence, as struggle against authoritarian controls may, but rather a kind of cloying paralysis; a sweet imprisonment without pain. Looking at the matter from another point of view, we might say that, were these children not fearful of loss of love, they would be indifferent to the teacher's messages. In a sense what the teacher's signals are really saying is: "This is the way to be loved by me; and this is the way I want you to love me."

6

Chicanos and the Schools*

DAVID L. BACHELOR

The purpose of this paper is to describe some of the processes that appear to be contributing to the poor school performance of Chicano children. Much has been written concerning the fact that Chicano children generally do badly in school, but there has been relatively little interest shown in describing the specific school practices that seem to contribute to the poor performance. Until we are able to describe some of the injurious school practices it will be difficult, if not impossible, to design alternative practices that will help the Chicano child fulfill his potential.

The descriptions in this report are based on some intensive but necessarily narrow research done at the University of New Mexico.[1] The research began almost by accident when the investigator invited some Chicano university students to talk to him of the problems they could recall experiencing when they were public school students. The interest of the university students and the possible flaws in such retrospective data led us to interview high school students. Another investigator, in the course of his participant observation study, kindly supplied us with some data collected from elementary and junior high school students. The "sample" whose testimony provides the basis for this paper is made up largely of male high school students, though some of this data is from younger students. Since the interviewees were not selected according to any plan to insure representativeness, our descriptions and observations may not be generalizable, though we treat them as such in this paper. All of the interviews were collected in 1969.

Although we interviewed four girls (two high school students, one college student, and one adult nonstudent), we have not included female students in our analysis. We had difficulty in eliciting responses from the female interviewees and the sessions were not very informative. It was therefore decided to concentrate on male students and reserve the investigation of female students' experiences for the future.

The male students who supplied us with this information were all from a single urban area of over 300,000 population. All had been born in the United States and most had lived in the state and in the city for several years. All lived

---

*An unpublished paper written for this volume.

with their families, and though family income was low there was an organized home life and a noticeable degree of family support. In short, we are describing the experiences of boys from low-income, blue-collar homes, perhaps representative of the large middle portion of the Chicano community in the Southwest. The boys were not from "multiproblem" or "clinical" families.[2]

THE CHICANO MILIEU

In this section we will describe the student's background as it provides the basis used to evaluate the school. We will attempt to identify some of the ways in which the school affects the student and how he interprets and reacts to these school influences.

The typical Chicano, from a low-income and urban setting, enters school from a milieu in which the evaluation of school is at best ambivalent. School is seen as the means to many things that are desirable to Chicanos, as to many other groups. But the desirability of and value attached to an education are partially offset by the school experiences that are typical in the community. The student's parents, older brothers, sisters, and friends have also been to school. It is likely that their attendance was marked by few successes and many bitter memories. Their remarks may still honor education but at the same time ridicule the local school and particular teachers.

Despite the rationalizations that may be used to explain away failure in the community, it is likely that education is valued and teachers generally respected by Chicano parents and other adults. The interview data indicates, however, that there is a gap between the general verbal support given to the abstraction "education" and the practical support given to class work. It is not that the Chicano parents are unwilling to back word with deed, but that they are so often distracted by the demands of keeping a home together on insufficient funds,[3] by contending with the demands placed upon them by a majority culture they may only incompletely understand, that they have neither the strength nor the skill to lend practical help to their children. General verbal support and encouragement by the parents may be enough to help the child realize some success in the early grades, where enthusiasm counts heavily and where the child can actively participate in the work of the classroom. In later grades, however, the heavier stress on cognitive acquisition, memorizing and manipulating abstractions, and the greater mechanization of instruction, typically leaves the child and the parents far behind.

An ambivalent assessment of school is pervasive in the Chicano subculture. On the one hand, school is seen clearly as the initial step toward a good job and a better life. On the other hand, the experiences of the older children, passed on to the younger, must generate a good deal of apprehension in the younger student concerning his ability to perform well. In addition, the comments of the older children will provide the younger with a set of stereotypes of the school and a set of rationalizations, both of which are designed to explain, and explain away, Chicano failure in school.

This confusion and ambivalence is epitomized in a statement made by one of the university students during an interview. He mentioned that the educated Chicano is an enigma to his noneducated neighbors. The puzzlement may be compounded of both envy and dislike, the reaction to him by a need for the preservation of self-respect. The noneducated Chicano feels envy for one who speaks English well, is regularly employed, is well paid, and dresses nicely. The dislike may be due to the strangeness of the manner of the educated Chicano. The label of "sell-out" or worse may be attached to the educated Chicano because he has punctured some of the self-protective facade of the uneducated Chicano. The uneducated Chicano can be more comfortable with his failure as long as he does not see too many exceptions; when he sees an exception he has to rationalize it away in order to protect his own self-esteem.

THE CHICANO STUDENT

The ambivalence toward, and even the distrust of, the school which the Chicano child feels in his milieu takes on real form and substance when he attends classes. Once in school the stress he has felt indirectly in his neighborhood becomes objectified in the tools of the classroom communications and most painfully in the language of the school. In school begins that curious but not inexplicable positive-negative relationship of the Chicano to the language of the majority, the language of success: English. The Chicano child understands that facility in English is the means to success, to power and status in the school, and that ability in expression is the means to the teacher's approval and reward. He understands this but he cannot often handle this strange and (for him) clumsy tool. It is likely that at first he will try to express himself in the only way school has defined as proper. But his attempts will be colored by his apprehension. If he has no Anglo student in his class to provide a standard of facility, there still are the seemingly effortless words of the teachers. Compared to these examples of mastery, his own efforts will appear to him to be pitiful and laughable. He has something to offer but it is in the wrong code and therefore is usually inadmissable in the classroom.

Our interview data provide abundant evidence concerning the fear engendered in the Chicano child when he is called upon to recite or to give an oral report in class. His apprehension seems to stem as much from his concern that his efforts will be met with laughter as from his inexperience in the formal atmosphere of the school. When the laughter comes from his Chicano classmates the effect is worsened. Laughter, any laughter, in a sense validates the Chicano reciter as a stereotype, but when his Chicano classmates join the laughter the child is alone and even more vulnerable.

It is impressive that adult Chicanos can still recall their anxiety when as children they were called upon to report in class. They can recall their fear—one respondent called it terror—even now, long after the event. The hopelessness they felt as children in front of the classroom has now been distilled into resentment that they ever had to undergo such an experience. It is clear that their accent and their lack of confidence in their ability to express themselves in English generated these fears. It is also clear that the typical Chicano child in this stressful situation does not feel he can look to the teacher for sympathy or understanding. The classroom work becomes one long experience in the validating of a stereotype for the typical Chicano student.

The formalism of the classroom, the organization of the school, add to the confusion and to the detachment of the child. He feels strange and inept in the school's world of bells, schedules, textbooks, and universalistic rules. These procedures have not been a common part of his experience yet he is often expected to act as if they had, often expected to understand the rules and to subscribe to them and to their rationale. Standardized and hierarchical distances between people in school, between students, school teachers and administrators, are supported by the supposed expertise of the teacher and by the requirements of bureaucratic rationality. These formalities act to increase the distance between the Chicano student and his teacher: a distance that is crucial in the performance of this student. Other students, including Anglos, must also cope with this distance and this formality, but they have other resources, skills, and abilities that help them to survive. The Chicano student typically has no other resources to help him survive in his new and often confusing role. The result, according to the interview data, is that the child feels little immediacy, little active participation, in what goes on in class. Involvement and the feeling that the work is somehow important to him and for him is not developed, hence school work means little and takes on the character of arbitrary, disconnected impositions.

This feeling of confusion and detachment probably does not develop steadily from the first day of school onward. In kindergarten and the early grades the generally looser rules, greater variety of activities, and closer, more personal relations allowed with the teacher may result in generally happier experiences for the student and some progress. It is in the later elementary years, perhaps from fourth or fifth grade on, and in high school, when there is a growing concentration on "work" (test performance, cognition, achievement, and grades) and on increased classroom formality and regimentation, that the child experiences more injury than support.

Detachment leads to disenchantment, and both developing responses tend to devalue the Chicano child's self-image and, as a result, depress his school performance. As a young child in a class with Anglos or with an Anglo (or anglicized) teacher, the Chicano begins to receive abundant evidence of what he takes to be his general ineptness with the tasks assigned. This will not be entirely new or surprising to him, for the growing disharmony he feels in school has been foreshadowed by the ambivalence in his milieu. His sense of being a failure, his declining self-evaluation, will have found support in the subtle community prejudices against Chicanos, in the readily visible stereotype of the sleepy Mexican. The cultural slights and insults will deepen his sense of being inferior, of being from an inferior culture.

In school, as one interviewee put it, the Chicano student becomes accustomed to the meaninglessness of it all, to the feeling that nothing really, *really* related to him. In assessing his own future performance, measuring his own aspirations, it becomes a habit to expect that someone else will do it better. It will not be a random someone who will do, and be, better—it will always be a member of that demonstrably superior group, the Anglo majority culture. The school, in effect, begins to provide rapidly accumulating experiences by which the Chicano child learns that the Anglo child will always be his superior. The Chicano child sits in class quietly, albeit uncomfortably, and is convinced of his own defectiveness (as the interviewee described it).

Any child can stand only so much devaluing, or damage to his image of himself, before he begins to react and to seek ways in which he can maintain some measure of self-respect, some measure of status in the eyes of others. He cannot communicate comfortably in English, nor can he confidently navigate across that formal distance that separates him from the teacher, and the breakdown of these channels has the effect of closing off legitimate accesses to respect and status for the Chicano student in the formal school situation. It becomes much easier to live up to the stereotype than to compete in a contest that seems to be held only to prove the Chicano's unworthiness.

Typically this process of exclusion is experienced as a group phenomenon by the individual Chicano student. At least he is not alone, and he can seek the solace that shared misery can afford. From this shared exclusion grow group attempts to seek out alternative paths to status, a different prestige rationale, in order to offset the devalued self-image arising from failure in school. Indeed the community ambivalence toward school and other aspects of the majority culture, the student's own early anxieties concerning communication, the lack of practical support at home, and the growing meaninglessness of the classroom all conspire to increase the Chicano child's need for constructive data telling him how he fits into it all. His needs and those of his fellow students are greater, and neglect of those needs constitutes a great failure by the school.

One way to deal with a damaging situation is to define it as illegitimate, irrelevant, or inane, and if that definition is shared it will then take on some semblance of a "true" judgment. We can see in this phenomenon the proximate origins of the "anti-intellectualism" that is so often identified as a general characteristic of lower socioeconomic groups and specifically of Mexican-Americans.[4] It is a more elaborate rendering of "anti-schoolism"; it is emphasizing one-half of the ambivalent assessment assigned to the school by the Chicano community. It may be posited that the developments we have outlined here and the Chicano student's intuited reaction to them are related to the "fatalism" and to the particular brand of *machismo* so often attributed to Chicano gangs and to the Mexican-American subculture in general. The individual Chicano student may be characterized as "fatalistic" because he feels he is being subjected to disconnected and meaningless demands in the classroom, demands whose only purpose appears to be to demonstrate his lack of ability, to frustrate him. The student has no chance to influence these demands on him, no power to control them. He may be identified as a practitioner or adherent of *machismo* because these practices (fighting, sexual episodes, elaborate masculinity, and codes of personal honor), all supported to a degree by his milieu, provide the *alternative means to status which the school has failed to provide.* This latter concept, furthermore, provides the rationale by which the school's judgments of the Chicano students, the explicit and implicit assessments, can be defined as irrelevant. The characterization of individual teachers as "pansies" or as generally asexual individuals epitomizes the stereotype of the school among Chicanos. Interviewees, for instance, spoke of such typical school dicta as "learn to fit in with your peer group," "develop the ability to get along with others" (the sense of such phrases if not the exact wording pervades most classroom and school activities) as "queer little words," as denoting demeaning, unmasculine behavior. The interviewees, in this case all adults, further responded that you do not share and share alike: "You don't take turns, you take it!" In effect, by emphasizing masculinity, the feminine and cooperative ethic of the school is defined as illegitimate. This stance, of course indirectly generated and nurtured by the school, pretty well insures the ultimate failure of the Chicano student.

THE ANGLO SCHOOL

The purpose of this section is to describe some teacher practices and school procedures that seem to be responsible for many of the Chicano student's problems. In describing these typical school procedures we will also attempt to detail what we feel will be the student's interpretation of them and reaction to them.

Operationally defined, teaching means dispensing information.[5] In the early grades the information deals largely with proper student behavior and skill development. Later in school the emphasis is almost exclusively on subject matter, even to the extent of leaving behavior correction to nonteachers (principals, coaches, counselors). We do not take issue here with the information-dispensing function of the school but we believe that the way the information is presented, and the content of that information, creates difficulties for the Chicano student and ultimately contributes to his failure in school. We do not believe that the typical classroom methods and procedures are well suited to facilitate communication with the Chicano student or to encourage his intellectual development.

Much of the classroom work, the dispensing of information, is accomplished by means of lectures, or at least by having the teacher tell the students all about it. Lecturing means that the teacher is the active participant, the student is the passive one. To the student who has no doubts about the value and relevance of the school to his aspirations (whatever his sentiments concerning a particular class), lecturing presents no crisis. To the student whose auditory discrimination allows him to tune out distractions, whose past training has enabled him to fit phrases and sentences in English into a meaningful idea, and whose experience has trained him to handle and appreciate abstractions of the order used in the classroom, lecturing may be a learning experience. These capabilities, however, are more commonly descriptive of the Anglo, not the Chicano student. To the Chicano student lecturing presents many problems. In common with most students from low-income homes, this child has probably learned in the past concretely and actively, by touching, by feeling, and by exploring with his senses rather than with his intellect. He is more practical, his hands are used to handling real things, his intellect is unused to handling abstractions of the order used in the classroom.[6] Therefore the passivity of his role as student is doubly strange and especially galling. The world of ideas, of abstractions, stupefies him and the strange language of instruction completes his detachment.

Lecturing and the general sense of social distances between the active (teacher) and the passive (student) participants mean that the special problems and expectations of the Chicano student are rarely recognized by the teacher. In effect the teacher appears to expect, and generally does expect, all students to know and to do certain things that the Chicano child in fact does not know or cannot do. The teacher's expectations for all are the same, are equal, but the result of that expectation is to insure inequality! The expectation of the teacher, the bland assumption that all children will do the same things and in the same way, indicates to the Chicano students that the teacher is not aware of their problems, that she does not understand them or their troubles. The classroom can become an anxious place full of dreary defeats when it is found that there is no recourse, when the work is seen as a continual exercise in frustration. The teacher is seen by the Chicano student as the only one able to alleviate his frustration, but he is also aware that she does not even know about it.

Dispensing of information is not the only aspect of the school's basic function that appears to affect the Chicano students adversely; difficulties also develop from the nature of the information itself. Typically the information transmitted by the school to (or sometimes only *at*) the students contains an Anglo, middle-class, suburban bias. The Chicano child is taught, for example, that "good"—*i.e.* health and nutrition—is synonomous with a typical Anglo meal. The obvious implication is that the meal the Chicano child sits down to in his home is not worthy, is not "good". Typically he is presented with the suburban story of Dick and Jane, a situation that has little relevance to Ricardo and Juanita who live in the barrio. Despite the fact that most Chicano students know that Spaniards and Mexicans have had a 400-year role in the development of the Southwest, they read history books that mention little if any of this contribution. In these books Christianity in the New World begins with the Pilgrims and not with the Spanish colonizers. Conquistadores conquered while the English immigrants "settled". If mentioned, Mexico is presented as a comic opera country of revolutions and bandit chiefs, and the major moral is usually that one Texan is worth three or four Mexicans in a battle. The role of Spain and Mexico in these Anglo-dominated versions of history seems to be to provide examples of the Manifest Destiny of the United States to rule the territory from one sea to the other (including some of the territory beyond). Extolling the greatness and uncritically relating the accomplishments of the United States blots out the non-Anglo contributions and generally places a negative connotation on any mention of Hispanic influences.

What we have outlined here is a fund of material which, at the minimum, will be distant and meaningless to the Chicano child. At the maximum, it will further devalue his already weakened self-image.

The relationships between people, their impact on one another and the impact of the school on both, that we have described must be seen as dynamic, changing and deepening through time. Many of the student and teacher reactions we have hypothesized will develop slowly and almost unconsciously on the part of both. It is clear that these reactions, often only half-recognized by the people involved, produce an uncomfortable situation damaging to learning.

The detachment and disenchantment of the student, caused by the forces outlined above, cause him to react in self-protective ways by means of stereotyping the school and the teachers. It is unlikely that the teacher remains unaware for long of this student evaluation of her. The stereotype of teachers as "pansies," as being "out of it," as "not knowing anything," provides the rationale for a variety of student actions designed to disrupt the class or to retreat from it. These actions, in and of themselves dangerous to the teacher's control of the classroom, tend to cut off any possibility of working out compromises. They illustrate a growing disdain for the teacher and finally cut off any basis for teacher-student understanding or cooperation. As a means of preserving her control and defining the student's stereotype of her and the school as illegitimate, the teacher builds her own stereotypes and rigidifies the social distances in the classroom.[7] She accomplishes the latter by means of greater emphasis on the custodial aspects of the teaching role and by the increased mechanization of instruction. Order, regularity, finishing the chapter on time, sitting straight in the seats, being quiet and insuring that all forms are filled out properly, become the ruling principles in the everyday affairs of the classroom. In addition the teacher "feels" the judgment of her Chicano students and takes disciplinary steps to deny it legitimacy. Classroom rules multiply and stiffen; disciplinary rules obviate understanding and automatically assign motives for student acts. Punishment is carefully graded and inexorably applied. Classroom time is taken up with a cat-and-mouse game as the teacher tries to catch the lawbreakers and so protect her power, while the student tries to gain points with his gang by transgressing without being caught.

Quite naturally the teacher (and the school, as we shall see) responds with her own categorizations, her own stereotypes. As a "professional" she feels the need to bolster her assessments with objective (or at least objective-appearing) support; hence they will be rationalized by some half-remembered behavioral science data. Chicano students will be feared because they are "tough"; they will be disliked because of their "smart" actions; they will be despaired of by the teacher because they are "unresponsive" and "unmotivated".

Teachers learn to accept the failure of these students, an acceptance at least partially developed from the stereotype. "What can you do when those kids have so little sleep, when there is so much noise at home, when it is so dirty there? They don't have any books in their house!" Such phrases as these provide the justification for the teacher's not expecting too much from her Chicano students. They also provide the teacher with an excuse for her own failure—the child or the home is at fault, not the teacher.

Stereotyping by individual teachers becomes general among the staff, and assessments of individual students are shared, by means of conversations in the teachers' lounge and by means of standards of behavior widely shared among the staff. Formally the school imposes stereotypes of its own by several methods. "Streaming" or homogeneous grouping may be officially supported by test results or previous class work. Formally described polar groups may be called "Fast" or "Slow," "Accelerated" or "Compensatory," but the real meanings of these designations to the children are not obscured by the euphemisms. For the Chicano student to find himself in a "Remedial" class is for him to find still another judgment against himself: he has something for which the school has to find a remedy. That the "Remedial" class will be a watered-down version of the "Accelerated" classes will not only testify again to his lack of ability, to his ineptness; its irrelevance will amost insure his continued failure.

Later in his school stay the Chicano's choice of high school elective courses will add to his classification as a failure. His past lack of success with academic classes, repeated indignities experienced with the tools of class communication, and his enduring propensity for concrete learning will usually result in the Chicano student's opting for the vocational or the commercial program rather than the college prep one. Chances are he will want to go to college (he is still fully aware of the real rewards that avenue promises), but he is either convinced by now that he cannot expect to go or else he just does not know how to go about doing it. His ignorance of specific job or career alternatives is not likely to be remedied by a few sudden and unsatisfying sessions with a counselor. The Chicano student has not been informed, except typically in terms so general as to be meaningless, about vocational options; he has not accumulated either the experience of success upon which to build positive anticipations of the future, nor has he acquired the necessary confidence and sophistication to approach and deal successfully with the large, impersonal bureaucracies that serve as gatekeepers to the better life. On the contrary, the sum of his experiences in the school bureaucracy has taught him that he cannot deal with them, understand them, or hope that they will understand him. When he is faced with these options it is not hard to understand that the Chicano child, now a young adult, will choose to leave school at the first possible chance and select the "immediate gratification" of a job—and freedom.

6. NOTES

1. The author wishes to acknowledge the help of Chicano students Armando Quinones, Joe Sedillo, and Robert Gonzales in collecting data for this article.

2. Eleanor Pavenstedt (ed.), *The Drifters: Children of Disadvantaged Lower-Class Families* (Boston: Little, Brown, 1967), pp. 257 and 229.

3. O. E. Leonard and H. W. Johnson, *Low-Income Families in the Spanish-Surname Population of the Southwest* (Washington, D.C.: Economic Research Service, U.S. Department of Agriculture, Agricultural Economic Report No. 112, April 1967), Table 7, p. 12. The data shows that 30.8% of the Spanish-surname urban population in the five Southwestern states of Arizona, California, Colorado, New Mexico, and Texas had incomes under $3,000 a year.

4. Albert K. Cohen and Harold M. Hodges, "Lower-Blue-Collar Characteristics," *Social Problems,* Spring 1963, pp. 303-34.

5. " 'Covering' the year's worth of current academic content remains a gatekeeper of the present system and is to all intents and purposes the primary objective of urban education." Mario Fantini and Gerald Weinstein, *Making Urban Schools Work* (New York: Holt, Rinehart and Winston, 1968), p. 13.

6. Frank Riessman, *The Culturally Deprived Child* (New York: Harper and Row, 1962).

7. "It is the 'slum' child who most deeply offends the teacher's moral sensibilities. In almost every area mentioned, these children, by word, action, or appearance, manage to give teachers the feeling that they are immoral, and not respectable. In terms of physical appearance and condition, they disgust and depress the middle-class teacher." Howard Becker, "Social-Class Variations in the Teacher-Pupil Relationship," in Robert Bell and Holger Stub (eds.), *The Sociology of Education* (Homewood, Dorsey Press, 1968), p. 164. These observations were based on experiences in the Negro ghetto of Chicago. We would argue that the situation is similar in the Southwest; it is not color differences that repel teachers as much as the variation between their standards and tastes and those of their charges.

7

Social-Class Variations in the Teacher-Pupil Relationship*

HOWARD S. BECKER

The major problems of workers in the service occupations are likely to be a function of their relationship to their clients or customers, those for whom or on whom the occupational service is performed.[1] Members of such occupations typically have some image of the "ideal" client, and it is in terms of this fiction that they fashion their conceptions of how their work ought to be performed, and their actual work techniques. To the degree that actual clients approximate this ideal the worker will have no "client problem."

In a highly differentiated urban society, however, clients will vary greatly, and ordinarily only some fraction of the total of potential clients will be "good" ones. Workers tend to classify clients in terms of the way in which they vary from this ideal. The fact of client variation from the occupational ideal emphasizes the intimate relation of the institution in which work is carried on to its environing society. If that society does not prepare people to play their client roles in the manner desired by the occupation's members there will be conflicts, and problems for the workers in the performance of their work. One of the major factors affecting the production of suitable clients is the cultural diversity of various social classes in the society. The cultures of particular social-class groups may operate to produce clients who make the worker's position extremely difficult.

We deal here with this problem as it appears in the experience of the functionaries of a large urban educational institution, the Chicago public school system, discussing the way in which teachers in this system observe, classify and react to class-typed differences in the behavior of the children with whom they work. The material to be presented is thus relevant not only to problems of occupational organization but also to the problem of differences in the educational opportunities available to children of various social-classes. Warner, Havighurst and Loeb[2] and Hollingshead[3] have demonstrated the manner in which the schools tend to favor and select out children of the middle classes. Allison Davis has pointed to those factors in the class cultures involved which make lower-class children less and middle-class children more adaptable to the work and behavioral standards of the school.[4] This paper will contribute to knowledge in this area by analzying the manner in which the public school teacher reacts to these cultural differences and, in so doing, perpetuates the discrimination of our educational system against the lower-class child.

The analysis is based on sixty interviews with teachers in the Chicago system.[5] The interviews were oriented around the general question of the problems of being a teacher and were not specifically directed toward discovering feelings about social-class differences among students. Since these differences created some of the teachers' most pressing problems they were continually brought up by the interviewees themselves. They typically distinguished three social-class groups with which they, as teachers, came in contact: (1) a bottom stratum, probably equivalent to the lower-lower and parts of the upper-lower class; (2) an upper stratum, probably equivalent to the upper-middle class; and (3) a middle stratum, probably equivalent ot the lower-middle and parts of the upper-lower class. We will adopt the convention of referring to these groups as lower, upper and middle groups, but it should be understood that this terminology refers to the teachers' classification of students and not to the ordinary sociological description.

We will proceed by taking up the three problems that loomed largest in the teachers' discussion of adjustment to their students: (1) the problem of *teaching* itself, (2) the problem of *discipline,* and (3) the problem of the *moral acceptability* of the students. In each case the variation in the form of and adjustment to the problem by the characteristics of the children of the various class groups distinguished by teachers is discussed.

I

A basic problem in any occupation is that of performing one's given task successfully, and where this involves working with human beings their qualities are a major variable affecting the ease with which the work can be done. The teacher considers that she has done her job adequately when she has brought about an observable change in the children's skills and knowledge which she can attribute to her own efforts:

> Well, I would say that a teacher is successful when she is putting the material across to the children, when she is getting some response from them. I'll tell you something. Teaching is a very rewarding line of work, because you can see those children grow under your hands. You can see the difference in them after you've had them for five months. You can see where they've started and where they've got to. And it's all yours. It really is rewarding in that way, you can see results and know that it's your work that brought those results about.

She feels that she has a better chance of success in this area when her pupils are interested in attending and working hard in school, and are trained at home in such a way that they are bright and quick at school work. Her problems arise in teaching those groups who do not meet these specifications, for in these cases her teaching techniques, tailored to the "perfect" student, are inadequate to cope with the reality, and she is left with a feeling of having failed in performing her basic task.

Davis has described the orientations toward education in general, and school-work in particular, of the lower and middle classes:

> Thus, our educational system, which next to the family is the most effective agency in teaching good work habits to middle class people, is largely ineffective and unrealistic with underprivileged groups. Education fails to motivate such workers because our schools and our society both lack *real rewards* to offer underprivileged groups. Neither lower class children or adults will work hard in school or on the job just to please the teacher or boss. They are not going to learn to be ambitious, to be conscientious, and to study hard, as if school and work were a fine character-building game, which one plays just for the sake of playing. They can see, indeed, that those who work hard at school usually have families that already have the occupations, homes, and social acceptance that the school holds up as the rewards of education. The underprivileged workers can see also that the chances of their getting enough education to intake their attainment of these rewards in the future at all probable is very slight. Since they can win the rewards of prestige and social acceptance in their own slum groups without much education, they do not take very seriously the motivation taught by the school.[6]

As these cultural differences produce variations from the image of the "ideal" student, teachers tend to use class terms in describing the children with whom they work.

Children of the lowest group, from slum areas, are characterized as the most difficult group to teach successfully, lacking in interest in school, learning ability, and outside training:

> They don't have the right kind of study habits. They can't seem to apply themselves as well. Of course, it's not their fault; they aren't brought up right. After all, the parents in a neighborhood like that really aren't interested.... But, as I say, those children don't learn very quickly. A great many of them don't seem to be really interested in getting an education. I don't think they are. It's hard to get anything done with children like that. They simply don't respond.

In definite contrast are the terms used to describe children of the upper group:

> In a neighborhood like this there's something about the children. You just feel like you're accomplishing so much more. You throw an idea out and you can see that it takes hold. The children know what you're talking about and they think about it. Then they come in with projects and pictures and additional information, and it just makes you feel good to see it. They go places and see things, and they know what you're talking about. For instance, you might be teaching social studies or geography.... You bring

something up and a child says, "Oh, my parents took me to see that in the museum." You can just do more with material like that.

Ambivalent feelings are aroused by children of the middle group. While motivated to work hard in school they lack the proper out-of-school training:

> Well, they're very nice here, very nice. They're not hard to handle. You see, they're taught respect in the home and they're respectful to the teacher. They want to work and do well. . . . Of course, they're not too brilliant. You know what I mean. But they are very nice children and very easy to work with.

In short, the differences between groups made it possible for the teacher to feel successful at her job only with the top group; with the other groups she feels, in greater or lesser measure, that she has failed.

These differences in ability to do school work, as perceived by teachers, have important consequences. They lead, in the first place, to differences in actual teaching techniques. A young high school teacher contrasted the techniques used in "slum" schools with those used in "better" schools:

> At S————, there were a lot of guys who were just waiting till they were sixteen, so they could get out of school. L————, everybody—well, a very large percentage, I'll say—was going on to secondary school, to college. That certainly made a difference in their classroom work. You had to teach differently at the different schools. For instance, at S————, if you had demonstrations in chemistry they had to be pretty flashy, lots of noise and smoke, before they'd get interested in it. That wasn't necessary at L————. Or at S———— if you were having electricity or something like that you had to get the static electricity machine out and have them all stand around and hold hands so that they'd all get a little jolt.

Further, the teacher feels that where these differences are recognized by her superiors there will be a corresponding variation in the amount of work she is expected to accomplish. She expects that the amount of work and effort required of her will vary inversely with the social status of her pupils. This teacher compared schools from the extremes of the class range:

> So you have to be on your toes and keep up to where you're supposed to be in the course of study. Now, in a school like the D———— [slum school] you're just not expected to complete all that work. It's almost impossible. For instance, in the second grade we're supposed to cover nine spelling words a week. Well, I can do that up here at the K———— ["better" school], they can take nine new words a week. But the best class I ever had at the D———— was only able to achieve six words a week and they had to work pretty hard to get that. So I never finished the year's work in spelling. I couldn't. And I really wasn't expected to.

One resultant of this situation—in which less is expected of those teachers whose students are more difficult to teach—is that the problem becomes more aggravated in each grade, as the gap between what the children should know and what they actually do know becomes wider and wider. A principal of such a school describes the degeneration there of the teaching problem into a struggle to get a few basic skills across, in a situation where this cumulative effect makes following the normal program of study impossible:

> The children come into our upper grades with very poor reading ability. That means that all the way through our school everybody is concentrating on reading. It's not like that at a school like S———— [middle group] where they have science and history and so on. At a school like that they figure that from the first to fourth you learn to read and from fifth to eighth you read to learn. You use your reading to learn other material. Well, these children don't reach that second stage while they're with us. We have to plug along getting them to learn to read. Our teachers are pretty well satisfied if the children can read and do simple number work when they leave here. You'll find that they don't think very much of subjects like science, and so on. They haven't got any time for that. They're just trying to get these basic things over. . . . That's why our school is different from one like the S————.

Such consequences of teachers' differential reaction to various class groups obviously operate to further perpetuate those class-cultural characteristics to which they object in the first place.

II

Discipline is the second of the teacher's major problems with her students. Willard Waller pointed to its basis when he wrote that "Teacher and pupil confront each other in the school with an original conflict of desires, and however much that conflict may be reduced in amount, or however much it may be hidden, it still remains."[7] We must recognize that conflict, either actual or potential, is ever present in the teacher-pupil relationship, the teacher attempting to maintain her control against the children's efforts to break it.[8] This conflict is felt even with those children who present least difficulty; a teacher who considered her pupils models of good behavior nevertheless said:

> But there's that tension all the time. Between you and the students. It's hard on your nerves. Teaching is fun, if you enjoy your subject, but it's the discipline that keeps your nerves on edge, you know what I mean? There's always that tension. Sometimes people say, "Oh, you teach school. That's an easy job, just sitting around all day long." They don't know what it's really like. It's hard on your nerves.

The teacher is tense because she fears that she will lose control, which she tends to define in terms of some line beyond which she will not allow the children to go. Wherever she may draw this line (and there is considerable variation), the teacher feels that she has a "discipline" problem when the children attempt to push beyond it. The form and intensity of this problem are felt to vary from one social-class to another, as might be expected from Davis' description of class emphases on aggression:

> In general, middle-class aggression is taught to adolescents in the form of social and economic skills which will enable them to compete effectively at that level. . . . In lower-class families, physical aggression is as much a normal, socially approved and socially inculcated type of behavior as it is in frontier communities.[9]

These differences in child training are matched by variation in the teachers' reactions.

Children in "slum" schools are considered most difficult to control, being given to unrestrained behavior and physical violence. The interviews are filled with descriptions of such difficulties. Miriam Wagenschein, in a parallel study of the beginning school teacher, gave this summary of the experiences of these younger teachers in lower-class schools:

> The reports which these teachers give of what *can* be done by a group of children are nothing short of amazing. A young white teacher walked into her new classroom and was greeted with the comment, "Another damn white one." Another was "rushed" at her desk by the entire class when she tried to be extremely strict with them: Teachers report having been bitten, tripped, and pushed on the stairs. Another gave an account of a second grader throwing a milk bottle at the teacher and of a first grader having such a temper tantrum that it took the principal and two policemen to get him out of the room. In another school following a fight on the playground, the principal took thirty-two razor blades from children in a first grade room. Some teachers indicated fear that they might be attacked by irate persons in the neighborhoods in which they teach. Other teachers report that their pupils carry long pieces of glass and have been known to threaten other pupils with them, while others jab each other with hypodermic needles. One boy got angry with his teacher and knocked in the fender of her car.[10]

In these schools a major part of the teacher's time must be devoted to discipline; as one said: "It's just a question of keeping them in line." This emphasis on discipline detracts from the school's primary function of teaching, thus discriminating, in terms of available educational opportunity, against the children of these schools.

Children of the middle group are thought of as docile, and with them the teacher has least difficulty with discipline:

> Those children were much quieter, easier to work with. When we'd play our little games there was never any commotion. That was a very nice school to work in. Everything was quite nice about it. The children were easy to work with. . . .

Children of the upper group are felt hard to handle in some respects, and are often termed "spoiled," "overindulged," or "neurotic"; they do not play the role of the child in the submissive manner teachers consider appropriate. One interviewee, speaking of this group, said:

> I think most teachers prefer not to teach in that type of school. The children are more pampered and, as we say, more inclined to run the school for themselves. The parents are very much at fault. The children are not used to taking orders at home and naturally they won't take them at school either.

Teachers develop methods of dealing with these discipline problems, and these tend to vary between social-class groups as do the problems themselves. The basic device used by successful disciplinarians is to establish authority clearly on the first meeting with the class:

> You can't ever let them get the upper hand on you or you're through. So I start out tough. The first day I get a new class in, I let them know who's boss. . . . You've got to start off tough, then you can ease up as you go along. If you start out easy-going, when you try to get tough they'll just look at you and laugh.

Having once established such a relation, it is considered important that the teacher be consistent in her behavior so that the children will continue to respect and obey her:

> I let them know I mean business. That's one thing you must do. Say nothing that you won't follow through on. Some teachers will say anything to keep kids quiet, they'll threaten anything. Then they can't or won't carry out their threats. Naturally, the children won't pay any attention to them after that. You must never say anything that you won't back up.

In the difficult "slum" schools, teachers feel the necessity of using stern measures, up to and including physical violence (nominally outlawed):

> Technically you're not supposed to lay a hand on a kid. Well, they don't, technically. But there are a lot of ways of handling a kid so that it doesn't show—and then it's the teacher's word against the kid's, so the kid hasn't got a chance. Like dear Mrs.————. She gets mad at a kid, she takes him out in the hall. She gets him stood up against the wall. Then she's got a way of chucking the kid under the chin, only hard, so that it knocks his head against the wall. It doesn't leave a mark on him. But when he comes back in that room he can hardly see straight, he's so knocked out. It's really rough. There's a lot of little tricks like that that you learn about.

Where such devices are not used, there is recourse to violent punishment, "tongue lashings." All teachers, however, are not emotionally equipped for such behavior and must find other means:

> The worst thing I can do is lose my temper and start raving. . . . You've got to believe in that kind of thing in order for it to work. . . . If you don't honestly believe it it shows up and the children know you don't mean it and

it doesn't do any good anyway. . . . I try a different approach myself. Whenever they get too rowdy I go to the piano and . . . play something and we have rhythms or something until they sort of settle down . . . .That's what we call "softsoaping" them. It seems to work for me. It's about the only thing I can do.

Some teachers may also resort to calling in the parents, a device whose usefulness is limited by the fact that such summonses are most frequently ignored. The teacher's disciplinary power in such a school is also limited by her fear of retaliation by the students: "Those fellows are pretty big, and I just think it would take a bigger person than me to handle them. I certainly wouldn't like to try."

In the school with children of the middle group no strong sanctions are required, mild reprimands sufficing:

> Now the children at Z———— here are quite nice to teach. They're pliable, yes, that's the word, they're pliable. They will go along with you on things and not fight you. You can take them any place and say to them, "I'm counting on you not to disgrace your school. Let's see that Z———— spirit." And they'll behave for you. . . . They can be frightened, they have fear in them. They're pliable, flexible, you can do things with them. They're afraid of their parents and what they'll do to them if they get into trouble at school. And they're afraid of the administration. They're afraid of being sent down to the principal. So that they can be handled.

Children of the upper group often act in a way which may be interpreted as "misbehavior" but which does not represent a conscious attack on the teacher's authority. Many teachers are able to disregard such activity by interpreting it as a natural concomitant of the "brightness" and "intelligence" of such children. Where such an interpretation is not possible the teachers feel hampered by a lack of effective sanctions:

> I try different things like keeping them out of a gym period or a recess period. But that doesn't always work. I have this one little boy who just didn't care when I used those punishments. He said he didn't like gym anyway. I don't know what I'm going to do with him.

The teacher's power in such schools is further limited by the fact that the children are able to mobilize their influential parents so as to exert a large degree of control over the actions of school personnel.

It should be noted, finally, that disciplinary problems tend to become less important as the length of the teacher's stay in a particular school makes it possible for her to build a reputation which coerces the children into behaving without attempting any test of strength:[11]

> I have no trouble with the children. Once you establish a reputation and they know what to expect, they respect you and you have no trouble. Of

course, that's different for a new teacher, but when you're established that's no problem at all.

III

The third area of problems has been termed that of moral *acceptability,* and arises from the fact that some actions of one's potential clients may be offensive in terms of some deeply felt set of moral standards; these clients are thus morally unacceptable. Teachers find that some of their pupils act in such a way as to make themselves unacceptable in terms of the moral values centered around health and cleanliness, sex and agression, ambition and work, and the relations of age groups.

Children of the middle group present no problem at this level, being universally described as clean, well dressed, moderate in their behavior, and hard working. Children from the "better" neighborhoods are considered deficient in the important moral traits of politeness and respect for elders:

> Where the children come from wealthy homes. That's not so good either. They're not used to doing work at home. They have maids and servants of all kinds and they're used to having things done for them, instead of doing them themselves. . . . They won't do anything. For instance, if they drop a piece of cloth on the floor, they'll just let it lay, they wouldn't think of bending over to pick it up. That's janitor's work to them. As a matter of fact, one of them said to me once: "If I pick that up there wouldn't be any work for the janitor to do." Well, it's pretty difficult to deal with children like that.

Further, they are regarded as likely to transgress what the teachers define as moral boundaries in the matter of smoking and drinking; it is particularly shocking that such "nice" children should have such vices.

It is, however, the "slum" child who most deeply offends the teacher's moral sensibilities; in almost every area mentioned above these children, by word, action or appearance, manage to give teachers the feeling that they are immoral and not respectable. In terms of physical appearance and condition they disgust and depress the middle-class teacher. Even this young woman, whose emancipation from conventional morality is symbolized in her habitual use of the argot of the jazz musician, was horrified by the absence of the toothbrush from the lives of her lower-class students:

> It's just horribly depressing, you know. I mean, it just gets you down. I'll give you an example. A kid complained of a toothache one day. Well, I thought I could take a look and see if I could help him or something so I told him to open his mouth. I almost wigged when I saw his mouth. His teeth were all rotten, every one of them. Just filthy and rotten. Man, I mean, I was really shocked, you know. I said, "Don't you have a toothbrush?" He said no, they were only his baby teeth and Ma said he didn't need a toothbrush for that. So I really got upset and looked in all their mouths. Man, I never saw anything like it. They were all like that, practically. I asked how

many had toothbrushes, and about a quarter of them had them. Boy, that's terrible. And I don't dig that crap about baby teeth either, because they start getting molars when they're six, I know that. So I gave them a talking to, but what good does it do? The kid's mouth was just rotten. They never heard of a toothbrush or going to a dentist.

These children, too, are more apt than the other groups to be dishonest in some way that will get them into trouble with law enforcement officials. The early (by middle-class standards) sexual maturity of such children is quite upsetting to the teacher:

> One thing about these girls is, well, some of them are not very nice girls. One girl in my class I've had two years now. She makes her money on the side as a prostitute. She's had several children. . . . This was a disturbing influence on the rest of the class.

Many teachers reported great shock on finding that words which were innocent to them had obscene meanings for their lower-class students:

> I decided to read them a story one day. I started reading them "Puss in Boots" and they just burst out laughing. I couldn't understand what I had said that had made them burst out like that.
> I went back over the story and tried to find out what it might be. I couldn't see anything that would make them laugh. I couldn't see anything at all in the story. Later one of the other teachers asked me what had happened. She was one of the older teachers. I told her that I didn't know; that I was just reading them a story and they thought it was extremely funny. She asked me what story I read them and I told her "Puss in the Boots." She said, "Oh, I should have warned you not to read that one." It seems that Puss means something else to them. It means something awful—I wouldn't even tell you what. It doesn't mean a thing to us.[12]

Warner, Havighurst and Loeb note that "unless the middle-class values change in America, we must expect the influence of the schools to favor the values of material success, individual striving, thrift, and social mobility.[13] Here again, the "slum" child violates the teacher's moral sense by failing to display these virtues:

> Many of these children don't realize the worth of an education. They have no desire to improve themselves. And they don't care much about school and schoolwork as a result. That makes it very difficult to teach them.
> That kind of problem is particularly bad in a school like ——————. That's not a very privileged school. It's very under-privileged, as a matter of fact. So we have a pretty tough element there, a bunch of bums, I might as well say it. That kind you can't do anything with them. And even many of the others—they're simply indifferent to the advantages of education. So they're indifferent, they don't care about their homework.

This behavior of the lower-class child is all the more repellent to the teacher because she finds it incomprehensible; she cannot conceive that any normal human being would act in such a way. This teacher stresses the anxiety aroused in the inexperienced teacher by her inability to provide herself with a rational explanation for her pupils behavior:

> We had one of the girls who just came to the school last year and she used to come and talk to me quite a bit. I know that it was just terrible for her. You know, I don't think she'd ever had anything to do with Negroes before she got there and she was just mystified, didn't know what to do. She was bewildered. She came to me one day almost in tears and said, "But they don't want to learn, they don't even want to learn. Why is that?" Well, she had me there.

It is worth noting that the behavior of the "better" children, even when morally unacceptable, is less distressing to the teacher, who feels that, in this case, she can produce a reasonable explanation for the behavior. An example of such an explanation is the following:

> I mean, they're spoiled, you know. A great many of them are only children. Naturally, they're used to having their own way, and they don't like to be told what to do. Well, if a child is in a room that I'm teaching he's going to be told what to do, that's all there is to it. Or if they're not spoiled that way, they're the second child and they never got the affection the first one did, not that their mother didn't love them, but they didn't get as much affection, so they're not so easy to handle either.

IV

We have shown that school teachers experience problems in working with their students to the degree that those students fail to exhibit in reality the qualities of the image of the ideal pupil which teachers hold. In a stratified urban society there are many groups whose life-style and culture produce children who do not meet the standards of this image, and who are thus impossible for teachers like these to work with effectively. Programs of action intended to increase the educational opportunities of the under-privileged in our society should take account of the manner in which teachers interpret and react to the cultural traits of this group, and the institutional consequences of their behavior.[14] Such programs might profitably aim at producing teachers who can cope effectively with the problems of teaching this group and not, by their reactions to class differences, perpetuate the existing inequities.

A more general statement of the findings is now in order. Professionals depend on their environing society to provide them with clients who meet the standards of their image of the ideal client. Social class cultures, among other factors, may operate to produce many clients who, in one way or another, fail to meet these specifications and therefore aggravate one or another of the basic problems of the worker-client relation (three were considered in this paper).

In attacking this problem we touch on one of the basic elements of the relation between institutions and society, for the differences between ideal and reality place in high relief the implicit assumptions which institutions, through their functionaries, make about the society around them. All institutions have embedded in them some set of assumptions about the nature of the society and the individuals with whom they deal, and we must get at these assumptions, and their embodiment in actual social interaction, in order fully to understand these organizations. We can, perhaps, best begin our work on this problem by studying those institutions which, like the school, make assumptions which have high visibility because of their variation from reality.

7. NOTES

1. See Howard S. Becker, "The Professional Dance Musician and His Audience," *American Journal of Sociology* LVII (September, 1951), pp. 136-44, for further discussion of this point.

2. W. L. Warner, R. J. Havighurst, and W J. Loeb, *Who Shall Be Educated?* (New York: Harper and Bros., 1944.)

3. August Hollingshead, *Elmstown's Youth* (New York: John Wiley & Sons, 1949).

4. Allison Davis, *Social-Class Influences Upon Learning* (Cambridge: Harvard University Press, 1950).

5. The entire research has been reported in Howard S. Becker, "Role and Career Problems of the Chicago Public School Teacher" (unpublished Ph.D. dissertation, University of Chicago, 1951).

6. Allison Davis, "The Motivation of the Underprivileged Worker," in William F. Whyte (ed.), *Industry and Society* (New York: McGraw-Hill Book Co., 1947), p. 99.

7. Willard Waller, *Sociology of Teaching* (New York: John Wiley & Sons, 1932), p. 197.

8. Although all service occupations tend to have such problems of control over their clients, the problem is undoubtedly aggravated in situations like the school where those upon whom the service is being performed are not there of their own volition, but rather because of the wishes of some other group (the parents, in this case).

9. Allison Davis, *Social-Class Influences Upon Learning,* pp. 34-35.

10. Miriam Wagenschein, "Reality Shock" (unpublished M.A. thesis, University of Chicago, 1950), pp. 58-59.

11. This is part of the process of job adjustment described in detail in Howard S. Becker, "The Career of the Chicago Public School Teacher," *American Journal of Sociology* LVII (March, 1952).

12. Interview by Miriam Wagenschein. The lack of common meanings in this situation symbolizes the great cultural and moral distance between teacher and "slum" child.

13. *Op. cit.,* p. 172.

14. One of the important institutional consequences of these class preferences is a constant movement of teachers away from lower-class schools, which prevents these schools from retaining experienced teachers and from maintaining some continuity in teaching and administration.

Part 2

TEACHERS

Introduction

As is pointed out in Part 4, the school is an institution that has been created, and is maintained, by society to help insure the continuance of that society, and social stability is preserved by providing continuity through a core of accepted values and practices. In America the values are those of the middle-class majority, and one of the main agents for transmitting those values to the younger generation is teachers. In the United States the local control of schools and the vulnerability of schools to local ad hoc pressure groups insure that the school's control of values by the middle-class majority is preserved. Additional insurance that this important function is carried out derives from the fact that teachers are strong and usually unquestioning adherents of the middle-class majority culture.

Many children, however, enter school with little or no commitment to the values teachers have to offer. The children do not share the teacher's values because they are from minority groups or, if the children are from middle-class homes, because they believe the school "offerings" are outmoded. Hence, because of the gap between what teachers have to offer and what pupils consider important and relevant, teachers often fail to communicate anything, even subject matter, to their pupils and thus they fail to help children realize and fulfill their potential.

It does not have to be so. There is hope that teachers can be relevant and fulfill their promise. The first three readings in Part 2 provide an abundance of information upon which the new teacher can build fruitful relationships with students. Le Baron's article gives some hints about how the teaching role itself may be modified and improved.

But these readings will not do the job alone. They contain many good words, but teachers are masters of using good words and failing to utilize the methods described by the good words. The job of becoming more relevant is much harder than learning to repeat nice phrases or transmit subject matter memorized in college "Arts and Sciences" courses. Teachers have the much harder job of learning how to be understanding and human in situations that may seem to them impossible. Here are Ulibarri's direct evidence and Manuel's interviews to show that in the Southwest teachers rarely concern themselves with understanding the needs, strengths, and shortcomings of children from minority backgrounds. What is needed, of course, is for teachers to understand their own values and to suspend easy judgments of children. In other words, teachers must try to separate themselves from their own commitments in order to understand their students' commitments. Only then will they understand the prejudices and fears and expectations they bring to school with them. Only by mediating their own values with the desire to *understand* will teachers ever be able to react to all students as human beings. This is an especially difficult job because it askes the teacher to do some things that seem to run directly counter to his experiences and training. Fortunately, we have the testimony of men like James Herndon, Herbert Kohl, and Jonathan Kozol who show us that it *is* possible to be understanding and human in a classroom.

The new teacher should not think that change will take place quickly, that understanding will be easy to develop. College training often does not prepare the new teacher to adjust and react constructively to new and different situations. In public schools the senior faculty members will tend to resent proposals for change. And a teacher safely within the walls of his own classroom is a master at frustrating even the best of plans. Genetics is another easy out for the teacher. It is much more convenient to stigmatize as "dumb" the students who do not learn than it is to try to find out why they are not learning. In the 1930s and 1940s progressive educators tried to point toward individual differences in children as the place to begin educational planning. Teachers resisted that policy and argued that the classroom did not permit them time or scope to deal with individual differences. Their responsibility was to the "entire class," and often this meant the psychologically average and the culturally middle-class. The years of World War II, the Cold War, and the Korean War gave teachers a readymade excuse for ignoring the particular in favor of the mass. The people who should have been doing the most to develop individual differences in children were, in fact, doing the most to homogenize us. "National survival depended upon it."

Well, we survived. And it turns out that it was the environment that was dying, not the national character. Happily for the country, it was the young people who woke up first and who threw back into the teeth of teachers and their petty conventions and their complacent security supported by academic experts, middle-class parents, and middle-class politicians—people who were doing better than ever before economically. When James Baldwin told teachers at an NEA convention that many of their students hated them because of what they represented, the teachers were incredulous. Slowly the lesson has come home. The teachers should have been in the vanguard, but they were in the rear. Baldwin was pointing out a new meaning for American society. It goes beyond the psychological differences of children to their cultural differences as well. When teachers recognize this, perhaps they will draw back from their present position. Open up themselves as well as their classrooms. Recognize the full richness of the human condition, and work *with* students as partners in a grand experiment of life. Perhaps then the school will become a place of learning rather than a house of hatred, ugliness, and fear.

8

The Key Word Is Relevance*

WILLIAM VAN TIL

Let us begin with an admission: Some of the content we teach in American schools is not as relevant as it might be to the lives of the young people we teach, to the society in which they are growing up, or to the clarification of democratic values.

Some illustrations are obvious. For instance, one of the many Puerto Rican schools I visited during a New York University survey of education in Puerto Rico was in a village high in the mountains of the interior. The villagers were very poor and afflicted with the problems that go with poverty—poor nutrition, inefficient agriculture, dilapidated housing, bad health, and the rest. ·

Only a handful of young people of the village and the surrounding country-side ever enrolled in any kind of educational institution beyond high school. Yet, what were the young people studying in the secondary school in this little mountain village? In a social studies class, they were memorizing lists of products of South American countries. Their mathematics work had no relationship to the problems they might encounter in the school shop or at home or elsewhere. In an English class, students were reading eighteenth and nineteenth century British novels: At the time of my visit one class was dissecting *Ivanhoe*. (This mountain school and community, I hasten to say, was not typical; many other Puerto Rican schools were more relevant to learners, society, and values, and many other communities had higher living standards.).

Recognizing the lack of relevance in education in an exotic, faraway setting is easy. Such was the case when I visited a home economics class in a town of mud hovels in Iran: The girls were making scrapbooks of pictures (clipped from very old magazines) that portrayed the clothes and foods of prosperous Americans and Europeans.

The closer to home we get, however, the harder it becomes for a teacher to recognize irrelevance. Take Doris Smith and Harry Jones, for instance. She teaches in the suburbs in the Midwestern United States; he in the slums of a West Coast city. Both of them would quickly recognize the lack of meaning in the

*Copyright 1969 by the National Education Association. Reprinted by permission of the publisher from *Today's Education,* January 1969, pp. 14-17.

two faraway examples cited. Yet both might have difficulty recognizing that they have their own problems in making the content of their classes meaningful to some students.

Doris Smith teaches social studies in an affluent suburb that is among the first places where new national projects and proposals are tried. A genuine innovator, she uses a variety of methods and materials with versatility. She uses simulation techniques, for example, and has just completed an academic game with her eleventh graders. The game deals with economics; the players adopt roles and the ones who make the most money are the winners.

Margaret, one of Miss Smith's better students, went through the motions of the game but was fundamentally uninvolved. Why? Because, like Benjamin in *The Graduate,* Margaret had painfully learned from the lives of her parents and their friends that affluence did not necessarily result in a good life. Why, wondered Margaret, were teachers blind to what was most relevant to young people? For instance, why didn't the teacher see that the most important thing about this game would be to examine the materialistic goals which were taken for granted as desirable?

During follow-up discussions, Miss Smith raised questions with the class about the strategy of moves made during the game. Margaret's responses were correct but unrelated to her concern for values.

Harry Jones teaches language arts in an intermediate school in a slum neighborhood. Though Mr. Jones is white and most of his students are black, racial differences have not been a barrier to mutual liking and respect. The class is now reading a selection in a new anthology which is quite appropriate to the level of the students' reading abilities. Mr. Jones notices that Jess isn't reading the assigned selection, but instead is simply leafing through the pages. It isn't as though I'd asked the class to read dull, difficult material simply because it's supposed to be an English classic, Harry thinks. I guess Jess just doesn't care.

Jess is thinking: I can't find black men in this book. Where's the brothers? This is Whitey's book. How can a good guy like Mr. Jones be so dumb? Not for me, baby.

"What are you doing, Jess?" asks Harry. "Just lookin'," says Jess.

Good teachers though they are, even Miss Smith and Mr. Jones sometimes attempt to teach content that is unrelated to the lives of learners. Some teachers have even greater difficulty in achieving relevance than do methodologically skilled Doris and well-liked Harry. Classes do exist in your community and mine in which an uninterrupted academic content bores young people. Classes do exist where subject matter is quite unrelated to the dilemmas and struggles and aspirations of many prospective learners.

The teacher who realizes that his content of instruction isn't meaningful has two viable alternatives. He can change his content from the irrelevant to the relevant. Or, if he cannot change the required content, he can teach it in such a way as to give it relevance.

Yes, a third possibility does exist. One can continue with the meaningless content, break his heart trying to teach, and achieve very little.

A teacher does not need extensive instruction in educational psychology to realize that his teaching must be connected with the student's background, drives, and life if any learning is to take place. Experience soon teaches a teacher this axiom.

The obvious and sensible thing to do is to replace the irrelevant with the relevant through changing the content. Remember, for instance, the poverty-stricken Puerto Rican mountain village in which the students were memorizing products, being taught mathematics without application, and reading *Ivanhoe*. Here was a setting characterized by a host of problems in the areas of health, sanitation, housing, nutrition, safety, use of resources, production, and consumption. Here were Puerto Rican youngsters who would face bewildering life problems including those presented by the continuing restless migration from the rural ways of the barrio to the urbanized ways of San Juan; from the hospitable island of their birth to the impersonal, tenement-lined canyons of New York City, with its strange folkways and less-than-warm welcome to those regarded as "foreigners."

Reality could be introduced into their education. In social studies, students might well learn of the real problems of the village, the island, the mainland. In mathematics, they might see a relationship between mathematics and the problems they encounter in school, shop and in their homes. In English classes, students might well acquire the bilinguality they need by reading English-language newspapers and magazines, as well as books of fiction and nonfiction by Puerto Rican and mainland Americans, plus a sampling of British authors. Fortunately, the better Puerto Rican schools do introduce such realities into their programs.

In mainland America, too, the obvious and sensible approach is to change the content if it is not germane. Most educators will readily grant that a teacher must begin at the actual level of accomplishment of those who are to be educated—not to stay there but begin there. Most will grant that pitching the learning at an unreachable level is an exercise in futility. But additionally we must recognize the vital importance of selecting suitable content.

The curriculum should be made more relevant to the lives of the children and youth for whom the curriculum exists. Through their reading materials, for example, city children must often meet people like themselves, rather than always encounter the legendary Dick and Jane and Spot of suburban life. The world of the city must itself become part of the subject matter if young city dwellers are to improve human relations, develop citizenship, widen horizons, and meet the problems of urban living. In Harry Jones's class, and those of his colleagues, surely the contributions of Negro/Americans should be an integral part of the American literature curriculum for both Negroes and whites.

Nor are the suburbs exempt from the blight of irrelevance. Though some suburban young people have an economic head start in life, they too are sometimes cheated. When communities are bland and homogenized and indifferent to reality, the young are sometimes cheated of the opportunity to know people of varied races, religions, nationality backgrounds, and social classes.

When high school students are regarded as college fodder, they are sometimes cheated of sufficient experience in home economics, music, fine arts, and industrial arts. When the only god worshipped is academic success in formal learning, students are sometimes cheated of the opportunity to explore seriously their allegiances to values, their relationships to the adult world, their ways of finding satisfaction, and their participation in political action and social change.

"But," a teacher may say, "I cannot change the required content to make it relevant. I am not a board of regents or a local board of education or a curriculum bigwig attached to the central office staff." He may add, "I am just a humble teacher, a prisoner of the syllabus, the required textbook, and the system in which I am caught. Deviation is not permitted. *They* would not allow it."

Maybe so, but I doubt it. Before the teacher resigns himself to a prisoner's life, he might wish to re-examine his chains. Perhaps they are not as strong as he assumes.

In today's world, more and more educators and laymen are realizing that not all of the answers to the problem of curriculum are in. Since the early 1960s, increasing numbers of educators have attempted to develop curriculums that are more important to the culturally disadvantaged or, in a plainer phrase, the poor.

Now recognition is growing that we are far from having achieved the best of all possible worlds with respect to the education of the economically advantaged. In 1969, still more educators will be looking for curriculums appropriate for young people from affluent backgrounds. Paradoxically, today's disenchanted young people, including democratic activists and serious and sensitive students as well as hippies and nihilists and revolutionaries, come mostly from the middle and upper classes.

Possibly the chains of established content are not as binding as assumed. Teacher power grows. In a time of teacher shortage, few need stay as teachers in repressive atmospheres, for some administrators are seeking change-minded teachers.

In those cases where, through a variety of circumstances, the chains do prove real and teachers simply must use some prescribed content which is not as relevant as they would wish it to be, how can they make their work more meaningful?

Rather than making fundamental changes in the content, some teachers use the second alternative mentioned and adapt the content to make it more relevant. Illustrations are legion: In literature, teaching *Julius Caesar* in relationship to contemporary dictatorships; in history, preparing and contrasting attitudes toward past American wars with present attitudes on war in Viet Nam; in biology, relating the study of human blood to false claims and misleading mythologies as to blood differences between races; in modern languages, teaching the culture as part of the culture's language; in language arts, stressing those readings in anthologies which have most meaning to the particular learners. Miss Smith, for instance, could have discussed with the class the value assumptions behind the economic game that was the required content.

Some readers may ask for the prescription good teachers use for adaptation of content. There isn't any. Sorry about that. If there were a single sovereign remedy, it would have been discovered long ago. The good teacher uses his intelligence in relating the required content to the world of the learner. Good teachers have been doing so for a long time; adaptation is no revolutionary doctrine.

In making content more relevant, there is no substitute for knowing the social realities which characterize the environment of the student. There is no substitute for knowing the learner as an individual. There is no substitute for having a philosophy which gives direction to the educational enterprise. So armed, one can relate much of the content to the learner, the class, the school, and the community.

9

Teaching in Inner-City Schools*

BERNICE WADDLES and DALE ROBINSON

Teaching in an inner-city school can be one of the "hippest" experiences an educator can have or one of the most devastating.

The plight—or blight—of the urban school is a national problem, compounded of unemployment, grossly inadequate housing, discrimination because of race or religion, chronic illnesses, malnutrition of adults and children, violence, crime, alcohol, drugs, and sex problems. One teacher, isolated in an inner-city classroom, cannot solve society's ills between 8:30 a.m. and 3:30 p.m.

This article, however, does propose to concentrate on what that one teacher in his inner-city classroom *can* do to meet the needs of today's urban youth more adequately.

Unfortunately, Betty Crocker does not publish a book of teaching recipes guaranteed to succeed in the big city classroom. No book contains all the know-how a teacher needs. Nor does a book exist about big city teaching which "tells it like it is."

What teacher is prepared to answer a fifteen-year-old girl who asks, "Mrs. H., how many months should you be pregnant before you can have an abortion?"

How adequately are current preservice or inservice teacher training programs preparing teachers to handle such situations? Traditional ways of teaching will not suffice in the ghetto schools. Teachers must be pupil-oriented, not subject-matter-enslaved.

The day-by-day, hour-by-hour, minute-by-minute explosive climate of the urban school demands teachers who have almost Herculean qualities: great flexibility, uncommon physical stamina, patience, creativity, sensitivity, tolerance, ego strength, and a genuine belief that there is good in every human being, plus the ability to accept progress in small doses, to communicate with alienated youth and parents, to handle emergencies, and to laugh at oneself.

As for inner-city students, research indicates that a positive self-image is essential to academic success. Sensible changes in teaching methods must be developed to help students form positive attitudes toward school and toward themselves. For Negroes, developing pride in Negro cultural heritage is an essential component in creating attitudes of positive self-worth. Urban curriculums—and teachers—cannot continue to ignore this fact.

Success must build on success. Every day every child should go home with at least one success under his cap—no matter how minor the achievement. For some students, the goal must be easily attainable.

One way that teachers can build positive school expectations is by letting students help plan what is going to happen in class the next day. Other suggestions include telling them their help is needed, letting them have "secrets," avoiding use of threats, giving them needed security, using role playing and playlets, putting a suggestion box in the classroom (with red forms for emergencies), smiling often, and laughing.

Trust is imperative. Teaching inner-city children requires utmost honesty. Students spot a hypocrite easily and dismiss him quickly. "I respect teachers who respect me" is the motto of urban youth.

Admitting human frailties can be a source of strength for teachers: A teacher gained a more sympathetic reception for antismoking literature after he confessed he had found it difficult to break the smoking habit.

Tasks that establish the child's identity and develop responsibility are essential. School jobs—as switchboard operators, teachers' helpers, cafeteria workers, bookroom assistants, assistant secretaries, and office helpers—help build a student's confidence in himself.

Some educators are guilty of trying to provide students, especially ghetto-scarred Negro youth, with qualities that the teachers want rather than with the ones these students need. Strict adherence to middle-class standards in a ghetto school is a cause of unnecessary conflict and has brought about irreparable harm.

Far too much fuss is made over supposed way-out modes of dress and hair styles, over things like moustaches, sunglasses, miniskirts, and fishnet stockings.

One rather shy Negro girl received an attractive hairpiece, a "fall," as a Christmas gift. It enhanced her appearance considerably and she began to emerge as a person. Unfortunately, however, her teacher—failing to see how the fall was giving this girl needed confidence—disapproved of her wearing it and ordered her not to wear it to school. Rebuffs such as this are unnecessary and they *hurt.*

Unfortunately some inner-city parents and students feel that certain educators do not respect them as fellow human beings. Regrettably, incidents occur that validate this attitude. Some of these result from innocent misunderstandings. In one school where the children went home for lunch, many students returned tardy in the afternoon. The students resented having to remain after school to make up time. Then a teacher walked home with the children at noon and discovered that a forty-car freight train blocked the students' path to school almost daily.

It may be sacrilegious to suggest that not all school rules and policies are in the best educational interests of urban youth. Inflexible rules can break teachers and students alike. If rules in inner-city schools must not be broken, they should be changed to meet *actual* educational needs (which do not necessarily coincide with administrative convenience).

Administrators frequently frown upon direct communication between parents and teachers without clearing through the front office first. They also often require that teachers get permission before keeping students after school or visiting them in their homes. Teachers who hold "bull sessions" with students are frowned on by other teachers. Teachers are discouraged from transporting students in private cars even though making other transportation arrangements for field trips often involves time-consuming red tape.

On the surface, the above rules are logical. But pure logic aside, the logistics, pressures, and urgencies of ghetto situations demand more expediency, efficiency, and enlightenment.

Unwise policies can hinder growth. One major school system in Michigan prohibits field trips near the close of any semester. When a special cultural enrichment art exhibit, geared just for children, came to town for one week, which unfortunately corresponded with the semester's end, no students could go.

At a parent-teacher conference at another school, a parent whose child read slowly but determinedly was reluctant to suggest that school library lending practices for slow learners might be adjusted to fit their special needs. (The parent had received a stern note from the librarian about her child's overdue book, with the unhappy consequence that the child stopped checking out books.)

Some years ago George S. Counts, in discussing how schools must meet individual needs, said: "You must back the wagon up to the load."

This observation is particularly true for students in ghetto schools. Unfortunately, standardized curriculums and tests do not always take into account students' individual abilities, backgrounds, needs, and goals. Something has to give. Is it essential that students learn all the products of Yugoslavia when a more burning consideration is learning to get along with others? It may be more important to answer students' questions on how their parents could apply for more adequate housing facilities than to lecture on the economy of Chile.

Peer pressures can be utilized. Students can help other students learn, as the author Bernard Asbell pointed out in 1965 at the Second National NEA-PR and R Conference on Civil and Human Rights in Education:

"We know that while large numbers of the children of poverty are failing to learn from the teachers in the classroom, they do succeed in learning from each other in the streets. . . . We have not brought ourselves to face the fact that the teachers who are succeeding in slum neighborhoods are the children themselves. These children possess the two magical secrets of successful teaching: They know that their young friends can learn and they know how to begin where the pupils really are. If the A-B-C's and the 1-2-3's of school work are simple enough for children to learn, they are simple enough for older children to teach—but always, of course, with the adult teacher as guide and supervisor."

Reasons are many for teachers' lack of success in ghetto schools. Grossly overlarge classes, lack of understanding of the community, lack of communication with parents, false standards, or reluctance to discard old teaching practices that were successful in other surroundings partially explain why some teachers fail in the inner city.

One teacher of long experience with children of high socioeconomic backgrounds, accustomed to a higher level of quiet and order, made an inner-city class just sit still for one entire hour because they had entered her room in a "disorderly" fashion. Had she discussed the matter with the children, the teacher would have learned that they were excited because a foreign visitor was to be their guest in another class. One hour of penance somewhat dampened their enthusiasm for the visitor.

Teachers must recognize the frustrations parents experience with schools. Inner-city parents communicate very little with the school. Many remained silent because they cannot express, in words, what they wish to say. *Meaningful* parent-school "know each other" programs need to be provided on a continuous basis. Writing in the *Saturday Review* (November 18, 1967), Edgar Z. Friedenberg warns, "Improvement in the urban schools will come when—and only when —the residents whose children attend those schools demand and get enough political power either to destroy and replace the present school bureaucracy or to impress upon it that they can no longer be patronized."

Teachers need to be fully prepared for inner-city conditions before they actually face them. They must be exposed to front-line experiences. Urban sociology must be stressed. Today's teacher-preparation courses virtually ignore the dimensions of poverty. (How does a bag of potato chips and a bottle of pop for breakfast affect a child's willingness to learn?) Teachers for inner cities need courses in how to teach basic skills up to the tenth grade level, especially reading.

The preceding comments should not be interpreted as a blanket condemnation of large cities for failing to look objectively at their complex school problems.

Detroit, for example, has recognized the need for integrated textbooks which show whites and Negroes working together, for family living classes, for school centers where teachers can go for specialized help, for curriculums adapted to meet inner-city needs, and for vocational guidance programs. Detroit has made a start.

Two Detroit locations—the Public Schools Center and the Special Projects Building—where teachers can go for special help (preparing audiovisual materials, research, etc.) are open Mondays through Thursdays from 8:15 a.m. to 6 p.m. and on Fridays from 8:15 a.m. to 4 p.m.

Specially noteworthy is Detroit's junior high television series, "Of Cabbages and Kings," which began in September 1966. This humanities-oriented series (36 programs in 25-minute segments) integrates music, art, and dance to provide enriching literary experiences for junior high students. Each unit is designed to focus on the basic humanistic theme of self-identification. The program uses the Socratic method, asking more questions than it answers.

Improved vocational guidance is imperative for youth from poverty areas. Detroit is moving in this direction with its Career Guidance Program, a project to help inner-city youth develop an adequate self-concept and to expose them to existing job opportunities. School personnel in one of Detroit's nine regions are receiving special assistance to help make vocational guidance a central force from the elementary level through senior high school.

On visits to industries and places of business, students learn about occupations they may never have heard of. They do role playing in employer-employee relations (how to apply for a job, how to dress).

In these ways, Detroit has made a start, but a start is not enough. Untrained personnel should not be permitted to enter inner-city classrooms. These schools must have teachers with the highest qualifications, not "substitutes" allowed to teach full time. They must have more teachers and smaller classes. Colleges of education must take steps to encourage more prospective teachers to accept inner-city positions where needs and rewards are the greatest.

To solve the schools' problems, we must cure the ills of the inner city, and to do this requires massive commitment—both individual and collective—now. Wars cost billions. Space programs cost billions. Highway programs cost billions. Where on our national list of priorities are the billions to save our large cities and, perhaps, Western civilization as well?

10

Characteristics of Good Teachers and Implications for Teacher Education*

DON HAMACHEK

It is, I think, a sad commentary about our educational system that it keeps announcing both publicly and privately that "good" and "poor" teachers cannot be distinguished one from the other. Probably no issue in education has been so voluminously researched as has teacher effectiveness and considerations which enhance or restrict this effectiveness. Nonetheless, we still read that we cannot tell the good guys from the bad guys. For example, Biddle and Ellena[1] in their book, *Contemporary Research on Teacher Effectiveness,* begin by stating that "the problem of teacher effectiveness is so complex that no one today knows what *The Competent Teacher* is." I think we *do* know what the competent—or effective, or good, or whatever you care to call him—teacher is, and in the remainder of this paper I will be as specific as possible in citing *why* I think we know along with implications for our teacher-education programs.

WHAT THE RESEARCH SAYS

By and large, most research efforts aimed at investigating teacher effectiveness have attempted to prove one or more of the following dimensions of teacher personality and behavior: (1) personal characteristics, (2) instructional procedures and interaction styles, (3) perceptions of self, (4) perceptions of others. Because of space limits this is by no means an exhaustive review of the research related to the problem, but it is, I think, representative of the kind and variety of research findings linked to questions of teacher effectiveness.

Personal Characteristics of Good Versus Poor Teachers. We would probably agree that it is quite possible to have two teachers of equal intelligence, training, and grasp of subject matter who nevertheless differ considerably in the results they achieve with students. Part of the difference can be accounted for by the effect of a teacher's personality on the learners. What kinds of personality do students respond to?

Hart[2] conducted a study based upon the opinions of 3,725 high school seniors concerning best-liked and least-liked teachers and found a total of forty-

---

three different reasons for "liking Teacher A best" and thirty different reasons for "liking Teacher Z least." Not surprisingly, over 51 percent of the students said that they liked best those teachers who were "helpful in school work, who explained lessons and assignments clearly, and who used examples in teaching." Also, better than 40 percent responded favorably to teachers with a "sense of humor." Those teachers assessed most negatively were "unable to explain clearly, were partial to brighter students, and had superior, aloof, overbearing attitudes." In addition, over 50 percent of the respondents mentioned behaviors such as "too cross, crabby, grouchy, and sarcastic" as reasons for disliking many teachers. Interestingly enough, mastery of subject matter, which is vital but badly overemphasized by specialists, ranked sixteenth on both lists. Somehow students seem willing to take more or less for granted that a teacher "knows" his material. What seems to make a difference is the teacher's personal style in *communicating* what he knows. Studies by Witty[3] and Bousfield[4] tend to support these conclusions at both the high school *and* college level.

Having desirable personal qualities is one thing, but what are the results of rigorous tests of whether the teacher's having them makes any difference in the performance of students?

Cogan[5] found that warm, considerate teachers got an unusual amount of original poetry and art from their high school students. Reed[6] found that teachers higher in a capacity for warmth favorably affected their pupils' interests in science. Using scores from achievement tests as their criterion measure, Heil, Powell, and Feifer[7] compared various teacher-pupil personality combinations and found that the well-integrated (healthy, well-rounded, flexible) teachers were most effective with *all* types of students. Spaulding[8] found that the self-concepts of elementary school children were apt to be higher and more positive in classrooms in which the teacher was "socially integrative" and "learner supportive."

In essence, I think the evidence is quite clear when it comes to sorting out good or effective from bad or ineffective teachers on the basis of personal characteristics. Effective teachers appear to be those who are, shall we say, "human" in the fullest sense of the word. They have a sense of humor, are fair, empathetic, more democratic than autocratic, and apparently are more able to relate easily and naturally to students on either a one-to-one or group basis. Their classrooms seem to reflect miniature enterprise operations in the sense that they are more open, spontaneous, and adaptable to change. Ineffective teachers apparently lack a sense of humor, grow impatient easily, use cutting, ego-reducing comments in class, are less well-integrated, are inclined to be somewhat authoritarian, and are generally less sensitive to the needs of their students. Indeed, research related to authoritarianism suggests that the bureaucratic conduct and rigid overtones of the ineffective teacher's classroom are desperate measures to support the weak pillars of his own personality structure.

Instructional Procedures and Interaction Styles of Good Versus Poor Teachers. If there really are polar extremes such as "good" or "poor" teachers, then we can reasonably assume that these teachers differ not only in personal characteristics but in the way they conduct themselves in the classroom.

Flanders[9] found that classrooms in which achievement and attitudes were superior were likely to be conducted by teachers who did not blindly pursue a single behavioral-instructional path to the exclusion of other possibilities. In other words, the more successful teachers were better able to range along a continuum of interaction styles which varied from fairly active, dominative support on the one hand to a more reflective, discriminating support on the other. Interestingly, those teachers who were *not* successful were the very ones who were inclined to use the same interaction styles in a more or less rigid fashion.

Barr[10] discovered that not only did poor teachers make more assignments than good teachers but, almost without exception, they made some sort of textbook assignment as part of their unyielding daily procedure. The majority of good teachers used more outside books and problem-project assignments. When the text was assigned they were more likely to supplement it with topics, questions, or other references.

Research findings related to interaction styles variously called "learner-centered" or "teacher-centered" point to similar conclusions. In general, it appears that the amount of cognitive gain is largely unaffected by the autocratic or democratic tendencies of the instructor. However, when affective gains are considered, the results are somewhat different. For example, Stern[11] reviewed thirty-four studies comparing nondirective with directive instruction and concluded:

> Regardless of whether the investigator was concerned with attitudes toward the cultural out group, toward other participants in the class, or toward the self, the results generally have indicated that nondirective instruction facilitates a shift in a more favorable, acceptant direction.

When it comes to classroom behavior, interaction patterns, and teaching styles, good or effective teachers seem to reflect more of the following behaviors:

1. Willingness to be flexible, to be direct or indirect as the situation demands.

2. Ability to perceive the world from the student's point of view.

3. Ability to "personalize" their teaching.

4. Willingness to experiment, to try out new things.

5. Skill in asking questions (as opposed to seeing self as a kind of answering service).

6. Knowledge of subject matter and related areas.

7. Provision of well-established examination procedures.

8. Provision of definite study helps.

9. Reflection of an appreciative attitude (evidenced by nods, comments, smiles, etc.).

10. Use of conversational manner in teaching—informal, easy style.

Self-Perceptions of Good Versus Poor Teachers. We probably do not have to go any further than our own personal life experiences to know that the way we see, regard, and feel about ourselves has an enormous impact on both our private and public lives. How about good and poor teachers? How do they see themselves?

Ryans[12] found that there are, indeed, differences between the self-related reports of teachers with high emotional stability and those with low emotional stability. For example, the more emotionally stable teachers (1) more frequently named self-confidence and cheerfulness as dominant traits in themselves, (2) said they liked active contact with other people, (3) expressed interests in hobbies and handicrafts, (4) reported their childhoods to be happy experiences.

On the other hand, teachers with lower emotional maturity scores (1) had unhappy memories of childhood, (2) seemed *not* to prefer contact with others, (3) were more directive and authoritarian, (4) expressed less self-confidence.

We can be even more specific. Combs,[13] in his book *The Professional Education of Teachers,* cites several studies which reached similar conclusions about the way good teachers typically see themselves, as follows:

1. Good teachers see themselves as identified with people rather than withdrawn, removed, apart from, or alienated from others.

2. Good teachers feel basically adequate rather than inadequate. They do not see themselves as generally unable to cope with problems.

3. Good teachers feel trustworthy rather than untrustworthy. They see themselves as reliable, dependable individuals with the potential for coping with events as they happen.

4. Good teachers see themselves as wanted rather than unwanted. They see themselves as likable and attractive (in a personal, not physical sense) as opposed to feeling ignored and rejected.

5. Good teachers see themselves as worthy rather than unworthy. They see themselves as people of consequence, dignity, and integrity as opposed to feeling they matter little, can be overlooked and discounted.

In the broadest sense of the word, good teachers are more likely to see themselves as good people. Their self-perceptions are, for the most part, positive, tinged with an air of optimism and colored with tones of healthy self-acceptance. I dare say that self-perceptions of good teachers are not unlike the self-perceptions of any basically healthy person, whether he be a good bricklayer, a good manager, a good doctor, a good lawyer, a good experimental psychologist, or you name it. Clinical evidence has told us time and again that *any* person is more apt to be happier, more productive, and more effective when he is able to see himself as fundamentally and basically "enough."

Perceptions of Others by Good Versus Poor Teachers. Research is showing us that not only do good and poor teachers view themselves differently, there are also some characteristic differences in the way they perceive others. For example, Ryans[14] reported several studies which have produced findings that are in agreement when it comes to sorting out the differences between how good and poor teachers view others. He found, among other things, that outstandingly "good" teachers rated significantly higher than notably "poor" teachers in at least five different ways with respect to how they viewed others. The good teachers had (1) more favorable opinions of students, (2) more favorable opinions of democratic classroom behavior, (3) more favorable opinions of administrators and colleagues, (4) a greater expressed liking for personal contacts with other people, (5) more favorable estimates of other people generally. That is, they expressed belief that very few students are difficult behavior problems, that very few people are influenced in their opinions and attitudes toward others by feelings of jealousy, and that most teachers are willing to assume their full share of extra duties outside of school.

Interestingly, the characteristics that distinguished the "lowly assessed" teacher group suggested that the relatively "ineffective" teacher is self-centered, anxious, and restricted. One is left with the distinct impression that poor or ineffective teachers have more than the usual number of paranoid defenses.

It comes as no surprise that how we perceive others is highly dependent on how we perceive ourselves. If a potential teacher (or anyone else for that matter) likes himself, trusts himself, and has confidence in himself, he is likely to see others in somewhat this same light. Research is beginning to tell us what common sense has always told us; namely, people grow, flourish, and develop much more easily when in relationship with someone who projects an inherent trust and belief in their capacity to become what they have the potential to become.

It seems to me that we can sketch at least five interrelated generalizations from what research is telling us about how good teachers differ from poor teachers when it comes to how they perceive others.

1. They seem to have generally more positive views of others—students, colleagues, and administrators.

2. They do not seem to be as prone to view others as critical, attacking people with ulterior motives; rather they are seen as potentially friendly and worthy in their own right.

3. They have a more favorable view of democratic classroom procedures.

4. They seem to have the ability and capacity to see things as they seem to others—i.e., the ability to see things from the other person's point of view.

5. They do not seem to see students as persons "you do things to" but rather

as individuals capable of doing for themselves once they feel trusted, respected, and valued.

WHO, THEN, IS A GOOD TEACHER?

1. A good teacher is a good person. Simple and true. A good teacher rather likes life, is reasonably at peace with himself, has a sense of humor, and enjoys other people. If I interpret the research correctly, what it says is that there is no one best better-than-all-others type of teacher. Nonetheless there are clearly distinguishable "good" and "poor" teachers. Among other things, a good teacher is good because he does not seem to be dominated by a narcissistic self which demands a spotlight, or a neurotic need for power and authority, or a host of anxieties and tremblings which reduce him from the master of his class to its mechanic.

2. The good teacher is flexible. By far the single most repeated adjective used to describe good teachers is "flexibility." Either implicitly or explicitly (most often the latter), this characterisitc emerges time and again over all others when good teaching is discussed in the research. In other words, the good teacher does not seem to be overwhelmed by a single point of view or approach to the point of intellectual myopia. A good teacher knows that he cannot be just one sort of person and use just one kind of approach if he intends to meet the demands of the moment. They seem able to move with the shifting tides of their own needs, the student's, and do what has to be done to handle the situation. A total teacher can be firm when necessary (say "No" and mean it) or permissive (say "Why not try it your way?" and mean that, too) when appropriate. It depends on many things, and good teachers seem to know the difference.

THE NEED FOR 'TOTAL' TEACHERS

There probably is not an educational psychology course taught which does not, in some way, deal with the highly complex area of individual differences. Even the most unsophisticated undergraduate is aware that people differ in readiness and capacity to handle academic learning. For the most part our educational technology (audio-visual aids, programmed texts, teaching machines, etc.) is making significant advances designed to assist teachers in coping with intellectual differences among students. We have been making strides in the direction of offering flexible programs and curricula, but we are somewhat remiss when it comes to preparing flexible, "total" teachers. Just as there are intellectual differences among students, there are also personality and self-concept differences which can have just as much impact on achievement. If this is true, then perhaps we need to do more about preparing teachers who are sensitive to the nature of these differences and who are able to take them into account as they plan for their classes.

The point here is that what is important for one student is not important to another. This is one reason why cookbook formulas for good teachers are of so little value and why teaching is inevitably something of an art. The choice of instructional methods makes a big difference for certain kinds of pupils, and a search for the "best" way to teach can succeed only when learners' intellectual *and* personality differences are taken into account. Available evidence does not support the belief that successful teaching is possible only through the use of some specific methodology. A reasonable inference from existing data is that methods which provide for adaptation to individual and group differences, encourage student initiative, and stimulate individual differences, encourage student initiative, and stimulate individual and group participation are superior to methods which do not. In order for things of this sort to happen, perhaps what we need first of all are flexible, "total" teachers who are capable of planning around people as they are around ideas.

IMPLICATIONS FOR TEACHER EDUCATION

Research is teaching us many things about the differences between good and poor teachers, and I see at least four related implications for teacher education programs.

1. If it is true that good teachers are good because they view teaching as primarily a human process involving human relationships and human meanings, then this may imply that we should spend at least as much time exposing and sensitizing teacher candidates to the subtle complexities of personality structure as we do to introducing them to the structure of knowledge itself. Does this mean personality development, group dynamics, basic counseling processes, sensitivity training, and techniques such as life-space interviewing and encounter grouping?

2. If it is true that good teachers have a positive view of themselves and others, then this may suggest that we provide more opportunities for teacher candidates to acquire more positive self-other perceptions. Self-concept research tells us that how one feels about himself is learned. If it is learned, it is teachable. Too often, those of us in teacher education are dominated by a concern for long-term goals, while the student is fundamentally motivated by short-term goals. Forecasting what a student will need to know six months or two years from now, we operate on the assumption that he, too, perceives such goals as meaningful. It seems logical enough, but unfortunately it doesn't work out too well in practice. Hence much of what we may do with our teacher candidates is non-self-related—that is, to the student it doesn't seem connected with his own life, time, and needs. Rather than talk about group processes in the abstract, why can't we first assist students to a deeper understanding of their own roles in groups in which they already participate? Rather than simply theorize and cite research evidence related to individual differences, why not also encourage students to analyze the individual differences which exist in *this* class at *this* time and then allow them to express and discuss what these differences mean at a more personal level? If one values the self-concept idea at all, then there are

literally endless ways to encourage more positive self-other perceptions through teaching strategies aimed at personalizing what goes on in a classroom. Indeed, Jersild[15] has demonstrated that when "teachers face themselves," they feel more adequate as individuals and function more effectively as teachers.

3. If it is true that good teachers are well-informed, then it is clear that we must neither negate nor relax our efforts to provide them with as rich an intellectual background as is possible. Teachers are usually knowledgeable people, and knowledge inculcation is the aspect of preparation with which teacher education has traditionally been most successful. Nonetheless, teachers rarely fail because of lack of knowledge. They fail more often because they are unable to communicate what they know so that it makes a difference to their students. Which brings us to our final implication for teacher-education programs.

4. If it is true that good teachers are able to communicate what they know in a manner that makes sense to their students, then we must assist our teacher candidates both through example and appropriate experiences to the most effective ways of doing this. Communication is not just a process of presenting information. It is also a function of discovery and the development of personal meanings. I wonder what would happen to our expectations of the teacher's role if we viewed him less as dispenser, answerer, coercer, and provoker and more as stimulator, questioner, challenger, and puzzler. With the former, the emphasis is on "giving to," while with the latter the focus is on "guiding to." In developing ability to hold and keep attention, not to mention techniques of encouraging people to adopt the reflective, thoughtful mood, I wonder what the departments of speech, theater, and drama on our college and university campuses could teach us? We expose our students to theories of learning and personality; perhaps what we need to do now is develop some "theories of presentation" with the help of those who know this field best.

This paper has attempted to point out that even though there is no single best or worst kind of teacher, there are clearly distinguishable characteristics associated with "good" and "bad" teachers. There is no one *best* kind of teaching because there is no *one kind* of student. Nonetheless, there seems to be enough evidence to suggest that whether the criteria for good teaching is on the basis of student and/or peer evaluations or in terms of student achievement gains, there are characteristics between both which consistently overlap. That is, the good teacher is able to influence both student feeling and achievement in positive ways.

Research is teaching us many things about the differences between good and bad teachers and there are many ways we can put these research findings into our teacher-education programs.

Good teachers do exist and can be identified. Perhaps the next most fruitful vineyard for research is in the classrooms of good teachers so we can determine, by whatever tools we have, just what makes them good in the first place.

10. NOTES

1. B. J. Biddle and W. H. Ellena, *Contemporary Research on Teacher Effectiveness* (New York: Holt, Rinehart and Winston, 1964), p. 2.

2. W. F. Hart, *Teachers and Teaching* (New York: Macmillan, 1934), pp. 131-32.

3. P. Witty, "An Analysis of the Personality Traits of the Effective Teacher," *Journal of Educational Research,* May 1947, pp. 662-71.

4. W. A. Bousfield, "Student's Rating on Qualities Considered Desirable in College Professors," *School and Society,* February 24, 1940, pp. 253-56.

5. M. L. Cogan, "The Behavior of Teachers and the Productive Behavior of Their Pupils," *Journal of Experimental Education,* December 1958, pp. 89-124.

6. H. B. Reed, "Implications for Science Education of a Teacher Competence Research," *Science Education,* December 1962, pp. 473-86.

7. L. M. Heil, M. Powell, and I. Feifer, *Characteristics of Teacher Behavior Related to the Achievement of Children in Several Elementary Grades* (Washington, D.C.: Office of Education, Cooperative Research Branch, 1960).

8. R. Spaulding, "Achievement, Creativity, and Self-Concept Correlates of Teacher-Pupil Transactions in Elementary Schools" (University of Illinois, U.S. Office of Education Cooperative Research Project No. 1352, 1963).

9. N. A. Flanders, *Teacher Influence, Pupil Attitudes and Achievement: Studies in Interaction Analysis* (University of Minnesota, U. S. Office of Education Cooperative Research Project No. 397, 1960).

10. A. S. Barr, *Characteristic Differences in the Teaching Performance of Good and Poor Teachers of the Social Studies* (Bloomington: The Public School Publishing Co., 1929).

11. G. C. Stern, "Measuring Non-Cognitive Variables in Research on Teaching," in N. L. Gage (ed.), *Handbook of Research on Teaching* (Chicago: Rand McNally, 1963), p. 427.

12. D. G. Ryans, "Prediction of Teacher Effectiveness," *Encyclopedia of Educational Research,* 3rd Edition (New York: Macmillan, 1960), pp. 1,486-90.

13. A. W. Combs, *The Professional Education of Teachers* (Boston: Allyn and Bacon, 1965), pp. 70-71.

14. Ryans, *op. cit.*

15. A. T. Jersild, *When Teachers Face Themselves* (New York: Bureau of Publications, Teachers College, Columbia University, 1955).

II

Technological Forces and the Teacher's Changing Role*

WALT Le BARON

INTRODUCTION

A great deal of confusion exists about the application of modern technology to education: most discussions either uncritically praise its use or condemn its destructive influence. Separating the two extremes is a growing literature about educational change processes that either suggests only minor alterations in the system or indicates that technology dehumanizes education.

This article attempts to resolve some of the confusion by looking at two aspects of the problem: (1) the meaning of technology for education and (2) the changing role of the teacher. From this perspective, a process model of teaching will be suggested and some suggestions made about the role of school boards in planning for technology.

Anyone talking about change or innovation, technology or humanness, school organization or aims and goals, especially in the abstract, is automatically putting his head on the block! Some ideas associated with technology require radical—perhaps impossible—changes in our ways of thinking about education; on the other hand, others may appear old hat. Also, in discussing technology, a serious defense ploy can sometimes interfere with communication. Called the "process of reduction," it operates, usually subconsciously, to protect against the threat of stange new ideas by automatically translating them into a nonthreatening form. The technique may operate in two ways: either it views the new as simply the reexpression of something that's been there all along, or it seeks to append the new without changing the basic concept of the system.

In education, however, technology requires a complete review and evaluation of our ways of thinking. Hilton sums this up very nicely:

> The danger I see for our society and, therefore, for the whole world, is the danger that we may not be able to adjust to change as quickly as change occurs, because we are afraid of the unknown. Fear is not conducive to clear thought. When one is afraid, one might think one has choices that are no

*Copyright 1969 by the National Education Association. Reprinted by permission of the publisher from *Journal of Teacher Education*, Winter 1969, pp. 451-64.

longer available and ignore the choices that ought to be made. Among the choices that are no longer available is the choice between change and no change, between cybernation and no cybernation . . . [because] nothing that has been invented can ever be uninvented. . . .[1]

It is in this spirit that this paper approaches technology and education.

THE PRESENT STATE OF TECHNOLOGY AND EDUCATION

A prolonged study of classroom multi-media problems has provided an opportunity to visit closed-circuit television installations, computer-assisted instruction experiments (in all modes), student-response systems and multimedia classroom dial-access systems, learning resource centers, learning laboratories, experimental schools, and recognized experts in the various phases of multimedia design. These visits have led me to an important conclusion:

Almost all present media applications have been based on traditional concepts of the teacher-learner relationship. It is unfortunate that there has been a consistent failure of multi-media (including telemedia) to increase the range of interactions within the learning situation. . . . Every current example of multi-media is based on the presenting of information from a single source (or group of mediated sources acting in concert) to one or a group of students. These students may or may not interact with the source. . . . There is, however, little evidence of change in the teacher's role as a result of mediated environments. No mediated classroom so far has made provision for comfortable interaction of groups of students, or for direct student-to-student interaction within the context of the subject matter. Yet it appears that the true vitality of the new media rests on the ability to promote just such new and exciting modes of learning interaction both among individual students and other persons and between the individual student and the technological system. . . .[2]

Although the catalogue of multimedia successes is long, the relation of a particular project to a total system always seems to remain questionable. This situation seems to stem from a resistance to broadly based institutional changes which will permit total systems planning. Since advancing technological design requires a kind of planning that permits of functional analyses, the greatest need at this time is for careful descriptions of total educational systems which facilitate the development of alternative plans for dealing with persistent problems.

The design of technological systems, especially for application to problems of repetitive learning and training, has yielded highly sophisticated engineering systems, but this process has only occasionally been functionally interrelated to either the system environment or the change and implementation process. Consequently, the application of such systems in schools finds them not achieving the objectives envisioned for them, not cost-effective, and causing problems not initially anticipated. These conditions suggest that the technological systems must now be combined with new designs for the educational system, the training of new kinds of teachers and other personnel, reevaluations of costs and the investment in education, and perhaps most of all, a major explication of aims and goals.

FORCES OPPOSED TO CHANGE AND INNOVATION

This paper will concentrate on two aspects of educational technology: the meaning of technology and its consequences for the role of the teacher. As a preface to this, a somewhat general list of the forces opposing technological change might be useful. These can be organized efficiently within five broad categories:

The Nature of the Institution. There are great strengths in the present organization and structure of American public education, but the pretechnological framework has not provided an adequate environment for technological implementation. Indeed, the organizational structure, institutionalized professionalism and labor-intensive economics, financial levels and governmental concern, and philosophical outlook of the schools are frequently in conflict with advances in technology. Radical structural changes in the schools may be required, but this condition has so far resolved itself in favor of maintaining the status quo rather than using technology effectively.

The Objectives of the School System. Much confusion exists over aims and objectives for public education. The tasks assigned to the schools, the changes in relevant populations, the increasing needs for knowledge and skill training, and the constant problems of providing these within the framework of scarcity budgets present such serious questions that a consensus on roles and functions of the schools seems almost impossible. Nevertheless, some perspective is necessary if the dialogue is to continue. In a recent book, Coombs suggests:

> A dispute about the technology of education which is confined to the question of whether or not to use machines . . . poses the wrong question. The real issue is whether all the ways of doing things carried over from the past are still relevant and sufficient to education's needs, or whether certain subtractions and additions would improve the situation.[3]

Briefly, the new technologies make possible new aims and goals (both quantitatively and qualitatively), but there exists strong conflict between some aspects of the new and the entrenched forces of the old.

Change and Development Models. During the past few years, a number of studies on change and innovation have appeared. Some of these have proposed models for change and others have significantly improved our understanding of change factors. Perhaps the great value of Title III, ESEA, was its provision of funds for experimentation with innovative ideas. Despite these developments, however, a change in one aspect of the school is still assumed not to change the whole school. In other words, we assume that the addition of a new technological device, a new course, or a new set of techniques will leave unaffected the rest of the educational program and institution. Indeed, if the change conflicts with the institution it is sloughed off or pushed into a corner; the system is protected against too broad a spectrum of change.

Management and Resources. Coombs states that the greatest single need throughout the world is for adequate management skills and personnel within the educational enterprise. Although there has been considerable improvement in the past ten years, there appears to be a gross neglect of the concepts of technological management, especially in such areas as man-machine systems, new educational formats to challenge basic classroom and school building organization, or new interrelationships among the public schools and other organizations providing education. What seems to be required, especially if we are to discuss advancing technology seriously, is a complete reorganization of input-output relationships within an understanding of the processes involved. Work is proceeding in this direction, but only rarely can a school district permit such a thorough rethinking.

Understanding the Learning Process. The basic need for the application of technology to education is an understanding of what is meant by learning; although there is a vast and growing literature in this field, we have perhaps not come to grips with the basic research questions about learning. The crux of any discussion of the uses of technology in education is the contribution technological devices can make to learning. There are many varieties of learning and many functions in the learning process. These require careful analysis and explication in a context which assumes that technology can contribute to the improvement of the process.

THE CONCEPT OF TECHNOLOGY IN EDUCATION

To understand this concept, we must first come to grips with the *idea of a machine*. This is necessary because the primary difficulty in applications of technology to education so far has been a concentration on the devices rather than the processes involving the devices. Heinich has pointed out that "the machine is only the visible manifestation of a process so implicit in our society that we take it for granted," and he finds that "too many educators point with pride to the machine without an understanding of, or a commitment to, the process."[4] The major guideline, therefore, for technological discussions must be a prior understanding of the processes represented by the machine. Ellis states this condition clearly:

> Machines execute procedures and each machine is the embodiment of the procedure it executes. This is an important relationship that exists for all machines, but people are just not in the habit of speaking about machines in this way. It means, of course, that knowing in detail what a particular machine does—how it works—is enough in theory to know what procedure it

is executing. This is true because when we say that a machine is the embodiment of the procedure it executes, we are saying, in effect, that a statement of procedure describes the machine needed to carry out the procedures. Thus, mechanizing means *thinking about procedure,* not about hardware, and once we state a procedure explicitly we should not really be surprised that a machine can be built to execute it.[5]

Two changes in technology must be recognized as they affect the present structure of education: (1) from mechanical to electronic, and (2) from nonsystematic to systematic; that is, the effective interrelationship of all parts is critical to the operation of any of the parts within the system. This electronic systems technology causes radical alterations in ways of both thinking and acting. Heinrich suggests that the "sophistication of technology is directly related to the number of decisions that are made in the design states ... [but] education is now structured so that emphasis is placed on use rather than on design."[6]

These shifts from use to design, from machine to procedure, from the casual to the basic, are creating significant problems in the advance of educational technology. The persistence of traditional thinking can be judged from what (it is hoped) may be an editorial oversight in a caption beneath a picture in the October 1968 issue of *Audiovisual Instruction:* "Appearance of Individualized Learning in Typical Classroom Environment with Technology Clustered at the Rear." If we acknowledge change and the problems stemming from it, the critical question for technology may be: To what degree, based on what values, should the present system of education be protected or the power of the technology released when the two are in conflict? The answer will depend to a large extent on our understanding and acceptance of the role of technology in modern life and a sufficient strength of desire to plan positively for the maintenance of human values.

But what are the values of the machine? And what are the human values we wish to retain? These are two of the perplexing questions of our times; yet, underlying them is our understanding of changes involving the uses of technology. As far as the machine is concerned, if a process can be defined as repetitive and routine, a machine can be designed to perform it. If this generality describes the function of the machine, how can we then describe the unique role of the human? This is a difficult task, because traditionally humans have been responsible for production, for doing the routine, so that we have come to think of humanness in routine terms. Man has been "man the producer" until modern times. He has designed his machines to assist his production rather than to replace those aspects of it that are essentially nonhuman; consequently, he has yielded some part of his right in favor of the machine. As Hilton asks:

> Why didn't man adapt the pattern of the machine to his needs rather than seek to adjust his needs to the pattern of the machine? The patterns of machines are not absolutes but potentials, but to take full advantage of

the potential productivity of the machine, the machine must be occupied to full capacity: and man wanted to take full advantage of the machine's potential productivity.[7]

It seems clear that we can best arrive at an understanding of humanness if we first ask what functions, tasks, or processes the machine cannot do. Thereafter we might ask what functions the machine can accomplish are better left as human responsibilities, and why. These two questions lead directly to consideration of the effective interaction of men and machines in a system designed to achieve specified goals and requiring the resources of both. It would seem that this philosophy should underly the design of future educational systems that can promote human values and provide effective and efficient operating environments.

However, to overcome the dependence on routine inherent in man the producer will require a new, and certainly not automatic, era of humanness. Too much of our human security (indeed, cultural stability) is dependent on this view of man; yet it has not always been easy for man to tolerate routine. He has sensed a greater role, but since there was little he could do about it, he has rationalized routine as a necessary part of his search for higher values. Horace Mann's comment, written in 1846, has particular significance:

> Essential requisites in a teacher's character are a love of children and a love of his work. To exclude the feeling of monotony and irksomeness, he must look upon his work as ever a new one; for such it is. The school teacher is not, as it sometimes seems to be supposed, placed upon a perpetually revolving wheel and carried through a daily or yearly round of the same labors and duties. Such a view of his office is essentially a low and false one. . . . What if he is required to explain the same principles, and to reiterate the same illustrations, until his path in the accustomed exercises of the schoolroom is as worn and beaten as the one by which, morning and night, he travels to and from it? Still, in the truest and highest sense, his labor is always a new one; because the subject upon which he operates is constantly changing.[8]

In modern-day education there are similar efforts to justify and glorify the teacher's role without discriminating between the monotonous and irksome and the human and unique, but modern technology can transfer the routine and inhuman to machines.

Before asking why this situation exists, we need to consider the question of human uniqueness—the qualities of man that cannot be transferred to a machine. Benne suggests that "man's dignity lies in the irreducible fact of human responsibility."[9] He finds that man is at present victimized by an "overpotent agent," the technology he has created, and that "the problem of humanizing the humanities remains a central element in contemporary tragedy."

Hilton asks: "What is to become of man [in this age of cybernation]? If he no longer be Man the Producer, will he become merely Man the Consumer? Or could he possibly become Man the Creator?" She goes on to point out that "our social difficulty is not the impending wholesale liberation from toil and scarcity, but our total lack of preparation for freedom."[10]

It would seem that technology offers teachers a terribly exciting opportunity. Let's suppose that 70 or 80 percent of what the teacher now does is mechanized. This means that the remaining 20 percent—the truly human aspects of teaching—can receive 100 percent of the teacher's attention. It is difficult to speculate about what new educational horizons might emerge; we have remained so enmeshed in our traditional thinking that it is virtually impossible to see beyond the reef.

The essentially human functions, then, are *choosing*—developing and reacting to unique situations; *feeling*—being emotional and loving, a total person as it were; *creating*—designing the machines to relieve the routine and release the chance to feel; and *cognating*—discovering and relating experience so that art and philosophy emerge to direct human awareness of self, of others, and of environment. These are acts that induce fear because they suggest confrontation with the unknown. But that is what man is all about; he is not all about the unfearful —the routine and monotonous that can be passed to the machine. But accepting the chance to be human will never be easy; as Erich Fromm put it, man tries often to "escape from freedom" rather than face himself and his world.

The concept of technology in education begins with an understanding of the machine as properly undertaking the routine repetitive functions, so that the teacher is left free to perform the unique human activities. Assisted by other specialists, the teacher controls and manipulates the machine processes, some of which aid him in the performance of tasks and others replace him in the least human of functions.

The role and functions of the teacher will more closely relate to the nature of the institution employing him than to either the professional autonomy based on education and outlook or the broad view of human nature suggested here; therefore, growth awaits changes in the nature of the institution. As a profession, teachers seem unwilling to take the lead in initiating such changes. The recent New York teachers' strike makes clear that efforts toward teacher professionalism are directed at security and role maintenance, although the present generally accepted concept of "teacher" is patently antiquated. When education is approached in a deliberate way, new theories will emerge to guide the selection and training of teachers for roles as leaders of technologically supported teaching systems.

THE EMERGING ROLE OF THE TEACHER

Historically, in America, the concept of teaching has included teaching a faith; a morality, a loyalty; teaching for basic literacy, public responsibility, occupations, physical health, social facility, general knowledge, and personal development. Although these roles reflect the changing mission and direction of

American education, they do not yield the kind of description required for a systematic analysis of teaching. Yet, as Green points out:

> The concept of teaching is like a blurred picture. It is a vague concept. Its boundaries are not clear. However accurately we may describe the activity of teaching there will, and always must, remain certain troublesome borderline cases. In admitting this, the point is not that we have failed to penetrate the darkness and to discover that juncture at which an activity ceases to be teaching and becomes something else. The point is rather that beneath the darkness there is simply no such precise discrimination to be found. There is, therefore, an initial presumption against the credibility of any analysis which yields precise criteria, which, without a trace of uncertainty, assigns to every case a clear identity.[11]

In brief, teaching is *a system of actions intended to induce learning.* This definition suggests that teaching may be analyzed in terms of the behaviors that contribute to learning. La Grone undertook such an analysis, and it appears extremely useful, but he cautions that "any effort to group teacher behaviors by categories tends to minimize the complexity of teaching and the interrelationships of behaviors."[12] In the emerging role, McKeachie sees the teacher becoming an "educational planner—one who has available a variety of resources to meet the varying objectives of his teaching and the varying needs of the learner."[13] Loughary feels that the "teacher's function as a presenter of information could be eliminated easily, but he will continue to interpret, synthesize, and clarify information displayed in another mode."[14] Biddle points out that "often the teacher is thought of simultaneously as a director of learning, as a friend and counselor of pupils, as a member of a group of professional persons, and as a citizen participating in various community activities."[15] For Schueler, "teaching is a social function, its aim being to guide desirable growth in others. ... Its method is communication."[16] Gagné defines the teacher in the simplest of educational systems as "the manager of the conditions of learning." He points out, significantly, that "this managing function does not change when the system is made more complex by incorporating certain technological improvements."[17]

Joyce, in a short essay that comes as close as any current attempt to deal with technological implications of the teacher role, describes the teacher variously as the student's "academic counselor, his personal guide, facilitator, alter ego, and friend"; in addition, he will function as a "diagnostician and prescriber." He will also "lead an inquiring group and help it become a self-propelling miniature democracy whose members improve their interpersonal development in the course of their academic inquiry." This teacher is supported by a direct-instruction team, including teacher, paraprofessionals, interns, and teacher aides; and by a support center where specialized resources (personnel and equipment) are available for computer operations, self-instruction, inquiry, materials creation, human relations, and guidance and evaluation. The teacher and his staff function to "orchestrate the environment,"[18] their aim being the individualization of various learning modes.

Joyce offers an exciting analysis of the future organization of teaching functions and roles. His essay, however, tends to concentrate on organization rather than on process. His role analysis seems based on a rather general discription of a career ladder for the school, and his functional descriptions are at best poetic. The pamphlet deserves wide attention because of its attempt to challenge a very knotty problem and perhaps to present a viewpoint for the profession that is sufficiently nonthreatening to be acceptable.

MAN-MACHINE SYSTEMS FOR EDUCATION

Man-machine systems imply the interrelationship and joint functioning of men and machines for the accomplishment of particular goals. Where this concept is applied, certain tasks are assigned to machines and others are reserved for men. Each is held responsible for the achievement of its functions; full operation is achieved only when both are functioning properly. Since both men and machines can fail on occasion, back-up systems are designed to cover emergencies.

The development of man-machine systems for education will affect both the functions of the teacher and the relation of the machines to the educational process. Joyce's essay envisioned the teacher as the generalist who orchestrates the resources at his disposal, but many writers see the future as increasing the specialized functions of the teacher. In this context, Gagné suggests that close attention should be given to the "kinds of teacher functions that are most highly dependent on dynamic interpersonal relationships for their success." He sees the teacher functioning as a decision-maker in the areas of motivation, transfer of knowledge, assessment, conditions of learning, and the structuring of knowledge to be learned. This kind of functional analysis, based on the nature of decisions, is a useful first step in developing the context for man-machine analysis. In their analysis of the teacher functions, Ward and Jung state:

> Direct man-machine interaction will provide a major part of the instructional function more efficiently than has ever before been possible. The teacher will have time to focus on more valuable functions such as (a) diagnosing learner abilities and needs, (b) creating an appropriate range of learning experiences, (c) helping pupils learn how to learn, (d) personalizing learning, (e) fostering unique individual potentials, (f) developing higher thought processes, (g) maximizing the learners in creating knowledge, applying principles, exploring life styles, and valuing explicitly.[19]

A functional analysis for purposes of a man-machine system would not necessarily consign a total function to either a man or a machine. For many funtions, the machine will support and assist the teacher; some progress, for instance, has been made in the use of the computer to assist the guidance function. Instructional management systems, i.e., systems for recording, updating, and storing information about pupil progress, have improved the teacher's ability to make decisions; they have not replaced it.

On the other hand, computer-based drill-and-practice modes suggest another aspect of man-machine interaction. Assuming the operations to be as competent as their developers claim, there is little reason to have a teacher do any drill and practice; he will, however, still organize the requisite learning experiences that must precede it. The teacher role that emerges most clearly is one of managing and planning for effective learning through the use of human and technological resources.

A FUNCTIONAL ANALYSIS OF TEACHING

No analysis of teaching based on functions describable in terms of the nature of the processes appears to exist at this time. The very idea of the task seems formidable; yet, if progress is to be made in this area, the first step will be a satisfactory description of the occupation of teaching that must be relatable to the emerging processes of mechanistic design, but certainly not limited to it. This section will attempt a rough description—no more than a plan of action—for developing an understanding of the teaching process appropriate for the emerging technological systems.

The primary assumption underlying this description is that, from the viewpoint of the teacher, there are basically two forms of activity within the present classroom: learning situations and other situations (for the present being considered less significant). Within these classroom situations, the teacher's functions may be divided into two major kinds of activities, which, for this analysis, have been labeled *curricular* and *interpersonaler*. This division is based on a further assumption: the curricular aspects of the teaching situation are basically "people functions" (activites related to dealing with the person as an individual and a member of a specifically defined group) require a different orientation. The teacher then behaves in support of one or the other (or both) of these areas, or is supported by a specialized team of assistants performing or assisting in these functions. The value of this dichotomy appears in its reflection of the basic differences in activities and support mechanisms involved in each area.

These activities, however, exist only within the "real world of the teacher," and it is necessary to understand the special dynamic of an individual working with a group of subordinates (as in the classic teaching role). A planning mechanism is needed if further (and specific) information is to be developed within such a schema. The model (Figures I, II, and III) expands the areas of function. On the curricular side of the model, processes are derived for concepts of information organization, storage, transmission, etc., and knowledge is organized primarily by the requirements of the disciplines as presently conceived for effective teaching. On the interpersonaler side, processes are derived from an understanding of human interaction, and knowledge is organized in relation to individual experience. Support systems represent the psychosocial aspects of the

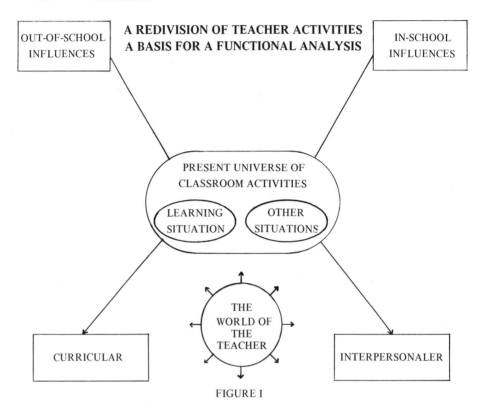

FIGURE I

classroom interaction. Emphasis on one side or the other would depend on the goals and nature of the particular learning situation, but it is assumed that the classroom activity implies a dynamic whose primary purpose is learning, which is understood as either the acquiring of knowledge or the application of this knowledge to the improved control of the environment.

The model does not point to job titles familiar with the school environment, as did Joyce, although some of these will come quickly to mind. Strong efforts will be required to examine what functions (processes relating to the teaching role) underlie the title and to relate these to the act of teaching. The concept of support teams permits the free location of functions within or quite distant from the school, to be determined by their efficient and effective performance. It is important, however, that these functions be related to the same or similar activities being carried out in other institutions and that there be cooperation among the agencies contributing to a function. Such planning would cause other levels of complication, but the explication of such overlap could lead to new methods of effectively accomplishing tasks within cost-effective (and other) parameters.

The model also includes feedback and reorganization functions for the system

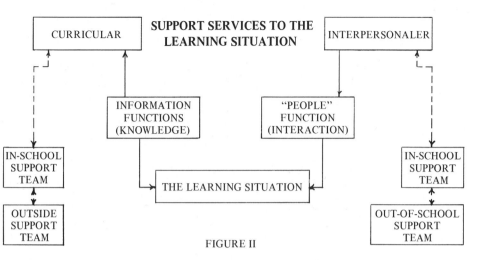

FIGURE II

it seeks to create for the analysis of teaching. This is important. Teaching is never a static act; indeed, the suggestion of such a model should not be taken to imply that teaching can become a mechanical process. It can, however, show which aspects of the total teaching role are routine, mechanical, and unworthy of the time and effort of a highly trained professional; such functions may then be delegated either to a machine or to paraprofessionals. It will also be found that many functions can be established outside the classroom, but in direct support of the teaching effort. The model, which definitely places the teacher in the role of a manager of learning, requires a competent, creative individual working with students in close interpersonal contact. Such a framework can open up exciting new vistas for teaching.

THE ROLE OF THE SCHOOL BOARD

The forces opposing change and innovation may be classified under seven headings: (1) the nature of the institution, (2) the objectives of the system, (3) the problems imposed by present change and development models, (4) the management of resources, (5) our present understanding of the learning process, (6) the emerging nature of man imposed by technological awareness, and (7) the changing role of the teacher. From this context, the design of man-machine systems of teaching is posited as necessary for the maintenance of human values and the efficient use of resources. This direction of educational planning has received neither sufficient research attention nor development within school districts, but we will lose the benefits inherent in the technologies unless we come to grips with the need for planning.

The present organization of educational personnel mitigates against this forth-right technological planning for some apparently justified reasons: inadequate research, insufficient resources (and taxpayer unwillingness to increase funds),

THE LEARNING SITUATION

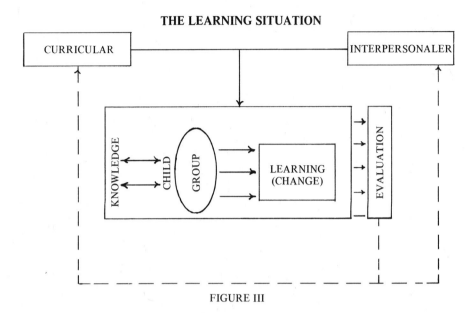

FIGURE III

lack of appropriate education and training, and the nitty-gritty problems of implementing technological advances under present school conditions. On the other hand, many reasons advanced by the profession (and, incidentally, I am including teachers, administrators, and many others) are simply defensive measures favoring retention of the status quo. Teachers seem to be fighting for their right to maintain routine.

Despite the tragic response of the profession to the New York City educational situation—one built up over years of closed bureaucracy and diminishing communication with nonprofessional forces—there are indications that ideas about technological change are taking hold. Especially exciting in this respect are the new concepts in teacher education presently being developed through U.S. Office of Education research grants. These programs will take time, however, and there is much that can be done now. It seems to me that school boards can help by:

1. *Encouraging positive thinking about technology.* If the professional staff is confident that job cuts, salary reductions, longer hours, or increased burdens will not be the results of planning for technology, they will feel free to undertake such planning. Indeed, the school board could perhaps motivate comprehensive planning by encouraging teachers to define the nonprofessional aspects of their roles so that new combinations of manpower and machines can be employed in the district.
2. *Seeking thoroughgoing analysis and change.* The major impediment to effective technological implementation is the idea that changing one part of a system will not affect the rest. In point of fact, any single change will

require that the whole system accommodate itself, either by adapting to the change or by inhibiting its force, which is what usually occurs unless careful planning precedes implementation.

3. *Implementing PPBS, systems analysis, and other positive planning procedures.* Developing these capacities within the district may be difficult. Planning should receive direct support as a distinct activity; it should not occur only in ad hoc committees which see the activity as detracting from other responsibilities.

4. *Developing outside lines of communication.* The school district, at both the board and administrative levels should develop the capacity to see beyond itself. This means relating to colleges training teachers, using consultants when appropriate, and keeping abreast of developments in technology and education.

5. *Promoting and supporting in-service education programs.* No one questions regular maintenance and repair for school buses or other major equipment. Indeed, service contracts are a regular purchase item; yet, teachers usually have to fight for in-service education and continuing education. Formal and informal programs can be developed within the district through the use of outside agencies to help build support for change and innovation.

6. *Concentrating on the processes, not the institutions.* The greatest inhibitor to change is an inability to separate the form from the function of the activity. As the processes of education change, formal arrangements should be free to adapt themselves to these changes.

7. *Building community support through information about change.* Most communities expect from the schools what they are told or what their own experience has led them to expect. Change mechanisms must be developed for community attitudes through a positive approach to information about technology and other changes.

Thinking about technology and education requires changes in our attitudes toward, and our understanding of, what is a man and what is a machine. Acceptance of this distinction can lead to the kinds of analyses of teaching and learning suggested by the model. Failure to accept this basic orientation can mean losing the opportunity to plan positively for the future.

11. NOTES

1. Mary Alice Hilton, "Cybernation and Its Impact on American Society," in Paul W. F. Witt (ed.), *Technology and the Curriculum* (New York: Teachers College Press, 1968), p. 11.

2. W. P. Kent, W. A. Le Baron, and R. Peterson, *Feasibility of Using an Experimental Laboratory for Identifying Classroom Multi-Media Problems and Requirements.* (Falls Church, Va.: System Development Corporation, 1968, Final Report, USOE Contract OEC-1-071143-4419).

3. Philip H. Coombs, *The World Educational Crisis: A Systems Approach* (New York: Oxford University Press, 1968), pp. 111-13.

4. Robert Heinich, "Technology of Instruction: Impetus and Impasse," in Edgar L. Morphet and David L. Jesser (eds.), *Planning for Effective Utilization of Technology in Education* (New York: Citation Press, 1969), pp. 75-76.

5. Allen B. Ellis, "Educational Technology: New Myths and Old Realities," *Harvard Educational Review* 38 (Fall 1968), pp. 724-30.

6. Heinich, *op. cit.,* p. 81.

7. Hilton, *op. cit.,* pp. 7-8.

8. Horace Mann, *Ninth Annual Report, Massachusetts State Board of Education* (Boston: Dutton and Wentworth, 1846), p. 83.

9. Kenneth D. Benne, *Education for Tragedy: Essays in Disenchanted Hope for Modern Man* (Lexington: University of Kentucky Press, 1967), p. 10.

10. Hilton, *op. cit.,* pp. 18 and 27.

11. Thomas F. Green, "A Topology of the Teaching Concept," in C. J. B. Macmillan and Thomas W. Nelson (eds.), *Concepts of Teaching: Philosophical Essays* (Chicago: Rand McNally, 1968).

12. Robert F. La Grone, *A Proposal for the Revision of the Preservice Professional Component of a Program of Teacher Education* (Washington, D.C.: American Association of Colleges for Teacher Education, 1964).

13. Wilbert J. McKeachie, "Higher Education," in Peter H. Rossi and Bruce J. Biddle (eds.), *The New Media and Education* (Garden City, Anchor Books, 1966), p. 323.

14. John W. Loughary (ed.), *Man-Machine Systems in Education* (New York: Harper and Row, 1966), p. 213.

15. Bruce J. Biddle and William J. Ellena, *Contemporary Research on Teacher Effectiveness* (New York: Holt, Rinehart and Winston, 1964), p. 3.

16. Herbert Schueler and Gerald S. Lesser, *Teacher Education and the New Media* (Washington, D. C.: American Association of Colleges for Teacher Education, 1967), p. 2.

17. Robert M. Gagné, *The Conditions of Learning* (New York: Holt, Rinehart and Winston, 1965), p. 241.

18. Bruce R. Joyce, *The Teacher and His Staff: Man, Media, and Machines* (Washington, D.C.: National Commission on Teacher Education and Professional Standards and Center for the Study of Instruction, National Education Association, 1967), pp. 7 and 21.

19. William T. Ward and Charles Jung, "Implications of Technology for the Preparation and Changing Roles of Educators," in Morphet and Jesser (eds.), *op cit.,* p. 309.

12

Teacher Awareness of Sociocultural Differences in Multicultural Classrooms*

HORACIO ULIBARRI

The public schools in the United States were created to serve all the children of all the people in order that youth might more ably participate in American society. With the acceptance of the principle of educating the whole child, the functions of the schools have been greatly expanded. Ideally, all these services are primarily aimed to help the individual child develop to his full potential. The practical application, however, is different. Upon closer analysis, one may find great discrepancies in the educational opportunities available to the children of different social and cultural backgrounds.

Among the variables jeopardizing equalized educational opportunity are the social-cultural backgrounds of the students. The schools have been complacent to a large degree in presenting only a small aspect of the American culture, namely, the middle-class values and orientations, as the sum total of the curricula in the schools. The teachers themselves, generally, have a middle-class orientation. These two factors, the middle-class orientation of the curriculum and the middle-class life-style of the teachers, place students of lower-class and/or different ethnic backgrounds at a disadvantage when competing with middle-class students.

The problem of equalizing educational opportunity may be resolved to the extent that teachers have empathy for, and insight into, classroom behavior and to the extent that they provide a curriculum that satisfies the needs of students from all sociocultural backgrounds.

In New Mexico, the problem is greatly accentuated because of the large number of children coming from Indian and Spanish cultural backgrounds. These minority groups—namely, the Navajo, Apache, and Pueblo Indians, and the Spanish-Americans—are in a state of transition and moving rapidly toward acculturation and assimilation. The extent of acculturation, however, seems to vary from almost no acculturation to complete acculturation. As with most other minority groups, these minority groups in New Mexico are being assimilated into the lower classes of Anglo society. Thus they present some of the same problems that the lower classes present as well as some unique problems of their own. There are a number of children coming from traditional homes who enter school with all the cultural orientations of the parents and with no knowledge of the English language. Nor is the problem resolved as the child progresses through school. It seems that the child is able to absorb some of the values promulgated by the school while still retaining, in large measure, the orientations of the traditional culture.

On first observation, this dual participation in both cltures would not seem to constitute a problem. But as the child develops into maturity, he finds himself confronted with orientations and expectations from the home and the school that are often opposing and contradictory. This factor engenders a personality conflict and disorganization in the individual which has expression in more basic behavioral patterns.

Thus in New Mexico the teachers need, for maximum effectiveness in their teaching, not only an understanding of child growth and development but also a deep insight into the cultural orientations and value configurations of these groups as they are expressed in traditional and transitional behavioral patterns. This study[1] has attempted to measure the extent to which teachers are aware of sociocultural factors that impinge on the education of children of these minority groups. A major premise of the study was that the ineffectiveness of the public schools in the education of minority groups such as the Indians and the Spanish-Americans has been due in large measure to the failure to consider sufficiently the cultural orientations, the value configurations, and the behavior arising therefrom, in the development of the curricula.

A stratified sample of 100 teachers, who were currently teaching Anglo, Spanish-American, and Indian children, was selected for interviewing. The interview schedule was made with the use of a questionnaire that covered the following areas: (1) psychological needs of children in relation to sociocultural differences; (2) cultural orientations as they affected children's classroom behavior; (3) social conditions prevailing among the groups; and (4) educational problems pertinent to the three ethnic groups. Each item had three five-point scales—one for each group—which enabled the subjects to draw comparisons among the three groups. The following is an item from the questionnaire used in the interview:

11. The concept of life-space entails the following three aspects: (1) the physical environment that the child lives in; (2) the artifacts, i.e., the material things that he manipulates; and (3) the persons with whom he interacts.

In your way of thinking, how enriching is the life-space of the following children?

Indian	1	2	3	4	5
Spanish-American	1	2	3	4	5
Anglo	1	2	3	4	5

To encircle "1" on the continuum would indicate that the teacher feels that the life-space is extremely meager and limiting; to encircle "5" would indicate that the teacher believes that the child has a very rich background of experience for understanding concepts taught in school.

Each item was analyzed statistically. The mean for each scale gave a rank to each ethnic group. The standard deviation showed the extent to which teachers agreed in assigning such a rank to each group. The coefficient of concordance indicated the amount of agreement or disagreement in assigning similar ranks to the three ethnic groups. A high coefficient of concordance indicated the amount of agreement or disagreement among teachers in assigning similar ranks to the groups. A low coefficient of concordance indicated a low agreement in assigning similar ranks.

When this analysis was completed, the results were compiled in terms of implications for education. This was done because several items had a bearing on several educational areas. Educational areas covered in the analysis were (1) curriculum, (2) language, (3) life-space, (4) motivation and achievement, (5) intergroup relations, and (6) personality disorganization.

Curriculum. All the items in the questionnaire had some relationship to the problems in curriculum. The teachers' responses on all items indicated consistent lack of awareness of the effect of sociocultural factors on pupil behavior. The teachers' responses also indicated that some teachers were not in agreement with practices and recommendations advanced by educational theorists.

The general lack of sensitivity on the part of the teachers in the sample indicated that they were not sure of the nature of sociocultural problems presented by these ethnic groups. This lack of awareness points to a strong probability of having a general curriculum for everybody regardless of sociocultural backgrounds. If these teachers follow the general trends in the country, the possibilities are that the curriculum implemented will be geared strongly toward middle-class values.

Language Differences. One item in the questionnaire considered oral proficiency in the use of the English language among the three groups. The teachers showed marked awareness in indicating that real and wide differences existed among the groups. However, in response to another item, the teachers failed to show that there existed any differences among the three ethnic groups in ability to use the regular textbooks for instructions.

Lack of proficiency in the use of oral English is rather self-evident, hence the sensitivity may be really superficial. This suggests an awareness of an obvious phenomenon without an understanding of the underlying causes or the adapting of methodology because of it. The teachers' responses to the item concerning differences in ability to use regular textbooks seem to confirm this supposition. The results of this item point to the possibility that the same textbook is being used within a grade level regardless of differences in reading abilities of the children.

Life-Space. Several items attempted to measure teachers' awareness to differences in life-space of the pupil groups considered. One item compared the out-of-school environment of the various groups with the school environment. The teachers appeared to be strongly aware of the effect of the differences of out-of-school environment upon pupils. The teachers indicated that the Anglo pupils have a superior out-of-school environment; that is, one which is closer and more compatible to the school environment than that of the Spanish-Americans or Indians. The teachers, in another item, failed to show sensitivity toward richness or meagerness in the life-space of the three groups. A third item relating to the concept of life-space attempted to interrelate the vicarious experiences in the classroom with the direct firsthand experiences of the children. In this item, the teachers again failed to differentiate, with any assurance, how meaningful the classroom experiences became to the children because of their firsthand experiences out of school. The teachers, in other words, believe that all children get equally meaningful experiences in the classroom despite the differences in direct life experiences of the three groups.

Thus, the last two items tended to negate the responses of the first item, in which the teachers showed marked sensitivity to differences in out-of-school environment of the three groups. The contradictions in responses to the three interrelated items indicate that, while teachers may be aware of out-of-school factors as they affect pupils, they apparently do not see any connection of these factors with in-school performance, nor do they know what to do about them.

Lack of sensitivity toward the child's life-space indicates that the curriculum may not be meaningful to a large number of children. When children have only a meager range of direct experiences to which they can relate the vicarious experiences of the classroom, the formulation of meaningful constructs is very difficult. There is a great possibility that teachers will start with what they consider common experiences for all, but which may actually exclude the majority. Thus teachers may think their teaching is quite effective. Apparently teachers are prone to believe that there is a commensurate amount of learning with a given amount of pedagogy.

Motivation and Achievement. Several items attempted to measure whether teachers are sensitive to factors affecting pupil motivation and achievement. Two items showed that teachers did not differentiate between the types of curricula needed to meet the psychological differences of the three ethnic groups. They stated that the same type of curriculum could essentially satisfy the psychological needs of Indian and Spanish-speaking children just as it did for the Anglo children. They further stated that the present curriculum was meeting these needs.

The teachers were somewhat undecided with respect to the true value placed on education by the parents from the three ethnic groups. The teachers failed to recognize any substantial differences in the amount of motivation the children from each ethnic group received from the parents. A large number of teachers thought that there was some difference in the financial means at the disposal of each ethnic group for further education, but many did not. Furthermore, the teachers believed that most of the children, regardless of ethnic origin, were achieving at grade level.

The lack of sensitivity regarding values placed on education by minority groups points to the possibility that teachers may not know obstacles or aids that may thwart or enhance the motivation of children from different ethnic groups for maximum school achievement. Generally, teachers reflect middle-class values. These middle-class values are comprised in part of achievement and success, competition, and aggressiveness. The teachers therefore use praise, competitiveness, and pressure as some of their motivating practices. Children from different cultural backgrounds may not have internalized any of these values and may not respond to these types of motivation. Hence, if teachers are unaware of cultural differences in the motivation of children, motivational structures such as drive, reward and punishment, and level of aspiration may become very unreal to children with cultural orientations different from those of middle-class society.

Intergroup Relations. Two items considered intergroup relations among the different ethnic groups. In one item, the teachers agreed very strongly that the children were practicing school-taught concepts of citizenship in their out-of-school life. In another item, the teachers agreed that the three groups, the Indian, the Spanish-American, and the Anglo, were interacting with a minimum of tension and intergroup conflict.

The possible outcome of unawareness regarding problems of intergroup relationships is that the intergroup cleavages will remain indefinitely and will perhaps become more rigid. In effect, instead of helping the situation, the schools will be perpetuating the minority status of the Indian and Spanish-American. The need exists for orientation of teachers concerning majority-minority human relationship problems as well as to find ways and means of establishing better relations among the groups. This is imperative if the groups acculturating through the educational process are not going to be denied the rights and privileges that the school teaches them to appreciate and desire.

Personality Disorganization. An attempt was made to measure teachers' sensitivity toward differences in satisfying the psychological needs of the children from the three ethnic groups. These items have a relationship to personality disorganization of minority group members.

The teachers very strongly agreed that the psychological needs of all the children in school could be met within a singular curricular design. Moreover, the teachers strongly indicated that the school was essentially meeting the psychological needs of the three ethnic groups equally well.

The outcome of these items may indicate that teachers are not exactly sure of the nature of psychological needs or of the process of personality development. How the total sociocultural background defines the psychological needs of each child, and to a great extent prescribes the manner in which these needs should be met, incorporates an era of knowledge drawn from anthropology, sociology, and psychology that teachers need to know in much more detail than they appear to know at present.

Similarly, as evidenced from the responses, teachers need an understanding of the concept of marginality, the processes of disassociation, and of personal disorganization. Without these concepts, the behavior of children from minority groups may not be fully understood. At the same time, no preventive steps can be taken without an appreciation of the dual roles that the children are playing—at home and at school. There is real danger that the school will un-consciously bring about personality disorganization among its students because of its insistence on inculcating middle-class values and its belittling or ignoring of the subculture.

CONCLUSIONS

At least three levels of sensitivity were detected among the teachers in the sample toward sociocultural differences of the three ethnic groups considered. At one level, the teachers revealed a tremendous amount of awareness; at another, the teachers were somewhat aware but not really sensitive to socio-cultural factors; and at still a deeper level, the teachers were not sensitive at all to sociocultural factors as they impinge on classroom behavior of the different ethnic groups.

The level at which the teachers showed great sensitivity was the area con-cerned with overt behavioral practices and artifacts of the three cultures. Thus they were very sensitive to differences in oral proficiency in the use of the English language, and were quite ready to differentiate between the home and school environment in relation to the three ethnic groups.

At the second level, which perhaps is more abstract and of deeper significance, the teachers tended to show very little awareness of sociocultural factors affecting classroom behavior. They showed very little sensitivity to differences among the three groups in issues concerning health, meaningfulness of classroom experiences, values placed on education, and reading abilities.

The third level at which teachers indicated little or no sensitivity to socio-cultural differences was concerned with psychological needs and their satisfac-tion in relation to sociocultural orientations, scientific interpretation of natural phenomena, civic responsibility, intergroup relationships, economic efficiency, and achievement at grade level.

12. NOTES

1. Research study entitled "The Adjustment of Indian and Non-Indian Children in the Public Schools of New Mexico," College of Education, University of New Mexico, Albuquerque.

13

Problems as Seen by Parents and Teachers*

HERSCHEL T. MANUEL

A sampling of the opinions of parents relative to the problems of their children was secured with the assistance of the principals of a few schools. A letter addressed to the parents invited their comments; the form enclosed for their reply was entitled "The Education of Spanish-Speaking Children—Experiences and Opinions of Parents." Two questions asked were:

"As a parent what do you find to be the special problems of Spanish-speaking children?"

"What should I tell teachers and the public about schools for these children?"

A COMMON GOAL FOR ALL CHILDREN

We desire for our children, said some, the same things that other parents desire for their children. One of the Denver parents stated it this way:

We like to enjoy the better things in life. We want our children to be well educated and successful. We want them to lead good, clean, moral lives.—Like any other parent I want what is best for my children.

An Arizona parent voiced the same feeling:

I believe every parent wants the same things for his children—no matter what race or color.

There was evident also a strong desire to be accepted, to belong, to be a full member of the community. The not-belonging feeling of their children was a matter of deep concern. A California parent showed a keen perception of the effect of rejection and the significance of the attitudes generated by rejection:

My husband and I many times feel we do not fit in certain groups or are not accepted because we are of Mexican origin. We realize most of the time we are wrong. Yet, I'm afraid they [the children] will begin to feel the same way.

Her concern was further expressed:

The one thing I wish [is that] my children would grow up to feel more true loyalty for our country. To feel they are actually a part of this nation, not just a

*Copyright 1965 by the University of Texas Press. Reprinted by permission of the publisher from Herschel T. Manuel, *Spanish-Speaking Children of the Southwest*, pp. 73-81.

113

Mexican that happened to be born on this side of the border. To be proud of their origin, but to keep it in its place.

Another parent showed her attempt to guard her children against the effect of prejudice toward them:

I've always told my children, "You are only what *you* make of yourself. Nobody is better than you, and you are no better than anybody." . . .Spanish children should be proud of what they are.

Another, remembering her childhood in a little town where prejudice was shown toward the Spanish-speaking people, noted her own good fortune:

I have been very lucky because I had red hair, freckles, and a light complexion.

She offered no suggestions on the special educational treatment of Spanish-speaking children. Instead:

All I can say is, Teach the children; we are all God's children, no matter what we look like or who we are.

An Arizona father expressed a strong view against segregation of Spanish-speaking children in separate schools, rooms, or even groups, adding:

I believe that every Spanish-speaking [child] knows he is different and does not need reminding.

ECONOMIC CONDITIONS

Lack of money was said to be a source of difficulty. A Texas mother expressed the opinion that "the economic conditions of the Spanish-speaking have a direct bearing on the ability of their children to learn English." Another expressed two unfavorable results of insufficient income: lack of educational materials at home and having to withdraw children from school so the parents may find work in another community:

With six children I am unable to provide educational toys, records, or books for them. . . . More jobs are needed in our hometown for Spanish-speaking people so we could become permanent residents of this or any community. So many times we must withdraw the children from school in order to look for jobs elsewhere.

Another parent expressed the point of view that lack of money or failure to use it for education is a serious problem:

The most important problem is money. Many of the Spanish-speaking Americans don't have enough money to help their children through school. Some people do acquire enough money but will rather use it on something of less importance, ignoring their children's education.

The complicated relation of prejudice and economic conditions is suggested in the remarks of one parent:

If a Spanish kid gets into some mischief with the law, the reaction is usually, "Well, what can you expect; he's Spanish, isn't he?" The public should be educated to the fact that many times these kids get into trouble because of family financial troubles or environment. Many times their parents cannot get higher paying jobs because of their nationality. Society rather than the individual is more often than not responsible for poverty.

I think that the Spanish group has come a long way in the way of improvement, but it has a long way to go yet. Establishing anything like economic equality with other groups will mean increasing their number in skilled trades and professional and clerical work.

The responsibility of parents for an active part in the education of their children was recognized in various statements. Some felt that teaching English to their children at home was a parental responsibility. One expressed regret that she had done so little to contribute to the language development of her children:

I see the mistake I have made now, because my children are not progressing as fast as I thought they would. I have started to speak English to my five-year-old hoping that by the time he enters school, he will be better prepared than the others.

One parent expressed the need for teamwork on the part of parents and teachers in these words:

Most teachers will not help children because the parents do not cooperate, and most of the Spanish people are not interested in school activities. I think that the parents need to help more and encourage the children better.

Another expressed the need for cooperation in these words:

We cannot expect the teacher to do our job for us. They are wonderful to try to understand them, but the foundation is the home; the next step is the school.

LANGUAGE DIFFICULTIES

The problem of language was recognized in various comments, some of which have already been given. Individual differences among children on this point were clearly evident. A Denver mother wrote that her husband and her children did not speak Spanish. In fact, at the time of writing, her husband and one son were "taking Spanish" by television. Another parent expressed the opinion that if people would speak English to their children at home, their children would be more confident. She commented that her little son was taught English first and now can express himself much better in English than in Spanish.

Some parents expressed the need for a school program for five-year-old children. A father said that one year of kindergarten or pre-school education is worth as much as three years later on:

I believe that one year at the start for a Spanish-speaking child will be as effective—if not more so—as about three years at the age when a child loses interest in school (ages 13 to 16). I believe that, if a Spanish child at this age had the kindergarten background, he would very likely continue through high school and possibly college.

The problem of keeping children in school was recognized by another parent in these words:

The number-one problem with the Spanish-speaking children is [that] they go as far as the eleventh grade, and then they quit. They lose all interest with only a year or two to go.

She feels that schools should make it "almost impossible" for a child to leave school.

That different children have different needs is evident from various comments. One parent remarked:

I have ten children, among them a set of twins, and not even the twins are alike in any of their habits or ways of thinking.

One way in which children are different, it is pointed out, is in their feeling of security or insecurity, of trust or timidity.

It is obvious that the parents who made the comments quoted here are of an economic and cultural level above that of a large number of less fortunate people who have children in the schools. In general, however, the problems listed are problems also of the children from poverty-stricken and culture-deprived homes. Some of the problems, such as achieving status, acquiring a new language, and finding money to support children in the schools, are frightfully magnified in groups of lower economic levels. In these homes there is often a lack of understanding and a resulting lack of aggressive interest in the education of their children. There is a certain hopelessness and lack of ambition fostered by continued poverty and frustration. On the other hand, there are many very poor people who have a vision of better days for their children and who are struggling forward, perhaps groping from lack of direction.

PROBLEMS AS SEEN BY TEACHERS

In general, teachers emphasize problems related to their work. The principal of an Arizona elementary school presented a group of problems as a summary of questions listed by his teachers. Naturally, some of the questions dealt with policies and methods of teaching. For example, should Spanish-speaking children be allowed to speak Spanish to one another in class? Do teachers tend to make class work easier for Spanish-speaking children? Should drill be used to correct the speech errors of the five-year-old, or should he be encouraged to speak the best English he can by simply listening to other children and to the teacher? When an older child enters without knowledge of English, how should he be taught? Should he be enrolled in grade 1 and work through grade-by-grade to the grade in which he otherwise belongs? What is the best procedure to use when a child has shown no desire and made no effort to talk?

Some of the questions were directed toward an understanding of cultural difficulties and the ways to deal with them. One teacher expressed the opinion that "there is a strong pressure in each class to keep all individuals at the same level of achievement. Slow learners are not especially looked down upon, but fast learners must be careful not to achieve beyond the group as a whole. Humor is often used to keep an individual in line."

Emotional difficulties, perhaps related to cultural background in the thinking of the teachers, were suggested by some of the comments and questions. What cultural or other factors, excluding the language barrier, tend to influence Spanish-speaking children to be timid and withdrawn in learning situations? How can greater self-expression be developed? One teacher pointed to feuds among girls in the upper grades, remarking that in her opinion girls fight worse than boys. In two comments the opinion was expressed that Spanish-speaking children tend to be either extremely shy or very bold. If this observation is true, it was asked, what kinds of activities and room atmosphere should be planned to meet the situation?

One question pointed to an emotional conflict which seems to stem from a difference in school procedures and home culture. The school, it was said, teaches children to care for themselves, but the home teaches the older children to look after the younger. The result: fourth-graders "beat up" first-graders! Another suggested that the families have a "strange defeatist attitude" toward the behavior problems of the children, accepting the difficulties as a "cross they have to bear" rather than attempting to understand and help the children.

A few questions related to special characteristics or handicaps of Spanish-speaking children more or less creative than are other children of the same socioeconomic level? How does the physical and mental maturity of these children compare with that of other children? How can horizons be expanded for children of very limited experience?

ANOTHER LIST OF PROBLEMS

A number of Texas teachers, responding to an invitation to list "problems in the education of Spanish-speaking pupils," took the opportunity to stress the techniques of language teaching. For one thing, they called attention to difficulties arising from differences in Spanish and English. Illustrations of differences include pronunciation of the vowel *i;* verb-subject sentence order; inflection of words to show tense, gender, and number; and stress, rhythm, and intonation in sentences. Other problems of teaching technique which occur in teaching Spanish-speaking children, they reported, include building vocabulary, teaching silent reading without vocalization, teaching abstract words, timing progress from one stage of learning to another (for example, from oral work to reading), providing reading materials of appropriate difficulty, stimulating effort toward accomplishment, finding the right amount of drill, using music in language teaching, using Spanish in teaching English.

Three types of factors were pointed out as adding to the difficulties of teaching Spanish-speaking pupils. The first was a group of practices in the schools themselves: promoting pupils, for social reasons, to grades beyond their levels of ability, holding Spanish-speaking pupils to a speed established for English-speaking pupils, enrolling in the same class pupils of very different ability in the use of English, failing to allow time for teachers to give individual help, not providing opportunity for practice in English at school outside the class.

The attitudes and abilities of pupils were considered another source of difficulty. In many cases there seemed to be a lack of motivation for school work. Many seemed to have a feeling of insecurity in the use of English and in dealing with the English-speaking environment. Another depressing factor was said to be the lack of concepts, not only in English but in Spanish as well, and the lack of experience on which concepts must be built. Pupils tended to learn words without grasping the ideas which the words should suggest.

Finally, it was thought that home and community conditions were often a hindering factor. Teachers pointed to a frequent lack of parental cooperation and to difficulty in trying to confer with parents. Many pupils come from homes of poor cultural background, and looming large in the difficulties was the lack of practice in English. Sometimes the use of English is resisted by the child's parents and even by his peers. Continuing immigration of Spanish-speaking persons tend to perpetuate the use of Spanish as the language of the community and of large numbers of children. On the positive side, television was pointed to as being of significant assistance in the teaching of English.

Here are the comments of two teachers of Spanish-speaking children. The first speaker is a person transplanted to the Southwest from another section of the country; the second is herself of Spanish name.

1) Being a ——, I was quite unprepared for what I assumed was a "foreign accent." And more shocking to my system was the fact that these children speak Spanish as a colloquial language!

Almost all of the children in my class have a pronounced accent which in *this* classroom situation bothers no one but me. However, I have had the experience of teaching in a school for military dependents [elsewhere]. I had the privilege of having in my class a boy born in [the Southwest] and who had spent most of his life here. T—— was considered to be extremely dull and of course was a discipline problem. Closer observation (at the *end* of the school year) proved that T—— was in fact not dull but that he could not "speak English." Rather than have his classmates laugh at him, T—refused to speak! I realize now, that T—was a boy I could have found *right here,* but never having been in Texas, I was not aware of this problem. Unfortunately, none of his other teachers were aware of it either. These children—here—can "get by," but taken out of this "border land" they are just as much foreigners—on first observation—as DP's. My sympathy is with these children who once having left their own safe little "world" [here], find that they are looked upon with amazement, if not downright ridicule!

2) Personally, I think that the greatest problem encountered by teachers of Spanish-speaking children in the first grade is that of the language handicap. A great number of our children in the southside schools have recently come from Mexico, and, naturally, have never been exposed to the English language. As we all know, oral language is a prerequisite to reading as well as to other subjects taught in the first grade. Here is where our problem lies—teaching them sufficient oral English in as short a time as possible in order that they will be able to cover all the first grade work in one year. The problem of these children can be justified by the mere fact that their parents are Mexican citizens, do not know the language and therefore cannot help them.

However, we have a number of children whose parents were born in the United States, have lived here all or most of their lives, and can speak the English language fluently. Yet these children do not speak a word of English when they first come to school. I don't think there is any excuse whatsoever for these parents' not teaching their children at least a few words of English so they will not feel lost when first they come to school. Other teachers and I have talked to some of these parents about this but they all give us the same answer—because of social reasons.

It seems that they live in a neighborhood that is strictly Latin American—many of their neighbors do not speak English. When these people hear them speaking English to their children, they regard them as pretentious and conceited and will cease speaking to them. Therefore, in order to maintain friendly relations with their neighbors, these parents refrain from speaking English to their children. I hope this problem of jealousy on the part of neighbors will be solved some day.

THE PROBLEM LIST

The problems of Spanish-speaking children are many and serious, whether enumerated by their parents or by their teachers. The parents were eager that their children receive a good education, and they were keenly aware of their own responsibilities and limitations. They regarded acceptance in the community and the learning of English as major problems. The teachers were struggling with detailed problems of teaching and guidance. They were concerned with techniques with their emotional development, and with parental cooperation. Like the parents, they saw language as a major problem of the Spanish-speaking group as a whole.

Part 3

PUPILS AND FAMILIES

Introduction

Whenever a child enters formal schooling he brings with him beliefs, attitudes, prejudices, expectations, aspirations, likes and dislikes, behavioral patterns, and learning styles in various degrees of development. The process of enculturation begins for the infant as soon as he is born, perhaps before. Because of the long period of dependence for humans, the effect of environmental influence upon the children is severe. Parents, siblings, extended family, neighbors, geographic locations and features, cultural milieu, peer groups, community organizations, and the mass media all exert pressures upon children and limit the direction of their actualized potential. This process is not considered deterministic here because each child reacts to these influences with reference to his heredity. But the immature child is not always able to exert control or direction over the environment. Most, if not all, of a child's behaviors have been culturally conditioned before the child enters school and before he has reached that existential moment when he is aware of his own responsibility and his power in the decision-making process. This sociocultural conditioning also has an effect upon the perceptual screen of each child as he experiences schooling in the formal and informal sense. Teacher behaviors may have as many different interpretations and effects upon students as students have upon one another.

American schools began as rural-oriented institutions and only gradually modified their structure and practices toward a modern, organizational, industrialized, urbanized society. Because the school is a conservative institution, and because there is an Eastern-Midwestern flavor which dominates research and curriculum development in public education, there has been a large cultural lag in the school's development. The school as a social agency with unique sociocultural climates fosters cultural shock for those whose orientation differs from the middle-class "Anglo" pattern. If educators are to ameliorate this shock and to foster the optimum development of each unique individual within the American society, teachers must be aware of the different sociocultural patterns and learning styles of peoples and be able to structure learning environments predicated upon those styles. It is to this end that the following readings are directed. Each selection views a different aspect of the problem, with several directed toward specific minority groups whose cultural patterns vary greatly from the stereotyped middle-class orientation.

The myth of America as the great melting pot has been rudely exploded in this century. In the Introduction to *Beyond the Melting Pot,* Glazer and Moynihan set the scene for their investigation of the significance of ethnicity on American life. New York City, the largest, most complex, and most heterogeneous urban center, is their focus of attention. The continuity of Irish, German, Jewish, Italian, Negro, and Puerto Rican immigrant traditions is traced. Although the loss of native languages and cultures in later generations renders "cultural pluralism" as impossible as the "melting pot" ideal, differential rates of assimilation as each group interacts with Americanizing influences assures the continued existence of "new" ethnic groups. This "new ethnicity is not a purely biological phenomenon but a group style of life. Ethnic groups act as interest groups as well as thus affect education politically (see Part 1.) And of course identification with an ethnic group can have both advantages or disadvantages, depending upon many social circumstances, as Shakespeare suspected and Hitler proved.

The second theme of Part 3 adds ethnicity in social class. Grace Graham defines social class in terms of social prestige cutting across religious, ethnic, and political lines. She examines studies of social class groups and some of the difficulties encountered in applying her concepts. A useful summary of the general characteristics of the upper, middle, working, and lower classes is later used to demonstrate how class differences affect schooling. She also examines problems of lower-class youth with school cultures and the importance of a school's social class ethos, which varies with location. A dim view of homogeneous grouping and tracking as patterns which isolate middle-class youth from the lower class is explored to the surprise of many educators. Graham believes that it is possible to ameliorate class distinctions and that social distinctions are probably inevitable and even desirable in the development of youth's talent.

In a more specific way James Meyer describes suburban youth as intelligent, amoral, sophisticated individuals with disturbing behavioral tendencies. They find their insulated, anesthetized, affluent lives essentially meaningless and useless. Their suburban education does not expose them meaningfully to the variety of American life. Teachers are intimidated by these precocious youths and their affluent parents. Meyer is much more disturbed by these trends than Peter Wyden was in *Suburbia's Coddled Kids,* and he recommends a kind of compensatory education in reverse which would develop supplementary reality and sensitivity in human relations.

Far from the affluence of suburbia are the small rural schools, the concern of Horace Aubertine. He collected his data from thirty-five volunteer college students from the Rocky Mountain states, who responded to an open-ended question on tape. Such a group is a very biased sample, probably unrepresentative of the masses, because only a small percentage of rural students continue on to higher education. Their comments, however, tend to verify many of the observations this writer has made in the rural high schools of New Mexico. A large segment of the student body has potential for cohensive personal relationships and social fulfillment. But disadvantages stem from the narrow, presumably college-oriented educational opportunities traditionally and thoughtlessly offered, and even from the quality of that education. Aubertine suggests regional center for teachers to supply specialized instruction and services—centers similar to those of the Ford Foundation Small Schools Project and ESEA Title III centers.

Ethnic communication in social discourse among whites and American Indians is described by Wax and Thomas. Whites are characterized as using experimental approaches, coercive actions, and an aggressive type of defensive behavior. American Indians, on the other hand, are trained for a social sensitivity from birth—trained to observe a situation carefully until they know what the expected behavior is, to employ noninterference in the actions of others no matter how foolish, and to withdraw from disturbing situations in order to avoid embarrassment. The author suggests that "accommodating" informal contact situations without an authority figure are optimum for communication with American Indians.

Herschel T. Manuel's focus is on the improvement of education for Spanish-speaking boys and girls. In order to gain insights into this task, Manuel asked Spanish-speaking high school students to reply to his letter on this problem. Again the sample is biased by educational success within the system and predates the militant Chicano lower-class movement. Student replies stressed the difficulties and the need to learn English well; they recognized economic problems in education and discrimination in and pressures for social acceptance. They also recognized the positive effects of a sympathetic, sensitive, and interested teacher.

Classroom situations are greatly affected by sociocultural backgrounds. Ruth Strang investigated motivational behavior in concrete terms as revealed by high school sophomores and seniors in their compositions. Eight motivational influences are described. Strang concluded that motivation is a complex matter which varies because of many interrelated factors. We need to know the motivational stimulus in real learning situations, past responses and consequences in similar situations, and the deprivations of each student.

In keeping with the earlier work of Arthur T. Jersild, Sol Gordon comes with a mental health point of view. He shows how the home environment can be a psychologically disturbing influence for children. The school must, in Gordon's opinion, be a positive climate. Teachers should accept fantasy in children because to criticize it engenders feelings of guilt and insecurity which retard the learning process for a disturbed child. Teachers must not confuse the difference between behavior and fantasy. Teachers should become sensitive to human relations and their own needs. There are, of course, some children whom the school cannot help and who need clinical assistance.

In the final essay we return to New York City. Harvard Graduate School of Education's Laboratory of Human Develpment conducted a research study with

320 first graders from four ethnic groups in the lower and middle classes. These children took the Diverse Mental Abilities Test with four measures: verbal, reasoning, numerical, and space conceptualization. Middle-class children were more alike than their lower-class counterparts. There were different general strengths among the four ethnic groups in relation to the mental abilities which were assumed to be related to preschool experiences and ethnic behavioral patterns. The Harvard group is continuing their research to remedy the dearth of information on cultural learning styles. This study returns us to the purpose of Part 3. We must individualize instruction, a goal of democratic education. We must be able to match methodology and content with learning styles. In short, the classroom is a complex psychological and, especially, sociological phenomenon. To suppose that one goes in merely to teach a "subject" is always a mistake. To suppose that one can go into a classroom without a knowledge of the human complexity of the students in that classroom is an even worse mistake.

14

Influences of Social-Class Differences in Schools*

GRACE GRAHAM

> *Every man is in certain respects: a) like all other men; b) like some other men; c) like no other man.*
>
> —Clyde Kluckhohn and Henry A. Murray[1]

Social distinctions among groups of persons are not new in America. In early colonial days a farmer or an artisan of humble standing in the community was called "goodman," and the title of "mister" was reserved for gentlemen. The deference afforded a plantation owner, a wealthy merchant, or a minister in the Massachusetts theocracy was quite different from the treatment given indentured servants, slaves, and free men of limited means. Long before sociological studies of social class were made, everybody knew that some people had a "higher standing" or a "lower standing" than others. Nevertheless, the earliest studies of class in this country, particularly those of the Warner School in the 1930s and early 1940s, created great interest among sociologists and educationists. A popularized discussion of the theme, *The Status Seekers* by Vance Packard, published in 1961, and other descriptions of social class appearing in popular magazines at about the same time have been widely read in this country and abroad.

The initial reaction to studies of social classes by many Americans was resistance to the findings because they outraged the basic American belief in equalitarianism. Even though everybody knew that there were and always had been social distinctions in this country, Americans did not like to admit their existence. Social-class differences negate claims that every man has an equal chance to rise if he works hard enough and that "I am as good as the next man." Despite resistance to studies of social classes, the concept of differing classes has been gradually accepted and by the 1960s references to "upper class," "middle class," and "lower class" in the mass media and everyday conversation were commonplace.

Many studies of the influences of social classes upon pupils in schools have been made. Such studies resulted in labeling schools and teachers as "lower-middle class" and in charging schools with not meeting the educational needs of "lower-class" children. In an attempt to clarify such charges, the first section of this chapter deals with the concept of social classes, the second section, with the beliefs and practices commonly attributed to the major social classes, and the final section, with implications of such distinctions for school practices.

THE CONCEPT OF SOCIAL CLASSES

Many social scientists have been disturbed by glib presentations of social class that distort the concept into a rigid deterministic mold. As Max Lerner says, "To draw a profile of American social strata is more elusive than almost anything else in American life."[2] Social scientists do not even agree on the meaning of the term "social classes," the number of such classes, or how to measure the differences among such classes as may exist. They do, however, ascribe to complex, industrialized societies a web of dynamic relationships that involve and influence individuals and institutions. These relationships, they say, tend to be shaped by hierarchical positions of groups in a society. In other words, they see a society as stratified (arranged in layers), with individuals and groups holding higher or lower or equivalent positions in relation to one another.

Finding the bases of such stratification is not simple. Obviously American society has never been class-conscious in the Marxian sense, which pits those who work for others against owners and managers, i.e., proletarian vs. bourgeoisie. Milton M. Gordon suggests that three factors or variables, all intertwined, account for stratification in the United States. First, economic power that is determined by income, credit rating, steadiness of employment, employment control over others, and similar elements. Second, political power defied in terms of control, direct or indirect, of formal governmental structure and of opinion-forming agencies, such as the mass media, churches, schools, and civic organizations. Third, social status that may arise from a specific position, occupational or avocational, that a person holds, the respect or esteem that he gains from the success with which he carries out the role associated with this status, and his general reputation that he earns because of his individual qualities. Of the three factors, Gordon believes that social status, which he tends to equate with social class, is the most significant factor producing social divisions. In addition to economic power, political power, and social status that stratify all Americans, he says that a further differentiation is made on the basis of ethnic origin, national backgrounds, and religious differences. The latter variables crisscross the other factors in stratification, giving a different position in the social structure to individuals and families who are not "typically American," irrespective of their occupations, wealth, and political influence.

One can explain differences in the social structure of subcommunities, Gordon theorizes, by variations in four dimensions: (1) social class, determined largely by economic power and associated with political power; (2) ethnic, religious, and national backgrounds; (3) rural-urban location; and (4) regional area.[3]

Definitions of Social Class

The average American probably sees differences among social classes largely in terms of material accumulations. He believes that some individuals and some positions deserve higher financial rewards than others. Assuming that a man's gains have been won honestly, his neighbors are as likely to admire and applaud his achievements as they are to begrudge him the fruits of his success. Until recently almost all Americans accepted this view and regarded class differences as moral and proper because they believed they had equality of opportunity, even if it existed in fantasy to a greater extent than in fact. Recent charges of middle-class exploitation of the lower classes have, however, largely discredited this assumption of equalitarianism particularly among lower-class Negroes and idealistic college youths.

Although many scholars use the term "social class," few of them specify precisely what they mean by it. Do the terms "social class" or "socioeconomic level" as used by some scholars merely refer to a statistical aggregate of people in the same income bracket or at the same occupational level? Are there, in fact, well-defined classes in the United States into which people can be categorized? Is "social stratification" actually only another way of referring to a continuum of prestige ratings? If classes exist, why do many people not know to what class they belong? Why are so many people deviants from the norms of their social class? These are the kinds of questions that many sociologists are asking. They are also questioning the methodology of much of the research.

The term *social class,* as used herein, refers to a large number of the population who hold similar positions in respect to prestige within their society, who hold many beliefs and values in common, and who are willing to accept others within the same aggregate as equals or intimates. Obviously such a stipulative definition does not make sorting persons into classes any less difficult.

Researchers in towns and smaller cities have used numerous techniques to establish class categories, such as informants' ratings, interviews, observations, and studies of participation, organizational memberships, and genealogies. Warner developed a short-cut method called the Index of Status Characteristics, which correlates highly with the more costly and time-consuming methods that require extensive interviewing. By the I.S.C. method a person is given weighted scores for occupation, source of income, house type, and dwelling area.[4] Hollingshead's Index of Social Position, another simplified method of determining social class, uses ecological area of residence, occupation, and education as factors.[5] Still another method, developed by Ellis, asks a person to identify his father's or his own occupation in specific detail.[6] Other investigators get a rough measure of social classes from demographic studies of occupational and income levels.

The stress placed on income and occupations as indices of social strata in the United States seems to be justified. Numerous studies have demonstrated that income and occupational groups consistently differ in their activities, values, and attitudes and that from study to study occupations are given similar prestige ratings. Nevertheless, social-class position is not directly comparable to either wealth or occupational stratum. It may be true, as Baltzell's study in *Philadelphia Gentlemen* suggests, that wealth held by families over a span of generations does assure upper-class placement, but new money does not earn such status for its possessor. The rating of occupations is not directly related to income earned in that many skilled workers earn more than some white-collar employees, yet the latter are likely to be rated higher in social class. Nor do persons within an occupational group actually hold the same social rating. Notwithstanding these limitations to using income and occupation as determinants of social class, it is agreed that social class in this country has an economic foundation and that occupation is the best single clue to social class.

Number and Size of Social Classes

The number of social classes identified by a researcher and the size of each depends upon several factors such as the method used in determining social-class, location of the community studied, and the principal occupations of people who live there. In 1941 Warner and Lunt's study of "Yankee City" in New England revealed this distribution: upper-upper class, 1.4 percent; lower-upper class, 1.6 percent; upper-middle class, 10 percent; lower-middle class, 28 percent; upper-lower (working) class, 33 percent; and lower-lower class, 25 percent.[7] Other researchers in the East and Midwest using the Warner technique have arrived at similar distributions except for, in some instances, the distinction between upper and lower class. The chief disadvantage of studies of the Yankee City type is that the methods of research depend in part upon persons knowing one another and therefore are best adapted for small cities and towns. Warner's shortened I.S.C. Method, although usable in large cities, cannot be validated without a sample study of informants' judgments. His criteria, "house type" and "dwelling area" are also not very meaningful in mass-produced housing tracts.

Other researchers using different techniques sometimes encounter other problems. For example, Gross found in a Minneapolis survey that when persons were simply asked to what class they belonged, 14 percent said "no class," 20 percent said "don't know," 5 percent gave no response, and 15 percent gave responses other than upper, middle, lower, or working class.[8] In other words, over half of the respondents seemed to have not seen themselves as members of a social class.

In 1960 Havighurst estimated the following distribution of five social classes in the United States:[9]

Class	Percent
Upper	2
Upper-middle	8
Lower-middle	30
Upper-lower	40
Lower-lower	20

Havighurst's classifications and estimates are probably as good as any that can be made, but like the studies on which his estimates are based, his figures suggest clearcut lines between the various social classes. Actually, even in small towns, informants were unable to agree on a category for a number of persons and families. In such cases, researchers admittedly classified such persons arbitrarily. Researchers stress the conclusion that lines drawn between social classes are not real and that individuals and families are often inconsistent in their adherence to the behavior patterns and other characteristics associated with the class to which they are assigned.

The dangers of generalizing the findings of studies made in towns and small cities to metropolitian areas should be evident, and not many studies have been made of big cities or of communities in the Far West. There may be many more than five or six recognizable classes in large urban centers. (Some informants thought there were eight to eleven or more even in smaller places.) It should be readily apparent, too, that no one community can or does represent all the ramifications of the social-class system of the total population of the United States. Demographic studies show a larger percentage of lower socioeconomic groups in manufacturing and transportation centers; a larger percentage of white-collar workers in retail-trade, public administrative, entertainment and recreation centers, and in college communities.[10] Many smaller cities have no upper class in a national sense. Common sense observation reveals that lumbering towns and textile-mill villages have more people of lower-class status and fewer of middle-class than do trade centers in prosperous agricultural areas. Furthermore, American social structure is still in a state of flux. New occupations requiring special skill and knowledge are constantly emerging to attract workers from less skilled pursuits. To quote Lerner, "It may well be many years before one can formulate a coherent theory of power and class in America."[11] In the meantime let us not think of social class distinctions as real when they are only conceptual tools in analysis.

Let us not forget, too, that social class is not the sole determinant of one's status. The esteem that comes from a job well done, irrespective of what the job may be, and the respect that one earns as a father or mother, as a citizen, and as an honorable person of good repute are important factors in determining one's standing in his community. With these reservations in mind, we now move to a discussion of behavior patterns, values, attitudes, and motivations said to be associated with different social classes or life styles.

CHARACTERISTICS ATTRIBUTED TO VARIOUS SOCIAL CLASSES

Despite justifiable doubts about crystallized class formations in the United States, the Lynds, Warner and associates, and other researchers have performed a valuable service in describing differing life styles within the American society.[12] Although specific cultural traits may and do vary over the year, understanding the patterns of thought and behavior found within the social class of a child's family and neighborhood is significant to a teacher. Obviously discrepancies exist between what specific individuals and families do, believe, and value and what may be commonly accepted activities and thoughtways within a given social class. There are many deviants from social-class norms. Factors such as schooling, individual differences, and influences of the mass media make the process of socialization within any group something less than thorough. Many families are characterized by what sociologists call status inconsistencies; that is, they occupy marginal positions between classes and, as a consequence, may inculcate in their children selected cultural traits assigned to more than one social class. The adherence to class characteristics is found to be closer in a homogeneous than in a heterogeneous neighborhood where ethnic origin, religion, and the like, in addition to class differentials, complicate social relationships. It should also be remembered that the line between classes adjacent in rank is blurred if it exists at all, and that the differences may be relatively small. Thus the intent of the following discussion of class characteristics is not to stereotype individuals; rather its purpose is to provide insight into climates of opinion common among certain subcommunity groups.

The Upper Class

Not very much is known about the characteristics and values of the upper class. What researchers mean by the term *upper class* is ambiguous. Persons labeled upper class in small cities and towns are usually in no sense upper class on the national scene. They may be, however, very influential, socially and economically, within a limited sphere. Researchers in small towns and cities in New England and in the Deep South usually found that the local "aristocracy," who constituted only about 3 percent of the population, were divided into upper-upper and lower-upper classes on the basis of how long their preeminence as a family had lasted. Members of the upper classes of small cities, particularly along the eastern seaboard, are described as exceedingly proud of their lineage, eager for their offspring to marry within their own class and not disgrace the family name by being caught in illicit activities, conservative in taste, and not very active in community affairs except in behind-the-scene positions and philanthropic roles.

Members of the upper class are often cavalier in their attitudes toward matters of decorum and morality—the generally accepted customs of conduct and right living that prevail in this country. For this reason they are sometimes described as being more like the lower than the middle class. Their "moral" standards, notably in respect to extramarital relationships, are less rigid than those of the middle class. Friedenberg calls the "slum kid" the "last aristocrat" because he is arrogant, free and easy, expressive of his sexuality, and nonconforming. He believes that a talented boy from a slum would adjust more readily in an upper-class private school than in a public school.[13] Perhaps the positions of those at the top and those at the bottom of the social structure are similar in respect to nonconformity: Neither group is striving to be accepted; the elite does not have to, the disadvantaged person does not feel he would be accepted if he did try.

Probably the elite of small cities are more conforming, however, than the elite of metropolitan areas, who comprise most of the upper class when judged in terms of national influence. Baltzell described members of Philadelphia's old upper class. He said they belong to a metropolitan elite that includes fashionable old families from San Francisco to Boston, Philadelphia, or Baltimore.[14] They are a business aristocracy composed mostly of bankers and lawyers, and their families were educated at private schools and ivy league colleges. They live in the same wealthy metropolitan suburbs, belong to the same clubs and the same churches (Episcopal in Philadelphia), patronize the arts, and isolate themselves from contact with the lower class. Some of these Philadelphians are now for the first time in decades becoming interested in politics.[15] In his study of men of power behind the scenes in national government and economic life, Floyd Hunter found a small number of men in metropolitian centers throughout the United States who knew each other, exchanged ideas, and decided upon policies that they then tried to put into effect.[16] Presumably some of these men may be classified as upper class. There are other elite groups—leaders in politics, military affairs, corporations, labor unions, churches, the opinion industry, artistic pursuits, and education, some of whom are expense-account-wealthy "exurbanites." These individuals are men of power and prestige on the national scene but they are not members of the upper class, as usually defined, unless they have been born to that status. They marry into the upper class and, if exceptionally talented, they may move into the upper class.

Upper-class values are of little direct concern to public schools because few children from the upper class attend public schools, but indirectly the sociopolitical views of this group are very important to public education because of the relative power and influence of many upper-class people. In general, the high-income group (the upper 10 percent), some of whom are upper class, tend to be conservative, to disapprove of strong labor unions, to resist extensions of governmental influence, and to support special-interest groups that promote their interests.

The Middle Class

Studies made in small towns usually find an upper-middle and a lower-middle class. The demarcation between the two tends to follow differences in income and occupation (professionals and more successful businessmen being placed in the top category and sales persons, office workers, a few skilled and semiskilled workers, and less successful businessmen in the bottom classification). Their values and life styles differ in degree rather than in kind. Since the lower-middle class more or less imitates the upper-middle class, a broad classification of middle class would perhaps reflect characteristics more typical of the upper-middle than of the lower-middle class. Among the activities and values commonly attributed to middle-class status are aspirations to respectability and conventionality in family life, moral outlook, and sex behavior. They are the "joiners," the workers for community welfare, the pillars of well-established religious groups. They see wealth and education as the means to mobility and they seek to acquire both. Because they are especially eager to maintain their status above the lower class, they discourage their children from cultivating friends among those less advantaged from themselves. Parents are devoted to their children and ambitious for them. In fact, they often compete through their children and are therefore excessively concerned with school affairs and cultural activities that are thought to be good for the children. They insist upon high standards of cleanliness, neatness, punctuality, dependability, and responsibility. In the home they also emphasize correct English, good grooming, etiquette and manners, and the social amenities. They teach their children to settle their differences without fighting. They encourage their children to defer present pleasures for future rewards, to value education, and to respect authority and the law. Family relationships, particularly toward the upper end of the class, tend to be equalitarian.

Membership in the middle class has undergone marked change during the last two or three decades. Historically the old middle class was composed of farmers who owned land, small businessmen, professionals, shopkeepers, and other tradesmen. The new middle classes are composed of clerical workers, technicians, managers, new professional groups, government bureaucrats, distributors, advertisers, and other relatively new white-collar vocational groups. Members of the old middle class have diminished in relative importance in respect to determining the middle-class life-style. Many of the newcomers, upwardly mobile from the lower class, are said to value security and a good salary much more than did the independent, self-employed entrepreneurs of the old middle class. Numerous writers have painted a dim picture of middle-class life today. United by no bond other than the desire to maintain status, subscribing to different economic and political beliefs, living different life styles, losing relative position on the income scale to union-organized workers, members of the new middle classes are described as anxious conformists. They are said to be excessively concerned about their personalities because they sell only their skills to the companies for which they work. They are the "yes-men" who mask their real feelings and thoughts in order to curry favor. This description is oversimplified, of course, because in fact, the middle class is the "pivot class" setting the tone of the consumption and dominating the culture. People in this class are not the sources of power politically or economically, but from among them have sprung some of the most creative talents in America. They share in varying degrees what has been called a *corporate morality*—the idea that humanitarianism is more important than property. Thus they serve as a cushion between the wealthy and the poor, siding with management more often than with labor, but sometimes lending support to the less privileged. In recent years the alleged conservatism of persons in the middle class, especially of well-educated members of middle-middle and upper-middle class groups, is open to question.

There is much vagueness about membership of the middle class because in large urban centers there are so many middle-class groups of differing life styles. Social class status in the metropolis cannot rest upon intimate associations. Although city dwellers defy the easy classifications, they fall into many sub-classes that manifest in varying degrees some of the characteristics ascribed to the middle class.

The Working Class

The group of people called the working class in this discussion is usually called the upper-lower class, a term that conveys to most people and to them a stigma. Steadily employed blue-collar workmen in the United States do not identify with the lower class, or a proletariat, but rather with the middle class. The very small success of Communists in recruiting members among American working-men is clear proof of their identification. In some respects characteristics of the working class and the lower-middle class are much alike. Many working-class people cherish respectability, conventional morality, family life, and sex behavior, and such virtues as punctuality and acceptance of responsibility as much as do lower-middle class people. They are likely to be as ambitious for their children as those above them in social class. These similarities, which seem to be increasing, have led some writers to group the two classes together as "common man Americans."

Despite these similarities, members of the working class and the lower-middle class are sufficiently different in other ways to justify separating them into two classes. Whereas the lower-middle class is composed of persons holding ill-paid, white-collar jobs, members of the working class have jobs in the manual trades in which they may earn more money than do those in petty white-collar jobs. Often they spend their earnings for different purposes than would persons in the lower-middle class.

Other differences also clearly set members of the working class apart from the middle class. They are almost always less well educated than those in higher classes. They tend to have a pragmatic orientation to education—they want to learn what they regard to be useful and practical. The value of education to them is that education helps one learn how to deal with "red tape," to get and hold desirable jobs, and to avoid problems related to signing contracts and the like. They are not usually interested in literature, the arts, and the social sciences, but they have great respect for modern science.[17]

Working-class parents do not approve of progressive education because its methods of child training conflict with those to which they subscribe. Their homes tend to be patriarchal, with the father serving as disciplinarian. Although many of the differences between the middle-class and the working-class methods of child care seem to have disappeared in recent years, the stress upon child obedience remains in the working-class home. Physical punishment of the young is common in these homes. Children are also encouraged to resort to physical force in settling arguments rather than to exercise self-restraint and settle differences rationally. Children may have less continuous supervision and may roam the streets more at will than those in the middle class, but they are expected to obey their parents at home and their teachers at school.

Many working-class parents are ambitious for their children and want them to have a better education than they had, but these parents often lack the knowledge that they need to guide young people socially and vocationally. Poorly educated themselves, they do not know how to provide cultural advantages for their children or how to motivate their interests in academic areas. Until recent years, most families in the working class have usually lived close to a subsistence level. They have, therefore, not been accustomed to saving and making long-range plans for the education of their children. But there are exceptions among working-class families, and the number of students in college from this class is increasing steadily. Many teachers in public schools have their origin in the working class. The mobility of many working-class people into the middle classes is, in fact, one of the reasons for the lack of a feeling of class consciousness in this country.

Nevertheless, ambitious working-class children who aspire to middle-class status have to overcome a number of handicaps because many of the attitudes and social customs learned in working-class homes are inappropriate in middle-class groups. Their parents are antagonistic to "big shots" and usually not favorably disposed toward intellectuals. The relationships of their father and mother are less equalitarian than that of parents of middle-class children. People in the working class tend to be more hedonistic than those in the middle class; they spend freely when they have money. Their social interests are limited and few of them take an active role in community affairs except possibly in a church. Their leisure interests are likely to be confined to do-it-yourself projects, spectator and group sports, bowling, viewing television, church socials, and visits within their extended families. Males attend occasional stag parties in taverns, homes, and fraternal organizations.

Not all children from this class expect or want to move into the middle class. In some cases they may see their parents' life style as that which they prefer. In a number of ways it is indeed a comfortable way of life. It is noncompetitive, relaxed, equalitarian, and secure in its affectional relations within the extended family. The worries of working-class people are real (money to pay debts, illnesses, desertions, divorces), not the vague fears and pressures that haunt many in the middle class. Another significant characteristic in the life style of members of the working class is the so-called *ethic of reciprocity*—they give cheerfully of their time, money, and skills to one another without expecting repayment other than that some day others may do something for them.

The primary handicap that children who wish to remain in the working class may suffer is that they may fail to stay in school as long as they should. Many of them will not be able to find jobs with as little or little more education than their fathers had. Since automation is eliminating many skilled as well as semi-skilled jobs, working-class youths need to attain considerable competence in technical skills to attain the financial security that their fathers now have. More-over, automation is likely to reduce the hours in the work week. In this event, working-class pupils need to acquire skills and appreciations that help provide meaning in leisure pursuits. To become good citizens, they need also to develop greater concern than many of their fathers show for those less fortunate than themselves and for political and civic activites.

The Lower Class

Persons classified as lower-lower class are sometimes described as "not respectable," "poor white trash," "scum," or something else to indicate their lowly position. Lately, in an attempt to avoid the pejorative connotation, they have been called the "culturally deprived," the "underprivileged," or the "socially disadvantaged." They are indeed the unskilled, the unemployables, the poorly educated, the vagrants, the outcasts, and the unfortunates. If they must be labeled descriptively, the less offensive term is *socially disadvantaged* because it is neither disparaging in connotation nor inaccurate in denotation.[18] The War on Poverty is designed to improve the life-style of the poor, most of whom are lower-lower class.

It is a mistake, however, to assume that all very poor people share the beliefs and patterns of living prevailing among those of the lower-lower class. As already stated, occupation and income are not sole criteria for determining social class. Some persons who by definition are poverty-stricken are much like working class or even middle-class people. The differences between values and practices of those in the working class and those in the lower-lower class are, in fact, differences in degree more often than differences in kind.

Like working-class people, lower-lower class people value the ethic of reciprocity, the security of a large extended family, and punishment as a means of controlling children. They also resent snobbery and believe that one should fight with his fists for his rights. Parents, too, especially if they are Negro, may value education for their children, but they usually do not know how to motivate their children's interests in school nor can they financially afford to provide books, trips, and other educative experiences for them.

In the lowest social group, homes are crowded not only with children but also with relatives. Family life is likely to be disorganized by frequent divorces, desertions, and common-law marriages. Promiscuity and prostitution are not uncommon; obscenity and profanity punctuate conversations. Children are treated like little adults. Children are frequently responsible for the care of brothers and sisters only a few years younger. Under such circumstances children are informed early in life in respect to marital relations, the exigencies of life, and economic realities. They often learn, "You'll work hard enough, but you won't get anywhere." They share with their parents a fatalistic outlook that causes them to attribute whatever happens to good or bad luck. Like their parents, they usually acquire a low self-image not only because they realize their parents are not respected but also because they themselves suffer personal indignities at the hands of others.

In such situations children escape the unhappiness and discord in their homes by joining their peers on the street. Acceptance by age-mates becomes of great importance to these young people because they find among them warmth, status, and gaiety that they cannot find at home or at school, as will be later elaborated.

Some lower-class boys join with other emotionally disturbed youth of the lower and working classes in illegal activities. Albert K. Cohen's hypothesis, in which he seeks to explain the subculture of the delinquent gang, is that the gang simply reverses middle-class values. The youths know what these values are from television, movies, schools, and other sources. They are so frustrated, Cohen believes, by their inability to meet middle-class standards that they react by lashing out at society. The psychologists call this defense mechanism *reaction formation;* that is, one does exactly the opposite of what one really wants to do. The delinquent regains his self-respect by proving that he does not want to be middle-class. The gang commits vandalism because the middle-class ethic respects private property; it fights because the dominant ethic says it shouldn't fight; it is irrational and hedonistic because the middle class values long-term planning, forethought, and thrift; it is nonutilitarian, stealing "for the hell of it," because the middle class disapproves of purposeless activity and makes theft a crime.[19] There are, of course, other theories of the causes for delinquency. Cohen's theory is of interest at this point because it implies that middle-class values not only produce respectable young people but delinquent gangs as well.

Differences in motivations, values, social environments, and characteristic patterns of behavior of children from different social classes have significant implications to teachers. Although not many studies give clues as to why some children are deviants from the norms of their class, analyses of social-class influences upon children increase our insight into the complexities of human behavior in the classroom.

Notwithstanding the usefulness of such studies, social status is by no means the only variable that influences behavior. Whether the family lives in a rural or urban neighborhood is another factor; its religion is another; and the degree of discrimination to which a person is exposed still another. Persons of color— Indian, Mexican American, Puerto Rican, and Negro—are found in disproportionate numbers to whites in the lower-lower class. The attitudes and values of minority groups are also shaped by family systems that deviate from the norms assumed to be prevalent in the social classes. The lower-class Negro family, for example, differs considerably from the lower-class white family or the Mexican American family.

SOCIAL-CLASS DIFFERENCES AND SCHOOLS

The fluidity of the open-class system in the United States is presumably maintained largely through the ready access of all to educational opportunity. The chief avenues to social mobility lie in possessing outstanding talent, appearance, or superior education. Since many persons are neither physically attractive nor talented to a conspicuous degree, they must turn to education as the means by which they may rise in status. Since education is so important to mobility, many people are indignant when they hear that members of the lower classes do not, in fact, find equality of opportunity in American schools.

Schools in this country are described as middle-class institutions since the value system of the school culture is that of the middle class. Public school teachers are usually middle-class in orientation even if their class of origin was not middle class. The stress given to middle-class values is reasonable because these are the dominant values in American society and because many parents from the lower classes expect the schools to prepare their children for mobility. Despite such justification of common school practices, the lower-class child is disadvantaged in competing within a school culture that upholds values and patterns of behavior that conflict with those he has learned at home. He is handicapped by the cultural limitations of his home environment, economic hardships, and the low social position of his parents.

Socioeconomic Differences and Educational Statistics

The relationship of socioeconomic level, determined by occupation and income, and certain statistics in education is well established. Alfred Binet, the father of mental tests, recognized differences related to social backgrounds in the test scores made by children. In 1916 Terman wrote that children of the "superior social class" scored 14 points higher on the average than did those of the "inferior social class."[20] Allison Davis pointed out that tests of mental ability do not accurately measure the Intelligence Quotients of children from lower-class homes because the tests are culture-laden in a way favoring middle-class children.[21] Although overlaps of individual scores exist among socioeconomic levels, the averages of the upper classes are higher than the averages of the lower classes. There is still controversy about why these differences exist and just what the tests actually measure. It is generally agreed, however, that although the tests measure achievement as well as aptitude, they do not measure innate ability, and that they are useful, taken in conjunction with other evidence, in predicting scholastic success. In line with such predictions and perhaps partly because of them, children from the lower classes tend to make lower grades and earn lower scores on tests of achievement than do those from the upper classes.

The number of pupils who drop out of school before they graduate from high school is related to their socioeconomic level. Pupils whose parents are wage earners or unemployed are more likely to drop out of school than are children whose parents earn larger and more stable incomes. Children from less-privileged homes are more frequently absent from school, more often sick, and less active in cocurricular activities than are middle-class children. The educational and occupational aspirations of children from the lower classes are also generally low.

It is significant, however, that the number of school dropouts has been reduced in recent years, that the median grade level of American adults is rising, and that the number of young people from the lower classes in college is increasing. Havighurst estimates that between 1940 and 1960 the percentage of college entrants from the lower-lower class increased from 0 to 10 percent, of those from the upper-lower class increased from 5 to 25 percent, of those from the lower-middle class increased from 20 to 55 percent, and of those from the upper and upper-middle class from 80 to 85 percent.[22]

This trend is likely to continue because a technological society cannot meet its occupational need without a greater number of highly trained people than were formerly needed. Until this century, schools tended to perpetuate social-class lines by educating few from the lower classes beyond a minimal level. But, as Burton Clark points out, the role of the school and of the college in promoting social mobility grows when education becomes available to all and when technical competence is in great demand.[23] The poor, able working-class boy with access to government loans and scholarships can and does succeed via the community college and the state university. Nevertheless, his chances of doing so are less than those of a middle-class child.

Comparative Educational Advantages

In the following discussion, the contrasts are more nearly descriptive of children of the upper-middle and those of the lower class than they are of children of "common man" groups. We are talking, therefore, chiefly of pupils in schools like those in wealthy suburbia and in the slums, or of the coteries of upper-middle-class and lower-class pupils in comprehensive schools. Pupils of the lower-middle and working classes lie between these extremes.

When children from lower-class homes enter the first grade, their troubles in school begin. Unless they have lived in communities that have had Headstart programs, they are not likely to have had preschool experiences. Because they have not been read to, talked to, or had experiences in their homes that help develop concepts, they are usually not ready to learn to read. They may be unable to distinguish between sounds, particularly "b" and "p." They are likely to demonstrate what Bereiter and Engleman call the "giant word syndrome"— rather than learning individual words, they catch the main sounds of common phrases.[24] As a result, they cannot break phrases into words and use them in new sentences.

Children from disadvantaged homes are handicapped in their school work by their lack of the experiences middle-class children commonly have with ideas and language presented in picture books, stories, and trips to interesting places. A third-grade teacher after showing her class a picture of a lion in a jungle asked her pupils to tell a story about the picture.

Charlie said, "The lion lives in the jungle. She is laying a egg."

Bertha said, "The lion is crawling on the tree. The lion's name is Penny. He is a mother lion."

As they grow older, differences between disadvantaged children and the more privileged groups increase. They have learned to communicate in the "public language" of their home and neighborhood rather than in the formal language of the school. They cannot understand a teacher, Bernstein says, who uses a different language. The disadvantaged child understands "Shut up!" but not "I'd rather you made less noise." According to Bernstein, his language is a form of condensed and abbreviated speech that "encourages an immediacy of inter-action, a preference for the descriptive rather than the analytic, a linguistic form such that what is *not* said is equally and more important than what is said." His curiosity has been curbed by parents who refuse to answer "why" questions, and his capacity for rational thinking delayed by categoric statements ("Because I tell you") of his parents.[25]

Retarded linguistic development is perhaps the most serious handicap for a disadvantaged child in school, although he has others. He has not learned to concentrate; he has, in fact, learned in his noisy, crowded home to shut out sounds. Hence he has difficulty listening to a teacher, especially when she talks too much. Also, he has no place to study at home. Faced with a choice between studying and watching television in the same room with his family, he usually chooses TV. Deutsch found that the tasks that the disadvantaged child performed at home tended to be motoric, concrete, and of short duration.[26] Thus he is not prepared at home for verbal, abstract learning that extends over a relatively long period of time. He is likely to be a slow learner. If a very bright child can overcome all these handicaps he still may not want to do well in school. Loyalty to his peers, who may regard the good student as a traitor, may preclude his attempting to excel in school work.

The seeming inability to postpone present pleasures for future rewards is another serious handicap of disadvantaged children and of many working-class children. Although researchers have found somewhat conflicting evidence, the weight of such evidence shows a social-class relationship between deferred gratifications of needs (such as affiliation, sex, independence, material possessions, aggression) and the need to achieve.[27] Perucci suggests that upper-strata youths who do not have a great need to achieve may nevertheless achieve because their "general way of life" makes decisions concerning high school graduation and entering college for them.[28] Kahl points out that their trust of people smooths their way socially and their faith in their future encourages them to plan.[29] To succeed in school the lower-class youth, however, has to make independent decisions and develop social relationships and habits of planning foreign to his subculture.

Why do some children develop the need to achieve whereas others do not? McClelland found a high relationship between the need to achieve and "parents' high standards of achievement, warmth and encouragement, and a father who is not domineering and authoritarian."[30] These conditions are fairly common in middle-class homes. None of them is common in lower-lower class homes. Yet an increasing number of young people from disadvantaged as well as working-class homes do demonstrate the need to achieve and are graduating from high school and attending college.

Joseph A. Kahl tried to find the answer to why some intelligent "common man" boys are more ambitious educationally and occupationally than others. By interviewing the boys and their fathers, he decided that a core value in the homes of the ambitious boys was "getting ahead," whereas a core value in the homes of the boys who were not ambitious was "getting by." The fathers of ambitious sons usually were not satisfied with their own progress and blamed their inadequate educations for their lack of success. The fathers of less ambitious boys seemed resigned to their lot. The boys who planned to go to college but who came from homes that had not encouraged them to go had been influenced by friends. Kahl states that at the time an intelligent boy reaches the seventh grade he makes his initial choice as to whether or not he will do well academically.[31] (A survey by the College Entrance Examination Board also found the seventh grade to be the year when most pupils decide to go to college.)

A more recent study of California high school boys found that the ethos of the school is important to the aspirations of members of the student body. More middle-class boys go to college if they have attended predominantly middle-class schools than they do if they have attended predominantly working-class schools. Working-class boys tend to have higher aspirations when the ethos of their school is middle-class than when it is working-class.[32] They are more likely to plan for college if they have college-oriented friends and are active in school activities than otherwise.[33]

Other researchers have found that upwardly mobile young people are likely to have mothers who are better educated than their fathers.[34] Since most women in the lower class, however, are likely to have attended school longer than their husbands, some other factor such as dissatisfaction with her mate's job or her own white-collar job must be operative in such cases. Still other researchers have found that adults outside the family, particularly high school teachers, were very influential in raising the level of aspirations of lower-class pupils.[35]

Low self-concept is a final serious handicap to academic success of disadvantaged children. Brookover and Gottlieb cite research that shows a relationship between pupils' generalized self-concepts and their achievement in school.

The studies also revealed that the self-concepts of individuals varied by subject matter areas. In other words, a pupil is likely to get a better grade if he thinks he can. Whether he thinks he can is dependent, in part, upon what he thinks "significant others"—mother, father, teacher, and peers—think of his ability.[36] The self-concept of the disadvantaged lower-class child in respect to his academic aptitude is likely to be low. His frequent failures and often the attitudes toward him of his teachers as well as his parents confirm his low assessment of his talents. His peers are unlikely to encourage him to see himself as capable of good school work.

The obstacles to learning that the disadvantaged child brings to school with him are compounded by further obstacles that he meets in the school environment. On the other hand, the middle-class pupil, who experiences few obstacles to learning in his social environment, usually finds it relatively easy to adjust to the school's subculture. He may, of course, have psychological problems, limited academic aptitude, and difficulties in learning and in winning social acceptance, but his problems seldom arise out of a conflict between social-class values and practices in home and school.

Differential Opportunities in Schools

The comprehensive public school is praised by advocates on the grounds that it provides curriculums designed to meet the needs of all pupils and reduces differences among social classes because rich and poor "rub elbows" in the same academic classes in school. In many comprehensive schools such claims cannot be substantiated. The University of Pittsburgh's Project Talent survey revealed that in 1960 54 percent of the high schools had homogeneous grouping. The practice is also common in elementary schools. Grouping pupils homogeneously according to academic ability confers high status to those in the "bright" and "gifted" sections. In 1960, 49 percent of the high schools, according to findings of Project Talent, used a system of tracking. Assigning pupils to college-preparatory, general, and commercial courses tends to relegate those who are not taking courses designed for college entrance to inferior status. Tracking and homogeneous grouping have the effect, in general, of separating children from middle-class homes and those from lower-class homes. The best grades usually go to children from middle-class homes. Leadership positions in the cocurriculum tend to be held by the same children. Hence children from lower-class homes feel that the school brands them as "inferior."

In many ways teachers seem to tell children that all work is honorable but that some types of work are more honorable than others. The public school curriculum is geared largely to white-collar jobs. Individuals invited to visit schools as resource persons are usually professionals and businessmen, not blue-collar workers. A study of "community helpers" at a conceptual level appropriate to primary grades is common, but upper elementary children and high school pupils seldom learn about the work of mechanics, technicians, service workers, or semiprofessionals. Elementary school reading texts portray white-collar workers and their homes. As a consequence, children inadvertently learn that blue-collar jobs in which their parents work are not very desirable and that the school is not really interested in helping pupils prepare for such jobs. The general curriculum, a hodgepodge of classes, to which many youths of the lower classes are assigned seems to them to offer little of value vocationally.

Many young people from the lower classes feel that they are not learning anything worth learning. They may also feel left out of the social life of the school. Early researchers, such as Hollingshead in Elmtown, found that middle-class boys and girls dominated the cocurricular activities and that the chief reason young people from the lower classes dropped out of school was that they felt they did not belong. This situation still exists in most comprehensive schools, but in some schools what sociologists call "status upsets" have occurred. A recent study of ten Illinois high schools found that the social structure at Elmtown, one of the schools studied, had changed. The researcher learned that the leading cliques among the junior and senior girls were predominantly work-ing-class girls and that the leading boys' cliques in high schools were even less influenced by social class than were the girls' cliques.[37]

The preeminence of the middle class in the school's social life may change for several reasons. In smaller schools weak leadership in the middle class may be superseded by strong leadership in the working class. Continued prosperity that enables working-class parents to buy good clothes and other symbols of adolescent status may induce changes in the school status system. The school faculty may influence status upsets through its use of rewards, but the marked increase in the number of children from working-class and lower-class homes going to high school and college probably has the most effect.

Early researchers found that children in eastern and midwestern schools chose their friends largely from among children in their own social class.[38] In Califor-nia researchers arrived at different conclusions. They found that social-class membership had very little influence upon children's choices of friends.[39] Another study of adolescents in Ohio confirmed the California findings.[40] A reasonable conclusion is that the influence of family background in determining the social acceptability of children in comprehensive schools may vary from place to place.

Comprehensive schools, however, are more likely to be found in towns, small cities, and rural areas than in large cities. In cities, elementary schools and, to a lesser extent, high schools are likely to draw pupils from a limited range of social classes. In such schools, Coleman concluded, the importance of family back-ground in the school's status system is related to the number of upper-middle class children in the school.

In metropolitan schools, educational opportunities are more likely to differ between schools enrolling children of the middle class and those enrolling children of the lower classes than educational opportunities differ within a particular school. These inequalities will be discussed in detail in Chapter 11. At this point only the most commonly mentioned differences in opportunity will be noted. Schools in middle-class neighborhoods are more likely to offer curriculums in line with pupil needs, to have adequate facilities, counselors, and experienced teachers, and to spend more for education than for schools in lower-class neighborhoods. Teachers in middle-class schools are more likely to understand the behavior of their pupils and to achieve friendly and cooperative relationships with them than are their counterparts in slum schools.

Hopefully someday such differences will be erased. Since the mid-sixties, funds from the federal government have been disbursed to help the poor, to encourage research in learning problems of disadvantaged children and in methods of teaching, and to provide financial support for programs designed to upgrade education, particularly of disadvantaged children. It is still too early to assess results of these efforts.

SUMMARY

Several tentative conclusions about the influence of family background upon the social system within a school may be drawn. First, middle-class children have an initial advantage in acquiring status with their peers and teachers because they usually can succeed academically with less difficulty, have better clothes, and have more opportunity to develop their personalities. Second, the social advantages to children of family status varies with locality. Social class is more important in schools located in New England and the South than it is in the Far West, in older small cities and towns than in newly established places, and in schools with large upper-middle class enrollments than in schools where the student body is largely working class in origin. Third, status upsets are more common than they once were. And fourth, although the social system in the comprehensive school usually tends to follow socioeconomic lines, deviations can and do occur. The extent to which undesirable social distinctions exist in a school depends upon the school culture, the community and regional cultures, and upon the quality of faculty leadership.

In large city schools where pupils are segregated largely by the socioeconomic differences among their parents, the influence of social class may be more pernicious than it is in the comprehensive schools. Such segregation is dangerous because it tends to reduce social mobility of the lower classes and to encourage a rigid system of stratification. To a considerable extent, segregation of the disadvantaged has deprived them of equal opportunity because their schools have been found to be inferior in many ways.

An awareness of such inequities has motivated many persons to castigate teachers, school board members, or parents. Finding a scapegoat is not, however, a very enlightened approach to improving conditions. Nor is the reaction of college students who see evil in the whole system of stratification. In truth, a social system is dysfunctional if it permits some of its members, especially children, to suffer. Notwithstanding the frequent perpetuation of intellectual and social deadwood at the top, social stratification in a society as complex as that of the United States is not only inevitable but also desirable from the point of view of encouraging talent. Even if the abolition of social classes were desirable, it is not in the school's power to make such changes. All that school administrators and teachers can do is provide equality of opportunity at school for all children. Recognizing that the school has failed to do so is the first step toward mitigating the inequalities that exist.

14. NOTES

1. Clyde Kluckhohn and Henry A. Murray, *Personality in Nature, Society and Culture* (New York: Knopf, 1949), p. 35.

2. Max Lerner, *America as a Civilization: Life and Thought in the United States Today* (New York: Simon and Schuster, 1957), p. 473.

3. Milton M. Gordon, *Social Class in American Sociology* (Durham: Duke University Press, 1958), Chap. 8.

4. For a complete explanation of I.S.C. method, see W. Lloyd Warner, *Social Class in America* (New York: Harper Torchbooks).

5. August B. Hollingshead and Fredrick C. Redlich, *Social Class and Mental Illness* (New York: Wiley, 1958), pp. 387-97.

6. Robert A. Ellis, W. Clayton Lane, and Virginia Olesen, "The Index of Class Position: An Improved Intercommunity Measure of Stratification," *American Sociological Review* 28 (April 1963), 271-77.

7. W. Lloyd Warner and Paul S. Lunt, *The Social Life of a Modern Community* (New Haven: Yale University Press, 1941), p. 88.

8. Neal Gross, "Social Class Identification in the Urban Community," *American Sociological Review* 18 (August 1953), 402.

9. Robert J. Havighurst, "Social-Class Influences on American Education," in National Society for the Study of Education, Sixteenth Yearbook, Part II, *Social Forces Influencing American Education* (Chicago: University of Chicago Press, 1961), p. 121.

10. Otis D. Duncan and Albert J. Reiss, Jr., *Social Characteristics of Urban and Rural Communities, 1950* (New York: Wiley, 1956), pp. 272-73, 297, 338-42.

11. Lerner, *op cit.,* p. 473.

12. The studies by Robert S. Lynd and Helen Merrell Lynd, *Middletown* (New York: Harcourt, Brace, 1929) and *Middletown in Transition* (New York: Harcourt, Brace, 1937), were the first intensive studies of an American community. They describe the occupational, familial, educational, leisure-time and community activities of a "business class" and a "working class."

13. Edgar Z. Friedenberg, "The Schools: An Unpopular View," *American Child* 45 (May 1963), 5-10.

14. E. Digby Baltzell, *Philadelphia Gentlemen, the Making of a National Upper Class* (Glencoe: Free Press, 1958), p. 5.

15. *Ibid.,* pp. 385-95.

16. Floyd Hunter, *Top Leadership, U.S.A.* (Chapel Hill: University of North Carolina Press, 1959), Chap. 8

17. Frank Riessman, *The Culturally Deprived Child* (New York: Harper & Row, 1962), pp. 12-14.

18. The term *culturally deprived* is inaccurate because no one who lives in a human group is deprived of culture.

19. Albert K. Cohen, *Delinquent Boys* (Glencoe: Free Press, 1955), pp. 121-37.

20. Lewis M. Terman, *The Measurement of Intelligence* (Boston: Houghton Mifflin, 1916), Chap. 5.

21. Allison Davis, *Social Class Influences Upon Learning* (Cambridge: Harvard University Press, 1948), pp. 46-88.

22. Havighurst, *op cit.,* p. 123.

23. Burton R. Clark, *Educating the Expert Society* (San Francisco: Chandler, 1962), pp. 75-79.

24. Carl Bereiter and Siegried Engleman, *Teaching Disadvantaged Children in the Preschool* (Englewood Cliffs: Prentice-Hall, 1966), p. 34.

25. Basil Bernstein, "Social Class and Linguistic Development: A Theory of Social Learning," in A. H. Halsey et al., *Education, Economy, and Society* (New York: Free Press, 1961), pp. 293, 300.

26. Martin Deutsch, *Minority Group and Class Status as Related to Social and Personality Factors in Scholastic Achievement* (Monograph No. 2, Society for Applied Anthropology, 1960), p. 28.

27. See summary of research in Robert Perucci, "Education, Stratification and Mobility," in Donald A. Hansen and Joel E. Gerstl, *On Education–Sociological Perspectives* (New York: Wiley, 1967).

28. *Ibid.,* p. 132.

29. Joseph A. Kahl, "Some Measurements of Achievement Orientation," *American Journal of Sociology* 70 (May 1965), 677.

30. David C. McClelland, *The Roots of Consciousness* (New York: Van Nostrand, 1964), p. 39.

31. Joseph A. Kahl, "Educational and Occupational Aspirations of 'Common Man' Boys," *Harvard Educational Review* 23 (Summer 1953), 186-203.

32. Alan B. Wilson, "Residential Segregation of Social Classes and Aspirations of High School Boys," *American Sociological Review* 24 (December 1959), 836-45.

33. Robert A. Ellis and W. Clayton Lane, "Structural Supports for Upward Mobility," *American Sociological Review* 28 (October 1963), 754-55.

34. Seymour Martin Lipset and Reinhard Bendix, *Social Mobility in Industrial Society* (Berkeley: University of California Press, 1960), pp. 238, 249-50; Fred L. Stodtbeck, "Family Interaction, Values, and Achievement," in David C. McClelland (ed.), *Talent and Society* (New York: Van Nostrand, 1958), pp. 181-84, 189-91; W. Lloyd Warner and James C. Abegglen, *Big Business Leaders in America* (New York: Atheneum, 1955), pp. 77-78.

35. Ellis and Lane, *op cit.,* pp. 750-51, 754.

36. For summary of research see Wilbur B. Brookover and David Gottlieb, *A Sociology of Education,* 2nd ed. (New York: American Book, 1964), pp. 468-80; and Ruth C. Wylie, *The Self Concept: A Critical Survey of Pertinent Research Literature* (Lincoln: University of Nebraska Press, 1961).

37. James S. Coleman, *The Adolescent Society* (New York: Free Press, 1961), pp. 200-05.

38. Bernice L. Neugarten, "The Democracy of Childhood," in W. Lloyd Warner et al., *Democracy in Jonesville* (New York: Harper & Row, 1949), Chap. 5; and August B. Hollingshead, *Elmtown's Youth* (New York: Wiley, 1949), p. 212.

39. S. Stansfelt Sargent, "Class and Class Consciousness in a California Town," *Social Problems* 1 (June, 1953), pp. 22-27.

40. Harold R. Phelps and John E. Horrocks, "Factors Influencing Informal Groups of Adolescents," *Child Development* 29 (March 1958), pp. 69-86.

15

Introduction to "Beyond the Melting Pot"*

NATHAN GLAZER and DANIEL P. MOYNIHAN

In 1660 William Kieft, the Dutch governor of New Netherland, remarked to the French Jesuit Isaac Jogues that there were eighteen languages spoken at or near Fort Amsterdam at the tip of Manhattan Island. There still are: not necessarily the same languages, but at least as many; nor has the number ever declined in the intervening three centuries. This is an essential fact of New York: a merchant metropolis with an extraordinary heterogeneous population. The first shipload of settlers sent by the Dutch was made up largely of French-speaking Protestants. British, Germans, Finns, Jews, Swedes, Africans, Italians, Irish followed, beginning a stream that has never yet stopped.

The consequences of this confusion, soon to be compounded by the enormous size of the city itself, have been many. Not least has been the virtual impossibility ever of describing New York City or even the state in simple terms. By preference, but also in some degree by necessity, America has turned elsewhere for its images and traditions. Colonial America is preserved for us in terms of the Doric simplicity of New England, or the pastoral symmetry of the Virginia countryside. Even Philadelphia is manageable. But who can summon an image of eighteenth-century New York that will hold still in the mind? A third of the battles of the Revolution were fought on New York soil, but Bunker Hill and Yorktown come easiest to memory, as do Paul Revere and Patrick Henry.

History, or perhaps historians, keep passing New York by. During the Civil War "New York [State] provided the greatest number of soldiers, the greatest quantity of supplies, and the largest amount of money. In addition, New York's citizens paid the most taxes, bought the greatest number of war bonds, and gave the most to relief organizations." Yet it is recalled as a war between Yankees and Southerners. The Union preserved, the American mind roams westward with the cowboys, returning, if at all, to the Main Streets of the Midwest. The only New York image that has permanently impressed itself on the national mind is that of Wall Street—a street on which nobody lives. Paris may be France, London may be England, but New York, we continue to reassure ourselves, is *not* America.

But, of course, it *is* America: not all of America, or even most, but surely the most important single part. As time passes, the nation comes more under the influence of the city—consider the effect of television in the past fifteen years. As time passes, the nation comes more to resemble the city: urban, heterogeneous, materialist, tough; also, perhaps, ungovernable, except that somehow it is governed, and not so badly, and with a considerable measure of democracy.

With all this, our feeling for the city is at best remote. Even New Yorkers seem to avoid too direct an involvement. The taverns of the West Side of New York boast tunes as old and as good as many gleaned in Appalachian hollows, but when the latter-day folk singers of Morrisania and Greenpoint take to the night clubs, they give forth with "Barbree Allen" and the "Ballad of the Boll Weevil." Even the sociologists, wedded to complexity and eager for fresh subjects, have tended to shy away from the city. Chicago has been far more thoroughly studied in part because of the accident of the existence of a great department of sociology at the University of Chicago. But it is no accident that a department of equal distinction at Columbia University during the 1940's and 1950's had almost nothing to do with New York. Big as it was, Chicago still offered a structure and scale that could be more easily comprehended.

When magazines on occasion devote issues to San Francisco or Chicago or Houston, and publish pictures of well-dressed and distinguished people in elegant settings, and tell us that these are the important people in this city, it is easy to believe them. When the same magazines get to New York and do the same, the informed reader cannot help but think they are indulging in a game. True, there *must* be important people in New York, but are they this banker, this publisher, this playwright, this society leader? The head of a huge corporation or financial complex in Chicago or Pittsburgh or Boston does play an important role in his city. He will be a central figure in a great movement to reform city government or rebuild the city center. In New York, the man who heads an institution or corporation of equal size is only one of many. The men who can sit around a table and settle things in smaller cities would here fill an auditorium. Indeed, in New York one can fill an auditorium with people of many kinds, who in other cities can sit around a room—high school principals, or educational reformers and thinkers and leaders, police captains and experts on crime and law enforcement, housing project managers and experts on housing and urban renewal, hospital directors and specialists in any field of medicine, directors of societies that help the poor and organizations that raise money from the rich, professors of sociology and owners of art galleries.

Of course there are important people in New York. But they have been men like Robert Moses, who has no equivalent in any other city in the United States, and whose major virtue was that he was well enough connected with enough of the centers of power to get something done, to get things moving. Everyone was so astonished at this fact that for a long time it hardly mattered that what he was getting done on a scale appropriate to the city's size was brutal and ugly, and only exacerbated its problems. The Rockefellers are also important in New

York City. Perhaps only their combination of wealth and energy and political skill makes it possible for them to approximate the role that the Mellons play in Pittsburgh. But really there is no comparison. The Mellons can be a moving force in remaking the center of Pittsburgh, and in reshaping the image of that city. But all the wealth and skill of the Rockefellers, wedded to the power of Robert Moses, produce a smaller impact on New York. Robert Wagner, the mayor of New York, is an important man. He probably has never met, and never consults, men who in cities of a million or two million people would be movers of city affairs.

We must begin with this image of the city. New York is more than ten times as large as San Francisco, and twice as large as Chicago, but this does not suggest how much more complicated it is. For in the affairs of men, twice as large means four or eight times as complicated. Twice as large means that the man on top is perhaps four to eight times away from what happens on the bottom. But attempts at calculation understate the complexity. When you have 24,000 policemen in a city, it not only means that you need a few additional levels of authorities to deal with them—those over hundreds, and five hundreds, and thousands, and five thousands—but it also means (for example) that there are enough Jewish or Negro policemen to form an organization. And they too can fill a hall.

The interweaving of complexity that necessarily follows from its size with the complexity added by the origins of its population, drawn from a staggering number of countries and from every race, makes New York one of the most difficult cities in the world to understand, and helps us understand why so few books try in any serious way to understand it.

Ideally, if we are to describe one aspect of a city, in this case its ethnic groups, we should begin by spreading out as a background something about the city as a whole. We should speak about its politics, its economic life, its culture, its social life, its history. But none of these aspects of the city can be adequately described or explained except by reference to its ethnic groups.

Consider the politics of New York. Major changes are now taking place in the city. The power of the regular Democratic party—the "machine"—to name its candidates has been broken. In 1961 Mayor Robert F. Wagner, having been denied the nomination, ran in opposition to the regular party, and won. To explain what happened, we have to say that he won the support of lower-class Negro and Puerto Rican voters, and middle-class Jewish voters who together were enough to overcome the opposition of Italian, Irish, and white Protestant middle-class and upper-working-class voters. One could describe his victory and the political transition now underway in the city without using ethnic lables, but one could barely explain it. For in New York City ethnicity and class and religion are inevitably tied to each other. The votes of the poor and the well-to-do cannot be understood without looking into the question of who the poor and the well-to-do are, without examining their ethnic background.

Similarly, to describe the economy of New York fully, one would have to point out that it is dominated at its peak (the banks, insurance companies, utilities, big corporation offices) by white Protestants, with Irish Catholics and Jews playing somewhat smaller roles. In wholesale and retail commerce, Jews predominate. White-collar workers are largely Irish and Italian if they work for big organizations, and Jewish if they work for smaller ones. The city's working class is, on its upper levels, Irish, Italian, and Jewish; on its lower levels, Negro and Puerto Rican. Other ethnic groups are found scattered everywhere, but concentrated generally in a few economic specialties.

Despite all this, it remains something of a question just what role the ethnic groups play in the development of New York economy. New York is affected by the growth of suburbia, where it is easier to locate plants and shopping centers, and where the middle class prefers to live—and presumably this would be happening no matter what ethnic groups made up the city. New York is affected by the growth of the Far West and Southwest, for more and more productive and commercial facilities are located in those areas. New York is affected by the power of unions in old centers, just as Detroit and New England are, and this encourages some plants to move away. Its original growth was touched off presumably by the fact that it was the terminus of the best level route to the Midwest, both in the canal era and the railroad era, and that it has the best natural port on the Northeastern Seaboard. These factors are quite independent of the nature of its population.

But there are other elements in the relationship between the population of New York and the economic development of New York. New York is now plagued by low wages in manufacturing. In the years since the end of the Second World War, the city has declined, relative to other cities, in the wages paid in manufacturing industries. This is a very complicated matter. Yet it must be of some significance that its manufacturing wages have fallen at a time when it has had a vast influx of relatively unskilled and untrained manufacturing labor. If through some historical accident the immigrants of the period 1946-1960 had been of the same level of education and training as the refugee German and Austrian Jews of 1933-1940, might not the economic history of the city have been different? Clearly, the main lines of the economic history of New York have been fixed by great factors that are quite independent of the nature of the population. Yet obvious as this is, there are important connections between what a people are, or what they have been made by history and experience, and their economic fate, and as economists now become more and more involved in considering the development of people of widely different cultures, they may learn things that will throw more light on the economic development of New York.

New York's culture is what it is presumably because it is the cultural capital of the richest and most important nation in the world. If America's culture is important, New York's culture must be important, and this would be true even if New York were all Anglo-Saxon and Protestant. And yet, the fact that the city is one-quarter Jewish, and one-sixth Italian, and one-seventh Negro—this also plays some part in the cultural history of New York. Ethnic identity is an element in all equations.

The census of 1960 showed that 19 per cent of the population of the city were still foreign-born whites, 28 per cent were children of foreign-born whites, another 14 per cent were Negro, 8 per cent were of Puerto Rican birth or parentage. Unquestionably, a great majority of the rest (31 per cent) were the grandchildren and great-grandchildren of immigrants, and still thought of themselves, on some occasions and for some purposes, as German, Irish, Italian, Jewish, or whatnot, as well as of course Americans.

Of the foreign-stock population (immigrants and their children), 859,000 were born in Italy or were the children of Italian immigrants; 564,000 were from the U.S.S.R. (these are mostly Jews); 389,000 from Poland (these too are mostly Jews); 324,000 from Germany; 312,000 from Ireland; 220,000 from Austria; 175,000 from Great Britain; almost 100,000 from Hungary; more than 50,000 from Greece, Czechoslovakia, Rumania, and Canada; more than 25,000 from Yugoslavia, around 10,000 from the Netherlands, Denmark, Finland, and Switzerland; more than 5,000 from Portugal and Mexico. There were more than a million Negroes, and more than 50,000 of other races, mostly Chinese and Japanese. From almost every country in the world there are enough people in the city to make up communities of thousands and tens of thousands with organizations, churches, a language, some distinctive culture.

Let us introduce some order into this huge buzzing confusion. The best way to do so is historically. English stock has apparently never been in a clear majority in New York City. In 1775 one-half of the white population of the state was of English origin, but this proportion was probably lower in New York City, with its Dutch and other non-English groups, and with its large Negro population. After the Revolution and the resumption of immigration, English and Scottish immigrants as well as migrants from New England and upstate New York probably maintained the British-descent group as the largest in the city through the first half of the nineteenth century.

In the 1840's Irish and Germans, who had of course been present in the city in some numbers before this time, began to enter in much larger numbers, and soon became dominant. By 1855 the Irish-born made up 28 per cent of the city, the German-born 16 per cent of the city; with their children they certainly formed a majority of the city, and they maintained this dominance until the end of the century. In 1890 Irish-born and German-born and their children made up 52 per cent of the population of New York and Brooklyn (then separate cities).

In the 1880's Jews and Italians began to come in large numbers (there were of course sizable communities of both groups in the city before this time), and this heavy immigration continued until 1924, and on a reduced scale after that.

The Negroes began to enter the city in great numbers after World War I, the Puerto Ricans after World War II.

Thus six great groups have entered the city two by two, in subsequent epochs; and to these we must add as a seventh group the "old stock," or the "white Anglo-Saxon Protestants." The two terms are of course not identical, but the overlap among those they comprise is great. The "old stock" includes those New Yorkers who descend from families that were here before the Revolution. They were largely of English, Scottish, and Welsh origin, but also included Dutch, French, and other settlers from Northwestern Europe. It has been relatively easy for later immigrants of the same ethnic and religious background—from Canada and from Europe—to assimilate to this "old stock" group if they were in occupations of high status and of at least moderate affluence.

What is the relative size of these seven groups in the city today? For all except the Negroes and the Puerto Ricans, who are listed separately in the census, it is difficult to give more than a very general guess. The accepted religious breakdown of the city population, based on sample surveys and estimates by various religious groups, indicates that less than a quarter of the population is Protestant, and more than half of that is Negro. The white Protestants of course include many of German, Scandinavian, Czech, and Hungarian origins. It is thus not likely that more than about one-twentieth of the population of the city is "old stock," or "WASP." Public opinion polls which ask for "national origin" suggest that about a tenth of the population is Irish, another tenth German. The same sources suggest that about a sixth is Italian. Jewish organizations estimate that one-quarter of the population is Jewish. The census reports that Negroes form 14 per cent of the population, Puerto Ricans 8 per cent. We have accounted for about 90 per cent of the population of the city. These figures, aside from being inexact (except for Puerto Rican and Negro), also assume that everyone in the city can be neatly assigned to an ethnic category. Of course this is in large measure myth; many of the people in the city, as in the nation, have parents and grandparents of two or three or four groups.

Despite the immigration laws, old groups grow and new groups form in the city. Thus, Batista and Castro, as well as the growing size of the Spanish-speaking population, have encouraged the growth of a large Cuban community of 50,000. For despite the stringent immigration laws, the United States is still the chief country of immigration in the world, and 2,500,000 were able to enter this country as immigrants between 1950-1959. Very large numbers of these immigrants settle in New York and its region, where large communities of their compatriots make life easier and pleasanter. Buried in this vast population of the city are new groups (such as 18,000 Israelis) that in any other city would be marked and receive attention. In New York their coffee shops and bars and meeting places and political disputes and amusements and problems are of interest only to themselves. Only when an immigrant group reaches the enormous size of the Puerto Ricans does it become a subject of interest, attention, and concern.

New York cannot be read out of America because of its heterogeneity; but it is true its heterogeneity is to some extent extreme, even among the heterogeneous cities of the Northeast. The cities of the South, except for the presence of Negroes, are far more homogeneous. They are largely inhabited by white Protestants whose ancestors came from the British Isles. The cities of the Great Plain—from Indianapolis to Kansas City—are also somewhat less mixed. Their largest ethnic element is generally German; and Germans have also found it easiest to assimilate to the white Anglo-Saxon Protestant culture that is still the norm in American life. The cities of the Far West, too, are in their ethnic aspect somewhat different from the cities of the Northeast. Their populations, if we trace them back far enough, are as diverse as the populations of Northeastern cities. But these immigrants have come from the East, Midwest, and South of the United States, rather than from Europe. This second immigration to the Far West has made them more alike. If you ask people there, "Where did you come from?," the answer is Illinois or Iowa, Oklahoma or New York. In the Northeast, the answer is more likely to be Germany or Sweden, Russia or Italy. In terms of immediate origins, the populations of Far Western cities consist of Iowans and Illinoisans and New Yorkers, rather than Germans, Jews, and Italians.

But now what does it mean for New York that most of its population is composed of people who think of themselves—at least at some times, for some purposes—as Jews, Italians, Negroes, Germans, Irishmen, Puerto Ricans? Is New York different, because of this fact, from London, Paris, Moscow, Tokyo?

Do we not, in every great city, meet people from all over the world? We do; but we should not confuse the heterogeneity of most of the great cities of the world with that of New York. The classic heterogeneity of great cities has been limited to the elite part of the population. It is the small numbers of the wealthy and exceptional who represent in those other cities the variety of the countries of the world, not, as in the United States, the masses. This for the most part is still true of the great cities of Europe, even though large numbers of Irishmen and colored people now form part of the working class in London, large numbers of Algerians part of the working class of Paris. Those with very special skills and talents have always been drawn from all over the world into its great cities. Thus, the specialized trading peoples—Phoenicians, Syrians, Greeks, Jews—have formed, for thousands of years, part of the specialized commercial and trading classes of the Mediterranean cities. And even today, trade with foreign countries is still in large measure carried on by nationals of the countries involved, who have special knowledge of language and conditions and local laws and regulations. There is also to be found in all great cities the diplomatic corps, now enormously swollen by international agencies of all sorts. There are the people involved in cultural and artistic activities, who may be of any part of the world. These elites, commercial, political, cultural, today give such cities as London,

Paris, and Tokyo an international flavor. It is these people we think of when we say that people from all over the world flock to its great cities; they do, but they are relatively few in numbers.

The heterogeneity of New York is of the masses—numbers so great that Negroes are not exotic, as they are in Paris, Puerto Ricans not glamorous representatives of Latin American culture, as they might be in London, Italians not rare representatives of a great nation, as they are in Tokyo. Here the numbers of each group are so great, so steady and heavy a presence, that it takes an effort of mind to see that all these group names describe a double aspect: those one sees around one, and those in some other country, on some other continent, with a different culture.

Admittedly, even this heterogeneity of the masses is not unique to the cities of the United States. The cities of Canada and Latin America have also drawn their populations from varied groups (though none equals New York in its variety). Even in the great cities of the past one could find sizable differences among the masses. In Athens one might presumably find countrymen from every deme, in Paris workers from every province. There was probably a tendency for them to cluster together. Even though all spoke the same language, they spoke different dialects. Even though they were all of the same religion, they may have preferred to worship among friends and relatives. Even though they all participated in some forms of a growing national culture, they must have preferred their own provincial specialties in food, folk music, and dancing.

But in New York the masses that make up the city have come not from different provinces but different countries. Their languages have been mutually unintelligible, their religion radically different, their family structures, values, ideals, cultural patterns have been as distinct as those of the Irish and the Southern Negro, of urban Jews and peasant Italians.

This is the way it was, but will it be relevant for New York City much longer? The foreign-language press declines rapidly in circulation; the old immigrant quarters now hold only some of the old-timers. The immigrant societies play little role in the city's politics. The American descendants of immigrants diverge markedly from the people of the old country. American descendants of Germans seem no more committed to the unity of Germany and the defense of Berlin than other Americans, the foreign policy of the American Irish seems to have nothing in common any more with the foreign policy of a neutral Eire, and the political outlook and culture of Americans of Italian descent seem to have little more in common with what one can see in Italy. (New Italian movies exploring the limits of modern sensibility are as incomprehensible to Italian immigrants as to other immigrants.) And perhaps the Jewish commitment to Israel is best explained by the recency of the establishment of the state and the permanent danger surrounding it. American culture seems to be as attractive to the children of immigrants as the descendants of pioneers (and indeed, as attractive to Indonesians or Russians as to Americans). The powerful assimilatory influences of

American society operate on all who come into it, making the children of immigrants and even immigrants themselves a very different people from those they left behind. In what sense, then, can we put immigrants, their children, their grandchildren, and even further descendants into one group and speak of, for example, "the" Irish? Must we not speak of the middle-class Irish and the working-class Irish, the big-city Irish and the small-town Irish, the recent immigrants and the second and third and fourth generation, the Democrats and Republicans; and when we do, is there any content left to the group name?

Perhaps the meaning of ethnic labels will yet be erased in America. But it has not yet worked out this way in New York. It is true that immigrants to this country were rapidly transformed, in comparison with immigrants to other countries, that they lost their language and altered their culture. It was reasonable to believe that a new American type would emerge, a new nationality in which it would be a matter of indifference whether a man was of Anglo-Saxon or German or Italian or Jewish origin, and in which indeed, because of the diffusion of populations through all parts of the country and all levels of the social order, and because of the consequent close contact and intermarriage, it would be impossible to make such distinctions. This may still be the most likely result in the long run. After all, in 1960 almost half of New York City's population was still foreign-born or the children of foreign-born. Yet it is also true that it is forty years since the end of mass immigration, and new processes, scarcely visible when our chief concern was with the great masses of immigrants and the problems of their "Americanization," now emerge to surprise us. The initial notion of an American melting pot did not, it seems, quite grasp what would happen in America. At least it did not grasp what would happen in the short run, and since this short run encompasses at least the length of a normal lifetime, it is not something we can ignore.

It is true that language and culture are very largely lost in the first and second generations, and this makes the dream of "cultural pluralism"—of a new Italy or Germany or Ireland in America, a League of Nations established in the New World—as unlikely as the hope of a "melting pot." But as the groups were transformed by influences in American society, stripped of their original attributes, they were recreated as something new, but still as identifiable groups. Concretely, persons think of themselves as members of that group, with that name; they are thought of by others as members of that group, with that name; and most significantly, they are linked to other members of the group by new attributes that the original immigrants would never have recognized as identifying their group, but which nevertheless serve to mark them off, by more than simply name and association, in the third generation and even beyond.

The assimilating power of American society and culture operated on immigrant groups in different ways, to make them, it is true, something they had not been, but still something distinct and identifiable. The impact of assimilating trends on the groups is different in part because the groups are different—

Catholic peasants from Southern Italy were affected differently, in the same city and the same time, from urbanized Jewish workers and merchants from Eastern Europe. We cannot even begin to indicate how various were the characteristics of family structure, religion, economic experience and attitudes, educational experience and attitudes, political outlook that differentiated groups from such different backgrounds. Obviously, some American influences worked on them in common and with the same effects. But their differences meant they were open to different parts of American experience, interpreted it in different ways, used it for different ends. In the third generation, the descendants of the immigrants confronted each other, and knew they were both Americans, in the same dress, with the same language, using the same artifacts, troubled by the same things, but they voted differently, had different ideas about education and sex, and were still, in many essential ways, as different from one another as their grandfathers had been.

The initial attributes of the groups provided only one reason why their transformations did not make them all into the same thing. There was another reason —and that was the nature of American society itself, which could not, or did not, assimilate the immigrant groups fully or in equal degree. Or perhaps the nature of human society in general. It is only the experience of the strange and foreign that teaches us how provincial we are. A hundred thousand Negroes have been enough to change the traditional British policy of free immigration from the colonies and dominions. Japan finds it impossible to incorporate into the body of its society anyone who does not look Japanese, or even the Koreans, indistinguishable very often in appearance and language from Japanese. And we shall test the racial attitudes of the Russians only when there are more than a few Negroes passing through as curiosities; certainly the inability of Russians to get over anti-Semitism does not suggest they are any different from the rest of mankind. In any case, the word "American" was an unambiguous reference to nationality only when it was applied to a relatively homogeneous social body consisting of immigrants from the British Isles, with relatively small numbers from nearby European countries. When the numbers of those not of British origin began to rise, the word "American" became a far more complicated thing. Legally, it meant a citizen. Socially, it lost its identifying power, and when you asked a man what he was (in the United States), "American" was not the answer you were looking for. In the United States it became a slogan, a political gesture, sometimes an evasion, but not a matter-of-course, concrete social description of a person. Just as in certain languages a word cannot stand alone but needs some particle to indicate its function, so in the United States the word "American" does not stand by itself. If it does, it bears the additional meaning of patriot, "authentic" American, critic and opponent of "foreign" ideologies.

The original Americans became "old" Americans, or "old stock," or "white Anglo-Saxon Protestants," or some other identification which indicated they were not immigrants or descendants of recent immigrants. These original Americans already had a frame in their minds, which became a frame in reality, that placed and ordered those who came after them. It was important to be white, of British origin, and Protestant. If one was all three, then even if one was an immigrant, one was really not an immigrant, or not for long.

Thus, even before it knew what an Italian or Jew or an Irishman was like, the American mind had a place for the category, high or low, depending on color, on religion, on how close the group was felt to be to the Anglo-Saxon center. There were peculiarities in this placing. Why, for example, were the Germans placed higher than the Irish? There was of course an interplay to some extent between what the group actually was and where it was placed, and, since the German immigrants were less impoverished than the Irish and somewhat more competent craftsmen and farmers, this undoubtedly affected the old American's image of them. Then ideology came in to emphasize the common links between Englishmen and Germans, who, even though they spoke different languages, were said to be really closer to each other than the old Americans were to the English-speaking, but Catholic and Celtic, Irish. If a group's first representatives were cultured and educated, those who came after might benefit, unless they were so numerous as to destroy the first image. Thus, German Jews who arrived in the 1840's and 1850's benefited from their own characteristics and their link with Germans, until they were overwhelmed by the large number of East European Jewish immigrants after 1880. A new wave of German Jewish immigrants, in the 1930's, could not, regardless of culture and education, escape the low position of being "Jewish."

The ethnic group in American society became not a survival from the age of mass immigration but a new social form. One could not predict from its first arrival what it might become or, indeed, whom it might contain. The group is not a purely biological phenomenon. The Irish of today do not consist of those who are descended from Irish immigrants. Were we to follow the history of the germ plasm alone—if we could—we should find that many in the group really came from other groups, and that many who should be in the group are in other groups. The Protestants among them, and those who do not bear distinctively Irish names, may now consider themselves, and be generally considered, as much "old American" as anyone else. The Irish-named offspring of German or Jewish or Italian mothers often find that willy-nilly they have become Irish. It is even harder for the Jewish-named offspring of mixed marriages to escape from the Jewish group; neither Jews nor non-Jews will let them rest in ambiguity.

Parts of the group are cut off, other elements join the group as allies. Under certain circumstances, strange as it may appear, it is an advantage to be able to take on a group name, even of a low order, if it can be made to fit, and if it gives one certain advantages. It is better in Oakland, California, to be a Mexican than an Indian, and so some of the few Indians call themselves, at certain times, for certain occasions, "Mexicans." In the forming of ethnic groups subtle distinctions are overridden; there is an advantage to belonging to a big group, even if it is looked down upon. West Indian Negroes achieve important political positions, as representatives of Negroes; Spaniards and Latin Americans become the representatives of Puerto Ricans; German Jews rose to Congress from districts dominated by East European Jews.

Ethnic groups then, even after distinctive language, customs, and culture are lost, as they largely were in the second generation, and even more fully in the third generation, are continually recreated by new experiences in America. The mere existence of a name itself is perhaps sufficient to form group character in new situations, for the name associates an individual, who actually can be anything, with a certain past, country, race. But as a matter of fact, someone who is Irish or Jewish or Italian generally has other traits than the mere existence of the name that associates him with other people attached to the group. A man is connected to his group by ties of family and friendship. But he is also connected by ties of *interest*. The ethnic groups in New York are also *interest groups*.

This is perhaps the single most important fact about ethnic groups in New York City. When one speaks of the Negroes and Puerto Ricans, one also means unorganized and unskilled workers, who hold poorly paying jobs in the laundries, hotels, restaurants, small factories or who are on relief. When one says Jews, one also means small shopkeepers, professionals, better-paid skilled workers in the garment industries. When one says Italians, one also means homeowners in Staten Island, the North Bronx, Brooklyn, and Queens.

If state legislation threatens to make it more difficult to get relief, this is headline news in the Puerto Rican press—for the group is affected—and news of much less importance to the rest of the press. The interplay between rational economic interests and the other interests or attitudes that stem out of group history makes for an incredibly complex political and social situation. Consider the local laws against discrimination in housing. Certain groups that face discrimination want such laws—Negroes, Puerto Ricans, and Jews. Jews meet little discrimination in housing in New York but have an established ideological commitment to all antidiscrimination laws. Apartment-house owners are against any restriction of their freedom or anything that might affect their profits. In New York, this group is also largely Jewish, but it is inhibited in pushing strongly against such laws by its connections with the Jewish community. Private homeowners see this as a threat to their homogenous neighborhoods. These are largely German, Irish, and Italian. The ethnic background of the homeowners links them to communities with a history of anti-Negro feelings. The Irish and Italian immigrants have both at different times competed directly with Negro labor.

In the analysis then of the conflict over antidiscrimination laws, "rational" economic interests and the "irrational" or at any rate noneconomic interests and attitudes tied up with one's own group are inextricably mixed together. If the rational interests did not operate, some of the older groups would by now be much weaker than they are. The informal and formal social groupings that make up these communities are strengthened by the fact that Jews can talk about the garment business, Irish about politics and the civil service, Italians about the state of the trucking or contracting or vegetable business.

In addition to the links of interest, family and fellowfeeling bind the ethnic group. There is satisfaction in being with those who are like oneself. The ethnic group is something of an extended family or tribe. And aside from ties of feeling and interest, there are concrete ties of organization. Certain types of immigrant social organization have declined, but others have been as ingenious in remolding and recreating themselves as the group itself. The city is often spoken of as the place of anonymity, of the breakdown of some kind of preexisting social order. The ethnic group, as Oscar Handlin has pointed out, served to create a new form of order. Those who came in with some kind of disadvantage, created by a different language, a different religion, a different race, found both comfort and material support in creating various kinds of organizations. American social services grew up in large part to aid incoming immigrant groups. Many of these were limited to a single religious or ethnic group. Ethnic groups set up hospitals, old people's homes, loan funds, charitable organizations, as well as churches and cultural organizations. The initial need for a separate set of welfare and health institutions became weaker as the group became more prosperous and as the government took over these functions, but the organizations nevertheless continued. New York organizational life today is in large measure lived within ethnic bounds. These organizations generally have religious names, for it is more acceptable that welfare and health institutions should cater to religious than to ethnic communities. But of course religious institutions are generally closely linked to a distinct ethnic group. The Jewish (religious) organizations are Jewish (ethnic), Catholic are generally Irish or Italian, now with the Puerto Ricans as important clients; the Protestant organizations are white Protestant—which means generally old American, with a smaller German wing—in leadership, with Negroes as their chief clients.

Thus many elements—history, family and feeling, interest, formal organizational life—operate to keep much of New York life channeled within the bounds of the ethnic group. Obviously, the rigidity of this channeling of social life varies from group to group. For the Puerto Ricans, a recent immigrant group with a small middle class and speaking a foreign language, the ethnic group serves as the setting for almost all social life. For Negroes too, because of discrimination and poverty, most social life is limited to the group itself. Jews and Italians are still to some extent recent immigrants, and despite the growing middle-class character of the Jewish group, social life for both is generally limited to other members of the group. But what about the Irish and the Germans?

Probably, many individuals who by descent "belong" to one of these older groups go through a good part of their lives with no special consciousness of the fact. It may be only under very special circumstances that one becomes aware of the matter at all—such as if one wants to run for public office. The political realm, indeed, is least willing to consider such matters a purely private affair.

Consciousness of one's ethnic background may be intermittent. It is only on occasion that someone may think of or be reminded of his background, and perhaps become self-conscious about the pattern formed by his family, his friends, his job, his interests. Obviously, this ethnic aspect of a man's life is more important if he is part of one group than if he is part of another; if he is Negro, he can scarcely escape it, and if he is of German origin, little will remind him of it.

Conceivably the fact that one's origins can become only a memory suggests the general direction for ethnic groups in the United States—toward assimilation and absorption into a homogeneous American mass. And yet, as we suggested earlier, it is hard to see in the New York of the 1960's just how this comes about. Time alone does not dissolve the groups if they are not close to the Anglo-Saxon center. Color marks off a group, regardless of time; and perhaps most significantly, the "majority" group, to which assimilation should occur, has taken on the color of an ethnic group, too. To what does one assimilate in modern America? The "American" in abstract does not exist, though some sections of the country, such as the Far West, come closer to realizing him than does New York City. there are test cases of such assimilation in the past. The old Scotch-Irish group, an important ethnic group of the early nineteenth century, is now for the most part simply old American, "old stock." Old Dutch families have become part of the upper class of New York. But these test cases merely reveal to us how partial was the power of the old American type to assimilate—it assimilated its ethnic cousins.

There is also, in New York, a nonethnic city. There are the fields that draw talent from all over the country and all over the world. There are the areas, such as Greenwich Village, where those so collected congregate. On Broadway, in the radio and television industry, in the art world, in all the sphere of culture, mass or high, one finds the same mixture that one finds in every country. Those involved in these intense and absorbing pursuits would find the city described in these pages strange. Another area of mixture is politics. It is true that political life itself emphasizes the ethnic character of the city, with its balanced tickets and its special appeals. But this is in large part an objective part of the business, just as the Jewish plays on Broadway are part of the business. For those in the field itself, there is more contact across the ethnic lines, and the ethnic lines themselves mean less, than in other areas of the city's life.

How does one write about such groups? If one believes, as the authors of this book do, that the distinctions are important, and that they consist of more than the amusing differences of accent and taste in food and drink, then it is no simple matter to decide how to describe and analyze this aspect of American reality. For it has been common to speak about the ethnic groups in terms of either blame or praise.

It is understandable that as foreigners flooded American cities all the ills of the cities were laid on their shoulders. It is also understandable that the children of the immigrants (and they had the help of many other Americans) should have defended themselves. They had become part of America; they spoke the language, fought in the wars, paid the taxes, were as patriotic as those who could count more generations in the country—and just as they had become Americanized and good citizens, others would. There is no way of discounting the polemical impact of anything written on this question. How many and of what kind to let into this country is a permanent and important question of American public life. It is also a permanent question in American life what attitudes to take in matters of public welfare, public education, housing—toward increasing numbers of Negroes in American cities. This is a matter that involves the chance for happiness of many Americans, and mobilizes the deep and irrational passions of many others. On such issues, most people will simply have to use arguments and facts and ideas as weapons, and will not be able to use them for enlightenment. Even scholarship is generally enlisted in the cause, on one side or another. And yet beyond personal interest and personal commitment, it is possible to view this entire fascinating spectacle of the ethnic variety of the American city and to consider what it means.

At least, this is the point of view we have tried to adopt in this book. It is inevitably filled with judgments, yet the central judgment—an over-all evaluation of the meaning of American heterogeneity—we have tried to avoid, because we would not know how to make it. One author is the son of a working-class immigrant, the other, the grandson; there is no question where their personal interest leads them. On the other hand, we would not know how to argue with someone who maintained that something was lost when an original American population was overwhelmed in the central cities by vast numbers of immigrants of different culture, religion, language, and race.

But the original Americans did choose this course; the nation stuck with it for a hundred years; and despite the policy of 1924, which was supposed to fix the ethnic proportions of the population, then attained, these proportions change continually because the immigration policy of the United States is still the freest of any great nation. And enormous internal migrations continue to change the populations of the cities as rapidly and on as great a scale as in the era of free immigration.

A nation is formed by critical decisions, and the American decision was to permit the entire world to enter almost without restriction. The consequences of this key decision, despite the work of such major figures as Marcus Hansen and Oscar Handlin, have received surprisingly little attention. Popular writing, scholarly writing, novels, and plays, all seem to find the beginning of the process of assimilation most interesting. It is when the immigrants first arrive that everyone is aware of them. By the time the problems are less severe, or have become largely personal, local color has been dissipated in the flush of Americanization, and the writers find less to write about. Because of the paucity of the literature and the size of the subject, it has proved beyond our capacities to present our theses wholly in terms of objective and verifiable statements. It would be quite impossible to write a book such as this exclusively on the basis of concrete data which are either now available or which could, with reasonable effort, be obtained. We have nonetheless gone ahead out of the strongest possible feeling of the continuing reality and significance of the ethnic group in New York, and by extension, in American life. This is what we think we know about the subject: this is all we can say except that if we are subsequently proved wrong, we hope we shall have at least contributed to a continuing discussion.

Some of the judgments—we will not call them facts—which follow will appear to be harsh. We ask the understanding of those who will be offended. The racial and religious distinctions of the city create more than a little ugliness and complacency. But they are also the source of a good deal of vigor, and a kind of rough justice that is not without attraction. Melbourne is said to have expressed a particular fondness for the Order of the Garter, which was awarded, as it were, on the basis of blood lines "with no damned nonsense about merit." This, precisely, is the principle of the balanced ticket and a thousand other arrangements, formal and informal, that the people of New York have contrived to bring a measure of social peace and equity to a setting that promises little of either.

16

Cultural Background and Learning in Young Children*

JANE G. FORT, JEAN C. WATTS, and GERALD S. LESSER

For many years now school administrators, teachers, psychologists, and parents have been increasingly concerned about the manner in which intellectual evaluation of school children is conducted. The staggering increase in the numbers of children from minority groups entering the educational institutions of major American cities has intensified this concern. Educators and social scientists see an urgent need for new instruments to measure the abilities of children with diverse backgrounds. Just as urgent, if less obvious, is the need for instruments to evaluate variability in abilities within individual children and the related need to develop new instructional methods in response to these individual patterns of ability.

It is generally felt by laymen, and increasingly indicated by research, that individuals are differentially able to perform various tasks; some find the development of complicated theories a simple matter, but are completely inept at presenting their theories to an audience; others are quite articulate, but never manage to untangle the intricacies of a monthly budget. In a longitudinal study which now spans five years, we have found that a child's pattern of intellectual strengths and weaknesses is related to his ethnic-group background. Children in particular ethnic groups tend to be able to do certain kinds of tasks better than they are able to do others, whether or not they do either task particularly well.

THE ORIGINAL STUDY

When the project discussed here was begun in 1963, the purpose was to examine differential mental abilities in young elementary-school children and to ascertain what, if any, patterns of abilities were related to social class and to cultural background. The project directors set about the task of building a test which, when administered to first-grade children in the public schools in the Greater New York City area, would measure ability in four areas: verbal, reasoning, numerical, and space conceptualization. The children of the original sample

---

(N=320) were from lower-class and middle-class homes of Chinese, Jewish, Negro, and Puerto Rican origin.

The Diverse Mental Abilities test was administered to each child individually at school during the regular school session on three or four occasions over a period of one month. No reading or writing was required of the child and no assessment of the child's personality or private attitudes was included. The test consists primarily of a number of pictures and games which the child is asked to manipulate or to label.

The results of this study indicate that middle-class children are better able to perform on all tasks than lower-class children, that children from different ethnic groups show different constellations of abilities as well as different levels of performance for various tasks, and that the middle-class children from different ethnic groups in general perform more like each other than do lower-class children from different ethnic groups. The performance of the various ethnic groups on the four ability areas was as follows:

1. Chinese children perform spatial tasks better than they did any of the others. They performed verbal tasks least well, although the test was administered in their native dialect and/or English, whichever was preferred by the child. Their performance in the reasoning and numerical areas was essentially the same and only slightly lower than in the spatial area.

2. Jewish children evidenced their greatest proficiency in the verbal area and were next best in numerical concepts. Their spatial skills were their poorest, and reasoning scores were only a bit higher than spatial.

3. Negro children showed their greatest skill to be in the verbal area. They performed least well in the numerical area. Their reasoning and spatial scores were better than their numerical scores but not as high as the verbal scores.

4. Puerto Rican children evidenced the least difference among the four abilities. Their best area was space conceptualization, their worst verbal concepts. Again, these children were able to use both Spanish and English in the test situation, so that the language used had no effect on test performance.

A few years after the original study was completed, a group of forty Chinese and Negro children were tested in Boston, duplicating almost exactly the findings among the Chinese and Negro children in New York City. This replication reinforced our earlier conclusion that at least four mental abilities are organized in ways regularly related to cultural background.

SOME IMPLICATIONS

Stability of Patterns—These findings of different, ethnically related patterns of abilities raise many questions about the nature, the causes, and the consequences of such differences in school children. Since the children were first-graders when tested, it is assumed that their skills reflect experiences of pre-school years.

Once enrolled in school and exposed to the experiences and styles of teaching of the big-city public school system, the child's pattern of abilities may change in response to this new force. However, it is possible that the relative strengths of the skills evidenced in the first grade are quite stable and that the same pattern among the four areas will be found in later years and possibly throughout life. We are now evaluating this possibility by analyzing scores of our original group of first-graders tested on the same types of measures five years later.

Origin of Patterns—Although the relative contributions of genetic and environmental effects are unclear, we assume that the origins of differential development of abilities lie in part in the experiences of the child's early years. What early experiences produce the particular patterns of mental ability in different ethnic groups? Since we are only now beginning empirical research on this question, we can merely offer our preliminary speculations and observations.

One important factor may be the type and extent of activity to which the child is exposed, depending on the child's interaction with his parents and the values which the parents attempt to transmit through their system of rewards and punishments. In turn, the values of the parents, and subsequently the things which they feel it is important for the child to learn, may have been determined by the experiences the parents have had; the expectations placed by society on the parents and the outlets for expression of the abilities of the parents may have worked to mold a pattern of abilities for them.

As we consider the relative strengths and weaknesses of each ethnic group in the four areas tested, our observations of "real world" experiences and information on cultural styles seem to fit the patterns which we observed. For example, Chinese children in our sample performed best on the spatial tasks and least well on the verbal area. Preliminary observations indicate the prevalence in Chinese families of emphasis on spatial contexts: Chinese children often are taught the Chinese language, a highly spatial one; games most frequently played in the homes are spatial games; a large number of Chinese professionals are employed in areas which require and utilize strong spatial skills, such as architecture and engineering. On the other hand, there is relatively little reinforcement of verbal skills. In fact, a highly verbal, that is, talkative child may be considered a problem child in a Chinese home. (In our own research we found it most difficult to locate a Chinese psychologist to test the Chinese children; Chinese students were much more frequently found in the natural sciences than in such areas as psychology or education.)

The Jewish children in our original sample showed a high degree of verbal competence, in keeping with reports of verbal emphasis in Jewish homes. Many Jewish parents were in highly "verbal" occupations, such as teaching, law, and psychology, while few were in space-related occupations. In addition, the relatively strong numerical skills of these children may have reflected the fact that many of the Jewish parents were employed in businesses and stockbroking areas which provided contact with the manipulation of numbers and use of numerical concepts. Such exposure may offer to children of these parents an opportunity to become familiar with and skilled in these concepts.

Our sample of Negro children showed greatest competence in the area of verbal skills, while their poorest performance was in numerical concepts. Preliminary observations suggest that Negro homes may be more rich verbally than heretofore suspected; verbal interaction is frequent and is encouraged. Negro parents in our sample were more likely to be employed in "verbal" occupations such as teaching and law than in occupations requiring manipulation of numbers, perhaps leading to the poorer grasp of numerical concepts of the Negro children we tested.

The skills evidenced by the Puerto Rican children of our sample are the least differentiated. However, the children did give their best performance in the spatial area. Again, casual information indicates that spatial skills are reinforced in the culture; tasks such as close and intricate needlework performed by the women and varied technical jobs which occupy the men utilize and strengthen these spatial skills.

These facts suggest that the developmental origins of the different patterns of ability which we have observed probably lie in two main areas. The first is the occupational and social structure of American society which, historically, has forced different ethnic groups into different occupations and social roles. Hence the stereotype of the Jewish lawyer or businessman, the Negro teacher or preacher, the Chinese architect or engineer. Middle-class children are exposed directly (lower-class children aspirationally) to these models of success in their own ethnic groups. Relevant skills are differentially taught and reinforced in the pre-school years in the "hidden curriculum" of the home, and eventually the child "becomes father of the man."

The second major determinant of different patterns of mental ability may be more subtle, involving differences in general styles of child-rearing as these vary not with social class but with ethnic or cultural-group membership. Since we are currently testing this idea, we now speculate, for example, that the highly verbal child comes from a "talkative" home in which the mother has close contact with her child but may also be a shade too intrusive, too restrictive, and over-protective. In such a home the mother is the dominant figure, especially *vis-a-vis* the male child. Their emotional bond may be warm or hostile, but the effect is to restrict the child's autonomy and freedom to explore the world of objects and to structure the world for himself. In contrast, we suggest that the highly spatial child comes from a home in which his essential autonomy is preserved even if the reason for its being granted is often simply the parent's convenience or the old-fashioned belief that the worlds of children and adults should be kept separate.

At the moment we do not know how our ethnic or cultural groups vary on the child-rearing dimensions hypothesized or even whether these variables are critical. Lack of relevant research has encouraged us to undertake new research in which we directly observe young children (two to four years of age) in the home, to see how they interact with adults, how they play, and how and what they learn. This research should permit a much clearer idea of how aptitudes are transmitted to young children in the family circles of different ethnic groups.

INSTRUCTION AND ABILITY PATTERNS

The developmental psychologist is interested in questions of the stability and origin of the patterns of ability displayed by children from different ethnic groups. The school practitioner may be more interested in another question we are attempting to study: How can knowledge of a child's pattern of mental abilities be fitted to the content and timing of his instruction? How can instruction be adjusted to the child's particular strengths and weaknesses, or the child's abilities modified to meet the demands of instruction? In the context of individualizing instruction, we are attempting to fit instruction to particular forms of ability and vice versa. In the context of research design, we are searching for interactions between instructional treatments and abilities of the learner in order to determine how selected mental ability variables are related to learner performance under different conditions of instruction. Thus we are applying our analysis of patterns of mental ability to an issue which we believe has promise for classroom learning and teaching: how to match instructional strategies and individual differences in patterns of ability in order to produce effective learning performance.

SUMMARY

We have reported evidence that children from different ethnic groups (Chinese, Jewish, Negro, and Puerto Rican) display different patterns of mental abilities which probably begin to take form during the early years of life. Each ethnic group apparently transmits its own particular combination of intellectual strengths and weaknesses. Recognizing these differences in patterns of ability—and studying their family antecedents and their implications for school instruction—may help us to understand more fully and to capitalize upon the pluralism and diversity of our society.

17

Education and the Impulse Life of the Child*

SOL GORDON

For the most part, educators and the general public are tempted to think that the best way to improve the educative process is to offer new courses of study. As the need for greater numbers of highly trained people has increased, the rearrangement of textbooks and course outlines for the schools has multiplied, often without a real evaluation of the underlying problems created by a rapidly changing social order. I suspect that curriculum change is a worthwhile endeavor when teachers understand what they are expected to do, and when the school itself is operating at a "profit." By "profit" I mean the academic surplus that accrues when large numbers of children in the school appear to be learning, when a favorable teacher-student ratio is operative, when academic expectancy is high, and when both teachers and administrators appear genuinely receptive to new ideas. On the other hand, when students are functioning at a "loss," curriculum innovation does not have a very great impact unless it is grounded in a sound examination of the "here-and-now" problems particular to a given situation.

The school has enormously expanded its function as our society has become more complicated and more demanding. Today it is generally agreed that education should aim to develop students' abilities to write and speak clearly, to deal competently with numbers and figures, to think critically, to appreciate personal and cultural differences, and to enjoy the worlds of art and music. At the same time, the school should function as a "social conditioner," that is, it should prepare the young for entrance into the existing social order.

If we are to hope that every child reaches the optimum development of which he is capable, we must discover ways to show the child that he is a worthwhile human being, that he has a place in society, that he is needed and not surplus. We may develop the most advanced curriculum innovations, we may construct the most modern school buildings, but we still will fail to educate if we do not succeed in giving youngsters the self-confidence and essence of adequacy that is essential to the learning process.

In a sense, self-confidence and feelings of adequacy are transmitted by adults who are confident and comfortable with their own impulses. But too often our

*Copyright 1966 by Phi Delta Kappa. Reprinted by permission of the publisher from *Phi Delta Kappan*, February 1966, pp. 310-13.

society and culture operate in opposition to the "impulse" life of the child. Many mothers seem to have developed child-rearing practices based on notions inspired by popular women's magazines. Fifteen years ago we were supposed to be strict with children; ten years ago we were supposed to be permissive. Today we don't love them enough, but are allowed to beat them occasionally. Ten years ago a schedule was all the rage; three years later we were supposed to feed permissively. Recently, it was "discovered" that fathers are important.

I have seen homes where the parents were strict, homes where the parents were permissive, and other homes where both parents were neurotic. In each case their children were perfectly normal, and I *mean* perfectly normal. But the children do grow up confused, unhappy, and neurotic when the mother is insecure about her role as a mother, or when there is conflict between the mother and father about the management of the child. Parents have become paralyzed by an overabundance of advice from magazines, from their own mothers and fathers, and from neighbors. As a result, many parents can no longer respond in a spontaneous way to their own children.

One of the most dynamic aspects of spontaneity is the courage to accept the impulse life of the child. Let me illustrate that point with reference to parents and teachers.

The child has a nightmare. He wakes up in terrible fear and calls his mother. She says, "Oh, there's nothing to be afraid of." But the child is frightened. What we need to say to the child is, "Yes, it is very frightening to have a nightmare." Then, we need to reassure him that he is loved and that he is not alone.

Another example: Jimmy is six, his brother Johnny is four, and Jimmy doesn't like his brother. Mother says, "But you're supposed to like your brother; he *is* your brother"—as though this has any meaning whatsoever to the child. This mother should be saying, "You don't have to like your brother, but I still don't want you to hit him."

Sandra is seven and comes home from her first day in school and says, "I don't like my teacher. She is a nut." Too often Mother replies, "Oh, you mustn't say that!" As a matter of fact, Sandra may be right.

SPONTANEITY IS MENTAL HEALTH IN ACTION

Why are we unable to accept the free spontaneous statements of the child? They are often correct. Spontaneity is mental health in action. Acceptance provides the child with a sense of security. Children who are secure will learn in school with a good teacher, or a poor one. Characteristic of a secure child is his inner striving to become a more complete person. Characteristic of the maladjusted child is his struggle against the mother, father, and other authority figures.

To illustrate: Johnny is an underachiever. He has a very high I.Q. but his school work is poor. He is a lovely boy with blond hair and blue eyes and inspires a rescue fantasy in his teacher. He is noticed right away and she calls him aside at the end of the day and says, "Johnny, you're such a nice boy. You have a high I.Q. and could do the work if you tried." At that moment the teacher has eliminated herself as an educative influence in the boy's life. His mother and father have too often told him the same thing. As a matter of fact, he *cannot* do the work. He cannot study. He cannot concentrate. It would be better to say, "Johnny, I don't think you can do the work. It's just hard for you." Then Johnny might have thought, "Ah, a teacher who finally understands me." At that point, this child could become educable. But his teacher doesn't do this. She talks and talks, unaware that he is the victim of that most troublesome problem of the underachiever—*he is someone with a mother who talks too much.* The mother could be a charming middle-class woman, but to Johnny, she's like this, "Get up Johnny, you'll be late for school. Johnny, don't forget to brush your teeth, Johnny. . . ," talking, talking all the time. The child feels there is nothing he can do right. And when he comes home she is still talking! Imagine what happens when the teacher talks too much as well. Remember, if we have an insecure, maladjusted child, the teacher affects this child in the same way as the mother and father have. If the child is secure and well-adjusted, he can go home and say, "Boy, this teacher is for the birds," but still learn.

Another illustration: Susan is a beautiful, bright child. She was the teacher's pet in the first grade, and in the second grade as well. But in the third grade the teacher didn't like her and Susan developed severe psychosomatic disorders (stomachaches) which required hospitalization. Careful examination revealed nothing physically wrong. I had an opportunity to get to know her teacher very well. It turned out the teacher had suffered at the hands of a very beautiful sister and, without conscious intent, was determined that the "pets" in her class would be the fat ugly children. She just couldn't like the pretty girls in her class.

Consider Jimmy, a nine-year-old, who is caught drawing a "dirty" picture. The teacher gets very excited. She rushes and tears the picture from the boy's desk. Apart from harming Jimmy, the teacher has indicated to the class that she is threatened by sexually loaded material. She rushes the boy to the principal, who also gets very excited, indicating that he, too, is threatened by the question of "Sex." Now I ask you, just what kind of "education" is this?

I have experimented with children in trying to interest them in "pornographic" literature. They were just not interested and wouldn't read it. Who are the children in the greatest danger of committing sexual crimes? Children who do not know how to read or who do not read at all. I have yet to hear an authenticated case of a child or adolescent who, because of reading pornographic material, engaged in a sexual crime. If you examine the cases of these children you find that it is the wild curiosity, the inability to gratify any of their sexual needs in any way, that is responsible. The delinquents I treat start to get better when they start to read these books—if they start to read at all. Of course, we are not supposed to say things like that. It's not nice—but it's true. I am not for pornography, but I am not going to attribute to pornography the sum total of social evil.

INSECURE TEACHERS DEMAND ORDER

Why are so many teachers overly concerned with getting order and attention? Does this hint at the insecurity of the teacher, an insecurity that resolves itself in a demand for attention, for order? Some may think that the best teachers are the strict ones who get all this wonderful discipline. But we know a child can "tune out" a strict teacher as well as a permissive one. He can learn or not learn, from either.

Consider the teacher or parent who is terribly orderly and preoccupied with cleanliness. She worries about dirt most of the time. Why project concern with dirt upon children? Have you any idea of the enormous mental health implications involved? If children feel their thoughts are dirty, their ideas dirty, and their behavior dirty, they end up feeling guilty and insecure. They are well on the road to delinquency or emotional breakdown, and eventually become the statistics of social pathology.

NO SUCH THING AS AN ABNORMAL, DIRTY THOUGHT

There is really no such thing as an abnormal or dirty thought. What a powerful impact on the mental health of our society if only more of us could convey this to our children. Thoughts of sex, of death and aggression, stem largely from the unconscious and become "abnormal" only as a child feels guilty and becomes preoccupied with them. It is not hard to teach a child the difference between behavior and fantasy. We can get him to understand that while his fantasies are free and normal, his behavior needs to be modified by social custom and a sensitive appreciation of human worth and dignity. One of our real problems is that we are so unfree in matters of sexuality. While we tend to make a big thing of parents talking to their children about sex, I wish some of these talks could be tape recorded to discover what is really conveyed to the child. In the clinics we see children of middle-class, educated families whose distortion and confusions about sex are incredible. Yet, for parents who don't know how to tell them, who say, "I just don't know what to say," there are good pamphlets and booklets. *What To Tell Your Child About Sex* is an excellent publication by the Child Study Association. It is sensible, to the point, and quite undistorted. Of course, children usually know "the facts of life" before they are told. What bothers them are their feelings, their fantasies, and parents who avoid certain direct questions. Nor should the school avoid its responsibility for sex education.

I recently taught in a well-to-do suburban school where 80 per cent of the children go on to college and the other 20 per cent seem to become lost. I thought we should offer a program for this 20 per cent, the "lost" seniors. Most of them were uneducated and unable to read above a grade five level. They were troublemakers, 17-and 18-year old seniors who would graduate because the teachers got the signal, "Let this guy through." It was agreed that I might offer them an enrichment course, an "Introduction to Psychology," where we could talk about sex, hypnosis, the unconscious, etc. But I couldn't get them to listen to me. On the first day I was greeted with, "Hi Doc, I'm the class nut, analyze me." Another one said, "Hi Doc, I run this class. Nobody teaches anything without my permission." He was a six-foot-three leading basketball player. To my relief, he said, "I'm going to have a little snooze, so you just go ahead." Soon he was snoring. I finally said, "Jimmy, how would you like me to analyze you?" He woke up. Yes, he was interested, and so were the other members of the class who cheered him on.

Improvising, I said, "Jimmy, you have difficulty with your masculinity. You're trying to prove yourself all the time." After a moment he said, "You come to the bathroom and I'll prove it." I said, "I'm not interested in your physical self but in your feelings."

Considering this statement, he replied, "Doc, in this class I'm leader and speak for the hidden feelings of everyone in it. We are the generation nobody cares about. But I will never let anybody forget us. I'll cause so much trouble that no one will be able to." The class was astonished, the whole atmosphere charged, but they all knew what he meant.

Subsequent sessions revealed that this "dumb" class was every bit as bright as the senior class going on to college. Interesting things happened. I discovered that they couldn't pay attention to any teacher because they equated learning with submission. They seemed to feel their whole personality would crumble if they gave in and tried to learn anything. They would say of their mothers, "If I gave her an inch, she'd take a mile." They were quite unable to risk themselves and said "no" to everything. This is why these teenagers couldn't learn. It was no accident.

HOW INCULCATE RESPECT FOR THE INDIVIDUAL?

The central value of democracy is respect for the individual. In school it is through our activities and behavior, rather than by intellectualization, that we communicate this respect. In this same way, we prompt children to be creative. Yet too often just the opposite approach is taken by the teacher. I recall a group of five adolescent boys in a small-town high school, easily the brightest boys in the school. They were all in the academic program, but the chances were that they would not finish high school. It was obvious that these boys were brighter than their teachers and were bored with the school situation. They frequently held wild drinking parties. They presented quite a threat to their teachers.

Now, what happens with insecure teachers? Often they say in effect, "Look, I am the teacher and I know what's right" or, "I am the teacher and you do it my way," instead of saying to boys like these, "Say, that's really interesting" or, "I didn't know you knew about this. Tell us more about it" or, "That's something I don't know very much about. Would you like to spend more time on it?" Then I reflected on what these bright young men must have said in their primary grades: "Teacher, I found another way of doing this multiplication problem," and the irritated teacher may have replied that there was no other way, or that the youngster had to do it his way. The school system so brainwashes students that when they ask their parents for help with their homework and the parents show them another way of doing it, the children just can't accept it. The parents must be wrong.

CONFORMING PARENTS CAN CRUSH CREATIVITY

How many children have had their creativity crushed by rigid and conforming parents and teachers? I shall never forget my own child, who was late in everything, late in telling colors, in walking, talking, in everything; but he was a real artist. We grabbed onto that asset and encouraged him, and from the age of three he was drawing wonderful birds with heads and tails and personalities—really charming illustrations. Then some kindergarten teacher said, "You don't know how to draw birds!" Devastated, he came home crying and said, "I am not an artist anymore."

But it works the other way too. Far more teachers do good than harm. Sometimes the teacher is the single modifying influence in the child's life. Many children we see in the clinic are much more adequate and mature than their parents. When we look into it, nine times out of ten it turns out to be a teacher who has had this effect on them. Of course even the best teachers cannot assess in advance the impact they have upon children.

A little boy of ten, Bobby, came to our clinic and showed me a composition. His teacher, wishing to encourage her children to respond, had asked them to write a composition on "What Do You Think of the Teacher?" Bobby had used the theme: "My Teacher Is a Witch." I thought I should meet this "witch." On some pretext I went down to the school. The principal said, "Oh, you're going to meet Miss Jones. She's our best and most popular teacher." And indeed she was. But she told jokes, and Bobby thought they were all on him. So you see, you can have the finest teacher in the finest school, yet still have children who cannot respond positively. These children need help over and above what the school can offer. This is the role of the mental health clinic. When the child cannot respond to the very best that can be offered by a good school, the clinic can help. But when we think that perhaps only 1 per cent of maladjusted children will be seen by the mental health clinic, we have to reconsider the relative roles of the school and the clinic.

The teacher is responsible for the kind of classroom which supports feelings of personal adequacy in children. Through his relationship with the child, he can contribute toward the development of those positive feelings toward self and others which make learning possible. Certainly the more positive the child's perception of his teacher's feelings, the higher his achievement. It may be hypothesized that the child learns what he perceives he is able to learn, and that such self-perception is acquired during during the interaction with "significant others" who hold expectations of the child as a learner. Further evidence suggests that teachers, through their role as "significant others," can enhance the self-image of their students by creating an atmosphere of greater psychological security.

Though teachers generally pride themselves upon their objectivity and lack of prejudice, they are often influenced by subtle motivational forces, difficult to evaluate. Whether the teacher produces a class climate of success or failure and rejection depends on a configuration of his own feelings, attitudes, and beliefs of adequacy. Analyzing the teacher-learner "transaction," it develops that the teacher, like the learner, brings much more to the teaching-learning situation than a knowledge and skill in presenting subject matter. First, the teacher brings a certain degree of awareness, or lack of awareness, that the teaching-learning process is basically a delicate human transaction requiring skill and sensitivity in human relations. Second, the teacher brings an awareness of his own needs and motivations, and of their consequences to the learning process.

Third, the teacher brings an ability or lack of ability to accept the learner as a person. Such acceptance connotes the ability to respect and listen, and to segregate the individual from the disagreeable aspects of his behavior.

If we as educators are to have a meaningful impact upon children, we have to get through to the child first—through to his emotional life, through to his impulse life. It is no challenge to educate those who are already well motivated. The real challenge is to get through to the unmotivated child. Perhaps as educators we can convey to children such things as "there's no hope, no fantasy, no idea, no dream that is abnormal." All hopes, all dreams, all ideas, all fantasies are normal because the unconscious represents the primitive instincts of all human beings. There is morality; there is religion; there is human behavior—but not in thinking, not in dreams. Why should we operate against dreams and thoughts? Children have ideas, death wishes, aggressive thoughts, sexual thoughts, sexual ideas. We need to be a little more liberal in responding to children's fantasies, and if we can accept them, then we don't have to make them feel so guilty. We don't have to make them feel so angry. We don't have to make them feel so sullied. We don't have to make them feel that their very lives, their very existence, their very personalities, depend on blocking out adults, blocking out educators. If the adult is more receptive, the child can repress some of these primitive ideas and thoughts, and can sublimate and utilize energy in constructive channels. But if parents and educators convey to the children that their impulses are wrong, their ideas are sinful, their fantasies are wrong, then we create the climate for emotional disorganization in adulthood.

18

Motivation: As Adolescents See It*

RUTH STRANG

Few adolescents seem to be aware of deepseated, pervasive motivations of the type that psychologists recognize. High school sophomores and seniors in their compositions on "What Makes Me Tick" or "Why Do I Believe as I Do?" tend to account for their behavior in concrete, specific terms, rather than in terms of whole personality, self-concept, or egostructure.

To understand any instance of motivated behavior, we need to know what is stimulating the individual at present, what responses he has made to similar patterns of stimulation in the past, what consequences followed, and what deprivations he has experienced. Some of them say they "just couldn't figure out why they did such a thing." However, what seems to be a spur-of-the-moment response may have deep roots in the personality. One boy described his hidden motivations in this way:

"I really don't know what it is inside me, but it seems to push me to do my work. Maybe it's a 'doer' inside me that I train. Even though I don't feel like doing my work, my doer makes me do it."

In their descriptions of "critical incidents," a sampling of 100 high school sophomores has given us glimpses of the motivation process as they see it, as well as examples of specific motivation. The following is one student's analysis of the factors that motivated her in a specific situation:

"Last summer when I decided to go to work, I didn't want to. I loved the free time when I could take walks, sew, play tennis, read, and do anything I wanted to, including wasting time. I tossed the idea around for months, before I finally decided. I knew that I had to start accepting real responsibility and conditioning myself mentally for college. I realized that I was wasting so much time every day when I could be doing something beneficial to myself as well as to others.

"My parents had always told me that I didn't know how precious the second is, and for the first time I knew what they meant. I was simply staying in my bay where I was secure. I knew it was time to start crossing the ocean where I would start at the bottom and prove my every step. I loathed the idea of not being able to call my time my own, but I went to work to prove myself to myself."

Motivations may be arranged in a hierarchy. Over all are the most persistent, pervasive, and deepseated; below these stand motivations that are, in varying degrees, comparatively temporary, extrinsic, or superficial. Let us briefly examine some of the motivations expressed by adolescents.

SELF-ACTUALIZATION

The most basic motivation of all is the deep-seated desire to develop one's potentialities, to do what one is best fitted to do, to function as well as one is capable of functioning. One chooses the activities or courses of action that seem most likely to lead to self-realization or self-actualization. Though the individual may be motivated by the observed disparity between his self-ideal and his present achievement, if this disparity is too great it may simply lead to frustration and serious maladjustment. None of the students clearly recognized this pervasive kind of motivation.

VALUE SYSTEM

Some adolescents did recognize that values and standards may motivate one's behavior. In some cases their values were crystallized in a sentence. One boy quoted President Kennedy: " 'Ask not what your country can do for you, but what you can do for your country.' " Or they may be personalized in a hero or a model: "My motivation is to someday carry on the work and ideas of the man I most admire."

Seldom did an adolescent's value system coincide with his or her desires. However, one girl stated emphatically: "I have never had to do anything important that I did not want to do. This is the truth."

One boy decided to visit a friend in the hospital instead of going to a party. He explained his decision in this way: "I knew that my visits meant a lot to him, and I was the only one besides his parents who had been to see him. Yet the thing that made me go to see him wasn't pity. It was just that when I thought about going to the party or going to the hospital, the latter seemed important."

LONG-RANGE GOALS

More specific motivations include certain long-range goals. A college education was the one most frequently mentioned, as in the following fairly typical quotation:

"I have never been good at math, not *even* mediocre. The truth is I cannot stand math, or shall I say, my inadequacy to learn it. However, it was imperative that I take one last course in math, geometry, this year. My reason for doing so was that more of the colleges I have written to would accept me more readily with this subject under my belt. Being accepted to a good college means practically everything to me. For, let us face facts—those facts that are forever drummed in our ears—you can hardly get *anywhere* in our world without a college education. So, regardless of my dislike for my geometry course and the poor grades which come with it, I *have* to stick with it."

In trying to analyze her reasons for doing her homework, one girl wrote: "I certainly don't do my homework because I like to. Although the ideal is to study because you want to learn all you can, I don't think that is my motive either. Maybe I am motivated by pride, a feeling that if I don't get good grades, I won't be able to go to college and I will disappoint not only my parents but myself."

For other adolescents, college is only a halfway house on the road to lifetime goals. This is the way one boy expressed it: "Everyone at some time has felt a desire to do a really good job and work up the ladder—to do something worthwhile in life." Another said, "I wanted to go to college and try to make something of myself."

Daily tasks and responsibilities give rise to more immediate motivations.

OTHER PEOPLE'S EXPECTATIONS

Many adolescents feel that they must achieve goals that their parents have chosen for them. They frequently mention being motivated by their parents' expectations. If the parents really love the child and want the best for him, and if the child realizes this, he will put forth effort to live up to their expectations. However, if the child feels that he is merely a means to satisfy their ambition, he may be motivated, out of resentment, to try to frustrate their hopes. This often results in self-sabotage: the child fails to develop his own potentialities.

One youngster apparently resolved to accept her parents' plan until she got to college, and then launched out on her own:

"The biggest single thing that has motivated me all my life has been a responsibility to live up to my parents' expectations and the pattern of life they set for me—getting above-average grades, participating in worthwhile activities, making friends with acceptable people, going away to college next year to prepare for a career. All this is part of the plan my parents have had since before I was born. But soon I will have fulfilled my parents' expectations and will have to turn to myself for motivation. I plan on four years, while I'm in college, to find my direction. I then want to achieve some kind of individuality and purpose in my life."

Parental expectations sometimes become compulsions. As one girl said, "My motivation is my mother. I need a very strong motivation to do what I ought to do whether I want to or not. I guess that is what mothers are for."

PERSONALITY AND CHARACTER TRAITS

Curiosity is a prime motivation at any age; unless suppressed, it persists throughout life. Curiosity not only spurs an individual to achieve; it also increases his proficiency by heightening his interest and effort. It is alarming that so few high school students mentioned a desire to know, to discover, or to explore as the motivation for studying.

In some situations adolescents mention being motivated by fear. Sometimes this fear is physical. One boy described his motivation in a dangerous mountain climbing episode as a combination of fear and necessity:

"I feel that I was motivated by fear. The odds were against me. All I could think of was how the rock had gone crashing down. I could say I did perform the feat because it was a challenge or that I was brave, etc., etc. . . . . I did it because I was scared, and at the time it seemed the only way out."

These students mentioned social fears of many types—fear of becoming involved, fear of being called "chicken," fear of failure. They less often described the motivating effect of anxiety; perhaps they did not recognize that a mild degree of anxiety facilitates learning. One may study to relieve this anxiety; relieving it becomes a goal. On the other hand, intense anxiety is inhibiting; it disrupts learning.

Some adolescents are motivated by consideration for others. This feeling is related to a value system, but its intellectual aspect is strongly reinforced by an emotional factor. One girl hated dishwashing and housecleaning. However, she wrote:

"The reason I do these things is so that my mother won't have to until she gets well. Being a mother, she feels she must do things that need to be done. So I go ahead and do them, no matter how much I hate to, so that she can get all the rest she needs."

One girl's empathy with another motivated her to go to a party she would have liked to avoid:

"The girl who invited me to her party was of a poor family, so I knew the party would not amount to much and none of my friends would be there. The night of the party I thought I would tell her I would be unable to come. I was about to call when I realized that this girl must really have wanted me to come. I thought how I would feel if I were in her place, and I felt obligated to go."

One youngster mentioned "never having learned to be rude gracefully and always feeling embarrassed when I'm impolite to anyone." Another boy broke a date he had looked forward to because his club counselor was in need of help and he was the only one who could do the job.

Adolescents are often faced with conflicting motives; their own inclinations make it hard for them to maintain consideration for others. One girl was motivated not by sympathy but by a kind of callous calculation: "I wanted to get in good with some of the popular kids and if it meant having a few really boring evenings with the dull guy who invited me, I was willing to do it."

A few youngsters admitted harboring motives that are not socially acceptable. As one said, "I am a schemer and am motivated by other feelings than kindness and sweet-little-old-lady ideals. In one instance I was motivated by pure spite with some jealousy thrown in." Another girl admitted being motivated by selfishness": "I wasn't thinking of anybody else; I was thinking only of myself."

PRAISE AND CRITICISM

The students seldom mentioned being motivated by praise or criticism from adults. This may be because praise and blame have varying effects on various individuals. Praise may stimulate one student, but reduce the effort put forth by another. Praise given by a person whom the adolescent loves and respects will make him try harder, whereas praise given by a person whom he dislikes may have the opposite effect. Lavish, indiscriminate praise soon loses its value. It is also possible for a child to become so dependent on praise that he finds little "joy in the doing."

Some individuals respond better to blame than to praise. In other cases, being ignored may be as effective as being either praised or blamed. Neither praise nor blame is of much significance unless the student understands why his performance was good or bad.

The comments or expectations of one's peers, especially in an audience situation, seem to be more potent motivating forces than adult criticism. Comments like the following may explain much adolescent behavior:

"I wanted to be one of the fellows."

"I couldn't back out with everybody looking at me, so I dived off."

"I was afraid to do it, but everybody in the class was watching me so I got up my nerve and went ahead and did it anyhow."

PREVIOUS SUCCESS AND SATISFACTION

Success is generally motivating; it leads to further success, just as failure often breeds more failure. After one or more successful experiences, a student tends to raise his level of aspiration. However, his goal must be attainable and he must see that he is making progress toward it. He also needs to understand the process by which he arrived at his correct responses, and the reasons for his mistakes.

The individual who lacks the skills he needs for a given task, such as a reading assignment, becomes discouraged, and may soon try to "leave the field"— withdraw from the situation. On the other hand, the satisfaction that comes from increased competence is motivating. Increased confidence engenders increased confidence. Any pleasant and satisfying experience tends to motivate similar behavior when the next opportunity arises.

The underachiever is not necessarily lacking in motivation. He may be directing his efforts toward the satisfaction of needs other than the need to achieve in class. "The job is somehow to convince students that academic achievement in itself fulfills a need for self-expression."[1]

One needs understanding of adolescent motivations in working with individuals who are indifferent or resistant to learning. Take George, for instance. His reading teacher recognized the importance of discovering what is and has been stimulating him, and how he has responded to this stimulation. What is really important in his life? What has he wanted and never obtained?

Since George is antagonistic to teachers, a teacher's general praise does not motivate him. On the other hand, he responds well to specific and deserved approval from both adults and peers whom he admires. Disapproval and criticism tend only to increase his antagonism and intensify his feelings of inadequacy. If one gives criticism to George, it should be specific and constructive; it should show him just how to do better. Even slight objective evidence of improvement will spur him on to more achievement. Given sufficient experience of success, he may begin to think of himself as a more competent person.

MATERIAL THINGS

Most people work to make money. Adolescents are no exception. They often stick with unpleasant jobs in order to earn the spending money for something they want. With boys, this need or desire is most often for a car. One boy described his experience in this way:

"I think the thing that kept me working six days a week, five hours a night, was that gradually my car was beginning to look nice, and I was determined to have a nice car."

Girls give up certain social events to baby-sit because, as one girl said, "Baby-sitting is my only present source of income. I certainly do not want to baby sit, but I'm forced to in order to earn necessary spending money. My motivation in this case is not avarice, but necessity."

Motivation is a complicated matter. What motivates an individual at any particular time depends upon his physical condition, his goals, his self-concept, the pulls and stresses of his environment, and many other interrelated factors.

18. NOTES

1. William P. Wharton, "Attrition in College," *Allegheny College Bulletin,* October 1965.

19

The Rural Student Speaks Out*

HORACE E. AUBERTINE

The consolidation movement continues to reduce the number of small, rural schools, but in the plain and mountain regions of our nation the combining of school districts is not always feasible. Rural communities are satisfied with the advantages the small school offers, although acknowledging that improvements could be made in some areas of education. Funds for the new buildings, books, and buses which consolidation would require are lacking, and the rural resident does not favor possible tax increases. Moreover, if schools were consolidated the more remotely located student would spend unduly long hours traveling. His participation in extracurricular activities, a major feature of the rural school, would be limited; consequently, his isolation would be increased. These are reasons to consider the rural school as a continuing part of the educational picture.

Curiosity led me to seek student judgment of the advantages and disadvantages of a rural high school education. I was able to secure thirty-five volunteer college students who had attended rural high schools enrolling three hundred students or fewer. The states of Montana, New Mexico, Colorado, Nebraska, and Kansas were represented in the study. All but two of the thirty-five respondents had attended high school during the 1960s and were commenting upon current circumstances; however, the two older participants made essentially the same statements. Each person spoke into a tape recorder in private. The question was left open-ended: No specific areas of concern were mentioned. However, all focused their view upon personal relationships, participation in athletics and extracurricular activities, close contact with teachers, range of curricula, availability of resource materials and facilities, competition and challenge within the classroom, and quality of teaching.

Almost all the students praised the cohesive personal relationships possible in the rural schools, stating that "You learn to get along and work with people other than your friends. If you don't learn this in high school it will be a hard thing to learn later." "In a smaller school you can function as a group, not as a few individuals or as a clique . . . [It is] easier to live, to identify with and understand society, and to be a better American." In schools where cliques did exist it was noted that they interacted and in schools composed of mixed ethnic populations students developed greater insight into the situation of minority groups. On the negative side, two students expressed a desire for a wider range of contact with others and a greater choice of friends.

Those who had attended both urban and rural high schools confirmed that in the smaller school community they were more aware of a sense of personal value and felt more socially fulfilled and accepted. One stated that in the urban school, "Shy students just stayed introverts most of the time, due to large classes giving no opportunity or encouragement to bring themselves out." Furthermore, urban students separate during the day, whereas in the rural school they usually stay together, know each other better, and feel more at ease. This was noted as one of the outstanding differences between large and small school classes by a boy who attended sixteen different elementary and high schools.

General participation in athletics and extracurricular activities was a point of pride among the small-school students and all agreed it strengthened the bonds of the group. Their dependence upon one another for success in common enterprises brings a sense of achievement rarely found in the larger school, where only top students take part in extracurricular activities and only top athletes represent the school in sports. One student stated that the rural pupil willing to take on the responsibility matures faster than the urban pupil who cannot participate so freely, but at the same time it is easy to take on too many activities and fall behind in school work. All students, freshmen as well as seniors, are expected to expend a great deal of effort in extracurricular endeavors. Sometimes activities provide too ready a reason to leave the classroom and excuse slips from administrators or organization sponsors are seldom questioned by teachers.

In the main, the students participating in the study are convinced that the rural school environment is ideally suited to social interaction, the establishment of self-identity, and the development of character traits of value. They also voiced almost unanimous approval of the close association they enjoyed with faculty members. The smaller-sized class is conducive to personal contact between student and teacher; they are active together in general activities and frequently the teacher is a family friend as well.

In academic matters this close relationship can be faulted, as a teacher who has instructed a pupil for a period of several years tends to take improvement for granted. Also, those students assessed as academically able seem slated to receive top grades as a matter of course, while those viewed as average or below in scholastic ability sometimes are not encouraged to advance beyond these arbitrary limits. Furthermore, although many respondents noted the advantage of individual instruction made possible by the smaller-sized class, most agreed there was a dearth of advanced instruction for the student who wished to work on special projects. Many teachers were not competent enough in subject matter to supervise special studies, or were burdened with time-consuming extraccuricular duties.

Furthermore, seldom are there enough funds to permit employment of a greater number of qualified teachers in order to offer a more diversified curriculum. Accredited rural schools offer the "basics" and most of my respondents believed themselves to be as well prepared in this realm as students from urban schools; however, many commented upon the desirability of enlargement and enrichment of English and social studies programs and the addition of business and language courses. Many rural schools are making an effort to expand the science program, but generally basic courses in chemistry, biology, physics, and mathematics are not offered or are not taught by competent science teachers. As a result, students are often allowed to study texts or perform experiments on their own or with a minimum of supervision. One student recalled that "teaching myself out of the chemistry book was not quite the way I wanted to learn chemistry, but it didn't concern me that much. However, when enrolled in the university as an engineering student, I found in my first quarter in chemistry that it made a great deal of difference. I am presently an art student and am quite happy; perhaps engineering wasn't my stick after all, but I do feel inadequate preparation in high school had a part in my change of majors."

A narrow high school curriculum can constrict a student's choice of major in college or an inadequate background can handicap him in competition, perhaps forcing him to seek other academic pastures. Those who manage to overcome poor preparation experience a period of academic struggle, not made easier by involvement with social adjustment to the larger college population.

As college students, those interviewed tend to stress high school curricula in terms of college preparation, but consideration should be given to those graduates of rural schools whose formal education terminates with completion of the twelfth grade and for whom greater range in the programs mentioned above would be equally pertinent and profitable.

Limitations in curriculum are more unfortunate when material resources are lacking and when competition and challenge within the classroom is not evident. Incomplete school and town libraries bind the student to the textbook, which in many cases is not intended to serve as a sole source of information. When specialized, advanced courses are not available and special study materials are not provided, the student is confined to the classroom situation and the more gifted find it a simple matter to stay at the top of the class. Courses of study are structured to serve the needs of the class majority rather than to expand with the interest of the able and ambitious and stimulate them to pursue further study. Furthermore, there is a gap between the scholar and the average student which very few in the latter category attempted to close. One student said that work which earned her an "A" would have been evaluated at "B" level in a larger school where more students would have challenged her for the top mark. Another commented that this lack of competition deprives all concerned, as both superior and average pupils would profit from competition. It also was observed that the top student suffers from a side effect: He does not have to learn to study to maintain a position of scholastic honor, a shortcoming some found to be a serious handicap upon entering college.

The majority regretted the lack of scholastic rivalry during the high school years; having previously praised the spirit of competition in non-academic activities, the students' concern lay in the failure of cohorts to carry this attitude into the classroom. I would suggest that the failure lies at least in part with teachers who do not quicken the classroom tempo and motivate students to fulfill their academic potential. Teachers failed to perform well in other areas too; most of the respondents were not impressed with the quality of teaching in their rural schools.

Many rural school districts contend with geographical isolation, narrowness of curricula, poor classroom and laboratory facilities, and restricted funds for salaries. These factors, combined with community rigidity on academic matters, restriction of the teacher to the textbook, and unwillingness of many school boards or principals to support teachers on matters of discipline, cause a high rate of turnover. The better teachers can secure jobs in districts not faced with such drawbacks. One student stated that newer, more enthusiastic teachers will "buck the system," but most respondents took note that such teachers come to the rural district primarily for experience and soon move away. As another said, "Quality instruction is to be had in the rural school if you happen to be there at the same time as the good teachers." Often left in the wake of departing teachers is a staff composed of some who are weak in subject matter, some who hold no degree at all, and others trained in inferior institutions. Many are employed under the tenure system and have grown too old to function adequately as teachers. Sometimes women teachers are available because their husbands work in the locality. Be they good or bad teachers, they are there. One respondent mentioned that several teachers in her school were farmers who taught in the winter as a "sort of hobby."

A related problem is that the teachers are not prepared to give good counseling service. Since rural school budgets rarely permit employment of full-time counselors, it falls to the teachers to be adept in personal counseling and to have extensive information about requirements and offerings of various colleges and universities. Many respondents commented on the limitations of counseling services and one person expressed the view that there would have been fewer dropouts in her school and more graduates continuing into college if judicious counseling had been offered.

Limited curriculum, poor resource materials, and inadequate counseling are problems in the rural school, but the major disadvantage, in the opinion of the graduates of the system, is the poor quality of teaching. It would be difficult or impossible for each small school district to correct the circumstances that cause teacher turnover, yet consolidation presents difficulties of its own, as previously noted. However, it would be possible for several small school districts covering an area of perhaps several hundred square miles to join together to create a regional center composed of five or six teachers who would be specialists in their major fields. These teachers would travel among the schools, supplementing formal instruction and providing counseling services as well. Each school would set aside time blocks during which the visiting teachers would handle advanced instruction or give direction to individual study projects, present "special interest" material, and counsel teachers as well, in order to help the pupils realize their full potential. These teachers would arrange for teacher exchanges among the schools with the idea of offering once a week (or more often) music, language, or business and vocational instruction. This group should be knowledgeable about available resource materials and special aids and could arrange for occasional guest speakers to come into the area. Also, the regional teachers could arrange for students in outlying districts to take periodic trips to the best-equipped school in the cooperative area and could arrange for use of its facilities.

Such a regional group could be started with private foundation funds, "seed money," and could be paid for in future years with combined funds from the participating schools, thus distributing the burden of payment. State or federal agencies could augment the budget as well in cases where districts could not afford to contribute towards the employment of such a group. In order to remain aloof from adverse community conditions which affect the locally based teacher, this special team would be responsible to the state department of education, an administrative agency serving all of the cooperating schools, rather than to local school administrators.

The rural citizen's decline in political representation has lessened his ability to exert influence with state or federal agencies for funds to make improvements in education. It is left to prominent persons in the field of education to strive for more equitable distribution of resources, material and human, between the urban and the rural school. Every effort should be made to raise the quality of teaching in the rural school, so that this system with its multiplicity of advantages can be maintained in the future.

Many of the rural students I interviewed are in teacher training, and some have expressed a desire to return to teach in their home communities. Here is one possibility of upgrading instruction through the recruitment and development of a pool of teachers on the basis of ability, rural upbringing, and interest in teaching in a rural environment.

There is an acute need to bring rural education into a balanced qualitative relationship with its urban counterpart, and this equalizing process must be based upon greater allocation of state and federal funds to the rural schools. But equally important is the need for imaginative and efficient use of funds allocated to rural educational improvement. The creation of a pool of trained teachers aware of the uniqueness of the problems and needs of rural communities is the final touch to any positive movement toward rural educational renaissance.

Economists contend that education is one means of developing human capital which, properly invested, leads ultimately to raising a society's standard of living. It would seem appropriate to redirect some of our human capital back to the rural communities for reinvestment. If this could be done, it would help reverse the impoverishing effects of the talent drain. It would improve the quality of rural instruction and ultimately raise the standard of living in rural areas.

20

Suburbia: A Wasteland of Disadvantaged Youth and Negligent Schools?*

JAMES A. MEYER

The time has come to include our suburbias in any comprehensive assessment of the strengths and weaknesses of American education. At least among the vast middle classes, suburban life has long been thought of as ideal and suburban educational systems as exemplary; but there is mounting evidence that even by conventional standards such is not the case. One need look no further than the suburban youth—products of our so-called social utopias—to suspect that suburban societies and their educational institutions have been overrated and underproductive.

Indeed, suburban youth can no longer be taken for granted. How can they be, considering today's frightening world of aimless youth? The average suburban teenager is often pictured as either consumed with self-pity or alienated into withdrawal from society. He is said to know it all, to be intelligent and amoral, well-mannered yet merciless, cynical in a young-old way, and oh so sophisticated. Some suburban youngsters are in flight from their own lives; others are deeply worried about what the future holds for them; and some are in revolt against their parents' suburban values.

At first glance most of our suburban youth share a common background of comfortable homes, loving parents, "good schools," high intelligence, excellent health, and almost unlimited opportunities for self-development. They have almost all the advantages that many of their mothers and fathers growing up during the Great Depression and World War II were denied. Yet many of today's middle-class suburban youngsters exhibit disturbing character qualities—sexual libertarianism, vehement rejection of adult authority, and a widespread disposition to experiment with drugs.[1]

Is the older generation really at fault? Or is this rebelling suburban generation the product of an over-permissive educational system? Are modern suburbia and its so-called cultural attributes a myth? Do the hypocrisy and callousness of suburban living really distort the values of modern youth? Unfortunately, it does seem that the tremendous reservoir of young, creative talent located in suburbia is not being cultivated in a manner essential to effective growth of democratic ideals; and there are now some real doubts emerging about the kinds of leadership suburban youth might someday contribute to our society.

SUBURBAN DEPRIVATION

Our nation's suburbias are evidently becoming so segregated that children can grow up without genuine contact with others of different racial, religious, or social backgrounds. The result is a growing provincialism in spite of ease of travel and communication. Suburbia's children are living and learning in a land of distorted values and faulty perceptions. They have only the slightest notion of others; they judge them on the basis of suburban standards (such as "cleanliness" and "niceness"), generalize about groups on the basis of the few they might have known, and think in stereotypes. In short, they usually have little association with or knowledge of people who differ in appearance or attitudes.

Dan Dodson, director of the Center for Human Relations and Community Studies at New York University, addressing himself to the problems facing youngsters living in suburban societies, declared: "In the suburbs a significant hardship on youngsters is their essential uselessness. They are 'kept' people well into their teens and often longer. There is little a youth can do to contribute to his family's wellbeing except to make top grades. But this contribution can go to a limited number only."[2]

Dodson further claims that there is considerable evidence that life in the suburbs is harder on boys than on girls. One reason is that the fathers are away from home so much of the time that their sons have only a vaguely conceptualized father-figure with which to identify.

Similarly, the values, attitudes, and behavior of older generation suburbanites are often exposed by the mass media as superficial and empty. For example, youthful critics of the middle-class suburban society vividly illustrated their rejection of suburbanite values in their acceptance of *The Graduate,* a film which devastatingly portrays the affluent, banal, swimming-pool-and-corner-bar suburban set as seen through the eyes of its youthful "hero." The chief reason this film became such a social phenomenon is, perhaps, the forlorn manner in which the protagonist copes with the phoniness of a materially comfortable contemporary society. It says something about the meaninglessness of affluent life which distorts youthful aims and ambitions. It dramatizes the generation gap, portraying a youth almost paralyzed by the rapacious hedonism of his suburbanite parents.

Some authorities suggest that this alienation of the suburban child from "others" is a recent phenomenon stemming from the unique structure of suburban life. Discussing this idea, Goldman uses the words *sidewalk* and *station wagon* as keys to understanding:

The sidewalk [once] symbolized the avenue of communication between one child and another. In many areas this has vanished. . . . Sidewalks are no longer built . . . in some suburban housing developments. The response to the disappearing sidewalk is the mother-driven station wagon. Instead of relying upon informal mingling of children, the image of the station wagon implies a planned, structured mingling of children: the Boy Scout meeting at 7:30, the Little League game at 4:00, the music lesson at 5:00, etc. What is gained by structuring common activities for children may be lost by some of the concomitant results—the loss of spontaneity when games and recreation must be carefully scheduled and supervised, the early creation of the "organization man," etc. The increased number of nursery schools is part of the same response to the deprivation of young children.[3]

Other critics of contemporary suburban life have asserted that parents in suburbia pamper and spoil their children to such an extent that the children grow up without any real parental supervision. Halleck has declared that "some parents in suburbia have, through painstaking efforts to avoid creating neuroses in their children, abdicated their responsibility to teach and discipline their children. In so doing they have reared a generation of spoiled, greedy youth who are unable to tolerate the slightest frustration without showing an angry or infantile response."[4]

On the other hand, many critics put the blame for youthful unrest in suburbia on the way the children are overprotected and parentally dominated. This goes beyond an overabundance of material things. Rather, it consists of parental hovering and a reluctance to let their youngsters assume self-responsibility and self-direction. Perhaps some suburban parents fear their children will make mistakes and embarrass them. In any case, from an early age many suburban children are given little opportunity to use their own resources and make appropriate decisions.

Obviously, both extremes are unhealthy and undoubtedly contribute greatly to the restlessness and antisocial behavior patterns of rebelling suburban youth.

Of one thing we are sure, and that is that parental influence over suburban youth has deteriorated markedly; and children are cheated and deprived of experiences essential for effective development of wholesome ideals and attitudes. Unless more authentic human values are developed within our suburbias, the suburban style of life will significantly contribute to the further deprivation of suburban youth. While little can be done about the attitudes and values inherited from parents, the schools still have the opportunity to reach these restless youth and redirect their energies. But first the challenge must be recognized.

SCHOOLS SHARE THE BLAME

"Suburban children are underprivileged. . . . There is little in their education, formal or otherwise, to familiarize them with the rich diversity of American life." This judgment by Alice Miel in *The Shortchanged Children of Suburbia*[5] grew out of a series of research studies designed to explore life in suburbia and to determine what is being taught about human differences in our schools. Her findings were alarming and resulted in a sharp indictment of the suburban school for failure to do something about preparing suburban children for a healthy, wholesome life in our society.

The results of this study indicate that:

> The typical suburban elementary school student's life is almost totally insulated and circumscribed.
>
> Suburban youngsters learn, individually, to be bigoted and hypocritical about racial, religious, economic, and ethnic differences at an early age.
>
> Group prejudices, too, take root early—and go deep.
>
> Materialism, selfishness, misplaced aggression, fake values, and anxiety top the list of common characteristics.

Yet many educators today are neither adequately trained nor perceptive enough to cope with the problems experienced by adolescents growing up in our affluent suburbs, and these inadequacies of staff hamper efforts to provide compensatory treatment.

For example, on the basis of some recent career pattern studies, it is now estimated that about 85 out of every 100 secondary school teachers in our suburban schools are from family backgrounds that differ markedly from those of the majority of the students in their classrooms. These teachers are said to undergo an emotional trauma when teaching suburban pupils. Problems of adaptation and adjustment are many. Faced with an "affluence" and "sophistication" (as doubtful as it may be) that they themselves might never have experienced, teachers in suburbia often expect and accept different standards of behavior. It stands to reason that by condoning these unique standards of behavior, teachers must bear some responsibility for the distorted values and attitudes as well as the antisocial behavior patterns often displayed by suburban youth.

Not only are some suburban educators not emotionally equipped to teach suburban youth—they may not be intellectually equipped either. "Many secondary school teachers have lower I.Q.'s than those of the suburban children they teach." This is what S. Alan Cohen of Yeshiva University said about suburban educators when he suggested that:

> These teachers are unable to challenge their better students because they are afraid to. Many teachers are terrorized by the intellectual precocity of middle-class children. As a result, they cling tenaciously to rigid, lock-step pedagogies and mediocre materials to hold down the natural flow of intellectual curiosity.[6]

In asserting that suburban middle-class schools are not providing as good an education as they should, critic Cohen cites the growing evidence of educational inadequacy—the irrelevancy of curriculum content and the poor pedagogy—and concludes that superior test performances of children from "Scarsdales" tend to reflect the enriched verbal home environments rather than the school's educational program. "As a result," says Cohen, "the weak content and pedagogy in the middle-class schools are good enough, or perhaps more accurately, not bad enough to ruin these children."

Disappointingly enough, there are reports that school guidance counselors also experience difficulties when counseling in suburban schools. College counseling, for example, is theoretically only part of the total guidance function in secondary education. But in suburbia, college counseling becomes a major item of responsibility, and the counselor must become a master at it. Indeed, in the wealthy suburbs, where the citizenry have the money and desperately want to send their children to "good" colleges, they generally perceive counseling in "college" terms. Irvin Faust, a suburban counselor, has written that:

> The trouble with most college-oriented communities and the counselors they hire is that college placement rather than welfare of students proves the guidance program; it becomes the total force rather than the natural result of a developmental counseling experience. . . . Whatever else arises is subordinate. He's awash in the suburban syndrome that says it's worse not to get into college than to flunk out. And it's worse not to get into a particular college, or colleges, for collecting acceptances is part of the game.[7]

Suburban youths themselves have become progressively more sensitive to the lack of substance and meaning in the curriculum of their schools and are voicing strong concerns over the lack of relevancy. Many suburban youngsters, for example, are now said to be articulate, irreverent, humorless, and relentless in their contempt for what they honestly view as the meaninglessness of suburban education. They turn to one another when shaping beliefs or seeking advice, for they have learned to distrust both their parents and their teachers.

For some time now, the attentions and interests of most educators have been directed toward the educational problems relative to urban conditions of life. Recently, however, some concern has been given to shortcomings in rural education. But only little concern has been shown toward the possible needs of suburban youth, and the thought of any possible weakness in the education of suburbia's children has been virtually nonexistent. But the cultural circumstances of the suburbs are alive with challenges to the schools. Without compensatory approaches in the educational program, the suburban schools will fall far short of achieving the high purposes they are expected to achieve.

COMPENSATORY PROGRAMS

Occasionally school officials and boards of education in affluent suburban communities are perceptive enough to grasp the defects of contemporary suburban life and commit themselves to some form of action. There have been some noteworthy attempts to revitalize the suburban curriculum and bring meaning and substance to instruction. One major illustration of this is the growing tendency among suburban schools to emphasize a human relations approach to instruction in the classroom.

Indeed, human relations programs hold promise for the future of suburban youngsters. Without instruction relative to the human environment in the suburban schools, many suburban youngsters will grow up with little chance for wholesome personal development. But setbacks do occur. In one well-known Buffalo suburban community—Williamsville, New York—the board of education backed away from a regional Title III project which would have sent a corps of teachers into its schools to improve instruction in human relations. The reason? A band of more than 100 citizens opposed the program, claiming "it would interfere with parents' lessons in human relations." A sad day for Williamsville.

There are other programs suburban educators might seriously consider introducing in their schools if they would wish to see their students overcome the restrictive aspects of suburban life. Examples include:

Instruction about different groups and cultures which could help eliminate prejudices and misconceptions about others. Personal experience with children of other groups can show a disadvantaged suburban youth directly, immediately, and concretely that not all members of a different group are "stupid, dirty, or dishonest." Suburban youths need supplementary reality experiences to make it possible for them to "see" society as it really is so that they may develop the empathy and compassion essential for the development of wholesome values and attitudes.

More social, interscholastic, and subject-matter club activities in order to involve students in meaningful intergroup situations. Service clubs and school-community organizations serve as a very useful vehicle in relating the schooling process to community needs while restoring a sense of personal worth for our troubled suburban youth.

Suburban schools should actively assist in fostering a return of the "family unit" by encouraging child-parent attendance at school functions. Rather than tolerate parental isolation, the suburban schools must assist in creating a climate conducive to close family ties through school-centered activities, attempting primarily to entice fathers to share in these school events with their children.

The schools of suburbia must expand the counseling staff at both the secondary and elementary levels. Individual and group counseling is imperative—especially in the elementary grades when attitudes are still malleable. After-school counseling with parents also seems essential, in view of the alarming increase in family conflicts occurring within the suburban communities.

A major factor—perhaps the most important one—in providing suburban youth with direction and eliminating youthful prejudices is that of teacher attitudes. Suburban educators must teach suburban youth with warmth, respect, and understanding. This, however, can only follow self-examination and insightful knowledge of the problems and pressures experienced by suburban youth. The attitudes of teachers about themselves and their relationships with and responsibilities to the suburban disadvantaged must first be clarified through in-service programs. Suburban teachers must develop a more comprehensive understanding of the nature of suburban life and its inherent defects.

The schools should involve students more deeply in the task of teaching and curriculum construction, thereby serving two purposes: (1) determining just what aspects of the curriculum are indeed relevant from the student's point of view, and (2) improving the sense of worth of the student through responsible participation in the educational process. Why not have students contribute their views through the previewing of audio or visual materials; through examination of textbooks, library books, and other resource materials; through assisting in the instruction of slower or retarded children; through assuming leadership responsibilities in discussion groups and seminars? Why not delegate to the students more responsibility in designing school codes of conduct; supervision of study, library, or lunch areas; and enforcement of school discipline? Much could be gained—both by the schools and the students.

The defects of suburban society and the misconceptions brought by suburban students to the schools remain serious obstacles in the path of social progress. If the people of the suburbs—including suburbia's educators—would have their children grow up to respect all men and to seek for others the same scope of opportunity available to themselves, it is imperative that the suburban schools help develop the understandings and attitudes essential for constructive citizenship. Otherwise, the American Dream becomes the American Tragedy, and alienation and isolation become even more a way of life for youth trapped in their suburban environment.

20. NOTES

1. Yet Kenneth Keniston in *Notes on Committed Youth* (New York: Harcourt, Brace and World, 1968) asserts that these young radicals are unusually "healthy" youth who have solved their psychological problems to a higher degree than most and have achieved "an unusual degree of psychological integration."

2. Dan Dodson, "Are We Segregating Our Children?" *Parents' Magazine,* September 1963.

3. Louis Goldman, "Varieties of Alienation and Educational Responses," *Teachers College Record,* January 1968, pp. 331-44; Charles H. Harrison, "In the Suburbs," *Education News,* September 1968, pp. 15, 19.

4. S. L. Halleck, "Hypotheses of Student Unrest," *Phi Delta Kappan,* September 1968, pp. 2-9.

5. Alice Miel and Edwin Kieste, *The Shortchanged Children of Suburbia* (New York: Institute of Human Relations Press, American Jewish Committee, 1967).

6. S. Alan Cohen, "Local Control and the Cultural Deprivation Fallacy," *Phi Delta Kappan,* January 1969, pp. 255-59.

7. Irvin Faust, "Guidance Counseling in Suburbia," *Teachers College Record,* February 1968, pp. 449-58.

21

American Indians and White People*

ROSALIE H. WAX and ROBERT K. THOMAS

As the Hughes have pointed out, when people come into troublesome contact with each other, popular and scholarly attention is usually focused on only one of them. Thus the relationship between Indians and the persons of European extraction, known as whites, is commonly termed the "Indian Problem." While these authors agree that such emphasis is natural, they call attention to the fact that the unit of racial or ethnic relations is no single people, but the situation: the frontier of contact of the two or more peoples inhabiting a community or region.[1]

This paper is an attempt to describe one of the more intimate aspects of just such a frontier situation: namely, what happens when American Indians and white people meet in the course of their day-to-day activities and try to communicate with each other. It does not attempt to define the major areas of difference between Indian and white American culture or personality, nor does it discuss the major reasons for conflict and hostility between the two, but rather tries to explain how and why they find talking to each other difficult. It is, therefore, directed as much to the Indian as to the white reader.

We are aware that there are significant differences in behavior and personality among the various kinds of Indians and, likewise, among the various kinds of white men, and that interesting exceptions may possibly be found to all of our generalizations. Nevertheless, our observations have convinced us that most white men who live in the United States share ideas and practices about proper behavior that are very different from those shared by most Indians.

Social discourse is one of the areas where Indians and whites most easily misunderstand each other. Placed in an informal social gathering, such as a small party where he knows only the host, the Indian will usually sit or stand quietly, saying nothing and seeming to do nothing. He may do this so naturally that he disappears into the background, merging with the wall fixtures. If addressed directly, he will not look at the speaker; there may be considerable delay before a reply, and this may be pitched so softly as to be below the hearing threshold of

*Copyright 1961 by Atlanta University. Reprinted by permission of the publisher from *Phylon: The Atlanta University Review of Race and Culture* XXII, No. 4 (Winter 1961), pp. 305-17.

the white interlocutor; he may even look deliberately away and give no response at all.

In this same situation, the white man will often become undiscourageably loquacious. A silent neighbor will be peppered with small shop talk in the hope that one of the rounds will trigger an exchange and a conversational engagement. If the neighbor happens to be an Indian, his protracted silence will spur the white to ever more extreme exertions; and the more frantic the one becomes, the less likely he is to elicit a response from the other.

Ironically, both parties are trying hard to establish communication and good feeling. But, like Aesop's would-be friends the crane and the fox, each employs devices that puzzle, alienate, and sometimes anger the other.

From childhood, white people and Indians are brought up to react to strange and dangerous situations in quite different ways. The white man who finds himself in an unstructured, anxiety-provoking situation is trained to react with a great deal of activity. He will begin action after action until he either structures the situation, or escapes from it, or simply collapses. But the Indian, put in the same place, is brought up to remain motionless and watch. Outwardly, he appears to freeze. Inwardly, he is using all of his senses to discover what is expected of him—what activities are proper, seemly, and safe. One might put it this way: in an unfamiliar situation a white man is taught to react by aggressive experimentation—he keeps moving until he finds a satisfactory pattern. His motto is "Try and try again." But the Indian puts his faith in observation. He waits and watches until the other actors show him the correct pattern.

Once he has picked up the cues and feels relatively certain that he can accomplish what is expected, the Indian may respond with a sudden energy and enthusiasm that can bewilder his white partners. For example, at a party given for a group of Indian college students by the white members of a faculty, the Indian students sat and said virtually nothing. The faculty members did their best to draw out their expressionless and noncommittal guests. Even the stock questions of school and educational plans brought little response. At length, in desperation, the faculty members talked to each other.

After refreshments were served the party broke into small clusters of guests, and in each cluster an Indian student did most of the talking. He delivered a modest but well-organized address describing his educational plans. From questions put to him, each had concluded that his role at the party was to paint his academic future. When opportunity offered, he gave the faculty members exactly what he thought they wanted.

The active, experimenting disposition of many white men and the motionless alertness of Indians may be related to different cultural attitudes toward what white people call success or failure. Indian friends tell us that they do not praise or reward their children for doing what is proper or right; they are expected to behave well, for this is "natural" or "normal". Thus a "good" Indian child reflects no social credit on himself or on his parents. He is simply behaving as the child of his people should behave.[2] On the other hand, the "bad" or ill-intentioned child is censured and the child who makes mistakes is shamed, which, in an Indian community, is a grave punishment. As one sophisticated Indian remarked: "As a result of the way they are raised, very few Indians will try to do something at which they're not good [adept]. It takes a lot of courage."

As an example he cited a phenomenon, common in his tribe, of men gathering to help a relative build a house:

"You watch a housebuilding among my people. You see some men struggling with the work of erecting the structure, and over there, sitting on the grass, may be a man just watching, never lending a hand, even with the heaviest work. They get the structure up, and all of a sudden there's that man on the roof, working away, laying shingle—because what he knows how to do is lay shingle. All these men that were there are kin come to help with the housebuilding, but each person only offers his assistance in what he knows he can do."

He also reminded us of how an Indian girl who had been making tortillas at a picnic immediately stopped when two highly skilled girls began to help her. She excused herself and disappeared. But a white girl who knew nothing of Indian cookery pitched in and was quite unembarrassed by her lack of skill.

Many other examples of the Indians' reluctance to exhibit clumsiness or ineptitude before others appear in the literature. For example, Nash relates how a Maya girl learns to operate weaving or spinning machines in a factory by silently observing the operator. Only when she feels competent will the observer take over and run the machine.

"She will not try her hand until she feels competent, for to fumble and make mistakes is a cause for *verguenza*—public shame. She does not ask questions because that would annoy the person teaching her, and they might also think she is stupid."[3]

Gordon Macgregor mentions that an Indian school track team was reluctant to run because they knew they could not win, and a basketball team did not want their parents and neighbors to come to an interschool game for fear they would laugh at their mistakes and failure to win.

Perhaps it will be reassuring to the Indian to realize that the reckless torrents of words poured out by white people are usually intended as friendly, or at least social, gestures. The more ill at ease a white man becomes, the more he is likely to talk. He is not nearly so afraid of making mistakes as is the Indian and it is almost impossible (by Indian standards) to embarrass or "shame" him. By the same token, he will rarely hold an Indian's mistakes against him. Conversely, the white person who has had little experience in talking with Indians should find it heartening to know that the silence and downcast eyes with which the first conversational gambits may be received spring from shyness and, often, from courtesy. He is not being snubbed or ignored; on the contrary, his words and actions are being observed with minute care. Once the Indian has discovered what his response ought to be, he will make it. This may take a little time, but the person who is not willing to spend a little time ought not to try to talk to Indians.

The oversensitive white man may take comfort in the fact that the Indian who wishes to insult him will generally make his intentions quite clear. The Indian who looks away when you address him is being considerate—to stare into your face might embarrass you. But the Indian who treats you as if you were invisible is putting you beneath the notice of a highly observant man.

In every human relationship there is some element of influence, interference, or downright compulsion. The white man has been and is torn between two ideals: on one hand, he believes in freedom, to mind his own business, to make up his own mind; but, on the other hand, he believes that he should be his brother's keeper and not abstain from advice, or even action, when his brother is speeding down the road toward perdition, death, or social isolation due to halitosis. The Indian society is unequivocal: interference of any form is forbidden, regardless of the folly, irresponsibility, or ignorance of your brother.

Consequently, when the white man is motivated as his brother's keeper, which is most of the time when he is dealing with Indians, he rarely says or does anything that does not sound rude or even hostile to the latter. The white, imbued with a sense of righteousness in "helping the downtrodden and backward," does not realize the nature of his conduct, and the Indian cannot tell him, for that in itself would be "interference" with the white's freedom to act as he sees fit.

In a general sense, coercion has been and is a fundamental element in the social orders of the Western world. Social theorists have characterized the state as that national institution that effectively claims the legitimate monopoly of violence. Lesser institutions utilize a variety of corporeal and spiritual sanctions to effect cooperative action, and the economy prides itself on utilizing the lash of need and the lure of wealth. These characteristics of Western social structure have stimulated the more idealistic to the proposal of new communities in which the elimination of brute compulsion would ensure the release of the creative energies of man; but so deeply entrenched is this system of hierarchical organization that these are ridiculed as "utopian." In contrast, many of the Indian societies were organized on principles that relied to a great extent on voluntary cooperation and lacked the military or other coercive instrumentalities of the European.

Recent years have seen a marked shift in the general American social patterns. The use of physical violence has been curtailed and the emphasis has shifted toward verbal manipulation; this has been evident in such diverse areas as the armed services, business corporations, educational institutions, and the family. Educational movies shown to children at school impress them with the fact that the admirable leader is the boy or girl who can "get other children to do what he [the leader] wants them to do." Children are taught by parents and playmates that their success in most areas of life will depend on their skill as an influence on or manipulator of others. Thus white children begin to practice influencing other people very early in life and they conscientiously try to improve their skills, if we may judge by the letters sent to columnists asking for advice on how to get parents, dates, spouses, or children to do things that (one assumes) these parents, dates, spouses, or children are not particularly eager to do.

This ability is justly valued by the white people since a great deal of modern industrial and organizational work could not be carried on without it. For example, an office manager or foreman finds himself in charge of a group of people of different religious and ethnic backgrounds, different ages and temperaments, and widely varying moral and ethical views. If he is going to get the job done he must find some way of getting all of these folk to work together and he does this by being an extraordinary flexible, agreeable, and persuasive influencer.

Perhaps because these "human relations skills" are a social replacement for physical force, white people tend to be insensitive to the simple fact that they are still interpersonally coercive. The "nondirective" teacher still wants the children to work as a group and on the project for which she has the materials and the skills. Similarly, the would-be hostess who will not listen to an excuse and interprets a refusal as a personal affront may not realize she is forcing her guests to do what they do not wish to do. Even when white people do not wish to accomplish some end, their conversational patterns are structured along coercive lines. Thus, at a casual party, the man who remarks that he plans to buy a pear tree may anticipate that someone will immediately suggest that he buy a peach tree instead. If he remarks that he is shopping for a new car, someone will be happy to tell him exactly what kind of a car he ought to buy. The same thing happens if he ventures an opinion about music or politics. Someone is bound to inform him (in a friendly way, of course) that he ought to be listening to, reading, or attending something for which he has no particular inclination. Perhaps these patterns of conversation entertain white people because they play with the forms that are so serious in their society. The man who can out-advise the other is "one-up," and the loser is expected to take his defeat with good grace.

The Indian defines all of the above behavior, from the gentlest manipulation to the most egregious meddling, as outside the area of proper action. From earliest childhood he is trained to regard absolute noninterference in interpersonal relations as decent or normal and to react to even the mildest coercion in these areas with bewildermen, disgust, and fear.

Though most sensitive white persons who have lived with Indians are aware of this phenomenon, we have found none that have successfully described it in general terms. Under these circumstances it might be wise to follow the Indian pattern of communication and describe the Indian "ethic of noninterference" by examples.

One of the more spectacular examples is the behavior of Indian passengers in an automobile. If the car is the property of the driver, no passenger ever considers giving him suggestions or directions. Even though a rock slide or a wandering steer may have blocked the right of way, no one says a word. To do so would be "interference." In consequence, accidents can occur which might have been prevented had any one of several passengers chosen to direct the attention of the driver to the hazard or obstacle. As the car rolls merrily into the ditch, all that may be heard is a quiet exhalation of breath.

An example of this "ethic" was noted over thirty years ago among the Pit River Indians of California and recorded by Jaime de Angulo:

"I have heard Indians say: 'That's not right what he's doing, that fellow. . . .' 'What d'you mean it's not right?' 'Well . . . you ain't supposed to do things that way . . . it never was done that way . . . there'll be trouble.' 'Then why don't you stop him?' 'Stop him? How can I stop him? It's his way.' "[4]

A more personal example was given by an Indian friend. The friend was living with his wife's family and customarily drove to work every morning. One morning at breakfast he noticed that his sister-in-law, Mary, had dressed up as if she were going to town. Curious, he asked his wife, "Is Mary going any place?" "Oh yes," said his wife, "she's going to Phoenix." "Does she have a lift to the bus station?" asked our friend. "No," said his wife. Our friend then asked his sister-in-law if she would like him to give her a lift on his way to work and she accepted. After driving for some time, our friend suddenly became aware of the fact that he had automatically driven directly to work, passing right by the bus station without stopping. His sister-in-law was calmly looking out of the window. She had made no comment when he overshot the bus station and she made none now. Without a word, he turned the car around and took her to the bus station.

Characteristic Indian "noninterference" was shown by Mary, not only when she did not comment on the fact that her brother-in-law was passing the bus station, but also in her behavior before they set out. To have asked her brother-in-law to take her to the bus station would have constituted an indelicate attempt to influence him. Perhaps he would not wish to take her with him. By asking him she might "force" him to refuse and thus cause him embarrassment and discomfort. Again, if he took her unwillingly he would feel resentment toward her. By dressing up she could communicate her desires in a way that he could accept or reject without arousing any "bad feelings". That is, he could invite her to go along or he could "be occupied" and go without her.

Great delicacy and sensitivity of feeling are essential to even a moderate standard of Indian good manners. If one is extending invitations to a get-together one does not urge people to come; such urging would be "interfering," for if they wish to come they will come. Again, under ordinary circumstances, one does not address another human being unless he has given some indication that he is willing to give you his attention. Thus if one wishes to begin a conversation, even with a spouse, or relative, one first puts oneself in his line of vision. If he does not acknowledge your presence this is a sign that he is occupied and you wait or go away. To address him while he is talking to someone else or meditating would be gross interference. If one is talking with a friend and he unwittingly brings up a delicate or painful subject, one lets him know this by pretending not to hear, by looking away, or by changing the subject. Most Indians follow these rules of etiquette unconsciously. Even so-called assimilated Indians follow them in part, and are not aware that they do so.

A profound respect for the interests, occupations, and responsibilities of other human beings begins to show itself even in the very young Indian child. We have, for example, conversed with Indian parents for hours while half a dozen children played around us, and not once did any of the children address a word to us. A little girl of three or four might leave the playgroup for a while and lean against an adult relative or sit in a lap. But only in a grave emergency did she try to attract the attention of an adult and even then she tried not to interrupt what they were doing. Thus if a bold child wanted to know if it might have a piece of the watermelon that an adult was cutting, it might creep up and whisper into its mother's ear.

We have asked a number of Indians how it is that even very young children do not bother older people. We are usually told something like this: "When I think about it, I see you're right. We never did bother grown-up people when I was a kid. It's funny because I can't remember that anybody said anything to us about it. We just didn't do it."

Such statements suggest that the Indian child is taught very early not to interfere with or bother older people who are otherwise occupied and that both instruction and learning may proceed on a subconscious level. Indeed, we have noticed that even little toddlers do not make the loud and vigorous attempts to monopolize their parent's attention which are characteristic of so many white infants.

Since the human infant must be taught to demand the attention of its parents, and since Indian parents simply do not respond to "interfering" demand, it is possible that many Indian infants never learn some of the coercive and aggressive oral and verbal techniques available to children in other cultures. We do not suggest that Indian children lack aggression, but rather that their culture gives them virtually no opportunity to express it by interfering with the activities of others. On the other hand, they are taught consideration through the example of their elders, for Indian adults consistently treat children with the same respect they expect for themselves. To interrupt a child at play, or force it to do something against its will but "for its own good," are contrary to all precepts of Indian child-rearing. Indeed, Erickson tells of an Indian man reared by whites who felt that his wife ought to forbid his children to use profanity. His wife, reared as an Indian, regarded her husband's interfering attitude as evidence that he was sick in mind.

Indians rarely discipline their children in a fashion noticeable to white persons. In the few cases where Rosalie Wax has seen an Indian child punished, parental disapproval was directed against "interference." In one case an Indian boy of about six who had played a great deal with white children repeatedly interrupted a conversation between Indian elders. At first he was ignored or gently set aside. When after five or six rejections he was still persisting, his father addressed him directly: "Son," he said, "you're making it hard for all of us." This boy's father says regretfully that he thinks his son will grow up to be a white man. "When my wife or I show disapproval, it no longer makes any impression on him. He behaves just like the white boys he plays with."

In another case R. Wax was engaged in a conversation with an Indian man. His wife, a woman of notorious impatience, wished to go home. Not venturing to intrude herself, she sent her five-year-old daughter to tell papa to come home. Papa, though very fond of his little girl, behaved as if he neither saw nor heard her. I noticed that the child was very distressed and frightened, but I did not realize at this time how severely her father was rebuking her.

By this time some non-Indian readers may have concluded that the upbringing of Indian children must be harsh indeed and that the little tykes creep through their days behind a wall of silence created by adults. Nothing, of course, could be farther from the truth. Indian parents are by no means "busy" all the time, and when they are unoccupied they like nothing better than to coddle, play with, and talk to little children. Moreover, when an Indian gives anyone, child or adult, his attention, he gives all of it. Thus when he is interacting with an adult, the child is not only treated with the warmth and indulgence noted by so many observers, but is given an attention that is absolute. As we have already noted, this intense concentration on the emotional and intellectual overtones of a personal relationship also characterizes adult interaction. Thus there really is no such thing as a casual or dilatory conversation between Indians. If they are not *en rapport* they are worlds apart; if they are giving their attention, they use every sense to the utmost.

As we have noted, the first impulse of an Indian who encounters an interferer (with whom he is on terms of friendship) is to withdraw his attention. If the ill-mannered person does not take the hint, the Indian will quietly go away. If it is impossible for him to leave, he does his best to make himself inconspicuous. By disappearing he avoids provoking the disturbed individual to further outbursts and also avoids embarrassing him by being a witness to his improper behavior. Simultaneously he rebukes him in a socially sanctioned manner. In the past an entire community might withdraw from an incorrigible meddler and leave him quite alone.

Perhaps because these social sanctions are usually effective in an Indian community, Indians have not yet developed devices for dealing with an interferer who claims to be peaceable but aggressively refuses to permit them to withdraw. They can only marvel at his bizarre behavior and wish that he would go away. Sometimes, when prodded past endurance, Indian women will lose their self-control and try to drive out intruders with harsh words and even physical force.

Since the white man from infancy has been encouraged to defend himself and "face up" to unpleasant things, he almost invariably interprets the Indians' withdrawal from his verbal "attacks" not as an unostentatious rebuke but as evidence of timidity, irresponsibility, or even as a tendency to "flee from reality." This Indian trait more than any other seems to baffle the white man, for though the white man has been exposed to Christian doctrine for many, many centuries, he still cannot begin to understand the man who will not fight back.

We regret that some social scientists are among the least perceptive persons in this particular matter. (Perhaps their training makes them overprone to equate a disappearing informant with personal failure.) For example, we have seen a social scientist of some repute attempt to initiate a discussion with Indians by suggesting that they no longer possessed any culture of their own but were unrealistically clinging to an impoverished "reservation" culture. What they ought to do, he went on to say, was to leave the reservation and become assimilated. When this remark was received in expressionless silence, the scientist suggested that this "lack of response" supported his point, for no one present had been able to defend the existence of their culture. The faces of the Indians became even more impassive, but the scientist did not notice that the feet and legs of some of the young men from the Plains tribes had begun to tremble as with the ague. A white person in the audience could no longer control his impulse to interfere, and in the ensuing debate much of the Indians' tension was dissipated.

On another occasion a psychiatrist whose initial overtures had been observed in silence by his Indian audience began to prod them with remarks intended to arouse their anger. The Indian men, as usual, made themselves inconspicuous. A few stole out of the meeting. But some of the women lost their tempers and the session ended in a loud and rather vulgar brawl.

After these incidents we talked with both the white and the Indian participants. Both of the social scientists assured us that they had merely been trying to elicit a response from the Indians, and the second one seemed naively pleased with the "discovery" that "they'll only react if you get them mad." The Indians seemed to feel that it was best to ignore the whole thing. As one older man remarked, "You do not take the words of an insane person seriously or get angry at him."

The reader, by now, may be able to appreciate the blunt truth of a statement made by a middle-aged Apache who was attending a college class on the behavior of ethnic groups. Hoping to stimulate a discussion of accommodation and assimilation, the instructor asked, "What develops when two different peoples meet?" Laconically the Apache replied, "Bad feelings."

One cannot examine a situation as distressing as the Indian and white frontier of sociable contact without wondering what might be done to make it less painful for both parties. To tell most white people that they can get along with the Indians fairly well if they do not interfere is almost like telling them to give up breathing. It is, perhaps, equally difficult for an Indian to appreciate that the "mean" and "crazy" deeds of the white men do not necessarily have the same significance as the mean or crazy deeds of an Indian.

We have noted that there is less tension and distress in those situations in which the atmosphere of power and authority in which the Indian and the white man usually meet is mitigated or absent. Thus the white man often finds it easier to get along with the Indian when he is gambling, trading, partying, or simply "chewing the rag." This is because they represent some of the few remaining social situations in which the white man cannot always immediately assume an authoritative or interfering role. In such situations the Indian learns to make allowances for or take advantage of the white man's restlessness, his incomprehensible "pride," and his reckless "courage." The white man, for his part, learns to accomodate himself to the slow pace, sudden temperamental outbursts, and unexpected disappearances of the Indian.

We have noted that most white people who have a tolerably good relationship with Indians consciously or unconsciously subscribe to the notion that white men ought to keep their noses out of Indian matters. However else they may behave seems to make little difference. Thus one of the finest field workers known to us is an anthropologist of so gentle and unaggressive a nature that one sometimes wonders how he can maintain himself in the modern world. When he is in the field, the Indians spend a good deal of their time seeing that he comes to no harm. Another white man has no tact at all and breaks some rule of Indian decorum in almost every sentence he utters. Both men, however, subscribe to noninterference in Indian matters and both are admired and liked by Indians.

On the matter of interaction between groups composed of both Indians and whites, we have noted that "good feelings" are more likely to arise when the situation is clearly defined as one of contact. By this we mean that the participants from both groups come to realize that they are interacting in an entirely new situation, alien to both, and that their comfort, enjoyment, and accomplishment will depend on their ingenuity in inventing new forms and rules applicable to this new situation.

It is remarkable how rapidly and spontaneously new social forms comfortable to both parties may be defined, provided that both parties strongly desire to act or play together. We were, for example, unable to accomplish much in the Workshop on American Indian Affairs until we redefined the teaching-learning situation, and we were obliged to do that before we could participate in picnics and dances at which both white people and Indians could have a good time. It is possible that such "accommodating" contact situations are established more frequently than social scientists realize. Their recognition and study might help to throw light on problems of great importance.

We are aware that we have presented a picture and analysis of Indian child-rearing practices not entirely compatible with those of certain other observers. However, we think that the significant differences are quantitative rather than qualitative and rest on the fact that we emphasize what other scholars have overlooked.

We agree with Dorothy Lee that it is misleading to call Indian child-rearing practices "permissive" or "indulgent." It might be more accurate to say that it usually does not occur to Indian parents to permit or forbid their children to do anything, much less permit or forbid them to move their bowels. White parents, on the other hand, see themselves as "permitters" and "forbidders." Nevertheless, from the Indian point of view, they leave vast and very important areas of their children's behavior completely unstructured. Thus one might suggest that in both cultures parents and elders subject infants and children to an intensive and careful training, but that they use very different methods and emphasize very different skills.

Again, we believe that Erikson has overlooked something very important when he depicts Sioux upbringing as one in which the child is introduced to social discipline "in the form of a tradition of unrelenting public opinion" only after an infancy in which he "is allowed to be an individualist" and is subject to no frustration of impulse.

According to our observations, Sioux and other Indians begin to train their children to be highly sensitive social beings long before they can talk, and perhaps even before the age when white infants are subjected to oral and anal frustrations. Here we again agree with Lee in the view that Indian training in social sensitivity and in respect for others begins at birth and apparently is reinforced with every interpersonal experience.

Perhaps, on occasion, too intense a focus on a formidable theoretical framework may serve to blur important aspects of the phenomena one intends to observe. This may be especially so with an alien culture. Thus a people who do not practice the classic Freudian instinctual disciplines may be characterized as lacking in discipline, whereas the fact that they may practice a kind of subliminal "sleep-training" on their children (as do the Papago) may be overlooked. On the other hand, we may anticipate that in time cross-cultural studies will help to refine and develop our existing body of theory.

21. NOTES

1. Everett Cherrington Hughes and Helen MacGill Hughes, *Where Peoples Meet* (Glencoe: Free Press, 1952), pp. 18-19.

2. We have not heard an Indian use the old-fashioned term "decent" in this context though we note that Kluckhohn used it to describe the Indian point of view (cited in Dorothy B. Lee, *Freedom and Culture,* p. 130). We find it apt, since in the white society of a generation ago decent behavior was expected of children and brought no reward, while indecent behavior was severely punished.

The Indian conception that decent or proper behavior deserves no particular notice or praise is, nevertheless, rarely appreciated by white people. We have, for example, heard teachers and other professionals complain that their Indian students and clients never thanked them for their work and devotion. And Margaret Mead remarks that to Indians, "All government employees, no matter how honest, how tireless, how enthusiastic, would be voted as merely 'doing their duty' and given neither laurels or thanks." This Indian behavior does not reflect hostility or ingratitude. It merely reflects the Indian view that medals or laurel wreaths are not given to people for doing what they ought to do. (Margaret Mead, *The Changing Culture of an Indian Tribe,* cited by Erik H. Erikson in "Observations on Sioux Education," *Journal of Psychology* VII (1939), p. 123.)

3. Manning Nash, *Machine Age Maya,* Memoirs of the American Anthropological Association, No. 87 (1958), pp. 26-27, 46.

4. "Indians in Overalls," *Hudson Review* III (1956), p. 369.

Part 4

COMMUNITY

Introduction

Schools are a major social institution that can be understood only in relation to other social institutions. Schools exist because the special educational needs of society must be satisfied if society is to survive. Schools are therefore an important and integral part of the communities that support them; changes in the community are directly felt in the activities of the school and the problems of the community are unavoidably school problems. (A point educational theorists sometimes overlook.)

Although schools as an adapting agency support social change, communicating and justifying certain socially acceptable changes particularly in the material culture, it is important to note that the primary function of schools is to insure societal continuity by transmitting a core of values from one generation to the next. As society becomes more complex, schools assume a more crucial role in the enculturation and socialization of the younger generation.

Greer, in one of the following readings, points out one of the major societal needs performed largely by the school: selection of the "winners" and the "losers." But it is becoming increasingly clear that success or failure in American schools is largely predetermined by the student's socioeconomic status. In addition, there is an embarrassingly high correlation in the United States between low socioeconomic status and membership in minority groups. Hence a disproportionate number of Black, Puerto Rican, Indian, and Mexican-American children fail in school and are consigned to the occupational junkheap. This pattern of failure represents a profound problem, an aspect of what Gunnar Myrdal called the "American Dilemma," for a nation purportedly committed to a democratic society.

We are now witnessing some of the societal effects of this pattern of minority failure in the schools. The Watts, Detroit, and Chicago riots punctuate a growing theme of disenchantment among minorities, a theme that includes a measure of despair with the ways in which schools have served the minorities. Education cannot solve the country's immense social problems, but it is clear that the problems cannot be solved without a major overhauling of the system of education.

The essays in Part 4 raise for education the question of control: Who controls the schools and toward what end are they controlled? Citizens sometimes naively believe that schools are for children, overlooking the fact that schools are often a source of revenue, a base of power for politicians, and an important basis of the economic well-being of the community. But most importantly they are the instrument by which some groups can control the dissemination of values to other groups. It is in this spirit that some parents, especially among the minorities, have tried to restore to themselves the central control (school board) of their community schools. Recognizing that just putting a few Black faces among the pictures in a history won't change the fundamental environment of the school. Recognizing that speeches on Brotherhood Day won't change the environment of the school. Recognizing that legislation by itself won't change the school. But recognizing, rather, that education will change when the cultural and social thinking of the academic power structure is consistent with the needs of the children being educated.

22

Politics Without Power:
The Dilemma of a Local School System*

ROBERT T. STOUT and GERALD E. SROUFE

With rising tempo in recent years, educators have been entreated to "enter politics." Such exhortations have proven largely irrelevant, for, regardless of the ideological preferences of schoolmen, politics has come to education. It is the thesis of this paper that educators are being required to make decisions about one of the most sensitive political questions, segregation, and that they have almost no resources for dealing with this issue. This is to say that many local systems are finding themselves in the political arena without sufficient political power.

Why is it that the local school system is often devoid of political power in dealing with the segregation question? How does it seek to compensate for lack of a political base in making controversial decisions? What may be suggested as the likely outcome of conventional strategies adopted by local systems? We have tried to examine these questions through study of a local system which sought to resolve a situation of de facto racial imbalance, Daly City, California.

School desegregation is widely feared by school administrators and school board members as a dangerously disruptive issue. Such fears are well grounded, as conflict over desegregation often serves to mobilize persons who otherwise take no interest in the schools, and to antagonize elements of the community who normally support school bonds and tax referenda. Withdrawal of traditional support groups, coupled with opposition from elements about which the schools need not normally be concerned, often deprives the local school system of a power base sufficient to meet a political crisis.

In suburban communities such as the one we have studied, conflict engendered over the desegregation question may become intense. Here the schools are the most visible and expensive community service, and perhaps the most actively scrutinized by supporters and dissidents alike. The issue of a policy regarding racial balance in the Jefferson Union High School District illustrates both the explosiveness of the issue and the development of a power vacuum as a result of the controversy.

DEMOGRAPHY: CUSTOMARY VILLAIN

Prior to 1950 Daly City had been relatively small, white, and virtually self-sufficient. The advent of a new freeway resulted in rapid growth, and concomitant engulfment of the traditional political structure. Only 30 percent of the families living in Daly City in 1960 had lived there in 1955. Early "post-freeway" immigrants were typically lower-level white-collar workers who desired a home of their own, a yard, and "a good education for their children." Their desires were partially vitiated by their middle- to lower-middle-level incomes, but they appeared willing to tax themselves for "good education." Their median family income was about $7,700 a year and they had completed about 11.8 school years. About 65 percent identified themselves as white-collar workers. Almost 60 percent were either foreign-born or had foreign-born parents whose native tongues were predominantly German and Italian.

Since 1960 the population patterns have shifted somewhat. Because of its proximity to San Francisco, Daly City has been attractive to Negro families and families with Spanish surnames. While in 1960 less than 2 percent of the citizens were classified as nonwhite, now almost 20 percent are so classified. Typically, the major increase has occurred in "Old Daly City," where the purchase price of houses is $4,000 to $5,000 less than in other parts of the community.

"Old Daly City" is served by Jefferson High School, the original high school for the district. The newer sections of Daly City are served by Westmoor High School, which was occupied in 1957 following an immigration of over 6,000 persons in the years 1954-56. Although only about 20 percent of the total student population is nonwhite, more than 70 percent of the nonwhite students attend Jefferson High School, while less than 20 percent attend Westmoor High School. Seen another way, over 40 percent of the students at Jefferson are nonwhite, while less than 10 percent of the Westmoor students are so classified. Short of intervention by school officials, the percentage of nonwhite students attending Jefferson could be expected to increase substantially during the next few years; some of the elementary feeder schools had already become heavily nonwhite.

On August 23, 1965, the board of trustees of the Jefferson Union High School District appointed twenty-six citizens to an advisory committee. The board charged the committee with the study of overcrowding at both Westmoor and Jefferson High Schools, attendance boundaries for a proposed new high school, and "related ethnic and economic segregation problems." A member of the board of trustees appeared before the committee and asked them specifically to consider "how our district will prevent, if present trends continue, Jefferson High School from becoming a de facto segregated school."

The immediate antecedents for the board's action were a 1963 ruling by the California State Board of Education that ethnicity be considered in drawing school attendance boundaries, and the report of the Jefferson Union High

School Teachers' Association Committee on De Facto Segregation. The teachers' report requested that the board officially acknowledge the 1963 state board ruling and "create a study group on school boundaries . . . composed of teachers, administrators, and lay citizens."

Several features of the board's action are of special interest. First and most remarkable, the board was not forced to establish the committee as a last-minute effort to head off a crisis. Negroes were not sitting-in, marching, or even attending school board meetings. In fact, there was no organized minority group position, public or private. A second interesting point is that the board acted despite the unfortunate and well publicized experiences of two nearby communities. In these communities the desegregation efforts were of questionable success, and the political controversy of great magnitude.

Further, despite the fact that they were not forced to take any action, and despite the bitter experiences of nearby school systems, the Daly City board went far beyond customary limits in issuing their mandate to the citizens advisory committee. They did not ask the committee to decide whether desegregation was desirable or necessary, but to draw up a plan which would desegregate and which would prevent segregation in the future.

The citizens advisory committee worked for seven months, and in February and March of 1966 its recommendations were presented at three community meetings. The substance of the committee's recommendations was that an exchange of students take place between Westmoor and Jefferson. The community response was predictable and predictably onesided: the parents of Westmoor students did not want their children to attend Jefferson. The community had moved from a state of calm to a state of potential controversy.

The grounds for opposition to the exchange plans are familiar. Parents at Westmoor had a proprietary interest in *their* high school, an interest fostered by the system's policy of constructing small (1,500-2,000) high schools. One (white) citizen stated that as a taxpayer he had a right to send his children to Westmoor. A second source of opposition stemmed from the fear of a lower-middle-class group who envisioned a status loss if their children attended a school with lower-class children. One mother was quoted to the effect that her family had worked hard to be able to afford a home in the neighborhood served by Westmoor. This fear was exacerbated by the anxiety parents felt about sending children into the "tough" environment of Jefferson.

Opposition was also based upon more easily answered fears. These involved the distance from home to school, transportation, and the breaking up of friendship groups developed in elementary school.

In addition to these expressions of anger, the parents of Westmoor students accused the citizens committee of having arrived at its conclusions in secrecy and with disproportionately few representatives of the Westmoor position. Perhaps more than anything else, the charge of imbalance on the citizens committee effectively destroyed the usefulness of the committee report. The Board of Education, responding to its own long-held and public position of "democratic decision-making," voted to table the report.

EXTENDING SEARCH FOR SUPPORT

The powerlessness of the board in effecting its chosen strategy was now becoming apparent. The board believed that it could not simply disregard the opposition of the Westmoor parents, nor could it claim that the citizens committee report represented a consensus of the larger community.

In an attempt to share the decision-making responsibility with a larger segment of the community, the Board of Education invited 132 citizens to constitute a second citizens committee for the study of district problems. Only sixty-eight citizens agreed to serve, the great majority of whom were from areas served by Westmoor. Believing that this committee would be no more "representative" than the first, the Board of Education attempted to bolster its position by seeking assistance from a nearby university.

ANALYSIS OF POLITICAL PROBLEM

The board's problem was to find sufficient support to effect a decision of great importance to the larger community. As is suggested in the following analysis, traditional sources of power were unavailable to the board, and efforts to identify and encourage new sources proved exceedingly difficult because of the complexity of the "community" and the controversial nature of the issue.

The three traditional sources of power utilized in effecting school decisions were unavailable in dealing with the desegregation question. The power ordinarily accruing to the superintendency by virtue of the superintendent's presumed expertness was vitiated because many consider desegregation a social rather than an educational issue. The superintendent is hampered further by the fact that evidence of educational benefits accompanying desegregation, though increasing, is yet limited. The support of traditional backers of the schools, PTA's and other civic-minded boosters, was denied the board because these groups were themselves split on the question. That only sixty-eight persons could be recruited to serve on a committee to study the problem, most of these with a ready axe to grind, is evidence that there was little hope of relying upon accustomed support from the public-spirited. Finally, the board could not utilize the power of its own legitimacy as official decision-maker because it was unwilling to make a decision. The board was reluctant to make a unilateral decision which might embroil the community in conflict apart from evidence of strong outside support.

The board sought initially to garner additional power through the mechanism of a citizens advisory committee (hereafter CAC). Such an approach has earned educators' respect, partly because it satisfies the precepts of local control and democratic decision-making, and partly because it often works. The question of how it works is seldom considered. We must do so here because we have an instance in which the invoking of a CAC seems an inappropriate strategy in the face of a fractured power structure.

If one of the main purposes of a CAC is to promote consensus through cooptation during periods of political decision-making, it is well to explore some limitations of such a group. In the first instance, if its purpose is to engender consensus it can ill afford prolonged conflict. This means that its members must be carefully chosen on the basis of their shared values, or through selective attrition members will leave the committee, or compromises must be struck. In Daly City the last two phenomena occurred. However, as an issue becomes more crucial to a school, as time becomes less of a resource, and as the content of the issue becomes more emotion-laden, compromise may be both difficult to achieve and potentially disruptive. With respect to desegregation, for example, many persons on both sides of the issue are unwilling to compromise; they equate compromise with defeat.

A second limitation derives from the criteria for membership on a CAC. If membership is to be representative, how is a selection procedure to be devised? A suburban area such as Daly City is highly fractionized socially and geographically. There are perhaps a dozen "home owners' associations" devoted to keeping up the standards of their housing tracts, all located within somewhat larger municipalities. These groups identify primarily with their tracts, since for most of them the tract supplies personal and cultural support. Further, intermediary groups such as service clubs may enroll members who do not live in the school district. Unlike a self-contained community where small-business owners are residents, many of the local entrepreneurs live in other school districts.

Finally, the high rate of turnover among residents makes representation a curious concept. The basic question is, "Who is representing whom?" when over the course of a year or two a constituency changes radically.

On the other hand, if the purpose of a CAC is to allow local influentials to legitimize school decisions, selection is again a problem. The most interesting question concerns the basis of influence in a school district like Jefferson. In a small suburban community, unlike a major city, there are few rewards to be dispensed by the political leaders. The consequence may be that political control is unsteady and political leaders cannot be counted on to deliver their constituents. Thus political influentials may be influentials in name only. The local business elite, to the extent that it lives out of the community, is also a group of possible shadow influentials. Further, they cannot be legitimately included in a committee which does not directly consider business affairs. The corporate executives who commute to the city might be considered an influential group. But their influence is vitiated by their relative invisibility to the whole community and their residential instability. While they have occupational and educational status, it is difficult to attribute working influence to them. With a composition of quasi-influentials and some PTA leaders, a CAC has few mechanisms of control to assure its decisions will be accepted by the community. Other than personal ties, there are not restraints which can be used to "bring into line" dissenting residents who may also possess personal resources of occupational and educational prestige.

Finally, a CAC in such a community is highly vulnerable to charges of unrepresentativeness. Lacking substantial interlocking mechanisms among intermediary organizations, lacking political control over constituents, and with a high turnover of residents who have no occupational ties to the community, a suburban area such as this is fertile ground for a kind of mass-society response to decisions. Given the school's addiction to democratic decision-making defined as participatory decision-making, a school board cannot get true representation, nor can it ignore charges of autocracy. It is not surprising that the Daly City board rejected the report of its first CAC and attempted to appoint a second composed of 132 members, a number so large as to be almost meaningless when compared with such committees in Chicago or Pittsburgh.

FRUSTRATION OF POWERLESSNESS

The strategem of a CAC is successful when it combines the trappings of representativeness with the legitimacy of community influentials. In Daly City it proved impossible either to identify and garner true influentials or to obtain representativeness. Having failed to muster sufficient power through the citizens committee route, the board turned to another time-tested strategem, involving the prestige of a university.

The university was given what turned out to be a double role: to develop a plan or plans, and to gain community acceptance for it, or at least to try to prevent overt resistance to it. The latter role was never explicitly defined and sufficient resources were never invested to accomplish it. In effect, the university's role became one of identifying possible dissidents and attempting to persuade them that the plans which were developed were not threatening or were for the ultimate good of the community. Two problems are immediately apparent. Identification of possible dissidents or support groups is hampered by the mass-like political and social structure. Neighborhood groups seemed to be the most likely candidates for either role, but the multitude of neighborhoods requires a large investment of resources in order to insure contact. As a compromise strategy, especially vocal neighborhood groups were contacted and presentations were made to the members. In addition, meetings were held in the high schools under sponsorship of the PTA. This latter strategy seemed not to be effective because of the self-selection of the audience.

A second problem is that desegregation is threatening to many people and rationality is a weak argument. Further, the lack of a real "crisis" in the community (the concern was to *prevent* de facto segregation) robbed an argument of some of its urgency. Finally, an appeal to a mobile population with respect to the ultimate good of the community is almost ludicrous. If a man has been and expects to be mobile, his long-term interest in the health of the community is likely to be low. In addition, if by moving to the next suburb he can avoid sending his children to an integrated school and can continue to enjoy the conveniences of a suburban region, he has no reason to be concerned about community welfare.

The ultimate response of the university representatives was to present to the Board of Education three alternative plans for preventing de facto segregation. For each plan there was also presented estimates of educational consequences. The university personnel had not been successful in generating massive community support for any of the plans, although one had met with less resistance than the others. Nor had the Board of Education been convinced that it had to act immediately. Consequently, the university report was acknowledged by the board and no action was taken.

Subsequently, the board held more public meetings in order to gauge the desires of the community and to attempt to develop support for positive action. Unable to accomplish either objective, the board referred the university report to a teachers' study group and asked them to develop a plan. Lacking solid support from the community, lacking political or personal power to insure acceptance, having been failed by the university, and needing some influence resource to legitimize its action, the board's referral was predictable. Although without much power, teachers as a group have some influence. Further, the board in utilizing the recommendations of the teachers develops several new arguments. For example, the board could argue that the success of any educational plan depends on willing implementation by the teachers and that such willingness is more nearly assured when the plan is developed by them. The board can also argue that a recommendation based on the combined educational expertise of a group of professional educators is, for the board, an extremely persuasive recommendation. Not surprisingly, however, the teacher's recommendation was an extremely conservative one which does not resolve the issue; their recommendation defers the question until some unspecified future date.

CONCLUSION

What we believe we have observed in Daly City is the failure of four political strategies as the board attempted to insure a priori community acceptance of its action. We believe the strategies failed because they were predicated on the board's attempted reliance on traditional sources of support: the superintendent's expertise, educational well-wishers, and knowledgeable outsiders. This reliance, we believe, was further predicated on the board's public adherence to "democratic decision-making." The failure of the Jefferson High School board and the failure of other boards in dealing with controversial political questions requires us to reconsider schoolmen's understanding of the democratic process.

It would seem that participatory democracy is well established in American political ideology but that schools are the only public decision-makers continuing to rely on this model as standard operating procedure.

In so doing the board makes itself too accessible to citizens. Unlike a large city, access by citizens to this suburban Board of Education appeared to be relatively easy. The advantages of such an arrangement are obvious and have been extolled by many writers in school administration. However, there are some disadvantages. If we accept the notion that a board of education cannot satisfy the demands of all the citizens, the question becomes one of differentiating among demands. The board is then faced with the dilemma of choosing among demands with little information about their source. That an individual alleges that he is a spokesman for a group is not necessarily useful information. How is the board to gain knowledge of the size of the group, the spokesman's authority to speak for them and, ultimately, his ability to control them? More generally, how is a board to separate noise from demands which rest on a substantial support base? In many growing suburban communities the lack of mediating organizations casts the board onto its own resources and intuition to gauge the strength of a pressure group. Perhaps one of the reasons that suburban educational conflicts are often so intense is that the board must wait for extremely powerful groups of angry citizens who have coalesced around a long-brewing issue to make themselves known before it can estimate their strength. In a sense, there can be no accurate warning system based on a board's access to the leadership of stable pressure groups. At one moment a board faces a demand of unknown persons with unknown resources, and at the next moment it must face a movement. The intricate system of reliable and accurate pressure group channels evident in legislatures appears nonexistent.

Democracy requires total access to the decision-making structure (i.e., to the positions from which decisions are made). This is not at all the same as total participation in actual decision-making. Indeed, the policy of referring controversial questions to the electorate, for resolution outside the legitimate decision-making structure, is antidemocratic in that it is antigovernmental. Democracy requires that the electorate be in a position to hold public officials responsible; it presumes that elected decision-makers will make decisions.

Educators have long been entreated to enter the game of politics; it appears that now they must be entreated to play the game the way it is meant to be played.

23

Local Control vs. Professionalism: Formula for Inevitable Conflict*

ARTHUR E. SALZ

The Ocean Hill-Brownsville controversy, which apparently has been settled for the time being, will be viewed in retrospect as merely the opening round in what is destined to become a long and protracted struggle for control of public education in the United States. What has begun as a local conflict in one small district in the nation's largest urban area will spread to urban areas throughout the country. What is now essentially a city problem will, in the not too distant future, be a major concern of teachers and laymen in our suburbs. Albert Shanker, president of the United Federation of Teachers, realized this when he planned to go on a national speaking tour during last fall's teacher strike. David Selden, national president of the American Federation of Teachers, understood the sweeping implications of the controversy when he entered into the negotiations which eventually settled the third strike of the 1968 school year. For while the burning issue will not be settled in either-or terms, it is best to pose it that way to see what is at stake. Thus, who shall control our schools, laymen or professionals? Ten years ago the question was never raised; today it cannot be avoided. For in the past decade two major trends in the history of educational, social, and political thought have been on a collision course which was not discernible until quite recently: on the one hand, the movement toward self-determination for minorities in urban areas, focusing on community control of various institutions; on the other hand, the growth of teacher professionalism.

Self-determination is a very old notion. One needn't be reminded that it was the prevailing ideology of our own revolution, and supposedly the fundamental principle governing the settlement of World War I. Of even greater import, it has been the basic underlying concept of the post-World War II nationalism that has swept Africa and Asia, and it is not merely coincidental that Stokely Carmichael, Charles Hamilton, and others have applied the colonial model to the plight of the black man in the United States. For if the analogy holds, then self-determination is an appropriate antidote for the oppressed black man here, as it was for the disease of colonialism on the continent of Africa in the past two

*Copyright 1969 by Phi Delta Kappa. Reprinted by permission of the publisher from *Phi Delta Kappan*, February 1969, pp. 332-34.

decades. Interestingly enough, the thrust toward an integrated American society in the 1950's muted this concern for self-determination. However, with the failure of either school or housing integration in the 1960's (or was it never attempted?), the trend toward community control has developed momentum. Antipoverty legislation and the Office of Economic Opportunity formalized and sanctioned the concept of self-determination by calling for maximum feasible participation by those affected by the legislation. The movement was strengthened considerably when blacks in Harlem, realizing that the new Intermediate School 201 was not to be integrated as promised, shifted tactics and demanded control of their community school. Also of great importance was Mayor John Lindsay's appointment of a high-powered committee, headed by McGeorge Bundy, to study school decentralization. The trend is obvious. Whatever is finally implemented by way of legislation, the idea of self-determination and community control of institutions is now soundly imbedded in the conscience of blacks and Puerto Ricans in the urban areas.

Professionalism, on the other hand, is not an easy concept to define. Nevertheless, while some may differ as to definition, there is general agreement that the Milquetoast teacher who came hat in hand begging for salary increases, who had to wade through piles of low-level clerical work, who had to take lunch duty, lavatory duty, and the like throughout the school day, was hardly being treated as a professional. It has also become unprofessional for teachers to provide their services in situations which seriously militate against success—e.g., where there are huge classes, outdated textbooks, and inadequate facilities. To the extent that teacher militancy and collective negotiations have improved this situation they have contributed to furthering the professionalization of teachers. But these tend to be bread-and-butter matters, and while certainly not unimportant, they do not clearly distinguish the teacher unionist from other unionists.

On the matter of educational policy, however, a trend has developed which portends a major breakthrough. Heretofore, policy matters in education have been in the domain of the school board, as representative of the public. While one can argue with some validity that any collectively negotiated contract that calls for smaller class size, more remedial reading teachers, more guidance counselors, etc., has involved teachers in policymaking, these items still can be viewed as being in the area of improved working conditions. However, in the negotiations between the UFT and the Board of Education in 1967, the union pressed for expansion of the More Effective Schools program, which it has been instrumental in developing. The MES, begun in 1964, was an attempt to provide quality education to children with educationally deficient backgrounds by means of smaller classes and a host of remedial and supportive services. While the research as to its success had been mixed, the UFT pressed vigorously for additional appropriations for the program. What was at stake here, apart from the money, was the UFT's right to negotiate policy. Out of the settlement came an appropriation of $10 million for experimental programs involving smaller class sizes. Also significant was the fact that the committee to plan these programs was to be made up of two members of the board, two from the UFT, and two more community people chosen jointly by the board and the UFT. Based on proposals made by this committee last year, four different types of experimental schools are in operation during the current year. The importance of this is clear. Not as advisors, consultants, or suppliants, but as an equal voice at the negotiating table, the teachers of New York, through their union, have been involved in making policy for the entire school system. This is the trend toward professionalism which is of vital significance.

A professional, as Myron Lieberman has pointed out, does the following:

1. Practice a unique, definite and essential social service.

2. Emphasizes intellectual techniques in performing his service.

3. Requires a long period of specialized training.

4. Possesses a broad range of autonomy for both himself and for his occupational group as a whole.

5. Accepts broad personal responsibility for judgments made and acts performed within the scope of professional autonomy.

6. Places an emphasis upon the service to be rendered, rather than the economic gain to the practitioner, as the basis for the organization and performance of the social service.

7. Is a member of a comprehensive self-governing organization of practitioners.

8. Adheres to a code of ethics, developed by his occupational group, which has been clarified and interpreted at ambiguous and doubtful points by concrete cases.[1]

While teachers, individually and as a group, exhibit many of these characteristics, the glaring omission has been the lack of autonomy that has existed within the profession. As noted above, this weakness is obviously being rectified as teachers become increasingly militant and achieve collective negotiations arrangements. However, what has generally been overlooked is that when teachers act professionally—i.e., with the necessary autonomy to define the conditions within which they will provide their services—they come into direct conflict with those traditionally in control of education: the public. The professionalization of teachers and local, lay control of education are on a collision course. No matter how optimistic we are about cooperation between the community and its teachers, many issues will arise which will inevitably pit the desires of the professional teacher against the wishes of the community.

This analysis holds for education in general in the United States. The problem, however, is considerably more critical in New York City, where the public has never felt it truly controlled its schools. Under massive pressure from civil rights leaders and others, the Board of Education began a tentative decentralization program in order to eventually place control of the schools in the local communities. By the summer of 1968 the board had broadened its program by giving all local districts the power to select district superintendents and to hire and fire teachers under city-wide standards. Currently the city is operating under an interim decentralization plan, pending passage of legislation in Albany this spring. The crux of the problem, then, is that at the very moment local leaders are, for the first time, insisting upon and achieving increased power in educational decision making, the teachers, as professionals, are exerting their right to determine policy. Until very recently both teachers and minority groups have been quite impotent in determining their destinies. Suddenly they are getting a taste of power; unfortunately they both have their spoons in the same bowl.

The Ocean Hill-Brownsville dispute, which is still smoldering, is an example of the type of confrontation which will become more and more common. The issue, initially, was whether a community board of education could circumvent procedures established by the central board of education and remove teachers and supervisors from that district. The UFT, caught in the middle, obviously supported the interest of the teachers.[2] Job security has historically been the prime concern of trade unionism. But in reality the issue merely centered around the question of who had the power to remove the teachers, the local *lay* board or the central *lay* board. No one was questioning the right or the advisability of laymen performing this function.

A more significant development will come in the future when teachers are powerful enough to seek a voice in determining entrance into the profession, establishment of tenure procedures, and methods of policing these procedures. At our current point in history the only thing teachers can insist upon is that due process be followed and justice be meted out. This is not unimportant. But of far greater moment will be the confrontation that develops when teachers are ready to take a stand in determining who enters and remains in the profession. On this and many other issues like curriculum control, use of paraprofessionals, academic freedom, etc., professional autonomy will be pitted against lay control. Conflict must follow.

Obviously, there are serious racial overtones that exacerbate the current issue in New York. Nevertheless, it serves to sharpen the focus of the problem by indicating that where laymen feel intensely about the functioning of their schools, and teachers feel strongly about their professionalization, there will be areas of dispute. This would be true with or without the racial issue. That this condition has not erupted before can be attributed to a lack of public control in the cities, lack of strong feeling among local communities concerning their schools, and, most important, lack of real power among the ranks of the teachers. Once we remove our heads from the sand and acknowledge that there are areas of inevitable conflict between teachers and local communities over education, we can begin to deal with them. What will emerge in New York City in the future is not so much the concept that lay control and professionalization don't mix; rather, that a new form of relationship taking into account the growing autonomy of teachers *and* the growing urban concern for local control will be hammered out through negotiations and other forms of channeled conflict. This relationship will hardly be tension-free. The teachers of New York, who have taught their colleagues throughout the country so much concerning militancy, collective bargaining, and professionalism, will be forging a curriculum on the topic of realistic relations between the community and the professional teacher. It is important that those concerned with education in our cities watch carefully the events in New York; they may portend the future in our nation's other urban areas.

23. NOTES

1. Myron Lieberman, *Education as a Profession* (Englewood Cliffs: Prentice-Hall, 1956), pp. 2-6.

2. While this is being written, the dispute in the I.S. 201 complex is almost forcing Ocean Hill-Brownsville off the front page of the newspapers. It is most interesting to note that once again the controversy is between the local governing board and the central board of education. Specifically, the issue is whether the central board had the authority to assign teachers who had been out on strike to report to their schools on the day following Thanksgiving. The local board had ruled that schools in their district would be closed that day. Once again the teachers are caught in the center of what is essentially a power struggle between the two boards.

24

Public Schools: The Myth of the Melting Pot*

COLIN GREER

It is fashionable these days to point to the decline of the public school, as if there were a time in some golden past when the schools really served all of the people all of the time. Legend tells of the Little Red Schoolhouse that made equal opportunity available to children of every economic and social class, and, a little later in the nation's history, functioned as the primary instrument of the melting pot that offered poor immigrant children access to the fullness of American life. Today the schools are criticized for their failure to provide equality of opportunity to poor black children. The charge is true, but it is by no means the whole truth, nor is it new. The public schools have always failed the lower classes—both white and black. Current educational problems stem not from the fact that the schools have changed, but from the fact that they continue to do precisely the job they have always done.

What we are witnessing, in our current panic over urban education, is no more than an escalation of the criticisms made by school reformers since the turn of the century. The many innovations introduced over the past fifty years have made it easier for school systems to handle the huge numbers of students brought into the schools by compulsory attendance legislation and a job market requiring increasingly sophisticated talents, but they have not changed the basic function of the schools as the primary selector of the winners and losers in society.

The very fact that we can look with pride at more and more students going on to secondary and higher education reveals a system that with increasing efficiency benefits some and denies others in the bosom of its material prosperity. Public schooling cannot be understood, nor the current problems manifest in it, apart from a consideration of the predominant influence of social and economic class. For at least the last eighty years, socioeconomic class, as signified by employment rates and levels, has determined scholastic achievement, as measured by dropout and failure rates.

From 1890, at least, the schools failed to perform according to their own as well as the popular definition of their role. In virtually every study undertaken

*Copyright 1969 by Saturday Review, Inc. Reprinted by permission of the publisher from *Saturday Review*, November 15, 1969, pp. 84-86.

since that of Chicago schools made in 1898, more children have failed in school than have succeeded, both in absolute and in relative numbers. The educators who collaborated on the Chicago study found an exceedingly high incidence of poor school performance. They were quick to look to foreign births as an explanation, but immigrants spawned Americans and still, with each passing decade, no more than 60 percent of Chicago's public school pupils were recorded at "normal age" (grade level); the rest were either "overage" (one to two years behind) or "retarded" (three to five years behind). In Boston, Chicago, Detroit, Philadelphia, Pittsburgh, New York, and Minneapolis, failure rates were so high that in no one of these systems did the so-called normal group exceed 60 percent, while in several instances it fell even lower—to 49 percent in Pittsburgh, and to 35 percent in Minneapolis.

The truth is that the mobility of white lower classes was never as rapid nor as sure as it has become traditional to think. The 1920 census, for example, showed that even the favored English or Welsh migrants found half their numbers tied to the terrifying vulnerability of unskilled labor occupations. Americans of English stock (dominating national language, customs, and institutions) had 40 percent of their number working in coal mines and cotton factories.

And what of the school in all this? Clearly, according to the same body of data, a close relationship obtained between various group designations (native-born with and without foreign parents, and foreign-born), which revealed that levels of school retention in any given group coincided with that group's adult employment rate. Dropout rates for all groups, including the Negro, were in direct proportion to rates of adult unemployment. Further, the high degree of school achievement among Jews, which has confirmed our expectation of public schools, did not mean success for all Jews. Otherwise, why the remedial classes and dropout panic in several of the schools on New York's Lower East Side with as much as 99 percent "Hebrew" registration? Where the family was poor enough to take in boarders to cover rental costs and desperate enough to join the city's welfare roles, then delinquency, prostitution, and child-labor were as much the burden of Jewish families, for whom such characteristics were real if not typical.

With rising industrial unemployment and an expanded technological economy, the school-leaving age increased so that the problem of caring for all grades of ability on the elementary school level escalated to the high school level. Vocational instruction programs were an inevitable corollary to the academic program and quickly became a symbol of the schools' stratification role. Today, the junior colleges serve as the junior high school had served earlier, operating to a large extent as an extension of secondary education, with back-seat status justified by the democratic rationale of monumental numbers to be catered to.

The pattern of school failure has been perennially uniform, but concern for it was by no means as great as the concern on the part of educators to get more pupils into school. In 1917, and again in 1925, federal compulsory education legislation put added strength behind various state actions to this effect. Compulsory school-leaving age moved from twelve to fourteen and then to sixteen, but always with the proviso that the two years at the top were dispensable for those who either achieved a minimal grade proficiency determined by the classroom teacher or, more importantly, could prove that they had a job to go to.

In 1919 Chicago gave 10,000 such work permits, in 1930 only 987. Between 1924 and 1930 the allocation of work permits in a number of cities was reduced by more than two-thirds. The school had not suddenly become essential to mobility, but a shrinking unskilled job market required fewer men less early, and so the schools were expected to fill the gap.

The assumption that extended schooling promotes greater academic achievement or social mobility is, however, entirely fallacious. School performance seems consistently dependent upon the socioeconomic position of the pupil's family. For example, of high school graduates who rank in the top fifth in ability among their classmates, those whose parents are in the top socioeconomic status quartile are five times more likely to enter graduate or professional schools than those of comparable ability whose parents fall in the bottom quartile. Similarly, while American males born after 1900 spend more years in school than their nineteenth-century predecessors, federal and other estimates indicate no concomitant redistribution of economic and social rewards.

The factory, the union, the political machine were agents of mobility and Americanization before the school. Local stability for an ethnic group preceded its entry into the more prosperous reaches of society. The establishment of an ethnic middle class was basic to entry onto a wider middle-class stage via public education. It was the nation's demand for manpower that set the tone for assimilation, and the place of any one group on the economic ladder depended more on the degree to which the culture of the former homeland coincided with the values most highly prized in the culture of the new host society. Jews, Scandinavians, and Greeks, for example, were already practiced in the arts of self-employment, individual ambition, and the Puritan ethic with its corollary Gospel of Wealth. For the Catholic peoples, the Irish and Italians, padrone and party-boss authority seemed to go hand in hand with their being classified as dull, unambitious, and generally of low intelligence by urban teachers from the earliest days of heavy immigration. Bootstraps were not classroom resources.

The school failure problem was generally tucked away in xenophobic concern for expressions of loyalty and the management problems of running an "efficient" system. And efficiency was measured by the success schools enjoyed in getting more youngsters into the classroom, almost never by academic success or lack of it. "The ratio of the number of children in school to the number in the community who ought legally to be in attendance" was the measure, and academic success was by no means a necessary concomitant.

But if students were to stay in school longer, then the public school structure had to be stretched "by facilitating the progress" of those who were locked hitherto into repeating their grades. As surveyists in Chicago remarked, "vanishing opportunities of employment" meant that the time had come for "curricular offerings based on ability and purpose."

Once intelligence tests were considered "a measure of potential"—and this was precisely how surveyists, school supervisory personnel, and professors of education viewed IQ tests—it was a short step to the realization that the broadened base of high school admissions meant that academic work in the nation's high schools had to be reorganized. Very soon, it was observed, too, that the amount of academic work had been considerably reduced because there were so many more students who previously had not gone beyond the fifth grade. One survey team described them as "the boys and girls of secondary age who show little promise of being able to engage profitably in the activities commonly carried out by pupils of normal or superior ability."

Commitment to more and more schooling, beginning at kindergarten now (although only one in four of the eligible could go as yet) and continuing as long as possible, did nothing to modify the record of poor school performance. Compulsory attendance at higher levels only pushed failure rates into the upper grades throughout the 1920s and 1930s in such cities as Chicago, Boston, New York, Philadelphia, Detroit, and Washington, D.C.

Chicago noted a 65 percent increase among the "underprivileged" between 1924 and 1931. Elementary school backwardness stood at 61.4 percent, but 41 percent of all those entering ninth grade were seriously behind, too; in tenth grade the figure was 32 percent. Apart from such factors as pupil "feeble-mindedness" as an explanation, there were school difficulties to blame, too. Overcrowding in Detroit, where 13,000 were in half-day sessions and 60 percent in school were "inadequately housed" in 1925; in Philadelphia, Cleveland, and New York the same overcrowding, unsanitary conditions, and serious financial problems prevailed.

On a scale of nine semesters, Philadelphia high schools lost 65 percent of incoming students at the end of the first semester, lost another 32 percent at the end of the fourth, and were down to 19 percent of the total in the final semester. In one instance, of a 339-pupil sample established for survey purposes, only 91 survived two years. Federal data on schools published in 1937 showed clearly the nationwide "cumulative elimination of pupils in school." While 1,750,000 American youngsters entered grade nine, 86.7 percent were still in school one year later; by grade eleven, only 72 percent were left, and finally 56 percent were graduated. Separate data for New York City showed just over 40 percent of ninth-grade classes graduating. In the late 1940s, George Strayer recorded the same old story in Washington, D.C., New York City, and Boston. Fifty percent of Boston's ninth graders failed to graduate; in New York the figure was up to more than 55 percent. In James Coleman's assessment of *Equal*

Educational Opportunity in the nation (1966), in the Havighurst study in Chicago (1964), and in the Passow report in Washington, D.C. (1967), the narrative remains staggeringly unchanged.

The Negro, the individual farthest down, has epitomized the inexorable relationship of success and failure, inside and outside the school. The link between permanent unemployment or chronic underemployment and educational failure is black now, but blacks have inherited a whirlwind no less familiar to them than to lower-class whites. Employment conditions were most severe when it came to the Negro, and school failure rates were at once more glaring and more poignant. But, in effect, the public schools served Negro children as they served the vast majority of others; in Chicago, Philadelphia, Detroit, and New York, that has been the problem since 1890.

But if white lower classes have been vulnerable to the economic market place, the Negro, who worked sporadically and as a reserve force, was constantly a victim. If school success or failure had little meaning in the economic marketplace for whites, it bore no relevance whatever for blacks. As a result, Negro school failure was quickly isolated as a separate problem early in the twentieth century. When, in the 1940s, Negroes finally entered the lower levels of industrial employment from which they had been excluded, those levels had already become a shrinking sector of the economy, and the massive numbers of school dropouts had no place to go. And so it remained appropriate—even inevitable—to consider Negro school performance as a separate question. But the truth is that academic effort has never been relevant to the place of the poor in society.

In 1931, George Strayer, with a lifetime of school evaluations behind him, looked back on progress in public education over the twenty-five preceding years. Most clear in his assessment of that progress was that not only were the top 10 percent (in terms of IQ scores) in high school, but that 50 percent of all eligible students from nursery school through college were involved in formal education. That more of the nation's youngsters were in school was the point of his argument, but still more needed to be put there. He acknowledged that very high failure rates were "still characteristic" of the majority of school systems. That was not a high priority problem, however, but a job "we may certainly hope to accomplish within the next twenty-five years."

The fact is that we haven't, and we haven't precisely because the objectives and priorities of the first twenty-five years of the twentieth century have gone unexamined. Paul Mort, a school surveyist sensitive to the growing alienation of urban community groups from public schools in the 1940s, blamed both the alienation and school failure rates on the historic rigidity of the system, its patent failure to consider or to plan for modification for future needs, and the firefighting assumptions that offered more and more of the same, making progress in education no more than the "expansion and extension of the commonplace." The capacity for future innovation and modification has been assumed, because the contradiction between public school pretensions and the measure of its achievement has been entirely disregarded. Consequently, we have no valid education philosophy on which to build differently. And things are unlikely to be much different until we have first exposed our illusions, and finally addressed the problems whose symptoms we fervently wish would go away.

If the assumptions on which public education was founded have gone unexamined, the problem is now compounded by rising aspirations. We could afford failure in the schools as long as the economy had room for unskilled workers and as long as the lower classes accepted without protest what appeared to be their inevitable place. Now, however, there are practically no jobs left for the unskilled, and even if there were, the black lower class no longer is willing to accept only that kind of opportunity—not in a society in which real wealth is increasing so fast.

What this means, in effect, is that in a variety of different ways we have increased our demands on the schools. Thirty years ago the purpose of public education was culturally defined as little more than baby-sitting for all the children. Now, neither corporations, government, suburban parents, nor the black community are willing to accept the school as a mere custodian. Its purpose has been redefined by society: not only must it serve all children, but it must graduate them all with salable skills.

We criticize the schools and look for change in the present distribution of costs and benefits; we are aware that other social institutions educate, and we have been aware for a long time of the selective nature of public education, but we nevertheless accept the notion that public schools are an assumed asset in the regeneration of society. We have adopted a history based on men and events chosen from the history of democratic ideas in education, while we ignore other men, whom we have labeled anti-intellectual. David Crockett and Horace Greeley, for example, leveled scornful tirades against the creation of elite institutions that served an emerging meritocracy. The land and money, they said, might instead have contributed to a real experiment in universal public education, to make public education truly public in its services, not merely in its uses. Schools have been public only in the sense that what happens in them is typical of what happens outside.

Having assumed the salutary past of the school, we have engaged in discussion and debate over the present efficacy of schools with no question but that schools must be; they are generic to the American landscape. These assumptions preclude debate and scholarly inquiry as to why we maintain schools and what we can reasonably expect of them. Until we can question the validity of these assumptions, we cannot begin to achieve the social restoration of which we speak so eloquently, but for which there is little precedent. We can only continue to generate rationalizations across a variety of disciplines for a national commitment to an ideology that claims simply, but erroneously, that the public schools have always done what they are now expected to do. The truth is they never have.

25

The Politics of Black Separatism*

JASON EPSTEIN

Public hearings on questions of school policy in New York are typically ritual-istic and empty, the issues being either trivial or decided in advance by the interested parties. Lately, however, Negroes and Puerto Ricans have begun to come to these hearings and the tone, as a result, has considerably sharpened and become bitter, so that the Board of Education, which usually sends a representa-tive, now occasionally stays away. Last summer, for instance, the board decided not to attend a hearing held by the Mayor's Council Against Poverty to consider whether the Board of Education or the ghetto communities themselves should have charge of some $69 million in federal funds intended for the improvement of ghetto schools. Dozens of Negro and Puerto Rican leaders testified at this hearing, and one after another of them urged that sooner than give this money over to the board which, they argued, would inevitably use it against the interests of the ghettos, the city should give it back to Washington.

Most of these speakers represented community organizations within the ghettos; many of them were parents, and some were black school teachers. Nearly all of them described the public school system as a racist conspiracy to deny the children of the ghetto an education, and themselves, if they happened to be teachers, advancement. Their complaint was not that the schools had tried and failed, nor even that they hadn't bothered to try, but that they had deliberately or reflexively blocked and stupefied the children. Some of the speakers wanted the federal money spent on an alternative school system, run by the local communities within the city, responsible not to a distant and author-itarian central board of education, but to the parents themselves. What they wanted, in effect, was to get rid of the central school administration, with its complacent bureaus, its records of failure, and its insularity, and to take charge of the ghetto schools themselves.

Last fall these desperate and angry voices were joined by that of the formid-able McGeorge Bundy, who, having left the War Room of the White House, has been for the past year and a half head of the Ford Foundation. The so-called Bundy Report, which appeared in November 1967, became the first of several

*Copyright 1969 by *Current*. Reprinted by permission of the publisher from *Current*, August 1968, pp. 26-32.

plans for decentralizing the New York City public school system by proposing to turn its powers over to the various communities within the city. Mr. Bundy's proposal was to break the system into between thirty and sixty largely autonomous community subsystems, each with substantial control over its own budget, personnel, and curricula. Soon after the Bundy Report appeared, Mayor John V. Lindsay presented a modified school decentralization plan of his own which was more nearly calculated to appeal to the state legislators whose approval is required before any substantial changes can be made in the New York City system.

When the legislature ignored Mr. Lindsay's modifications, the state Board of Regents, which is ultimately responsible for the New York City schools, offered still another plan. The Regents' proposal would create somewhat fewer autonomous school districts, thus limiting the extent of decentralization, but it went beyond both the Bundy plan and the mayor's modification by offering to do away immediately with the present nine-member Board of Education and replacing it as of June 30 with a new, five-man board, appointed by the mayor. . . .

SCHOOLS VERSUS BUREAUCRATS

Whether the system should be broken down into thirty or sixty districts, as the Bundy plan suggests, or into twenty districts, as the Regents have advised, the urgent matter is to wrench the school system away from the bureaucrats who are now running it and whose failure now threatens the stability of the city itself. The children of the ghetto, who now comprise nearly half the total public school enrollment, are largely without a functioning educational system at all, and the present school administration has shown that it is incapable of supplying them with one.

Mr. Bundy's report represents his debut in urban affairs, but for the former White House official the political crisis which his report hoped to settle is nothing new. In the ghettos of New York as, a decade ago, in the Mekong delta, an angry and insurgent population feels that it has exhausted its last political options and is now ready for violence, even if violence means suicide. For the parents of the ghetto the schools are the only means by which their children can escape, but each year, as the failure of the schools becomes more apparent, the grip of the city's discredited education officials grows tighter. The city is thus faced with a classic revolutionary situation. The problem for Mayor Lindsay and Mr. Bundy is to keep the peace, but the present strategy is the opposite of what it had been in Vietnam. There we strengthened the mandarins. The plan now is to weaken them and to offer a form of self-government to the indigenous population. At the heart of the various decentralization programs is the dispersal of New York City's central educational bureaucracy, a pyramid of some 3,000 officials, so firmly impacted at its base and so remote at its summit that it promises to survive (unless it is destroyed by its angry clientele) longer than the pyramids of Egypt.

The proposed New York City school budget for next year is nearly one and one-third billion dollars. The strategy of decentralization is to turn much of this money, and thus much of the power to run the schools, over to the local boards of education, a majority of whose members will be chosen by the parents within the individual communities, while the rest will be appointed by the mayor from lists supplied by the central board in consultation with representatives of the various neighborhoods. Thus, in theory, the central board will be reduced largely to looking after labor relations, the protection of the children's constitutional rights, maintaining educational standards, data processing, citywide testing, and so forth. The real power—that is, the power to give out the 60,000 jobs within the system—will reside with the politically chosen local boards.

TEACHING VERSUS CONTROL

Though it is unclear from the report whether these local boards will, in fact, reflect the interests of their communities, or will accommodate themselves, as the central board itself does, to city-wide interests and pressures, resulting in the same inertia from which the system suffers now, it is clear that the proponents of decentralization are less concerned with what is taught in the schools than with who runs them. In this they share the attitude of the present school administration a century ago, before civil service reforms replaced a political spoils system in which school jobs were given out by local leaders in consultation with City Hall. The main assumption of the proposed new legislation is that, since the city's demographic center has begun to shift toward the ghetto, the distribution of power within the school system should now begin to shift accordingly.

As the Bundy Report itself acknowledged, the case for restricting the power of the central board is hardly original. A study issued in 1933 urged a form of decentralization and there have been others in 1940, 1942, 1949, 1962, and 1965. But the current proposals are unique in their urgency and aggressiveness, partly because their sponsors feel that it is no longer a matter merely of improving the schools but of saving the city, and perhaps, since the case of New York is typical of all large city systems, of saving the entire country. . . .

THE VESTED INTERESTS OF TEACHERS

There are, however, a number of difficulties with the plan, the most serious of which is that the board and its professional staff, supported in the present case by the powerful United Federation of Teachers, are unlikely to give up without a fight. Their political resources are formidable and, given what they stand to lose—that is, their jobs—they are likely to fight bitterly. To the administrators and teachers, as well as to their representatives in Albany, decentralization means that a largely Jewish bureaucracy with a strong residue of Irish flavoring, must now begin to make way, at least in the ghetto schools, for a largely Negro insurgency. White candidates for principal ($18,970-$25,795) or assistant superintendent ($30,000), who have served their time in the schools, passed their examinations, waited in line, attended the banquets, made the friends, and done whatever else the system expects of its future leaders, will, if the new legislation is enacted, have to stand by while Negroes and Puerto Ricans, appointed by community boards of education, take the jobs they feel they have earned. In Negro and Puerto Rican districts even the incumbent principals and superintendents, to say nothing of the individual teachers, will not be safe from the local boards, for while the proposed new legislation promises to maintain the tenure of these people, it does not guarantee to keep them in their present jobs. The local boards, under decentralization, will have the power to pluck the present staff members from wherever in the hierarchy they may now be perched and throw them, tenured but jobless, into cold storage until they resign or can be retired.

WHITE TEACHER REACTION

According to the Board of Examiners which administers the so-called merit system by which teachers and principals are advanced to higher positions (and which the new legislation proposes to abolish), the Bundy Report was "terrifying in its implications" for "white teachers." Privately, the report has been called antisemitic. Recently it was attacked by the Board of Rabbis. Last month Herman Mantell, president of the Council of Jewish Organizations in Civil Service, which represents 26,000 members of the Jewish Teachers Association, promised that his organization will campaign against persons who are implicated in "creating political chaos" in the school system, by which he presumably meant not only the mayor, the state commissioner, the Board of Regents, and the Ford Foundation, but also whichever state legislators are so bold as to vote for decentralization.

Though the language of the Bundy Report was conciliatory, as when its authors insisted that they had been "deeply impressed by the honesty, the intelligence and the essential good will" of the same educational leaders whom they intended to rusticate, the report's message was clear to the bureaucrats even before it was published. Their response was predictably critical, occasionally agitated, as in the case of the Board of Examiners, but reassured by the knowledge that the system has survived plenty of trouble so far, including its conspicuous and admitted failure to educate the children of the ghettos, and it will probably survive this crisis, too. Though the present school administration has tried to refute the report on such grounds as its implied attack on "professionalism," its main strategy has been to keep cool, avoid public arguments, and support the idea of decentralization in principle, though only in principle, while counting on representatives of the city's ethnic majorities, prodded by such statesmen as Mr. Mantell, to kill the proposal in the legislature. As if anticipating such a response, the Bundy Report chastised the board for its characteristic inertia, what the report calls its "negative power," the power to thwart its critics by ignoring them, on the proven assumption that sooner or later the critics will grow tired and quit.

BUREAUCRATIC NEGATIVE POWER

To experience this negative power directly, as anyone does who becomes entangled with New York City's educational bureaucracy, is often bewildering and usually infuriating. No doubt the authors of the Bundy Report, as they made their way through the enervated corridors of New York's school headquarters, past the bland or sullen officials, had plenty of chances to see this system at work and to conclude, quite apart from the larger political considerations which prompted the report in the first place, that whatever is wrong with the schools must begin with its central administrative staff. It is easy to see how the authors of the report may have felt that the first step toward reconstructing public education in New York must be to get rid of this frustrating organization, or at least to circumvent it, as the prosperous middle class had done years ago when it built its own system of independent schools, and as the population of the ghetto now wants to do when it insists upon running the ghetto schools itself. As it is already doing in a small way through its street academies and Harlem Prep, privately supported ghetto schools whose enrollment consists mainly of public school dropouts and whose aims are to send most of these students on to college.

Yet for all the anguish which the school bureaucracy inspires, it would be naive to assume that its negative power can easily be manipulated or sidestepped through institutional reforms, or that these reforms, assuming they can ever be legislated, can then, in fact, be implemented. One might have thought that Mr. Bundy had learned from his experiences in Saigon how stubborn an established hierarchy can be in the face of even the most zealous attempts to change it. But even if he had never heard of General Ky he had only to consider the miserable history of school desegregation in New York to know the many ways in which such bureaucracies protect themselves from the moral and political assaults of the outside world.

THE POWER OF SUBVERSION

Though school desegregation had been ordered, in effect, by the Supreme Court in 1954 and mandated, in turn, by the Board of Education as well as by the state commissioner, it became clear by the end of the 50s that the schools in New York were going to remain largely segregated not, as some sociologists have said, because there were not enough white children to go around, but because a number of principals and other administrators, fearful of the white parents and often because of their own prejudices, decided to ignore or subvert orders from the central board to integrate their schools. It would be unfair, however, to blame this failure solely on the headquarters officials who were charged with desegregation. A bureaucrat's power over his subordinates, and thus his strength within the hierarchy, is partly determined by whether these subordinates will carry out his orders. If enough of them resist or passively ignore what they are told to do, and if they are supported by forces—in this case the white parents—over whom the system has no control, then the responsible officials are likely to retreat, as in fact they did. That neither the superintendent nor the central board, armed with the authority of the Supreme Court, offered to discipline the rebellious principals suggests how stubborn the negative power of such a bureaucracy can be.

In this sense the problem in New York is not that there is too much central authority, as the various decentralization plans seem to imply, but that there is not enough, and that what central authority there is, is ineffective. In its resistance to integration the system showed that it was already "decentralized" to the point of anarchy. Aware that their power depended upon the compliance of a tenured field staff, the administrators at headquarters, when events required that they assert the authority of their offices, typically replied that "it is not our job to tell the principals how to run their schools," as if the responsibilities of leadership were somehow a violation of democratic procedure. (No reform is possible in New York City until the headquarters staff and the principals are made directly accountable for their performances. Neither the Bundy plan nor the Regents' proposal specifically provides for such direct accountability though both imply it. Middle-class parents who send their children to private schools take such accountability for granted. The headmaster's job depends directly upon the approval of the parents represented by their trustees. The five-man board proposed by the Regents will be effective only if it can find ways to hold the professional staff personally responsible for their performances. Under the system of tenured civil service it is hard to see how such a program of direct accountability can be implemented. Nevertheless, it should be the primary duty of any new board to assess the work of its professional staff and in consultation with local boards, replace incompetent personnel as circumstances require.)

THE SENSE OF BETRAYAL

Faced with this collapse of central authority, the leaders of the ghetto communities, who had been promised integrated schools, and who had conveyed these promises to the credulous, if restless, parents, correctly decided that they had been betrayed and that to depend any longer upon the board was useless. What they discovered was that for many school officials public education was not mainly a matter of teaching the children but of maintaining stable terms of employment for teachers, and, of course, administrators themselves. If these ghetto parents needed to be convinced further that negotiations with the system were a waste of time they had only to await the plans for Harlem's I.S. 201 to be announced.

The story of I.S. 201 is somewhat complex, but since it relates directly to the present move toward decentralization, and since it foreshadows the increasingly violent confrontations that can be expected between the community and the school authorities if decentraliztion is not enacted, it is worth outlining here. The initials I.S. stand for Intermediate School, an institution which includes grades six through eight, and is intended eventually to replace the present junior high schools, which include grades seven through nine. The point is to get the children out of their local elementary schools a year earlier and into the larger intermediate schools, which are supposed to draw their students from a wider community and thus, through this purely technical means, enforce a kind of integration. To do this the intermediate schools must be built in what the board calls "fringe areas," that is, between white and black neighborhoods. They must also be big enough to draw children from a number of elementary schools. At first I.S. 201 was to have been simply another mid-Harlem junior high school, built to relieve overcrowding in two adjacent junior high schools, and the Negro borough president of Manhattan approved the site accordingly. At this point, however, an officious administrator at headquarters decided, ostensibly in the interest of integration, to make the new school an intermediate school. But he neglected to change either the mid-Harlem site or the capacity of the building, with the result that Harlem's first intermediate school would inevitably be as segregated as a school in New York could possibly be. Probably this administrative decision resulted from nothing more sinister than the disingenuousness, together with the insensitivity, of the official who made it and from the tendency of the system to deal with its problems by changing their labels. Nevertheless, the Harlem leaders who had agreed to continue working with the Board were enraged. . . .

Some of the disenchanted parents whose children were enrolled in 201 decided that since they were stuck with the school they might as well run it themselves. The famous disorders followed in which the white principal was forced to leave and the board, since it was no longer a matter of offending the white parents and in order to avoid any further trouble in the ghetto, more or less capitulated to the militant Negroes. Shortly thereafter the Ford Foundation proposed that 201 become the pivot of a partly autonomous Harlem school district whose budget would be augmented by Ford. Ford also decided to finance two other "demonstration" districts, one in lower Manhattan and the other in Brooklyn, as further experiments in local autonomy. The school administration accepted these plans, partly in the spirit that, for the time being at least, it was getting rid of a headache, and perhaps also on the assumption that these "demonstration" districts would, like most other attempts at reconstruction within the system, come to nothing. Furthermore, the board had no choice. The alternative to capitulation was open warfare. The Bundy Report soon followed with its proposal that the authority of the central board be severely reduced throughout the city.

WILL THE SCHOOLS BE BETTER?

The question remains, however, whether the report and its subsequent modifications make sense in themselves: whether local autonomy offers a real solution to the crisis in public education. The answer goes beyond the question of who runs the school system, for the ultimate problem is not whether black officials replace white ones but whether the children will learn more in a system administered by several black school boards than in one dominated by a single, impotent white board. Unfortunately neither the Bundy Report nor the Regents' plan gives us much to go on, for they neglect to show how the inertia at headquarters leads to the disasters in the classrooms, or whether there are any meaningful links between the two phenomena at all.

As a result it is unclear how a formally decentralized system, replacing the present anarchy, based upon decaying, but still potent, traditions of mutual self-interest, will stimulate the 60,000 teachers, 30 percent of whom are substitutes, to outdo their present performances. Both the Bundy Plan and the Regents' proposal are content to assume that once the present bureaucracy is out of the way, talents and energies which heretofore have languished will awaken and find their way through the presumably enlightened local boards into the schools. That the various plans fail to show how decentralization might actually affect the children and their teachers in the classrooms is perhaps understandable, since their aims are largely political: to avert a revolution by redistributing political power and jobs. But the pedagogical question remains, for it would be foolish to reorganize the system only to discover that this sort of tinkering made no difference at all; that no matter how the system were organized and no matter who got the jobs, the problems in the classrooms would remain; that the real difficulty had lain in a different direction all along.

26

The Hispanic-American Superintendents of Northern New Mexico: Patron and Peon*

MARTIN BURLINGAME

In many important aspects, the Hispanic-American superintendents of schools in northern New Mexico appear to be a frustrated lot. As the professional educators in their small and often rural communities, their professional ideology flies in the face of local community norms. The expectations of their local constituents demand that they act as the village patrons. The political officials in their community and at the state level expect them to act like peons. These conflicting roles help produce an educational stalemate in the northern communities.

This brief paper seeks to explore the problems peculiar to Hispanic-American school superintendents in northern New Mexico. The first problem concerns the conflicts between the ideology of the professional educator and the rural norms of the Hispanic-American communities in the north. The second problem concerns the dual role of patron and peon played by these superintendents.

A PROFESSIONAL IN A NONPROFESSIONAL SOCIETY

According to Becker, "profession" is an honorific title. The title implies a set of characteristics which are esteemed by society. Becker indicates that this list of characteristics includes the following propositions:

(1) A body of esoteric and difficult knowledge exists.
(2) Such knowledge is based upon scientific research.
(3) Lengthy training is necessary to master the knowledge.
(4) The profession controls who may enter and practice.
(5) The profession has a rigid code of ethics.[1] This last point is often expressed by the notion of the professional spirit. This spirit is characterized by unselfish devotion to improve the conditions of the world. Professionals seek to bring truth, beauty, health, and justice to an imperfect world.

As Becker succinctly points out, it makes small difference whether so-called professionals really act as the criteria say they will act. The aspiring professional seeks to act this way and the public at large bestows the honorific title of "professional" as the gap between actuality and dream grows smaller.

---

*An unpublished paper written for this volume.

Hence the ideal professional image regards the school superintendent as a product of professional training and an examplar of a professional spirit which seeks altruistically to rebuild the world. Drawing on the authority of a scientifically developed body of knowledge, carefully trained to accept the authority of scientific inquiry, and guided by a code of ethics, the superintendent seeks to improve society. Attacking ignorance, prejudice, and intolerance, the professional educator is intent upon changing society for the better.

In contrast to this picture, most analysts of Hispanic-American rural culture stress its authoritarian and traditional nature. Indicators of this authoritarian mode are the patriarchal family, the power of the Roman Catholic Church, and the patron-peon system. These interlocking institutions stress not only loyalty to the leader but also a distrust for change. The Hispanic-American rural culture is replete with positions of dependency, with clearly defined statuses, with a distrust of competition and a fear of personal initiative, and with a distaste for cultural change.[2]

The concept of professional appears alien to the Hispanic-American rural culture. Rather than knowledge, authority appears to be vested in a paternalistic individual or institution. The traditional bent of the community counters directly the transforming aspects of a professional spirit. And the emphasis on local orientation and concern is in marked contrast to the professional interest in the activities of colleagues many miles away.

The Hispanic-American who is trained as a professional educator appears to face three alternative routes. First, he may reject his cultural heritage. The professional turns against the values and norms of his upbringing and instead argues for the absorption of the minority into the mainstream. This direction may be appealing to the minority group member who has been successful in school. Second, he may be frustrated by the conflict and develop some escape mechanism. This may range from a claim that no problem exists to the contention that the problem is insurmountable and may be resolved only by time. The third alternative, and the one this paper will describe, suggests that the educator adopts and rejects selectively certain professional attributes. To analyze this alternative, the roles of patron and peon must be understood.

THE SUPERINTENDENT AS PATRON

Although the terms "patron" and "peon" have often been used in a superficial and prejudiced sense, various social scientists have used them to describe the Hispanic-American rural culture of northern New Mexico. Holmes clearly distinguishes the "sometimes 'good' or at least kindly" patron from "the *jefe politico,* the political leader or boss (usually 'bad')."[3] He cites Mead's analogy of the patron as village father. The peon is also a well-defined role involving loyalty to a patron. However, the system depends upon norms of mutual reciprocity. The patron is not a dictator nor the peon a literal slave. The "politicking" involved in the relationship leads to mutual rights and responsibilities. The chief obligation of the patron is to help his village.

Critical to understanding the role of the superintendent as patron is the fact that schools are the major industries of most of the Hispanic counties of northern New Mexico. In many communities the school has replaced the farm as the economic backbone of the area. As the major economic force in the area, the superintendent has at his disposal a large number of jobs. He can provide employment for many of the local citizens. As the chief economic force in the community, the superintendent is a prime candidate to fulfill the role of village patron. For such a service the patron-superintendent can expect loyalty.

Yet the patron-superintendent must respect the customs and traditions of the local community. His employment pattern must be seen by the villagers as fair and just. As the father of his extended school family, he must care for all the members. If successful, the patron-superintendent can expect loyalty and an abdication of his staff's right to make professional decisions. The superintendent then can represent the system to the world. It is a system with carefully constructed and maintained hierarchical rights and responsibilities, with a strong person-to-person style and with a general unwillingness on the part of others to make decisions. As the patron of the village, the superintendent seeks to maintain the older cultural norms.

THE SUPERINTENDENT AS PEON

The superintendent, however, finds himself referring to another group. Because of a unique arrangement, the great bulk of operating funds for each local school district comes from the state legislature. The superintendent finds himself dealing with local and state politicians to secure the funds necessary to maintain his system. In dealing with these individuals, the superintendent finds himself in the role of peon.

As a peon, the superintendent is dependent upon the funds and the regulations distributed by the state government. The amount of funds directly affects the size of the system. If funds are cut, the patron-superintendent is forced to reduce his family of employees.

To avoid a reduction in funds, the superintendent can work closely with local political leaders. Most frequently this has meant that the superintendent provides certain jobs for local politicians. By allowing these positions to be filled by the members of the politician's extended family, the superintendent can expect favorable treatment. If the politician mistreats the superintendent's funds, the superintendent has the opportunity of reducing his personnel by firing the politican's appointees. In order to avoid such nasty encounters, the politician and the superintendent seek a reasonable compromise. The politician works for maximum funding for the local school while the superintendent provides maximum support for the politician.

The matter of state regulations provides more thorny issues. When the bulk of the legislature demands maximum output from the schools for minimum cash input, the superintendents and politicians of the Hispanic counties must protect their followers. The protection includes not only jobs but also the content and range of the school's activities. Programs designed to upgrade the curriculum by dealing with the problems of cultural change must be stifled. The superintendent and politician are on the safest grounds if they can maintain basic programs which do not challenge the traditional values of the community. Programs such as modern social studies or sciences might provoke the disloyalty of their personnel. If the legislature is able to extract promises of changes, the patron-superintendent and politican can mollify their people by pointing to Santa Fe, the seat of the New Mexico legislature, and claiming "they" did it.

The pressures of the local community also force the superintendent to go to Santa Fe and claim "they" won't stand for "it." Efforts to consolidate schools, for instance, run counter to the entire system. The centralized system also allows the state officials to become patrons whose behavior can be partially regulated by the peons. As a peon the superintendent is not helpless, but his range of activities is limited.

THE STALEMATE OF THE NORTH

If these contentions are accurate, the majority of Hispanic-American superintendents in the northern counties are beleaguered patron-peons. Unable or unwilling to adopt the role of professional educator, they seek to maintain the traditional and authoritarian culture of their ancestors. To do this, they find themselves playing the traditional roles of patron and peon. In their home communities, the superintendent bears the rights and responsibilities of a village patron. He must care for his peons of the school system. His responsibilities include providing employment, caring for all members of his system and enforcing the cultural norms which justify the patron-peon system. In dealing with politicians, the superintendent is a peon. Financially dependent upon the will of the legislators, he stands vulnerable to their wrath. Because he has jobs, however, the superintendent can modify the legislators' intentions.

In the long run, the basic value system of the Hispanic north has not been upset because it has meshed with the conservatism of a fundamentalist Protestantism in the state's "Little Texas." Coming by way of vastly different premises, these two sections often reach the same conclusions. Both sections stress authority, loyalty to family, and reluctance to change. Neither values education and educators as a vital force for social change. The two sections combine successfully into a "traditionalist" bloc whose energies are intent on defining professional educators within nonprofessional terms. Against this background, the emerging metropolitan centers of Albuquerque and Las Cruces stand helpless.

26. NOTES

1. Howard S. Becker, "The Nature of a Profession," in Nelson B. Henry (ed.), *Education for the Professions: The Sixty-first Yearbook of the National Society for the Study of Education,* Part II (Chicago: National Society for the Study of Education, 1962), pp. 27-46.

2. Clark S. Knowlton, "Patron-Peon Pattern Among the Spanish-Americans of New Mexico," in S. W. Webster (ed.), *Knowing the Disadvantaged,* Part I of *The Disadvantaged Learner* (San Francisco: Chandler, 1966), pp. 118-26.

3. Jack E. Holmes, *Politics in New Mexico* (Albuquerque: University of New Mexico Press, 1967), p. 21.

27

Intercultural Relations*

EVON Z. VOGT, with the assistance of MALCOLM J. ARTH

How long the Zunis as a separate and identifiable cultural unit have lived in their present territory along the banks of the Zuni River and its tributaries is not known. Certainly they were there when the Spanish conquistadores arrived in 1540, and archaeological evidence indicates that their cultural ancestors occupied the region for some hundreds of years earlier, extending back at least into Pueblo III times (A.D. 1050-1300) and probably much earlier.

It appears that the Zunis are one of several Western Pueblo cultures that developed over a long time span from earlier Basket Maker roots in the Colorado Plateau country. A few Basket Maker sites and many later Anasazi sites are found in the area. Although few of these have been excavated, the indications are that they were abandoned and the people concentrated in the historic six Zuni villages before any of the other present-day groups entered the region. By 1705 the six Zuni villages had been reduced to one main village. Later three outlying farming villages were established: Nutria ("beaver" in Spanish), so named because there used to be beaver dams near this village at the base of the Zuni Mountains; Pescado ("fish"), named for the fish found by the early Spanish explorers in the stream emanating from the springs near the village, which is located six miles below Rimrock; and Ojo Caliente ("hot spring"), twenty miles southeast of Zuni, where a warm spring bubbles up. The Zuni population on the Reservation in 1950 was 2486.

Compared to the Zuni, even the Navahos and early Spaniards are newcomers to western New Mexico. The Navahos may have had sporadic contact with the Zunis before the Civil War, but they did not arrive in any great numbers until later. Early accounts of raids against the Zuni cite Apache de Navajo or Navaho and/or Apache raiders. Whether the Navaho as a differentiated group engaged in such attacks is contingent on such disputed issues as when differentiation of Navaho from Apache occurred. It is probable that the raiders were generalized Apache. In the two decades before their removal to Fort Sumner in 1864, Navahos hunted in the Rimrock area and cultivated a few fields. After their release from captivity in 1868, a few related families came to the Rimrock region instead of settling on the Reservation to the north. They selected the well-watered valley which is now mostly covered by the Rimrock reservoir built by the Mormons, and later spread south and east into less desirable lands in the lava country. In 1950 the Rimrock Navaho population was 625.

The Spanish conquistadores were in the Rimrock area as early as the Coronado expedition, which arrived at the Zuni villages in 1540. Several later Spanish expeditions passed through the region, including that of Don Juan de Oñate, the colonizer and first governor of New Mexico, who left his inscription on the side of El Morro in 1605. The ancestors of the present Spanish-American inhabitants did not enter the Rimrock area until the early 1860's, when they began to migrate west from older settlements across the Zuni Mountains. By 1865 Tijeras was established as a frontier *ranchería*. Later, as other families came to settle and use the land, the winter sheep range was extended southwestward toward the Arizona line, where there were broad grassy plains. Along the route from Tijeras to the southwest several small *rancherías* were built, usually by one or two families who located in a canyon where a dam could be built and gardens cultivated. The larger settlement of Atrisco was founded in 1882. The Spanish-American population has decreased markedly in recent decades and in 1950 was only 89.

In 1876, Mormon missionary scouts first appeared in the region, visiting the Zunis at Zuni pueblo and at Pescado, and the newly settled Spanish-Americans at Tijeras. Eventually a site for colonization was selected at the base of the Zuni Mountains about five miles from the present village. In 1877, the colony was virtually wiped out by a smallpox epidemic. In 1882 a new band of Mormons settled, this time near the missionary establishment in the lower valley. The new settlement was first called Navajo and later Rimrock; by 1950 its population had expanded to 241.

Although a few Texan ranchers established cattle ranches in the area around the turn of the century, the main migrations from Texas occurred in the 1920's and 1930's. After World War I, Texans began to take up homesteads in the La Peña area. The number was much augmented during the depression of the early 1930's, when the community of Homestead was established near a rain-filled natural lake which the Spanish-Americans had fenced and had used for watering sheep and cattle since the 1880's. In 1950 the population of the Texan Homestead settlement was 232.

THE SPANISH CONQUEST

In the 1530's Cabeza de Vaca and three companions including the Moorish slave, Estevan, traveled across what is now south Texas and northern Mexico after surviving a shipwreck on the Gulf. When they finally reached Mexico City in 1536, they brought stories to Viceroy Mendoza of an "El Dorado" land north of the route they had traveled. As a result of these reports, a small party with Fray Marcos de Niza as leader and Estevan as guide was sent north in 1539 to look for the fabulous "Seven Cities of Cibola." Estevan, marching ahead of the main party, was killed by the Zunis at Hawikuh. It is not certain that Fray Marcos ever reached the Zuni pueblos, although he may have seen them from a distance as he reported. At any rate, he returned to Mexico with glowing tales of what he had seen and heard, and these stories helped spur on the organization of a larger expedition led by Coronado which did reach the pueblos in July 1540. Hawikuh was taken by the Spanish in a pitched battle which lasted only an hour but nevertheless broke organized Zuni resistance. The ruins of the village of Hawikuh are near the present Zuni farming village of Ojo Caliente.

After Hawikuh's conquest, the leaders of the other Zuni villages brought gifts and held lengthy conferences with Coronado. According to Spanish reports, the Zunis promised to become Christians and subjects of the king of Spain. However, after the conferences they packed up their property and with their women and children deserted their villages and took refuge on Corn Mountain, a high mesa which served as a refuge for them throughout the centuries of Spanish control. The Indians were finally persuaded to come down from the mesa, and Coronado and his troops made their headquarters in the Zuni villages and supplied themselves with Zuni food during the next few months while smaller expeditions were sent west to the Hopi pueblos and east to Acoma and the Rio Grande pueblos. In September 1540, the main army with sheep and cattle reached the Zuni country, and Coronado shifted his headquarters to Tiguex on the Rio Grande. In the spring of 1542, Coronado and his army passed through Zuni on their return to Mexico, having failed to find the gold, silver, and turquoise they had set out to discover.

The impact of Coronado's visit did not cease when he departed from Zuni. He left behind him three Catholic Mexican Indians, domesticated animals (sheep, cattle, horses, and mules), some Catholic paraphernalia, and possibly some wheat seeds. The Zunis also presumably retained vivid memories of the superior power of Spanish arms and of the potentiality of Corn Mountain as a sanctuary. For the next forty years the Zunis were not visited by any major Spanish expeditionary forces, and it was not until the 1580's that even small groups of Spaniards again reached Zuni. Chamuscado in 1581 and Espejo in 1583 found there the three Mexican Indians left by Coronado. However, Zuni did not feel the full force of Spanish power again until Governor Juan de Oñate, the colonizer of New Mexico, arrived in 1598. It was then that the Zunis formally made vows of allegiance and vassalage to Spain.

The first Catholic missionaries were established in 1629, at Halona and Hawikuh. Three years later Fray Francisco Letrado was killed at Hawikuh when he urged the Indians too strongly to attend Mass. The Zunis fled to the top of Corn Mountain where they remained for about three years. In the 1640's missionaries were re-established in Zuni, but in the general Pueblo Rebellion of 1680, the Zunis killed Fray Juan de Bal and once more took refuge on Corn Mountain. By 1680, the number of Zuni inhabited villages had been reduced to four. It was on Corn Mountain that General Diego de Vargas found and conquered them in 1692. After De Vargas' conquest missionaries were again placed at Zuni. However, in 1703, the Indians killed three Spaniards who were living in the Zuni villages and returned to Corn Mountain. When they descended, the Zunis consolidated into a single pueblo which has remained to the present. From the time of construction of the church at Zuni (in the late 1600's or early 1700's) until the mission was abandoned in 1821, resident missionaries were maintained more or less continuously in the Zuni country.

Parsons cites the danger from Navaho attacks and poor church attendance as the two main reasons for the abandonment of the mission. The factor of outside pressures, particularly the raids, has been of great importance in Zuni life, no doubt influencing the pueblo type of construction and the progressive consolidation of the villages. Bandelier has suggested that the Zunis offered little initial resistance to Spanish power and control because they hoped that the Spanish would serve as an unwitting ally against the continual Navaho-Apache attacks; they hoped the coalition would prove enough to counteract the raiders. Similar considerations probably played a role in their later acceptance of American power which did effectively end Navaho-Apache raids in the late nineteenth century.

These early contacts between the Zunis and the Spanish, extending over three centuries (1540-1846), have a number of significant features. There was only one major battle with Spanish troops, that between Coronado's men and the Zunis at Hawikuh in July 1540. Subsequent encounters between the two groups involved the isolated killings of Spanish priests when soldiers were not around to protect them, usually followed by attempts to evade Spanish retaliation by fleeing to Corn Mountain. At no time during these centuries did the Spanish establish settlements in the area. Contacts were limited to three specific types: Spanish expeditions coming to establish religious missions; Spanish expeditions passing through on their way elsewhere; and the resident Catholic missionaries.

Although the Zunis adopted elements of Spanish material culture, such as wheat and domestic animals, they were from the outset resistant to adopting the religious system. They looked particularly with hope to the Spanish religion, probably less as substitute for their own than as powerful magic which would help them "beat" the much dreaded "war-medicines" of their enemies. The early feelings of hostility over religious matters seem to be the historical root of the Zuni prohibition, still in force, that prevents Spanish-Americans from witnessing any of their ceremonials. On their side, the Spanish were motivated primarily by the hope of finding another Mexico or Peru with great riches and only secondarily by the desire to convert the natives. Neither goal was achieved. Closer and more enduring relationships between Zunis and Spanish-Americans were not established until the latter actually settled in the Rimrock area in the late nineteenth century.

THE NAVAHO ARRIVAL

Specialists are still debating the questions of when and by what routes the Athapascan-speaking peoples entered the Southwest and when differentiation into separate cultural groupings such as Navaho, Western Apache, and Jicarilla Apache occurred. Dates of arrival ranging from 1000 to 1500 have been proposed, and whatever dating is adopted, it is still an open question whether the Navaho entered the Southwest as Navaho or as generic Apache. These questions are intimately bound up with the historical reconstruction of early Navaho-Zuni contacts. For example, it is known that seventeenth-century Zuni life was punctuated by periodic raids. In discussing the raid on Hawikuh in 1670, in which the Spanish priest was killed and the mission burned, Bandelier states specifically that it was a raid by Navahos; Hodge disputes this, saying it is more likely to have been Apache raiding in 1670. In any event, there was general Athapascan (possibly Navaho) pressure on Zuni during the seventeenth century, and probably earlier, which was maintained intermittently until the middle of the nineteenth century. This external pressure is credited with reducing the number of Zuni villages from the original six or seven in 1540 to four in 1680, and finally to one site in 1705. Not only is the increasing consolidation of the Zunis attributed to Apache (or Navaho) attacks, but also the very architectural and settlement patterns which the villages took. The Zuni word, "apachu," meaning "enemies," applied to all Navahos and Apaches, seems aptly chosen.

Actual Navaho settlement in the immediate vicinity of Zuni is not recorded previous to the 1840's and 1850's. During the decade preceding the confinement of the Navahos at Fort Sumner, the Zunis were concentrated mainly in the central village, while the Navahos occupied the Pescado and Nutria valleys. When the Navahos were placed in captivity, the Zunis took advantage of their absence to establish Nutria, Pescado, and Ojo Caliente. When the Navahos returned, they settled in the Rimrock Valley and eastward along the southwestern base of the Zuni Mountains.

Looking at the two cultures for evidence of contacts, it may be seen that, although there is much in Navaho culture that appears to have derived from the Pueblo peoples generally, there is little that can be traced specifically to historical contacts with Zuni. Several local Navaho traits seem directly attributable to Zuni influences. At least four older men among the Rimrock Navahos speak Zuni and one knows the Zuni myth which "goes with" the Shalako. A few items of technology appear to have been acquired, such as outdoor bake ovens and painted pottery. The belief that Zuni gods and Zuni witches are able to influence events in Navaho life is further indication of contact. There is evidence of absorption of some Navaho traits by the Zunis, for example, hand-trembling techniques and the Yeibichai dance, as well as the speaking of Navaho by many Zunis.

The historical sequence of Navaho-Zuni interaction seems to fall into two main stages, one of hostility and the other of relative harmony. The first lasted from some time in the seventeenth century to the middle of the nineteenth; the second, characterized by permanent Navajo residence near Zuni and subsequent social and economic interaction, resulted in the transmission of most of the cultural elements noted.

SPANISH-AMERICAN SETTLEMENT

The next phase of intercultural relations opens with the arrival of the Spanish-Americans at Tijeras in the 1860's. They did not enter Navaho country as settlers until the Navahos had been brought under control by the United States government. Before then, the principal westernmost Spanish-American settlements were at Cebolleta and Cubero (at the base of Mount Taylor), out-posts at the edge of Navaho country for over a century.

During the 1860's, Spanish-Americans began to expand westward. In 1866 one family moved with its sheep from Cubero to Concho, Arizona. By 1869, several families had settled at Ojo del Gallo and founded the village of San Martín. Two families which settled at San Lorenzo (later called Tijeras) were joined by two more in 1870; from this small village, herds of sheep were grazed across the open country between Zuni and the Zuni Salt Lake. Atrisco, the second Spanish-American village in the area, was founded in 1882 by members of two related families from Cubero.

Since the Spanish-Americans occupied an area considerably east and south of the Zuni grazing lands, early contacts were few. Superficial contact occurred when the Zunis passed through Atrisco on their way to the Salt Lake on salt-gathering expeditions, but such journeys were infrequent. There was some inter-group trading, especially between Tijeras and Pescado and Atrisco and Ojo Caliente. The Spanish-Americans began quite early to make pilgrimages to the *Santo* at Zuni, an image of the Infant Christ of Our Lady of Atocha that was one of the items of Catholic religious paraphernalia retained by the Zunis after the mission was abandoned in 1821. Although at this time Spanish-Americans were welcome to visit the *Santo,* the taboo against their witnessing any Zuni cere-monials was strongly in force. Cushing, who lived at Zuni from 1879 to 1884, reports:

> There is one race, however—the Mexican—toward whom the Zuni, preserv-ing an outward calm, keeps up an inward and undying hatred. He so heartily despises and abhors these inoffensive representatives of a priesthood who persecuted the gods of his forefathers that any white man who resembles one of them even, will meet with but tardy welcome in the town of Zuni. The Zunis would as soon think of imbibing poison as of permitting man, woman, or child of that detested race to witness one of their festivals or sacred dances. If Don or "Greaser" chances to heave in sight while any of the tribal ceremonies are going on, he is met by watchful subchiefs and amicably but firmly escorted to such quarter of the town as is most remote from the scene

of celebration, and then locked up. He may rave and swear and call down the vengeance of "El Gobierno" on the Indians for detaining him, but so long as that festivity lasts, be it one day or four, he will be held strict prisoner. Yet so stringent are the customs of hospitality that the unhappy captive is supplied with every delicacy the Zuni cuisine can produce, his horses and donkeys are fed and watered, and nothing which a favored guest might anticipate is left undone.[1]

For their part, the early Spanish-American settlers regarded the Zunis with uneasiness. Florence Kluckhohn reports that when Atrisco was first settled, many people in the village, especially the women and children, feared the Zunis, for it was not known whether or not they would attack.

Despite mutual mistrust, the Zunis permitted some Spanish-American families to live in their villages. In the 1880's, Frank Montaño's great-grandfather lived in the pueblo, making his living as a smith, and later establishing a ranch north of the Zuni reservation. In the 1890's, three Spanish-American families, including Trinidad Marez's maternal grandfather, lived for a few years in Pescado, one of the outlying farming villages; they did smithing and were allowed to farm small plots of Zuni land while they resided there.

After the *patrón* of Atrisco went bankrupt in the late 1920's, the Spanish-American people of this village began trading more often at stores in the Zuni pueblo and interaction with Zunis became frequent and more important. The women of Atrisco started going to the government doctor in Zuni for delivery of their children, thus necessitating their living in the pueblo for a time. However, they usually stayed with one family, the Eriachos, the head of which is reputed to be half Mexican Yaqui Indian in origin. At least one Atrisqueño engaged the services of Zuni witch doctors during this period, though her community expressed disapproval.

The question of how the Zunis perceive the early Spanish conquerors' relation to the much later Spanish-American settlers is interesting. Linguistically they differentiate the early Spanish whom they call *Cipolo*[2] from the Spanish-Americans whom they view, accurately, as a mixture of *Cipolo* and *Mehikukwe,* Mexican people. However, they also perceive the continuity between the two, a fact demonstrated by their refusal to allow Spanish-Americans to witness their ceremonials.

For Spanish-Americans in the Rimrock area, early contacts with Navahos were more important than those with the Zunis.[3] The Spanish-Americans moved directly into Navaho territory when they settled at Tijeras, and Atrisco has had Navaho neighbors living within ten miles of the village. There is evidence that the Navahos at first may have been predisposed to steal Spanish-American livestock. However, the relationship soon reached a somewhat more reciprocally trustful level, with the Spanish-Americans actually carrying out *patrón* functions, and providing the Navahos with credit in their stores and in their saloons. Thus, from the beginning, Spanish-Americans were a main source of the Navaho liquor supply. In return, the Navahos worked as herders for them. Reciprocal trading and visiting relationships were established at both Tijeras and Atrisco. The Spanish-Americans engaged in some proselytizing in Tijeras.

As a result of this early interaction, many Navahos acquired Spanish names, learned to speak some Spanish, and copied Spanish-American techniques of handling sheep. There was relatively little conflict over land, such as occurred later when Mormons and Texans entered the Rimrock area. Spanish-American *patróns* made little fuss over the small Navaho herds that grazed in the open range. This was in part due to the fact that the range was still unfenced and uncrowded, but it no doubt also stemmed partly from the traditional Spanish attitudes of permissiveness and easygoingness. It seems unlikely that Texans or Mormons in the same situation would have responded to Navaho use of their land for grazing—or more literally have failed to respond—as did the Spanish-Americans. During this period there emerged an ecological balance among the Navahos, Spanish-Americans, and Zunis.

MORMON COLONIZATION

The Mormon entry into the Rimrock area was part of a purposeful church program to establish a missionary outpost to convert the Zunis and Navahos of the region to Mormonism. The first two missionaries arrived at Zuni in 1876. Later that year, Brigham Young "called" two additional missionaries to carry on the work, and they settled with their families at the Spanish-American ranching village of Tijeras. In 1877 seven families founded a settlement in the upper Rimrock Valley at the base of the Zuni Mountains. By that October it was reported that the mission numbered 116 Zunis and 34 Navahos who had been baptized. In the late autumn nearly a hundred converts from Arkansas arrived, placing such a strain on the food supplies that most of them were sent on to Mormon settlements in Arizona.

A smallpox epidemic broke out in Tijeras and Zuni, forcing the Mormon families to leave Tijeras and give up missionary work at Zuni. The disease spread to the upper Rimrock Valley and nearly a dozen Mormons died during the winter of 1877-78. One of the missionaries at Zuni "administered," according to Mormon doctrine, to over four hundred Indians in the pueblo, reputedly with great success. (This act of faith-healing is still stressed by Mormon missionaries and by Zuni converts to Mormonism in the contemporary missionary program.) By 1880 only one Mormon family remained in the area. To prevent complete failure of the colony, the church authorities "called" several families from Sunset, Arizona, to revive the New Mexican outpost, and in 1882 they moved to the Rimrock Valley. The new settlement established down the valley at its present site, a townsite laid out, a dam and irrigation ditches constructed, and an irrigation company formed.

By 1884, Rimrock had become a full-fledged Mormon community, ready to fulfill the purpose for which it had been created—to convert the Indians to

Mormonism. Missionary work was emphasized by church authorities until 1900 when all those who had been "called" to Rimrock as missionaries were officially "released" and allowed to go elsewhere if they so desired. At this point a goal which had emerged earlier now became prominent, that of "making the desert bloom like a rose." Missionary work continued, but the prime emphasis was placed upon building a permanent Mormon settlement.

The early relationships which the Mormons established with the Zunis, Navahos, and Spanish-Americans were heavily influenced by their definition of these groups as "Lamanites." The Mormons believe that all American Indians are descendants of Israelites who crossed the Pacific from the Old World and settled on the North American continent. According to the Mormons, the apostasy of these ancient Hebrews led to the degeneration of their religion and to the darkening of their skins; their conversion and "return to God," it is believed, will whiten their skins again. The Spanish-Americans are included in the category of "Lamanites" because of their mixed Spanish-Indian ancestry.

The Mormons who arrived in the Rimrock area, had a sincere desire to convert the "Lamanites," and the figures cited indicate considerable early success with both Zunis and Navahos. Among the 150 Zunis and Navahos baptized by the fall of 1877 were the headman of the Rimrock Navahos and a Zuni who later became governor of the pueblo. The formal acts of conversion and baptism may not have affected the value systems of those converted, but it is an indication that relationships between the Mormons and Indians were relatively friendly in these early decades.

A small group of Zuni families, including the convert who became governor, lived in Rimrock for a few years, helped the Mormons build the dam for their irrigation reservoir, and farmed a small plot of land the Mormons had promised them in exchange for their labor. Many of the Zunis from Pescado traded wheat in exchange for grinding services at the Mormon gristmill and lumber at the Mormon sawmill in Rimrock. Later, beginning in the 1920's, several Mormons worked for the Indian Service at the Zuni agency and developed close contacts with Zunis.

The difficulties between Mormons and Navahos began after 1900, when the Mormon emphasis shifted from missionary work to the task of building a permanent community at Rimrock. As the Mormon population increased, greater pressure was placed upon the lands that were being used by the Navahos. Eventually the Mormons gained control of much of the best Navaho land, and the resulting ecological conflict was not resolved until the Indian Service made allotments to the Navaho families in the 1920's. The situation has been legally stabilized, but the Navaho continue to feel that the Mormons, while talking about religion, have been taking the best Navaho lands. More recently the Mormons have also gained control of all of the local trading posts which handle most of the Navaho trade. This combination of developments has been at the root of the contemporary uneasy and mistrustful relationships between the two groups.

Like the early Mormon-Zuni contacts, the early relationships between Mormons and Spanish-Americans were free of the ecological conflict that emerged between Mormons and Navahos. Some early proselytizing was attempted by the Mormons, especially when they were living at Tijeras, but no successful conversions have been effected in the Rimrock area. Whereas the Navaho and Zuni traditions allowed them simply to add the Mormon religious label and such of the practices as they liked to their old religion, the Spanish-Americans could not become Mormons without renouncing Catholocism; and this they were unwilling to do. There were also some early economic arrangements between the Mormons and Spanish-Americans. Trade was carried on, and Mormons with technical knowledge were hired by the Spanish-Americans to build two dams in the Atrisco area.

TEXAN MIGRATIONS

The last of the five cultural groups to arrive was the Texan. This group came in three migrations: the first immigrants, a small number of cattle ranchers, arrived in the area around the turn of the century; the second, predominantly farmers, took up homesteads near La Peña in the early 1920's; and the third wave in the early 1930's established the community of Homestead. The Texans never developed close contacts with the Zunis, but relationships with the Mormons, Navahos, and Spanish-Americans have become important.

Contacts with the Mormons were initiated when the Texans traveled through Rimrock on their way to and from Railtown. At first there was a sense of relief when the Texans found that they were not the only "white folks" in the area. They wanted to believe that the Mormons were the same type of rural people that they were, held the same values, and were social equals. However, Rimrock had a longer and better established place in the region, higher material standards of living, and more community activities—qualities which made the Mormon community "superior" in the homesteaders' minds. Nevertheless, the Mormon religion was, from the first, considered very peculiar by the Texans, and the compact village pattern offended the Texan taste for privacy and wide-open spaces. For their part, the Mormons regarded their own way of life as distinctly superior. The Texan communities are usually considered "rough" and "immoral," because of the drinking, smoking, and fighting which take place and what is regarded as disorganization in Texan community life.

Before migrating to western New Mexico, most of the Texans had never seen an Indian, except in the movies, and they arrived with pioneer-type attitudes toward them: Indians were "wild and uncivilized" and "dangerous" if not closely watched, but they were destined to disappear as the land was settled by "superior" white people. The first contacts were established when Navahos were hired to work in the bean fields. Texan-Navaho relations in the La Peña area had developed on a markedly friendly and equalitarian basis. A number of the Texans in the La Peña area made "corn liquor" in homemade stills during

Prohibition days and engaged in an active bootleg liquor business with Navahos. With Homestead, however, Navaho contacts have always been characterized by more aloofness and less friendly interchange. In neither Texan settlement was there serious ecological conflict with the Navahos. The Texans settled on lands that were peripheral to those held by the Navahos, and unlike the Mormons, have never gone in heavily for trading posts oriented toward the Navaho trade.

Before the Texans migrated to New Mexico their only contacts with Spanish-speaking peoples were with the migratory workers who came in small numbers to the Panhandle each year to assist in the cotton harvest. These Mexican laborers occupied a depressed position within the social and economic structure. As one of the Texans expressed it: "Down in Texas, Mexicans are considered as niggers, and niggers are pretty low." This stereotype was reinforced through school lessons on Texas history and by folklore about the battle of the Alamo in which the Mexicans are pictured as treacherous villains and Texans as courageous and righteous heroes. It is not surprising, then, that the Texans were distressed when they settled in the Rimrock area to discover that almost all of the county and many of the state officials were "Mexicans" and that they would be living next to "Mexican" villages where their children had to attend school. From the beginning, the homesteaders manifested a distrust and fear of the Spanish-Americans.

The Spanish-Americans, on the other hand, had developed a modus vivendi with the older settlers in the area in which there were relatively tolerant and respectful relations among the groups. Although the Spanish-Americans made overtures of friendship to the *Tejanos,* many of whom they pitied because of their utter poverty, they stopped such gestures after being rebuffed. The Spanish-Americans were quick to sense the hate, prejudice, and superiority which the *Tejanos* felt toward them. The *Tejanos* soon posed a serious economic threat to their village, for the homesteaders began to acquire title to, and fence in, land which the Spanish-Americans had been grazing as open range for almost fifty years.

In the Homestead area there have been two important outbreaks of hostility between the two peoples. The first occurred in the fall of 1934 when a Spanish-American teacher (a son of one of the most respected families in Atrisco) was sent by the county to the newly constructed grade school in Homestead. This met with violent objections from the homesteaders. During the first few weeks of school, windows were broken at night and signs appeared on the door of the school which read: "We Don't Want Any Chile Pickers for Teachers." Finally, one night the schoolhouse burned down. Both Spanish-Americans and some of the homesteaders now claim that it was set on fire by one of the more rabid Mexican-hating homesteaders.

These events increased tension on both sides, but over the years as the older Homestead children went to high school in Atrisco, and as the homesteaders went to Atrisco to pick up their mail, the groups were brought into closer contact. However, most of the homesteaders continued to object to sending their children to high school in Atrisco, and talked openly of attempting to take both the school and the post office away from Atrisco. They looked forward to the day when their numbers would bring them political control over the Atrisco district. Eventually most of these came about. By 1936, Homestead had its own post office, although a small post office was still maintained in Atrisco. In 1938 the high school was shifted to Homestead, and a few years later the grade school in Atrisco was closed and the Spanish-American children had to go by bus to grade school in Homestead.

In the meantime, however, closer individual ties were developed between the two communities. Friendships between individuals were formed, and, despite objections from friends and relatives, two of the Texans married daughters of the former *patrón* of Atrisco; these families continue to reside in Homestead. One of the Spanish-Americans set up a bar in Homestead which in due course was well patronized by many homesteaders.

Just when it appeared that better relations between the two groups were developing, a second important outbreak of open conflict occurred in 1947. It began with a fight at one of the dances in Homestead and eventually involved almost all of the Spanish-American men and many of the Texans who were at the dance. The fighting continued off and on for several days, as one of the young Texans who was beaten in the first fight sought revenge on all of the young Spanish-Americans who had taken part in the fight. Although the open fighting stopped after a week or so, and many Homestead families who were not present at the dance regretted the incident (which they named the "Spanish-American War"), the conflict was another tension-producing event affecting adversely the relations between the two communities. It seems unlikely that these events will soon be forgotten by either group.

Thus, intercultural relationships in the Rimrock area during the period of the research had their roots in Southwestern history. From the arrival of the Coronado expedition at Zuni in 1540 to the most recent Texan influx during the depression of the 1930's, the successive entries of different groups have gradually filled all the ecological niches in the region and have sharply reduced the amount of life space available to any one people. By 1955, each of the cultures had had a substantial history of contact with each of the others and had developed patterned ways both of viewing and of interacting with its neighbors.

THE CONTEMPORARY INTERCULTURAL SYSTEM

Analysis of contemporary intercultural relations will focus on the generalized cognitive orientations which each group has developed to each of the others, and the intercultural role network which, paradoxically, provides both effective lines of communication and limits on the degree of intimacy between cultures. The term cognitive orientations refers to the ways in which one group perceives another: the symbols and elements of the other way of life which are selected, often unconsciously, to characterize it—the "cognitive map" each has of its neighbors. The cognitive orientations are independent of the facts of the perceived group's behavior or symbols. They designate what their neighbors *think* they do, and it is to their cognitive orientations that they adjust their own behavior.

The concept of an intercultural role network is needed, since whole cultures as such do not meet, but individuals as culture carriers do.[4] Out of intercultural contacts, a complex but limited number of roles are developed which establish a precedent for future meetings. Ultimately these roles achieve the status of channels through which the content of cultural systems *must* be communicated and transmitted one to the other. Like their internal counterparts, intercultural roles may be conceptualized as constellations of behavior patterns appropriate to particular situations, and, since they presuppose a social context, each calls for its complement if either is to be sustained. In an intercultural system, such reciprocal behaviors are paired cross-culturally; the performance of an act by a member of one cultural group evokes certain actions from a member of another. Underlying each set of actions in a paired set is a complex of beliefs and values. The pair constitutes a cross-cultural unit of mutually understood expectations founded upon a definition—probably implicit—of reciprocal rights and obligations.

ZUNI-NAVAHO RELATIONSHIPS

Zunis and Navahos are definitely cognizant of a bond between them. They recognize their cultural similarity—that both are American Indian tribes with many common customs. They are also aware that they have a long history of contact. Many Zunis and Navahos now believe that the ancestors of both people emerged from the underworld at about the same time. In the words of one Zuni:

> They [Zunis and Navahos] had contact when they first came up from the underworld. Just after they came up. The Navahos and Zunis actually came out of the underworld together, that's what the Zunis describe. The Navahos and Zunis went around looking for the middle place. When it came to the distribution of animals, the Navahos qualified to get the horse. So that's why the Zunis say the Navahos like to wrestle with horses a lot.

Another view is expressed by a Navaho informant who states: "The Zunis and Navahos came up separately from the underworld, and right after that is when they came in contact with one another." Not only are both groups aware of the early contacts, but they have definite ideas of what those contacts were like. The Zunis particularly recall that their early meetings with the Navahos were hostile. Navaho raids on livestock and stealing of crops are frequently cited. Only after the Navahos were placed in Fort Sumner were they finally "tamed" and transformed into peaceful neighbors. The Zunis still tend to look down on the Navahos as "crude" and "unsophisticated" people living in rude hogans scattered in the woods, rather than in "good" houses clustered in a pueblo. A Zuni woman expressed this general attitude at Shalako time in the following way: "Navahos who come can be fed on the floor or any place, but our fancy friends from Laguna have to be fed at the table with plates and knives and forks."

In other ways Navaho power is respected. For example, the Zunis believe that Navaho witches are effective against them in the same way that Zuni witches are. The Navahos hold similar beliefs about the power of Zuni witches. However, the Zunis do not hold that Navaho gods can affect the course of events in Zuni life, a position contrary to the Navaho belief about Zuni gods.

The Navahos, acknowledging that they were the aggressors, also view the early interaction with the Zunis as hostile. (Their name for Zunis is *na·ŝt' ézi,* which means "blackened enemies.") This stage of hostile interaction was superseded by peaceful relations, which persist to this day, with even a few cases of intermarriage. Navaho attitudes toward Zunis are marked by ambivalence. On the one hand, they consider the Zunis as a people with a superior technology and a more sophisticated, elaborate ceremonialism; here the Zunis represent a kind of ideal model. On the other hand, Zunis are "big witches," and all contacts with them must be handled with care. Ambivalence finds another expression in the conflict between the Navahos' admiration for Zuni industriousness and their feeling that Zunis are "soft" and slightly effete compared with the "tougher" Navahos, who spend more time on horseback and withstand long periods of cold and hunger. Yet Navaho life is seen as more desirable, permitting more freedom of movement and providing an easier daily pace.

Among the key intercultural roles in the Zuni-Navaho interaction system are guest-host, employer-employee, and intermarriage. The guest-host relationship is based on mutual hospitality and gift exchange. Unlike the ordinary trading situation, it involves no bargaining. Each Navaho family visiting Zuni, especially during the Shalako ceremonial but at other times as well, has one or more Zuni families regarded as "friends." Upon entering the pueblo, they go at once to the house of the "friends," where they leave gifts of mutton, rugs, pinyon nuts, or jewelry. The Zuni family in turn is expected to house and feed them throughout the visit and to return gifts of bread, corn, melons, or hay when they depart. Behavior during such visits is highly structured: there is handshaking upon arrival and again upon departure; there are mutual inquiries about the state of health of families, and about the condition of crops and herds. Communication is usually in the Navaho language rather than Zuni. Later in the year, the Zuni family may return the visit at the hogan encampment of the Navaho "friends." They are then expected to bring gifts, and it behooves the Navahos to house, feed, and give gifts to them when they leave.

Such guest-host "friendships" sometimes persist for several generations. However, they may be severed if one party fails to reciprocate with the expected hospitality or gifts. Though nothing is said at the time, the following season will find the family that was slighted either looking for other "friends" or merely failing to bring gifts to the same one.

The employer-employee roles reflect the socio-economic hierarchy of the Rimrock area and show the superior position of the Zunis. Navahos work as sheepherders and occasionally as field hands for the wealthier Zuni families. The reverse, Zunis working as hired hands for Navahos, almost never occurs. As herders, the Navahos live at the Zuni sheep camps and are especially in demand during spring lambing time and also during the fall Shalako season when the Zunis prefer the pueblo to the open range.

In the last half century there have been thirteen cases of Zuni-Navaho inter-marriage. (These cases include intermarriages with *all* Navaho communities, not just with Rimrock Navaho.) There may have been other cases before 1900 but we have no data on them. Of the thirteen cases, ten involved Zuni men married to Navaho women, three Zuni women married to Navaho men. The marriages were of varying degrees of success and lasted for variable periods of time, ranging from a few months to several years. Since both tribes have structurally similar matrilocal residence patterns and similar roles for sons-in-law living matrilocally, it might be presumed that intermarriage might work out well. But there have been two major difficulties. The Zunis do not practice the mother-in-law avoidance pattern, and when Zuni men live matrilocally but do not avoid their mothers-in-law, the situation is laden with tension. Furthermore, the Zuni men are accustomed to a much higher standard of living—stone houses with beds, tables, chairs, and other comforts of life—and are reluctant to spend their lives in a Navaho hogan. The result has been that most Zuni men have insisted upon living in Zuni, thereby taking their wives away from their Navaho families and traditional matrilocal pattern and creating great strain for the wives. Comparable difficulties arise when Navaho men live matrilocally in Zuni. They feel uncomfortable not observing the mother-in-law avoidance pattern, and they feel restricted by loss of the customary Navaho freedom of movement in the confines of settled Zuni life. In no case has a Navaho man moved his Zuni wife away from her matrilineal household and relatives in Zuni to live in a hogan with his Navaho relatives.

When differences in language, custom, and ceremony are added to these structural strains, it is rather astonishing that as many as thirteen marriages have occurred and have lasted as long as they did. When divorce occurs, the Navahos frequently attribute the difficulty either to witchcraft practiced by the Zunis or to a belief that a Navaho should not have married into a Zuni "animal clan," such as badger or eagle. To marry into a "vegetable or food clan" of the Zunis, such as corn or pumpkin, is regarded as good, but not to marry into the "animal or bird clans." We know of no comparable Zuni belief concerning differences among Navaho clans with respect to intermarriage. The children of divorced parents almost always stay with the mother and are reared as Zunis or Navahos, as the case may be.

INDIAN–SPANISH-AMERICAN RELATIONSHIPS

The orientation of the two Indian groups toward Spanish-Americans have much in common, since both feel a kinship with the Spanish-Americans who are also a subordinated group vis-à-vis the Anglos in the Southwest. The three groups share the guest-host intervisiting pattern and have common witchcraft patterns which extend across the cultural boundaries. But there is considerably more ambivalence in the Spanish-American–Zuni relationship than in the Spanish-American–Navaho relationship. A few cases of Zuni–Spanish-American intermarriage indicate a closeness of relationship, but the Zuni prohibition against Spanish-Americans attending their ceremonials indicates very ancient feelings of hostility. The prohibition is now glossed over with mythological justifications and is most commonly expressed by Zunis as "protecting" their Spanish-American friends from suffering supernatural harm. In the Spanish-American view, it is an arbitrary singling out of one group, and, while they generally accept the situation, they do not like it. Nevertheless, the Spanish-Americans feel a certain cultural kinship with the Zunis, especially since many of the Zunis are now nominally Catholic and live in the kind of houses and type of compact village settlement that are much like Spanish-American houses and villages. The Navahos, they say, "live in hogans in the woods" and are *muy tontos* (very stupid).

The key intercultural roles are: guest-host, employer-employee, bootlegger-customer, and intermarriage. The guest-host pattern described for the Navahos and Zunis is much the same in the relationships between the Spanish-American and these Indian groups. Spanish-Americans are frequently fed and housed by their Zuni friends when they come to trade or to visit the *Santo.*[5] Spanish-Americans feed and house Navaho and Zuni friends, but, due to the differential in living standards, they seldom stay all night in Navaho hogans, even though they do have meals with their Navaho friends. The Spanish language is the primary medium of communication between Spanish-Americans and the two Indian groups.

With respect to employer-employee relationships, Zunis hire Spanish-Americans to herd sheep and do other work for them. Spanish-American ranchers employ many Navahos as herders and ranch hands, but the reverse almost never happens. Navahos are regarded as potential laborers for both well-to-do Zunis and Spanish-Americans, and rich Zuni families also employ poor Spanish-Americans as laborers.

Before the repeal of Indian prohibition in 1953, the bootlegger-customer intercultural role was of crucial importance in relationships between the Spanish-Americans and Indians. It was clear that the best source of supply of liquor for the Indians was from Spanish-American saloonkeepers or storekeepers who sold liquor (without benefit of license) to both Navahos and Zunis. The mutual role expectations were that Indians could buy liquor from Spanish-American saloonkeepers by going to the back door or arriving under cover of darkness. In return for these bootleg services, it was understood that higher prices would be charged for the liquor. It was also understood that the Indians would not communicate news of the transaction to Anglos, who, it was thought, would be likely to report the Spanish-Americans in question to the law-enforcement officials. Since 1953, the law has changed, but it is significant in terms of cultural continuity of occupational role that the only saloonkeepers in the Rimrock-Zuni area are still Spanish-Americans who are now doing a good legal business selling liquor to both whites and Indians.

Some intermarriage between Indians and Spanish-Americans has taken place. We have data on five cases of Zuni–Spanish-American and on two Navaho–Spanish-American marriages. In the marriages between Zunis and Spanish-Americans, four have involved Zuni men and Spanish-American women. Three of these couples do not live in Zuni (except during visits) but live in Railtown where their husbands have jobs. The fourth couple lives in the pueblo where, despite the close affinal kinship tie, the Spanish-American wife is still prohibited from witnessing Zuni ceremonials. The children, however, are permitted to attend the ceremonials, although it is not clear whether or not they will be inducted into Zuni ceremonial positions when they grow up.

The fifth case is a special one and requires some explanation. The husband was a Yaqui Indian from Old Mexico who, in his youth, was captured by the Apaches. He escaped from the Apaches and came to Zuni where he spent the remainder of his life. He married a Zuni woman by whom he had several children and became a successful stockman and a governor of the pueblo. He later married a Navaho woman and had a large number of children by her in the Rimrock Navaho country. This polygynous family situation, involving persons from three cultural backgrounds, lasted for many years and was altogether a remarkable development. Many of the offspring (who were both biological and cultural hybrids) have had notably successful careers, especially in the livestock business, in both the Zuni and Navaho communities. One of the Zuni children later became the governor and a prominent leader of one of the political factions in the pueblo; one of the Navaho children became a large sheepowner, a "star" rodeo performer, leader of a large Navaho "outfit," and the father of at least seventeen children by two wives and countless "affairs" with other Navaho women until his career was prematurely ended when he died of typhoid fever in 1943. (It is perhaps questionable as to whether these marriages should be classed with the other intercultural marriages between Spanish-Americans and Indians, for the husband was biologically and culturally Yaqui rather than Mexican or Spanish-American.)

The only other record we have of a Spanish-American–Navaho marriage in the Rimrock area was that between the Spanish-American bartender in Homestead and his second wife, who was reputedly half-Navaho. If so, she highly acculturated to Spanish-American culture; hence, the marriage was not of the same character as one between a full-blooded, traditional Navaho woman and a Spanish-American. There have been many cases of extramarital relationships and a number of children fathered by Spanish-American men in the Navaho population, but no other cases of intermarriage involving social recognition and the full assumption of family responsibilities.

A few minor points of structured intercultural contact should be mentioned. When the Spanish-Americans first settled in the region some lay proselytizing among the Navahos and Zunis took place. Resultant baptisms involved the extension of the Spanish-American godparental pattern across cultural boundaries. More recently, Spanish-Americans have expressed little concern with missionary work, although one Zuni couple are godparents of a Spanish-American child.

There is some incidence of native "curers" crossing cultural boundaries, especially with cures for withcraft ailments. Spanish-Americans employ Zuni curers, even though the Zunis believe that curers should not practice on anyone who is not a Zuni. Sometimes the Spanish-Americans go to Zuni for treatment; on other occasions, the Zuni "witchdoctor" is brought to the Spanish-American villages. There are also cases in which Navaho "singers" have recommended the use of certain plants to Spanish-Americans for curing ailments—with good results, according to our informants. There is also one instance of a Zuni going to a Spanish-American "curer" for withcraft, but none of the Navahos going to Spanish-American "curers."

Certain important witchcraft beliefs are shared by Zunis, Navahos, and Spanish-Americans, and witches in each culture can effectively work across boundaries and bewitch persons in the other cultures. The techniques for curing can be effective across these cultural boundaries. This is especially important in the case of Zuni—Spanish-American relationships. Spanish-Americans hire Zuni curers to "suck out" objects shot into the body by witches, or to use the "smoke treatment " in which green boughs are burned in a room with door and windows shut, or to place various herbs on the body. Another patterned context for intercultural contact between these three cultures is the occasional taking of Navaho sweat baths with Navaho friends by certain Spanish-American and Zuni men.

INDIAN-MORMON RELATIONSHIPS

Both Zunis and Navahos recognize Mormons as a special class of Anglo-Americans; there are words in both languages designating them. The Zunis call them *Mumankwe* (Mormon people), the Navahos *Gamali.* Members of both Indian groups clearly remember the coming of the Mormon group to the Rimrock area. They view the Mormons both as missionaries and as important economic agents (traders, farmers, and ranchers). The conflict between the missionary and the economic aims of the Mormons reaches more intense form in their relationships with the Navahos than in their relationships with the Zunis, since the Mormons have replaced the Navahos on their best lands while no Zuni land has passed into Mormon hands. In terms of both the amount of contact and the economic and emotional investment involved, the Navaho-Mormon relationship is one of the most important points of intercultural contact in the whole region.

The Mormon view of the Indians is strongly colored by their conception of them as "Lamanites." The aims of the Mormons with respect to the Indians have been explicitly stated in many of the writings of their church. Talmage writes: "The Lamanites, while increasing in numbers, fell under the curse of divine displeasure; they became dark in skin and benighted in spirit, forgot the God of their fathers, lived in wild nomadic life, and degenerated into the fallen state in which the American Indians, their lineal descendants, were found by those who rediscovered the western continent."[6] In keeping with this conception of their origin, the Mormons believe that it is wrong to destroy the faith of the Indians, which is viewed not as a false but as degenerate form of the "true" religion. Mormons allow Indians to practice their own ceremonials and even attempt to relate elements of Indian religion to elements in the Bible and the Book of Mormon. They tend to interpret the Zuni *koyemci,* or "mudheads," who function partly as ceremonial clowns, as representations of the twelve apostles of Christ. (Since the *koyemci* are only ten in number and their ceremonial behavior is often obscene, establishing the connection takes a great deal of imagination.) Similarly, the Shalako ceremonial is viewed as a Zuni version of Christmas.

Missionary zeal to convert the "Lamanites" to Mormonism has been reawakened in recent years. Not only has the official missionary program been stepped up in tempo and numbers, but the establishment of a Nazarene Church among the Rimrock Navahos in 1954 has been a stimulus for local Mormon missionary activity. The missionary emphasis has also been important in stimulating Mormons to learn about Indian customs and to learn to speak Navaho and Zuni, although English is now the usual language of communication. As a result, the Mormons know far more about Indian culture than the Texans do.

While the official missionary view of the Indians has been of crucial importance in intercultural relations over the years, two other features of the Mormon "cognitive map" of Indians often offset the missionary attitudes. The Mormons share many of the general Anglo-American attitudes of superiority toward peoples who are different in language and customs, who are "dirty" and "uncivilized." Indians are not regarded as social equals when it comes to intermarriage, interdining, and other forms of close social interaction. There is some difference in attitudes toward Zunis and Navahos in these respects. The Mormons regard the Zunis as "a higher type of Indian," "an agricultural home-loving people," whereas "the Navaho is more of a nomad; stays where night overtakes him, in a little brush shelter." There is some speculation in Rimrock as to whether the Zunis might not be "Nephites" rather than "Lamanites." Further, the successful operation of the Mormon economic system depends upon Indian laborers and Indian customers, especially Navahos, in the local trading posts.

While the Zunis and Navahos perceive the conflicting attitudes and aims of the Mormons in their relationships with them, the Mormons do not perceive this conflict at all realistically and are often surprised by the negative responses they receive to their missionary efforts. The Mormon bishop expressed astonishment when we asked how he expected to convert the Navahos when he and his kinsmen had taken their lands in the past and were currently treating them as dependent laborers and customers in the Mormon economic system.

The key intercultural roles between the Mormons and the Indians are missionary-potential convert, trader-customer, and employer-employee. The local missionary work is directed by the head of the Stake Missionary Board, who lives in Rimrock and is the largest landowner and wealthiest Indian trader in the village. He was later chosen to be First Councilor of the President of the Mission Board for the whole Mormon church, a choice which seems strange considering his reputation for "exploiting" the Indians economically. The actual missionary work is done by local Rimrock people and by mission teams of young men sent in from other areas who work in pairs. The work is done by visiting Navaho hogans and Zuni homes, talking to the Indians, and urging them to come to church on Sunday. A mission church has been established for Sunday services in the Navaho area. The Zunis have rejected Mormon efforts to establish a mission chapel in the pueblo. The missionary efforts with the Navahos have been relatively successful in recent years. The local ward now carries some 112 Navahos on the rolls; one Navaho has been elevated to the Melchizedek priesthood, a second is a member of the Aaronic priesthood. The program has met with more resistance in Zuni. As of 1952, only five nuclear families had been converted and one man made a member of the Melchizedek priesthood.

The Mormon trader-Indian customer is the key intercultural role in the operation of both the Mormon and Navaho economic systems. The large trading post in Rimrock (with two smaller stores, one at La Peña and the other at the Navaho Day School) sells goods for a profit to the Navahos and buys Navaho wool, lambs, rugs, pinyon nuts, and other products, reselling them at a profit in the outside market. The trader advances credit to Navaho families for the purchase of food, clothing, automobiles, and other commodities. When an account becomes too large, the trader announces that there will be no more credit until some of the debt is repaid and, in his role as a recruiting agent for the railroad, urges the Navaho to go off and work on the railroad until he can pay his bill. Or the trader may accept a mortgage on the Navaho's sheep or on his automobile as a guarantee that the debt will be paid. The trader also controls sources of income coming into the Navaho community. He has strict control of the funds paid to the Navahos for the products they sell him; he also has matters arranged so that state welfare checks and off-season railroad unemployment checks come to the Navahos addressed in care of the trading post. By such measures the trader insures that bills are paid within a reasonable time—a fact of crucial importance to him since he usually pays cash each month to wholesale houses in Railtown that sell him the goods he resells to the Indians.

The two-way profit and the tight control over income and credit are standard operating procedures throughout Navaho country. Given the obligations which the trader has to the outside market and to the outside banks which finance him, the system is probably necessary for the successful operation of a trading post. But it has the effect of keeping the Navahos in a dependent economic status and of stifling their initiative to learn about and assume more economic responsibility.

The employer-employee relationship takes the form mainly of Mormons hiring Navahos to work by the day on farms and ranches, especially at harvest time, and to do various kinds of work on construction jobs in the village of Rimrock. In these wage-work situations, the Navahos are seldom fed and housed with the families of the Mormon employers; they either camp out at the edge of town or are given a small outlying shack or shed to live in. (This is striking contrast with Spanish-American and Zuni employers who often feed and house the Navahos in their own homes.)

The guest-host relationship shared by Zunis, Navahos, and Spanish-Americans is by and large absent from intercultural contacts between Indians and either Mormons or Texans. Occasionally an Indian will be given a meal in a Mormon home (usually fed separately) and sometimes will be invited to stay all night. On rare occasions, Mormon men eat meals in Navaho hogans. But the usual day-to-day contact takes place in the missionary situation, in the trading post, or in the wage-work situation.

Other minor forms of patterned intercultural contact occur sporadically. Mormons have been known to seek advice on herbal treatments for certain disorders from Navaho curers; one or two Mormon men have taken sweat baths with Navahos; there have been a number of illicit sexual affairs involving Mormon men and Navaho women. No intermarriage has occurred between the local Mormon and Navaho populations, and the sanctions are strong against such an occurrence. The Mormons frequently bury dead Navahos, a task which the Navahos, with their fear of the dead, are delighted to turn over to the Mormons.

INDIAN-TEXAN RELATIONSHIPS

The Zuni-Texan relationship is the most tenuous of the intercultural connections in this area. Most of the Zuni informants failed to characterize the Texans as a special group of Anglos, and it is apparent that contacts have been slight. The Zunis recognize that there is a group of people living in Homestead, a community they pass through on their way to Salt Lake to gather salt, who live by growing pinto beans. One Zuni family has come to know a number of Texan homesteaders who went to them for help when they were stuck in the mud near the Zuni ranch. The Navahos have had much closer contacts with the Texans, especially at La Peña, but also at Homestead. They designate the Texans as a separate group whom they call *Tejanos,* following the Spanish usage. Their image of them involves most centrally the fact of their engaging in bean-farming.

In the Texan group there is considerable variation in the image held of the Indians. Many informants in Homestead, after twenty years of residence in proximity to these two Indian cultures, could not clearly distinguish between Zunis and Navahos, but tended to think of them all alike as "Indians." Thus, although the dress styles of Zuni and Navaho women are distinctly different, the informants could not distinguish between them when they saw them on the streets of Railtown. Others could distinguish between the two tribes, usually thinking of the Zunis as a "higher type of Indian" and speaking of them as "more industrious farming people" who live "in better houses than the Navahos." The Navahos were commonly regarded as the "poorest and most ignorant people on earth." Finally, there were two Texan families who had previously lived in very close proximity to Navahos in La Peña area and had depended upon them as their closest neighbors. These Texans learned to speak the Navaho language—unlike other homesteaders, who speak neither Navaho nor Zuni—and continued to maintain close relationships with the Navahos. They not only employ them on their farms, but also the Navahos eat with them and have close and warm contacts with them. The other Texans single out these families for special comment, generally failing to understand how they "can stand to have Indians eating at their tables and sitting in their houses."

The most important role in the Navaho-Texan relationship is that of employer-employee. In years when the bean crop promises to be good and when the weeds threaten to take over the crop, large numbers of Navahos are hired to hoe the fields and help with the harvesting operations. But these relationships are (except for the two families mentioned above) strictly economic and highly formalized. Generally, the Navahos camp in the woods near the fields where they are working and contacts with the Texan families are slight.

It is highly significant that the trader-customer role and the missionary-potential convert role are unimportant in the Navaho-Texan relationship. Although a few Navahos trade at Homestead stores, the Homestead storekeepers have never encouraged their business. They do not like the idea of having Indians in their stores which are "for white folks," and they have never learned the language and the trading habits of the Navahos as the Mormons have. Nor is there any attempt on the part of the Homestead churches to do missionary work among the Indians. However, Homestead itself is regarded as a mission area by the churches and there is still much missionary work to be done among the homesteaders.

The homesteader-Navaho relationship is undergoing an important change.

With the shift from federal to state responsibility for Indian education, large numbers of Navaho children are now enrolled in the Homestead school system. The Texan community is ambivalent about this development. They do not like the idea of having Indian children in their classrooms; but the increased enrollment makes it possible to maintain the school system in the face of decreasing Texan population. This development is likely to have a strong influence on relations between these two groups.

MORMON-TEXAN RELATIONSHIPS

The Texans' contacts with Mormons back on the Plains were limited to acquaintances with a few missionaries. For the most part, they held the familiar stereotype of Mormons as people who had a "peculiar religion" and "more than one wife." In the Rimrock area, the Texans came to admire and envy the Mormons' economic organization, their irrigated land, and more promising prospects for crops each year. Although denominationalism is rife in the Texan communities, they do not regard the Mormon religion as an acceptable variety of Christianity. It was a shock for the Texans to discover that the Mormons dance in their chuch and that they open and close their dances with a prayer. In recalling the first time he attended a Mormon dance, one of the Texans commented:

> We didn't know anything about Mormons. Never been around them much. Well, we went to that dance and directly they said a prayer. All of our women were sitting around talking, yackety-yackety, and somebody tapped them on the shoulder and said, "they're prayin." And you should have seen the look on them women's faces when they saw them Mormons prayin' to start a dance!

The Texans also tend to regard the Mormons as "cliquish" and somewhat "unfriendly" and fail to understand why anyone "wants to live all bunched up the way them Mormons do."

The Mormons consider their way of life superior to that of the homesteaders. They commonly call them "Tejaners," a Mormon version of the Spanish usage *Tejano*. Some Mormons will admit that the Texans have the virtue of being more friendly, of "mixing more with others," and the Texan efforts in the face of severe farming risks are admired, but in general the Texan way of life is regarded as "rough" and "immoral." The Mormons have attempted to persuade the Texans to take up the "better" Mormon way of life. For a time they gave almost monthly sermons in the Homestead Community Church. There have been no converts in Homestead, the only two Mormons in the community being Mormon wives married into the group, but one family has been coverted in the La Peña community. This conversion is a particularly interesting case, since the man has an earlier record of making "bootleg corn likker" and selling it illegally to the Indians. But he gave up his "evil ways," and became a good Mormon, and in fact, did missionary work for the Mormons among the Navahos. One Texan woman from the La Peña group was also converted when she married a Mormon husband from Rimrock.

Although there is some trading in livestock, feed, and other crops, the most important contacts between the two groups are not economic but social and recreational. The recreational contacts take the form of baseball games scheduled between the two village teams and attendance at each others' dances and rodeos. But considerable strain in the relationship is evident; many "good Mormons" hesitate to attend Texan dances, because they risk coming into close contact with the drinking parties which are inevitable aspects of these affairs. Most Mormons who attend Texan dances regularly are "Jack Mormons" who enjoy the opportunity to escape the watchful eyes of their elders and have a good time at the Texan "hoedowns." And the Mormons dislike having too many Texans at their dances in Rimrock because they always bring liquor and not only get "likkered up" themselves but generously provide liquor for the "Jack Mormons."

The closest social contacts are maintained by the teenagers of the two communities who interdate. These courtships have led to eight intermarriages: four Mormon girls married Texan men, and four Mormon men married Texan girls. One of the latter type ended in divorce after a few years, but the others have been relatively successful. Although there has been considerable pressure on them to do so, the Texan husbands have not joined the Mormon church; one of the Texan women has joined the Mormon church but not the others. In almost all cases the children of these mixed marriages have been "blessed" and will probably become Mormons.

A ninth intermarriage has occurred between a Mormon girl from Utah and a Texan in Homestead. In this case the wife was previously married to a Mormon who was a Marine "buddy" of this homesteader. Before the Mormon was killed at Iwo Jima, his "buddy" promised to look after the wife if anything happened to him. After the war, the Texan went to Utah to call on the widow and later married her and brought her back to New Mexico. The intercultural strains in this marriage epitomized the conflicts between Mormon and Texan values. The Mormon wife (and her family) tried to persuade the Texan to become a Mormon and give up drinking and smoking. She was also worried by the fact that she was "sealed" to her first husband "for all eternity"; yet she loves her second husband more than the first. Meanwhile the Texan husband scoffs at the drinking and smoking taboos and the Mormon beliefs concerning the afterlife. The difficulties were finally resolved after ten years, when in 1956 the husband became a Mormon and the family moved to the Mormon community of Bluewater, New Mexico.

ANGLO–SPANISH-AMERICAN RELATIONSHIPS

From the point of view of the total populations involved, the Anglo–Spanish-

American relationship is the most important intercultural boundary in the contemporary Southwest. The state of New Mexico is about 40 percent Spanish-American in population, and Spanish is still an "official" state language in the sense that legal notices must be printed in both English and Spanish.

Various segments of the Anglo population have reacted quite differently to contacts with Spanish-Americans. This contrast is sharp with respect to the two varieties of Anglo-American culture represented in the Rimrock area, the Mormons and the Texans. The Mormons define the Spanish-Americans as "Lamanites," hence important potential converts. They are also thought to be in need of conversion in order that they might acquire the "good living habits" of the Mormons. The Mormons are bothered by the fact that the Spanish-Americans have been the main source of supply of liquor to the Indians. The Spanish-Americans are recognized as being strongly Catholic and the difficulty of persuading them to change churches is considered realistically. But, just as the Mormons have considerable knowledge of Indian culture stemming from their missionary interests, they have considerable knowledge of Spanish-American culture, and many Rimrock Mormons speak some Spanish, a few fluently. The knowledge of Spanish-American and Mexican culture is particularly impressive in the Rimrock families who lived in Chihuahua, Mexico, for a number of years before they settled at Rimrock.

The Spanish-American image of Mormons is less clear than their image of Texans. Few items stand out as characteristic Mormon symbols, except the fact that the Mormons attempt to proselytize them. The general picture is one of a rather distant and neutral relationship, from the Spanish-American point of view. The key intercultural roles are focused around economic trade, especially in livestock and in employer-employee situations: Spanish-Americans have worked in Mormon fields and Mormons have occasionally been hired by the richer Spanish-Americans. There have been no intermarriages in the Rimrock area.

In contrast, the Texan–Spanish-American relationship is characterized by affect on both sides, and both groups have well defined and explicit ideas of what they think the other is like. What is perhaps most persistent in the Texan cognitive orientations is their cultural "opaqueness." Despite close contacts with Atrisco for over twenty years, they know almost nothing about the essential elements of Spanish-American culture. Only a handful of the Texans speak more than a few words of Spanish. The Texans frequently attend the dances accompanying the annual fiesta, but none of the informants (other than the two Texans married to Spanish-Americans) had any conception of why the fiesta was held on a certain day each autumn, nor did they know that San José is the patron saint in whose honor the fiesta is given. The Texans manifest more intolerance towards the "Mexicans" than any group in the area and tend to think of them as "chile-pickers" or "greasers."

The Spanish-Americans, by contrast, are one of the most tolerant cultural groups in the region. They think of the other groups as having different *costumbres.* While they prefer their own *costumbres,* they feel that the others have a right to maintain their own customs. Almost all Spanish-Americans speak English which they have learned at school. They know more about *Tejano* culture than the Texans know about Spanish-American customs.

The key intercultural roles are storekeeper-customer, employer-employee, recreational (especially attendance at dances), teacher-pupil, and intermarriage. The stores in Homestead are owned and managed by the Texans, and, since Atrisco no longer has a store, the Spanish-Americans do a great deal of their trading there. They often stay to loaf and visit with the storekeeper and the Texan customers. The bartender-customer role is similar, except that in this case a Spanish-American owns the bar and his customers are both Spanish-Americans and Texans. In quantity of contact, the intercultural situations in the store and bar are the most important day-to-day contacts between the two groups. There is another economic intercultural role, for each year Texans employ Spanish-Americans to work in the bean fields. The Spanish-American fieldhands usually live at home and travel to and from work each day, but they may be fed by the Texan employer in his home at noon.

The most important intercultural recreation in the contemporary scene is provided by the dances which used to be held in both Atrisco and at La Peña. For the most part, the males who choose dancing partners from the other group are a few Texans who are either married to Spanish-American women or are for other reasons more tolerant in their attitudes toward other cultures, and a few of the most acculturated Spanish-Americans, such as sons of the former *patrón* of Atrisco, who may dance with Texan women. A more common Spanish-American response is that the Texan girls are *muy orgullosas* (very proud or haughty) and do not want to dance with a *Mexicano*. The political battle for control of the school system was finally won by the Texans as the Spanish-American population declined, and all Spanish-Americans of school age now attend school taught by Texan teachers in Homestead. The Spanish-Americans accept it as inevitable that their children will be attending a Texan-controlled school.

Despite the deep antagonism between the two groups, three intercultural marriages have taken place. One of these occurred between the daughter of a Texan schoolteacher and a young Spanish-American. This couple did not remain in the area, and there is little data on the success of the marriage. The other marriages occurred between Texan men and two daughters of the former *patrón* of Atrisco. These marriages have been successful, and the families are still living in the Homestead area. One couple is childless, but the other couple has four children, all of whom are being reared as Catholics, and the Texan husband has also joined the Catholic church. There is much discussion of these two marriages on the part of both groups. On the whole, the Texan husbands, as would be expected, are more fully accepted in the Spanish-American community than are their wives in the Texan community. Although the four children of the Texan—

Spanish-American marriage are fair-skinned and brown or blonde in hair color, there is a tendency of both groups to consider them as racial mixtures. The Texans think of the children as "halfbreeds"; the Spanish-Americans call them *coyotes,* with the connotation that although they are good children now, they may not turn out well in the long run.

Over and above the special historical events which have characterized the intercultural contacts in the immediate Rimrock area, there are many dimensions to the potential or actual conflict between Texans and Spanish-Americans in the Southwest which make long-range adjustments extremely difficult. There is important ecological conflict in the question of which group dominates the land base in this area, which was originally under Spanish and later under Mexican control but has become increasingly Texan. This conflict is especially acute when the traditional rancher-*versus*-farmer antagonism is added. In many areas, such as Homestead, the Spanish-Americans are predominantly Republicans, whereas the Texans are Democrats. The religious conflict between Catholics and Protestants is also involved. Racial and ethnic differences, real and supposed, have deep roots in Mexican and Texan history and are being perpetuated in the Southwest. Finally, the value-orientations of the two cultures are diametrically opposed at most points, with the Texans emphasizing future-time, mastery over nature, individualism, and a high degree of intolerance and opaqueness in intercultural relations, the Spanish-Americans emphasizing present-time, subjugation to nature, hierarchical and lineal social relationships, and a relatively high degree of tolerance in intercultural relations. It is not surprising that the local scene has been characterized by a great deal of difficulty between the "Mexicans" and *"Tejanos."*

INTERCULTURAL HIERARCHIES

In three important respects these interacting groups are segments of a larger system of relationships:

(1) From the point of view of the American national economic and political system, the five cultures must be regarded as subcultures. Each is related significantly to the prices, markets, factory goods, credit structures, and so on of our national economic system, and each is a segment of a political order in which the ultimate control of force is in the hands of the United States Government.

(2) Except in the case of Zuni culture, which exists only in our research area, the populations of each of the cultures studied are localized manifestations of cultural groups that have significant extensions outside the Rimrock area—the Rimrock Navaho are one band of the Navaho tribe; the Spanish-Americans in Tijeras and Atrisco form outlying communities of the Spanish-speaking population centered in the northern Rio Grande Valley; the Rimrock Mormons are a southwestern outpost of the intermountain Mormon "empire"; and the Texans are scattered from Texas itself westward to the Pacific Coast and elsewhere.

(3) In varying degrees the five groups are bound together in an internal areal system of relationships. Each tends to occupy one or more roles vis-a-vis the others, and a disturbance in intercultural relations between two of the groups will affect the relationships which each has with the other three cultures. For example, an increase in Mormon pressure upon the Navahos to join their church might result in more Navahos becoming Mormons, thereby disturbing the liquor business which the Spanish-Americans do with the Navahos and also disturbing Navaho-Zuni guest-host relationships (Zunis disapprove of Navahos joining the Mormon church).

Are the five cultures arranged in a social rank or prestige and power hierarchy? The answer is complicated because the cultures vary as to their definition of the nature of the hierarchical arrangements, but there are two basic interpretations. The Mormon and Texan view is that the rank order of the cultures in terms of both prestige and power is, in descending order: Mormans–Texans–Spanish-Americans–Zunis–Navahos. The Zuni and Navaho interpretation would tend to follow these lines:

They see the Anglo Mormons and Texans, undifferentiated in this respect, as "superior" to the Spanish-Americans; but they think of themselves as off to one side in a separate hierarchy with Zunis above Navahos and with Zunis ranking on a level with, or perhaps higher than, Spanish-Americans.

The Spanish-American interpretation is similar to that of the Mormons and Texans, except that, like the Indians, they do not clearly differentiate Mormons from Texans in a rank order and they often feel the Spanish-Americans are as "good" as the Mormons and Texans. They do, however, agree in placing the Zunis above the Navahos. There is general agreement that the Navahos are at the bottom of the rank order in both power and prestige in the Rimrock area.

One of the crucial bodies of evidence for this intercultural hierarchy is the over-all pattern of intermarriage. Going down the hierarchy, Mormons marry Texans but not Spanish-Americans or Indians; Texans marry Spanish-Americans but not Indians; Spanish-Americans marry Zunis but not Navahos (except for the two quite special cases described); Zunis marry Navahos.

This finding is buttressed by the data on employer-employee relationships. Going up the hierarchy this time, Navahos frequently work for the members of all the other groups; Zunis are employees of Spanish-American, Mormon, and Texan employers, but almost never work for Navahos; Spanish-Americans work for Mormons and Texans, rarely for Zunis, never for Navahos; Texans are frequently employed by Mormon employers, occasionally by Spanish-American employers, but never by Indians; Mormons sometimes work for Texans, in rare instances for Spanish-Americans, but never for Indians.

27. NOTES

1. Frank H. Cushing, *Zuni Breadstuff* (New York: Museum of the American Indian, Heye Foundation, Indian Notes and Monographs, Vol. VIII, 1920), pp. 534-35.

2. This term is probably derived from the historical search of the Spaniards for the Seven Cities of Cibola.

3. The Navaho term for "Mexicans" and "Spanish-Americans" is *Na-Kai*. Unlike the Zunis, the Navahos do not differentiate between "Spanish" and "Mexicans."

4. The concept of "intercultural roles" was developed by the SSRC Summer Seminar on Acculturation in 1953 in which Evon Z. Vogt was a participant.

5. The typical visit to pay respects to the *Santo* is a local manifestation of the widespread *promesa* (promise) pattern. A Spanish-American will pray to the *Santo* for some favor (e.g., to cure an illness or bring a relative safely back from the war) and make a *promesa* to undertake a pilgrimage to pay homage to the *Santo* after the favor is granted.

6. James Edward Talmage, *A Study of the Articles of Faith,* 12th ed. rev. (Salt Lake City, Church of Jesus Christ of Latter-Day Saints, 1924), p. 260.

28

The Mutual Images and Expectations of Anglo-Americans and Mexican-Americans*

OZZIE G. SIMMONS

A number of psychological and sociological studies have treated ethnic and racial stereotypes as they appear publicly in the mass media and also as held privately by individuals. The present paper is based on data collected for a study of a number of aspects of the relations between Anglo-Americans and Mexican-Americans in a South Texas community, and is concerned with the principal assumptions and expectations that Anglo- and Mexican-Americans hold of one another; how they see each other; the extent to which these pictures are realistic; and the implications of their intergroup relations and cultural differences for the fulfillment of their mutual expectations.[1]

THE COMMUNITY

The community studied (here called "Border City") is in South Texas, about 250 miles south of San Antonio. Driving south from San Antonio, one passes over vast expanses of brushland and grazing country, then suddenly comes upon acres of citrus groves, farmlands rich with vegetables and cotton, and long rows of palm trees. This is the "Magic Valley," an oasis in the semidesert region of South Texas. The Missouri Pacific Railroad (paralleled by Highway 83, locally called "the longest street in the world") bisects twelve major towns and cities of the Lower Rio Grande City, 103 miles to the west.

Border City is neither the largest nor the smallest of these cities, and is physically and culturally much like the rest. Its first building was constructed in 1905. By 1920 it had 5,331 inhabitants, and at the time of our study these had increased to an estimated 17,500. The completion of the St. Louis, Brownsville, and Mexico Railroad in 1904 considerably facilitated Anglo-American immigration to the valley. Before this the valley had been inhabited largely by Mexican ranchers, who maintained large haciendas in the traditional Mexican style based on peonage. Most of these haciendas are now divided into large or small tracts that are owned by Anglo-Americans, who obtained them through purchase or less legitimate means. The position of the old Mexican-American landowning families has steadily deteriorated, and today these families, with a few exceptions, are completely overshadowed by the Anglo-Americans, who have taken over their social and economic position in the community.

The Anglo-American immigration into the valley was paralleled by that of the Mexicans from across the border, who were attracted by the seemingly greater opportunities for farm labor created by the introduction of irrigation and the subsequent agricultural expansion. Actually, there had been a small but steady flow of Mexican immigration into South Texas that long antedated the Anglo-American immigration. At present, Mexican-Americans probably constitute about two-fifths of the total population of the valley.

In Border City, Mexican-Americans comprise about 56 percent of the population. The southwestern part of the city, adjoining and sometimes infiltrating the business and industrial areas, is variously referred to as "Mexiquita," "Mexican-town," and "Little Mexico" by the city's Anglo-Americans, and as the *colonia* by the Mexican-Americans. With few exceptions, the *colonia* in inhabited only by Mexican-Americans, most of whom live in close proximity to one another in indifferently constructed houses on tiny lots. The north side of the city, which lies across the railroad tracks, is inhabited almost completely by Anglo-Americans. Its appearance is in sharp contrast to that of the *colonia* in that it is strictly residential and displays much better housing.

In the occupational hierarchy of Border City, the top level (the growers, packers, canners, businessmen, and professionals) is overwhelmingly Anglo-American. In the middle group (the white-collar occupations) Mexicans are prominent only where their bilingualism makes them useful, for example, as clerks and salesmen. The bottom level (farm laborers, shed and cannery workers, and domestic servants) is overwhelmingly Mexican-American.

These conditions result from a number of factors, some quite distinct from the reception accorded Mexican-Americans by Anglo-Americans. Many Mexican-Americans are still recent immigrants and are thus relatively unfamiliar with Anglo-American culture and urban living, or else persist in their tendency to live apart and maintain their own institutions whenever possible. Among their disadvantages, however, the negative attitudes and discriminatory practices of the Anglo-American group must be counted. It is only fair to say, with the late Ruth Tuck, that much of what Mexican-Americans have suffered at Anglo-American hands has not been perpetrated deliberately but through indifference, that it has been done not with the fist but with the elbow.[2] The average social and economic status of the Mexican-American group has been improving, and many are moving upward. This is partly owing to increasing acceptance by the Anglo-American group, but chiefly to the efforts of the Mexican-Americans themselves.

ANGLO-AMERICAN ASSUMPTIONS AND EXPECTATIONS

Robert Lynd writes of the dualism in the principal assumptions that guide

Americans in conducting their everyday life and identifies the attempt to "live by contrasting rules of the game" as a characteristic aspect of our culture.[3] This pattern of moral compromise, symptomatic of what is likely to be only vaguely a conscious moral conflict, is evident in Anglo-American assumptions and expectations with regard to define what intergroup relations ought to be, and in the popular notions held by Anglo-Americans as to what Mexican-Americans are "really" like. In the first case there is a response to the "American creed," which embodies ideals of the essential dignity of the individual and of certain inalienable rights to freedom, justice, and equal opportunity. Accordingly, Anglo-Americans believe that Mexican-Americans must be accorded full acceptance and equal status in the larger society. When their orientation to these ideals is uppermost, Anglo-Americans believe that the assimilation of Mexican-Americans is only a matter of time, contingent solely on the full incorporation of Anglo-American values and ways of life.

These expectations regarding the assimilation of the Mexican are most clearly expressed in the notion of the "high type" of Mexican. It is based on three criteria: occupational achievement and wealth (the Anglo-American's own principal criteria of status) and command of Anglo-American ways. Mexican-Americans who can so qualify are acceptable for membership in the service clubs and a few other Anglo-American organizations and for limited social intercourse. They may even intermarry without being penalized or ostracized. Both in their achievements in business and agriculture and in wealth, they compare favorably with middle-class Anglo-Americans, and they manifest a high command of the latter's ways. This view of the "high type" of Mexican reflects the Anglo-American assumption that Mexicans are assimilable; it does not necessarily insure a full acceptance of even the "high type" of Mexican or that his acceptance will be consistent.

The assumption that Mexican-Americans will be ultimately assimilated was not uniformly shared by all the Anglo-Americans who were our informants in Border City. Regardless of whether they expressed adherence to this ideal, however, most Anglo-Americans expressed the contrasting assumption that Mexican-Americans are essentially inferior. Thus the same people may hold assumptions and expectations that are contradictory, although expressed at different times and in different situations. As in the case of their adherence to the ideal of assimilability, not all Anglo-Americans hold the same assumptions and expectations with respect to the inferiority of Mexican-Americans; and even those who agree vary in the intensity of their beliefs. Some do not believe in the Mexican's inferiority at all; some are relatively moderate or sceptical, while others express extreme views with considerable emotional intensity.

Despite this variation, the Anglo-Americans' principal assumptions and expectations emphasize the Mexicans' presumed inferiority. In its most characteristic pattern, such inferiority is held to be self-evident. As one Anglo-American woman put it. "Mexicans are inferior because they are so typically and naturally

Mexican." Since they are so obviously inferior, their present subordinate status is appropriate and is really their own fault. There is a ready identification between Mexicans and menial labor, buttressed by an image of the Mexican worker as improvident, undependable, irresponsible, childlike, and indolent. If Mexicans are fit for only the humblest labor, there is nothing abnormal about the fact that most Mexican workers are at the bottom of the occupational pyramid, and the fact that most Mexicans are unskilled workers is sufficient proof that they belong in that category.

Associated with the assumption of Mexican inferiority is that of the homogeneity of this group—that is, all Mexicans are alike. Anglo-Americans may classify Mexicans as being of "high type" and "low type" and at the same time maintain that "a Mexican is a Mexican." Both notions serve a purpose, depending on the situation. The assumption that all Mexicans are alike buttresses the assumption of inferiority by making it convenient to ignore the fact of the existence of a substantial number of Mexican-Americans who represent all levels of business and professional achievement. Such people are considered exceptions to the rule.

ANGLO-AMERICAN IMAGES OF MEXICAN-AMERICANS

To employ Gordon Allport's definition, a stereotype is an exaggerated belief associated with a category, and its function is to justify conduct in relation to that category. Some of the Anglo-American images of the Mexican have no ascertainable basis in fact, while others have at least a kernel of truth. Although some components of these images derive from behavior patterns that are characteristic of some Mexican-Americans in some situations, few if any of the popular generalizations about them are valid as stated, and none is demonstrably true of all. Some of the images of Mexican-Americans are specific to a particular area of intergroup relations, such as the image of the Mexican-American's attributes as a worker. Another is specific to politics and describes Mexicans as ready to give their votes to whoever will pay for them or provide free barbecues and beer.[4] Let us consider a few of the stereotypical beliefs that are widely used on general principles to justify Anglo-American practices of exclusion and subordination.

One such general belief accuses Mexican-Americans of being unclean. The example given of this supposed characteristic most frequently refer to a lack of personal cleanliness and environmental hygiene and to a high incidence of skin ailments ascribed to a lack of hygienic practices. Indeed, there are few immigrant groups, regardless of their ethnic background, to whom this defect has not been attributed by the host society, as well as others prominent in stereotypes of the Mexican. It has often been observed that for middle-class Americans cleanliness is not simply a matter of keeping clean but is also an index to the morals and virtues of the individual. It is largely true that Mexicans tend to be much more casual in hygienic practices than Anglo-Americans. Moreover, their labor in the field, the packing sheds, and the towns is rarely clean work, and it is possible that many Anglo-Americans base their conclusions on what they observe in such situations. There is no evidence of a higher incidence of skin ailments among Mexicans than among Anglo-Americans. The belief that Mexicans are unclean is useful for rationalizing the Anglo-practice of excluding Mexicans from any situation that involves close or allegedly close contact with Anglo-Americans, as in residence, and the common use of swimming pools and other recreational facilities.

Drunkenness and criminality are a pair of traits that have appeared regularly in the stereotypes applied to immigrant groups. They have a prominent place in Anglo-American images of Mexicans. If Mexicans are inveterate drunkards and have criminal tendencies, a justification is provided for excluding them from full participation in the life of the community. It is true that drinking is a popular activity among Mexican-Americans and that total abstinence is rare, except among some Protestant Mexican-Americans. Drinking varies, however, from the occasional consumption of a bottle of beer to the heavy drinking of more potent beverages, so that the frequency of drinking and drunkenness is far from being evenly distributed among Mexican-Americans. Actually, this pattern is equally applicable to the Anglo-American group. The ample patronage of bars in the Anglo-American part of Border City, and the drinking behavior exhibited by Anglo-Americans when they cross the river to Mexico indicate that Mexicans have no monopoly on drinking or drunkenness. It is true that the number of arrests for drunkenness in Border City is greater among Mexicans, but this is probably because Mexicans are more vulnerable to arrest. The court records in Border City show little difference in the contributions made to delinquency and crime by Anglo- and Mexican-Americans.

Another cluster of images in the Anglo-American stereotype portrays Mexican-Americans as deceitful and of a "low" morality, as mysterious, unpredictable, and hostile to Anglo-Americans. It is quite possible that Mexicans resort to a number of devices in their relations with Anglo-Americans, particularly in relations with employers, to compensate for their disadvantages, which may be construed by Anglo-Americans as evidence of deceitfulness. The whole nature of the dominant-subordinate relationship does not make for frankness on the part of Mexicans or encourage them to face up directly to Anglo-Americans in most intergroup contacts. As to the charge of immorality, one need only recognize the strong sense of loyalty and obligation that Mexicans feel in their familial and interpersonal relations to know that the charge is baseless. The claim that Mexicans are mysterious and deceitful may in part reflect Anglo-American reactions to actual differences in culture and personality, but like the other beliefs considered here, is highly exaggerated. The imputation of hostility to Mexicans, which is manifested in a reluctance to enter the *colonia*, particularly at night, may have its kernel of truth, but appears to be largely a projection of the Anglo-American's own feelings.

All three of these images can serve to justify exclusion and discrimination: if

Mexicans are deceitful and immoral, they do not have to be accorded equal status and justice; if they are mysterious and unpredictable, there is no point in treating them as one would a fellow Anglo-American; and if they are hostile and dangerous, it is best that they live apart in colonies of their own.

Not all Anglo-American images of the Mexican are unfavorable. Among those usually meant to be complimentary are the beliefs that all Mexicans are musical and always ready for a fiesta, that they are very "romantic" rather than "realistic" (which may have unfavorable overtones as well), and that they love flowers and can grow them under the most adverse conditions. Although each of these beliefs may have a modicum of truth, it may be noted that they tend to reinforce Anglo-American images of Mexicans as childlike and irresponsible, and thus they support the notion that Mexicans are capable only of subordinate status.

MEXICAN-AMERICAN ASSUMPTIONS, EXPECTATIONS, AND IMAGES

Mexican-Americans are as likely to hold contradictory assumptions and distorted images as are Anglo-Americans. Their principal assumptions, however, must reflect those of Anglo-Americans—that is, Mexicans must take into account the Anglo-Americans' conflict as to their potential equality and present inferiority, since they are the object of such imputations. Similarly, their images of Anglo-Americans are not derived wholly independently, but to some extent must reflect their own subordinate status. Consequently, their stereotypes of Anglo-Americans are much less elaborate, in part because Mexicans feel no need of justifying the present intergroup relation, in part because the very nature of their dependent position forces them to view the relation more realistically than Anglo-Americans do. For the same reasons, they need not hold to their beliefs about Anglo-Americans with the rigidity and intensity so often characteristic of the latter.

Any discussion of these assumptions and expectations requires some mention of the class distinctions within the Mexican-American group. Its middle class, though small as compared with the lower class, is powerful within the group and performs the critical role of intermediary in negotiations with the Anglo-American group. Middle-class status is based on education and occupation, family background, readiness to serve the interests of the group, on wealth, and the degree of acculturation, or command of Anglo-American ways. Anglo-Americans recognize Mexican class distinctions (although not very accurately) in their notions of the "high type" and "low type" of Mexicans.

In general, lower-class Mexicans do not regard the disabilities of their status as being nearly as severe as do middle-class Mexican-Americans. This is primarily a reflection of the insulation between the Anglo-American world and that of the Mexican lower class. Most Mexicans, regardless of class, are keenly aware of Anglo-American attitudes and practices with regard to their group, but lower-class Mexicans do not conceive of participation in the larger society as necessary nor do they regard Anglo-American practices of exclusion as affecting them directly. Their principal reaction has been to maintain their isolation, and thus they have not been particularly concerned with improving their status by acquiring Anglo-American ways, a course more characteristic of the middle-class Mexican.

Mexican-American assumptions and expectations regarding Anglo-Americans must be qualified, then, as being more characteristic of middle- than of lower-class Mexican-Americans. Mexicans, like Anglo-Americans, are subject to conflicts in their ideals, not only because of irrational thinking on their part but also because of Anglo-American inconsistencies between ideal and practice. As for ideals expressing democratic values, Mexican expectations are for obvious reasons the counterpart of the Anglo-Americans'—that Mexican-Americans should be accorded full acceptance and equal opportunity. They feel a considerable ambivalence, however, as to the Anglo-American expectation that the only way to achieve this goal is by a full incorporation of Anglo-American values and ways of life, for this implies the ultimate loss of their cultural identity as Mexicans. On the one hand, they favor the acquisition of Anglo-American culture and the eventual remaking of the Mexican in the Anglo-American image; but on the other hand, they are not so sure that Anglo-American acceptance is worth such a price. When they are concerned with this dilemma, Mexicans advocate a fusion with Anglo-American culture in which the "best" of the Mexican ways, as they view it, would be retained along with the incorporation of the "best" of the Anglo-American ways, rather than a one-sided exchange in which all that is distinctively Mexican would be lost.

A few examples will illustrate the point of view expressed in the phrase, "the best of both ways." A premium is placed on speaking good, unaccented English, but the retention of good Spanish is valued just as highly as "a mark of culture that should not be abandoned." Similarly, there is an emphasis on the incorporation of behavior patterns that are considered characteristically Anglo-American and that will promote "getting ahead," but not to the point at which the drive for power and wealth would become completely dominant, as is believed to be the case with Anglo-Americans.

Mexican ambivalence about becoming Anglo-American or achieving a fusion of the "best" of both cultures is compounded by their ambivalence about another issue, that of equality versus inferiority. That Anglo-Americans are dominant in the society and seem to monopolize its accomplishments and rewards leads Mexicans at times to draw the same conclusion that Anglo-Americans do, namely, that Mexicans are inferior. This questioning of their own sense of worth exists in all classes of the Mexican-American group, although with varying intensity, and plays a substantial part in every adjustment to intergroup relations. There is a pronounced tendency to concede the superiority of Anglo-American ways and consequently to define Mexican ways as undesirable, inferior, and disreputable. The tendency to believe in his own inferiority is counterbalanced, however, by the Mexican's fierce racial pride, which sets the tone of Mexican demands and strivings for equal status, even though these may slip into feelings of inferiority.

The images Mexicans have of Anglo-Americans may not be so elaborate or so emotionally charged as the images that Anglo-Americans have of Mexicans, but they are nevertheless stereotypes, overgeneralized, and exaggerated, although used primarily for defensive rather than justificatory purposes. Mexican images of Anglo-Americans are sometimes favorable, particularly when they identify such traits as initiative, ambition, and industriousness as being peculiarly Anglo-American. Unfavorable images are prominent, however, and, although they may be hostile, they never impute inferiority to Anglo-Americans. Most of the Mexican stereotypes evaluate Anglo-Americans on the basis of their attitudes toward Mexican-Americans. For example, one such classification provides a two-fold typology. The first type, the "majority," includes those who are cold, unkind, mercenary, and exploitative. The second type, the "minority," consists of those who are friendly, warm, just, and unprejudiced. For the most part, Mexican images of Anglo-Americans reflect the latter's patterns of exclusion and assumptions of superiority, as experienced by Mexican-Americans. Thus Anglo-Americans are pictured as stolid, phlegmatic, cold-hearted, and distant. They are also said to be braggarts, conceited, inconstant, and insincere.

INTERGROUP RELATIONS, MUTUAL EXPECTATIONS, AND CULTURAL DIFFERENCES

A number of students of intergroup relations assert that research in this area has yet to demonstrate any relation between stereotypical beliefs and intergroup behavior; indeed, some insist that under certain conditions ethnic attitudes and discrimination can vary independently. Arnold M. Rose, for example, concludes that "from a heuristic standpoint it may be desirable to assume that patterns of intergroup relations, on the one hand, and attitudes of prejudice and stereotyping, on the other hand, are fairly unrelated phenomena although they have reciprocal influences on each other . . . "[5] In the present study, no systematic attempt was made to investigate the relation between the stereotypical beliefs of particular individuals and their actual intergroup behavior; but the study did yield much evidence that both images which justify group separatism and separateness itself are characteristic aspects of intergroup relations in Border City. One of the principal findings is that in those situations in which contact between Anglo-Americans and Mexicans is voluntary (such as residence, education, recreation, religious worship, and social intercourse) the characteristic pattern is separateness rather than common participation. Wherever intergroup contact is necessary, as in occupational activities and the performance of commercial and professional services, it is held to the minimum sufficient to accomplish the purpose of the contact. The extent of this separateness is not constant for all members of the two groups, since it tends to be less severe between Anglo-

Americans and those Mexicans they define as of a "high type." Nevertheless, the evidence reveals a high degree of compatability between beliefs and practices in Border City's intergroup relations, although the data have nothing to offer for the identification of direct relationships.

In any case, the separateness that characterizes intergroup relations cannot be attributed solely to the exclusion practices of the Anglo-American group. Mexicans have tended to remain separate by choice as well as by necessity. Like many other ethnic groups, they have often found this the easier course, since they need not strain to learn another language or to change their ways and manners. The isolation practices of the Mexican group are as relevant to an understanding of intergroup relations as are the exclusion practices of the Anglo-Americans.

This should not, however, obscure the fact that to a wide extent the majority of Mexican-Americans share the patterns of living of Anglo-American society; many of their ways are already identical. Regardless of the degree of their insulation from the larger society, the demands of life in the United States have required basic modifications of the Mexicans' cultural tradition. In material culture, Mexicans are hardly to be distinguished from Anglo-Americans, and there have been basic changes in medical beliefs and practices and in the customs regarding godparenthood. Mexicans have acquired English in varying degrees, and their Spanish has become noticeably Anglicized. Although the original organization of the family has persisted, major changes have occurred in patterns of traditional authority, as well as in child training and courtship practices. Still, it is the exceedingly rare Mexican-American, no matter how acculturated he may be to the dominant society, who does not in some degree retain the more subtle characteristics of his Mexican heritage, particularly in his conception of time and in other fundamental value orientations, as well as in his modes of participation in interpersonal relations. Many of the most acculturated Mexican-Americans have attempted to exemplify what they regard as "the best of both ways." They have become largely Anglo-American in their way of living, but they still retain fluent Spanish and a knowledge of their traditional culture, and they maintain an identification with their own heritage while participating in Anglo-American culture. Nevertheless, this sort of achievement still seems a long way off for many Mexican-Americans who regard it as desirable.

A predominant Anglo-American expectation is that the Mexicans will be eventually assimilated into the larger society; but this is contingent upon Mexicans' becoming just like Anglo-Americans. The Mexican counterpart to this expectation is only partially complementary. Mexicans want to be full members of the larger society, but they do not want to give up their cultural heritage. There is even less complementarity of expectation with regard to the present conduct of intergroup relations. Anglo-Americans believe they are justified in withholding equal access to the rewards of full acceptance as long as Mexicans remain "different," particularly since they interpret the differences (both those which have some basis in reality and those which have none) as evidence of inferiority. Mexicans, on the other hand, while not always certain that they are not inferior, clearly want equal opportunity and full acceptance now, not in some dim future, and they do not believe that their differences (either presumed or real) from Anglo-Americans offer any justification for the denial of opportunity and acceptance. Moreover, they do not find that acculturation is rewarded in any clear and regular way by progressive acceptance.

It is probable that both Anglo-Americans and Mexicans will have to modify their beliefs and practices if they are to realize more nearly their expectations of each other. Mutual stereotyping, as well as the exclusion practices of Anglo-Americans and the isolation practices of Mexicans, maintains the separateness of the two groups, and separateness is a massive barrier to the realization of their expectations. The process of acculturation is presently going on among Mexican-Americans and will continue, regardless of whether changes in Anglo-Mexican relations occur. Unless Mexican-Americans can validate their increasing command of Anglo-American ways by a free participation in the larger society, however, such acculturation is not likely to accelerate its present leisurely pace, nor will it lead to eventual assimilation. The *Colonia* is a relatively safe place in which new cultural acquisitions may be tried out, and thus it has its positive functions; but by the same token it is only in intergroup contacts with Anglo-Americans that acculturation is validated, that the Mexican's level of acculturation is tested, and that the distance he must yet travel to assimilation is measured.

CONCLUSIONS

There are major inconsistencies in the assumptions that Anglo-Americans and Mexican-Americans hold about one another. Anglo-Americans assume that Mexican-Americans are their potential, if not actual, peers, but at the same time assume they are their inferiors. The beliefs that presumably demonstrate the Mexican-Americans' inferiority tend to place them outside the accepted moral order and framework of Anglo-American society by attributing to them undesirable characteristics that make it "reasonable" to treat them differently from their fellow Anglo-Americans. Thus the negative images provide not only a rationalized definition of the intergroup relation that makes it palatable for Anglo-Americans, but also a substantial support for maintaining the relation as it is. The assumptions of Mexican-Americans about Anglo-Americans are similarly inconsistent, and their images of Anglo-Americans are predominantly negative, although these are primarily defensive rather than justificatory. The mutual expectations of the two groups contrast sharply with the ideal of a complementarity of expectations, in that Anglo-Americans expect Mexicans to become just like themselves, if they are to be accorded equal status in the larger society, whereas Mexican-Americans want full acceptance, regardless of the extent to which they give up their own ways and acquire those of the dominant group.

Anglo-Americans and Mexicans may decide to stay apart because they are different, but cultural differences provide no moral justification for one group to deny to the other equal opportunity and the rewards of the larger society. If the full acceptance of Mexicans by Anglo-Americans is contingent upon the disappearance of cultural differences, it will not be accorded in the foreseeable future. In our American society, we have often seriously underestimated the strength and tenacity of early cultural conditioning. We have expected newcomers to change their customs and values to conform to American ways as quickly as possible, without an adequate appreciation of the strains imposed by this process. An understanding of the nature of culture and of its interrelations with personality can make us more realistic about the rate at which cultural change can proceed and about the gains and costs for the individual who is subject to the experiences of acculturation. In viewing cultural differences primarily as disabilities, we neglect their positive aspects. Mexican-American culture represents the most constructive and effective means Mexican-Americans have yet been able to develop for coping with their changed natural and social environment. They will further exchange old ways for new only if these appear to be more meaningful and rewarding than the old, and then only if they are given full opportunity to acquire the new ways and to use them.

28. NOTES

1. The term "Anglo-American," as is common in the Southwest, refers to all residents of Border City who do not identify themselves as Spanish-speaking and of Mexican descent. The Anglo-Americans of Border City have emigrated there from all parts of the United States and represent a wide variety of regional and ethnic backgrounds. The terms "Mexican-American" and "Mexican," as used here, refer to all residents of Border City who are Spanish-speaking and of Mexican descent. The term "Spanish-speaking" is perhaps less objectionable to many people, but for present purposes is even less specific than Mexican or Mexican-American, since it also refers to ethnic groups that would have no sense of identification with the group under consideration here.

2. Ruth D. Tuck, *Not with the Fist* (New York: Harcourt, Brace, 1946).

3. Robert S. Lynd, *Knowledge for What?* (Princeton: Princeton University Press, 1948).

4. For an analysis of Mexican-American value orientations and behavior in the occupational and political spheres, see Ozzie G. Simmons, "Anglo-Americans and Mexican-Americans in South Texas: A Study in Dominant-Subordinate Group Relations" (Ph.D. dissertation, Harvard University, 1952).

5. Arnold M. Rose, "Intergroup Relations vs. Prejudice: Pertinent Theory for the Study of Social Change," *Social Problems* 4 (1956), pp. 173-76.

29

Between the Tracks and the Freeway: The Negro in Albuquerque*

ROGER W. BANKS

In the summer of 1905 twenty-nine Negroes met near Niagara Falls and organized the Niagara Movement. This was the first cohesive and sustained effort by Negroes to alleviate and eliminate specific racial problems in America. Eventually these radicals, which included William Monroe Trotter, Oswald Garrison Villard, and W. E. B. DuBois, allied themselves with a small group of influential white liberals and founded the National Association for the Advancement of Colored People. Since the founding of this Northern-oriented organization, the civil rights movement as a whole has experienced two distinct phases and is now in the midst of a third. What has happened throughout the nation and what has not happened in New Mexico can best be understood through a review of the three phases of the civil rights struggle.

Twenty years ago the struggle for civil rights and dignity reflected the goals, aspirations and the methods of the National Association for the Advancement of Colored People, America's wealthiest and most powerful civil rights organization. The NAACP's persistent efforts, using legal and educational techniques to end racial discrimination met with success in 1954 when the U.S. Supreme Court handed down a decision overthrowing the separate but equal doctrine in public education. Twenty years ago other civil rights and racially oriented groups such as the Black Panthers, the Black Muslims, the Southern Christian Leadership Conference, and the Student Nonviolent Coordinating Committee were nonexistent. Other established organizations, the National Urban League, the Congress of Racial Equality and the Southern Regional Council were essentially unknown on a national level. Yet today, most of them enjoy national prominence, national membership and considerable publicity. They are not only familiar to most Americans, but because of communication media are familiar to the citizenry of the world.

The major method employed in the drive for civil rights from the turn of the century until 1954 was that of professionalism. The NAACP and other civil

*Copyright 1969 by the University of New Mexico Press. Reprinted by permission of the publisher from Henry J. Tobias and Charles E. Woodhouse (eds.), *Minorities and Politics,* pp. 113-31.

rights organizations established during this period (with the exception of CORE, which first involved the individual on a personal level and first initiated the use of the Gandhian concept of direct nonviolent action in America in the early 1940's) conducted civil rights activities via professional civil rights workers.

The significant difference today, compared to the civil rights activities which took place prior to 1954, is that now there is active personal involvement in the struggle for human dignity rather than a reliance on staff professionals to carry out the necessary activities. Today, because of the diverse and changing character of the civil rights protest, the individual Negro can take the initiative, set his own priorities, join the organization which to him seems most appropriate, and take part directly in the activities which he believes will shape and improve his future.

Prior to 1954 discrimination was blatant in the schools, shameful in the area of housing, vicious in employment and belligerent in public accommodations. The activities and programs designed to cure these socioeconomic and political ills were modeled after the NAACP approach and yielded only token results. This first phase of the struggle had lasted for half a century.

The struggle for civil rights and human dignity gained momentum with the successful implementation of the Montgomery, Alabama bus boycott in 1955-56. This event marked the beginning of the democratization of the civil rights struggle. The entire civil rights structure in the South underwent change. The control over activities, initiative, and involvement was transferred from the hands of professional civil rights workers to the hearts and backs of enraged, frustrated militants of every description. Historically, in such periods of democratization, dynamic, charismatic leadership emerges. Montgomery was no exception. The events of the boycott moved Dr. Martin Luther King, Jr., first into a position of local leadership and later into national prominence.

Further momentum developed in the early 1960's when four Negro students in Greensboro, North Carolina, were refused service at a lunch counter reserved for whites. Rather than walk away they quietly and stubbornly refused to leave their seats, an action that came to be known as "sitting-in." This action created immediate responses from students and organizations and unleashed a powerful social force which has disrupted and shaken our nation. It was at this time that most Americans, particularly the Negro, referred to the civil rights struggle as a movement. This sense of movement grew, and with it grew the number of civil rights organizations, the number of involved citizens, and the pressure on Congress to pass necessary legislation—the 1964 Civil Rights Act and Economic Opportunity Act—which would not only protect the rights of Negroes, but increase their opportunities to achieve dignity and acceptance. This was the second phase of the civil rights struggle.

The NAACP's legalistic-educational approach used during the first phase of the civil rights struggle and the direct nonviolent action approach used by SNCC, SCLC and CORE during the second phase were assimilation methods with limited usefulness and effectiveness. These methods achieved some success but only in areas where a large voting Negro populace was present. Desegregation in the areas of public education and accommodations occurred only where the Negroes had voting power which could be used to determine the outcome of an election. Public school desegregation in hardcore segregationist areas like Alabama and Mississippi, where the Negro continues to be disenfranchised, proceeds at a snail's pace, ignoring the mandate given by the U.S. Supreme Court in 1954 to proceed "with all deliberate speed."

The use of nonviolent direct action to dislodge discrimination in public accommodations was spearheaded by students and other mobility conscious groups within the Negro community. The goal to achieve desegregation in public accommodations was a hollow middle-class goal and its accomplishment provided a superficial sense of achievement for the mobility conscious, holding few benefits for the poor, static Negro majority which did not have the means to take advantage of this middle-class-guided adventure. It has become clear that the problems of assimilation facing the Negro populace cannot be solved through private, voluntary nonpolitical action. Particularly in the areas of housing, education and employment, the Negro community must be organized into political power units capable of effecting social and economic change. Thus it is not surprising that, on a national level, the Negro has become more involved and successful in politics, and that the civil rights protest is well into a third and essentially political phase.

Within a period of twenty to thirty years (1938-1968), the Negroes have become an urban people, thereby becoming a viable political force. The mayoralty elections in Gary, Indiana, and Cleveland, Ohio, are examples of this force. The growing number of Negroes who are becoming militant, embracing the concept of "black power," and the established civil rights organizations which are modifying their platforms and plans of action to a militant methodology are even more powerful indications of the desire for political solidarity among Negroes.

The cry of Black Power has evoked considerable controversy. It has alienated a large segment of the white liberal community, causing an unmistakable withdrawal of sentiment. It has shaken the Negro middle class who have been incorporated into the "white society." Essentially it has brought to the surface the fear, animosity and mistrust that has existed for centuries between the black and white communities. Black Power has been belittled, feared and damned, but it has not been understood. The extraordinary thing about this condition is that the concept of Black Power is extremely simple and is consistent with the traditional political course of action taken by other ethnic minorities. Both the Irish and the Italians used politics through ethnic solidarity to articulate their particular interests.

What does "black power" mean? It means dignity. It does not mean anti-white. It means feeling, thinking and acting black—and liking it. It does not mean separatism. It means cooperation with those communities who will co-operate. It is a reaction to the reluctance of White Power to make the kind of changes necessary to make justice a reality for the Negro. It is unrealistic to think that the Negro is desirous of going it alone.

Although the economic system of this nation has prospered within the past two decades, the Negro's economic and social plight has improved very little. Since 1954 there has been a drastic decline in the number of legal barriers between the Negro and full equality. Also during this period from 1954 to 1968 there has been an increase in de facto segregation in America's basic socioeconomic institutions. More than half the Negro families in America have an annual income of less than $5,000. Moreover, the unemployment rate of the Negro is twice that of the whites. In some cities, particularly in the ghetto areas, the rate of unemployment ranges from 20 to 50 per cent. To advance economically the Negro must have a solid political base, because the civil rights struggle is no longer a moral or ethical phenomenon. It is, for the most part, an economic and political problem.

The Negro is not the sole vocal minority in America. The Mexican-American, the Puerto Rican, the American Indian and poverty-stricken whites are increasingly vocalizing demands similar to those of the Negro. Funds to carry out meaningful antipoverty programs, employment training, adult basic and higher education, and adequate housing programs for the benefit of these disadvantaged groups in an egalitarian manner will not be made available, unfortunately, until appropriate pressure is put on Congressional representatives to support such measures or replace representatives with those who will. Having a political base of operation is essential if the Negro is to survive the third phase of the civil rights struggle. And he must also have allies. Above all, he must be understood if there is to be racial harmony in America. These prerequisites have been partially attained in some parts of this country—but not in New Mexico.

The Negro in New Mexico, and particularly in Albuquerque, possesses many Southern Negro characteristics. He is ambivalent in most of his politics, conservative in his religion, and has been timid in the struggle for racial equality and equal opportunity. This is seen in several areas. First, the size of the Negro population is small. There are 17,063 Negroes in the state and 4,652 in the Albuquerque area, according to the 1960 Bureau of the Census Report. The 4,652 Negroes in the Albuquerque area constitute 1.8 per cent of its total population, but make up over 27 per cent of the total Negro population in New Mexico. Second, there is a larger minority group present. New Mexico has a Spanish surname population of 269,122. Third, the Negro is essentially a new-comer to New Mexico and is somewhat transient and parochial in character; he had not participated in politics where he came from, and has not yet been incorporated into the political system of this state even though the Negro has a strong national lobby. Fourth, the Spanish-Americans have inherited a system of politics based on the *patron,* or political boss. They have a strong state lobby but are weak on the national level. Fifth, the Albuquerque Negro has had to use the existing dominant political system of the Spanish-American as his only means for making demands on the total political system.

The civil rights movement which began in the early 1960's pricked the conscience of this nation but sowed few seeds of change in New Mexico. This is not to say that no change was needed, or that there was no activity directed toward creating this change, or that there were not some token changes. The role the Negro in New Mexico has played in the struggle for civil rights has been minimal, and national and local civil rights victories elsewhere have left the Negro in New Mexico, and particularly in Albuquerque, without an identity, unchanged and uncommitted.

Albuquerque has had an NAACP chapter since the 1940's. Its membership is small, prestigious, mainly middle class, and racially mixed. Its approach has been educational rather than legal, with the church providing much of its membership and leadership. Its main appeal has been moralistic. The Albuquerque chapter is a defensive organization rather than an offensive one and its victories have been battles won for them by the national organization. Many of the victories had no effect on the local scene and its particular problems. The 1954 U.S. Supreme Court decision is a case in point. The Albuquerque Public School system has never had de jure segregation, but this is not because it was integrationist. The fact is that in the late 1930's a representative from the Albuquerque Public School system offered the Negroes of Albuquerque their own school. The Negro families of Albuquerque refused this invitation to segregate themselves. Although the Negro students were allowed to attend neighborhood public schools, they were not treated as equals. They were forced to sit in the back of the classroom and at graduation time they were not lined up in alphabetical order but placed en masse in the center of the procession so that they could not lead their graduating class in or out of the assembly area.

Albuquerque had only one public high school for many years. When a second high school was built in the late 1940's, the school board gerrymandered the districts by including the wealthy University area west of Yale and north of Central Avenue and by excluding the poorer area west of Yale and south of Central Avenue which lessened the possibility of Negroes and Spanish-Americans attending the new high school. Nothing was done by the local NAACP about this condition nor the housing pattern which is still existing and causing de facto segregation.

Discrimination in public accommodations in New Mexico was eventually outlawed with the passage of the 1964 U.S. Civil Rights Act. The involvement of the local NAACP in this problem area was minimal. The state of New Mexico adopted a public accommodations law in the early 1960's but there was no provision for penalty or enforcement in the law. It was as if there were no law, because discrmination in this area blatantly continued. The attempted action taken to solve this situation was through students at the University of New

Mexico, the GI Forum, the Archdiocese of Santa Fe and other religious organizations. Their efforts were in vain because a strong bloc of state legislators from the Little Texas area of the state maintained that such an enforcement and penalty provision were not needed.

Several attempts were made to have a state fair-housing law passed by the previously mentioned coalition. Their efforts again were in vain. A Fair Employment Practice Commission statute was passed, but it was not until 1966 that the state legislature approved an allocation which allowed the commission to function even marginally. The failures in action taken in various areas and the lack of action in other areas by the local NAACP has caused considerable frustration among the Albuquerque Negroes.

Albuquerque has been limited to one civil rights approach, the local NAACP approach, and it has been directed by middle-class Negroes for the Negro middle class. This has deepened the frustration of the lower-class Negroes because their goals and problems are different from those of the middle class. The differences between these two classes of Negroes are sharp, hindering necessary interaction and mutual concern.

The middle-class Negro resides and is employed outside the Negro slums of Albuquerque. His concern is not integration because he has become culturally, emotionally, economically, and geographically part of the white community. His primary concern is inconspicuously keeping what he has and getting more, and not drawing attention to the fact that he is a Negro. He has broken with his traditional black background. The vast majority of Albuquerque's Negro middle class are neither natives of Albuquerque nor from New Mexico. They are, primarily, transient professionals who have come to Albuquerque because it is an easy place to become part of the white community, if one has the educational qualifications, or because they were employed by certain firms or agencies which directed that they be stationed in Albuquerque. Because of the transient nature and relatively small numbers of the Negro middle class, they have provided the total black populace with little or no leadership. They have exhibited little or no concern about the plight of their lower-class black brothers and sisters and have become only marginally involved in activities which would benefit the total black populace. Because of these conditions, the black population in Albuquerque lacks concerned, knowledgeable, committed black leadership and is essentially a decapitated leaderless mass.

The lower-class black, on the other hand, has very little and is preoccupied with his own and his family's private problems, with unemployment, and other day-to-day frustrations that mirror the plight of the lower class. He is desirous of getting out of the cycle of poverty in which he lives, but is pessimistic about his situation. The basic characteristics of the black residential area in Albuquerque are poverty, apathy, inarticulate resentments and dormant hostilities.

The most densely populated black community in Albuquerque is census tract thirteen. It is located a mile south of the central business district between the tracks and the freeway. By using the data contained in the 1960 U.S. Bureau of the Census Report and analyzing the socioeconomic problems that the lower-class black in Albuquerque faces, the existence of these characteristics and lack of assimilation into the mainstream of Albuquerque life is understandable.

The Negro population of census tract thirteen, which can basically be described as poverty-transient area, was 1,218 in 1960. Of the 1,014 blacks that resided in this area in 1955, only 383 lived in the same house in 1960, 328 resided elsewhere in the city, and 284 lived outside of Albuquerque and New Mexico. The conditions which the transient residents of this area have to live in have inhibited the development of community and group identity and have had substantial consequences for black political activity.

In 1960 there were 300 Negro families in census tract thirteen. More than 10 per cent of these families had an annual income of less than $1,000 and 38 per cent earned less than $3,000 annually. The median income was $3,719, but there were only seventeen families which had incomes of $10,000 or more. The great majority of these families had resided in this census tract for more than fifteen years prior to the 1960 census. They own their homes and are generally conservative politically, but provide little leadership within their community.

Only twenty-three black residents of census tract thirteen have four or more years of college. The median educational level of attainment in the tract is 9.9 grades. The leadership role of the more educated blacks is minimal. They have participated little in politics and are almost totally absent in community action and development activities.

Of the 326 occupied housing units in census tract thirteen in 1960, 61.6 per cent were categorized as deteriorating or dilapidated. Employment conditions and opportunities facing the blacks in this community are on much the same order. There were 517 employed blacks in this census tract. Of these, 450 were employed in marginal income categories as laborers, private household workers, in service occupations and in clerical-sales positions. The black unemployment rate is estimated at over 8 per cent, twice that of the white unemployment rate.

After viewing the data from census tract thirteen, one can understand the problems facing the Albuquerque blacks. The conditions which exist in this census tract also exist in other areas of Albuquerque where lower-class blacks reside.

The lack of political involvement and social improvement activity, black leadership, and the plight of not having a mechanism to express their frustrations and aspirations have contributed to the invisible and uninvolved character of the Albuquerque Negroes.

The involvement of the masses in the struggle for civil rights as it occurred nationally has not become a reality in Albuquerque. This is not because there are no racial problems in Albuquerque, but because middle-class leadership is not trusted and is no longer acceptable to the poorer and larger segment of the black community, and because the poor have not developed their own leadership.

It was stated earlier that frustration within the Albuquerque Negro community is deepening. But at the same time, the white's concern about the Negro has quickened. Fear and resentment have replaced sympathy. Opportunities for the Negro in Albuquerque have decreased because of what happened in Watts, Atlanta, and Washington, D.C., and not because of any action taken by the Negroes in Albuquerque. This bit of overreaction has added fuel to the already existing frustrations of the Albuquerque Negro.

Lack of equal employment opportunity, decent housing, equal educational opportunity, as well as police brutality, were some of the conditions which caused the riots that left the ghettos across the nation smoldering these past summers. Conditions conducive to riots also exist in New Mexico and are getting worse. They exist and will continue until the Negro and white communities develop a means, through solidarity and coalition, to deal with these problems.

Because of the unique racial composition of Albuquerque—a small Negro population and the presence of a larger Spanish-American minority—much of the civil rights action taken has been in the form of a coalition. The NAACP and the GI Forum, the main civil rights organ for the Spanish-American, on several occasions banded together with the white liberal community to achieve a common goal. This was, however, before the Black and Brown Power or political phase. Prior to 1965 and the advent of the "War on Poverty" and other "self-help" federal programs, relations between the various ethnic groups were not desperate, but rarely harmonious. Because of the housing pattern, the majority of Negroes reside in the South Broadway area of Albuquerque isolated from the white community. The racial composition of that neighborhood was basically 33 per cent Negro, 66 per cent Spanish-American, and the relationship between the two groups was one of tolerance with occasional undercurrents of conflict. But essentially no great conflict developed because of the lack of opportunity for both minority groups. Both were discriminated against and oppressed. Both were faced with the same conditions of poor education, poor housing, high unemployment and underemployment.

Since 1965, however, the relationship between the Negro and the Spanish-American has become a problem in Albuquerque. This situation is the result of the competition and polarization stimulated by the Economic Opportunity Act of 1964 and other similar federally sponsored community self-help programs, reinforced by petty politics on the part of local program directors and the majority communities. Each year after 1964, Congress has committed an appropriation too small to launch a meaningful offensive to accomplish the enormous task of eliminating poverty and providing equal opportunity. This lack of funds has developed increasing competition and animosity that never before existed between the Albuquerque minorities.

The War on Poverty in the Albuquerque area began in March of 1965. One of the essential components of this program was the organization of the poor. The method used to accomplish this task was the development of the Neighborhood

Association plan. Attempts were made to organize all poor communities of the county into Neighborhood Associations. It was the function of such organizations to speak for and involve the poor in the development of community improvement programs to meet the needs of particular communities.

The first phase of this organizational plan brought considerable success: nine Neighborhood Associations were organized. There was a visible desire on the part of all communities to cooperate and busy themselves with the problems of poverty. Approximately one year later, however, factions in each of the communities were bidding for control of the Neighborhood Association. In the South Broadway area, where five associations had been developed, the struggle for control became an ethnic struggle between Negroes and Spanish-Americans. It reached a point where one group would not participate if another group was in control. Some residents would regularly attend meetings and participate in programs in another community rather than participate in their own Neighborhood Association where they had little or no voice. In the John Marshall Community, largely census tract thirteen, the confrontration grew to such a point that the Spanish-Americans withdrew and developed their own organization rather than deal with the largely Negro organization (large in the sense that the black majority controlled the organization which had an active membership of from twenty to thirty). The split that occurred between the two ethnic groups was stimulated by the desire for employment in the proposed Neighborhood Service Centers and other OEO county programs.

Since 1965 the Economic Opportunity Board, the Community Action Agency for the Albuquerque area, has employed 204 community residents (121 Spanish-Americans, 67 Anglos, and 16 Negroes) in various positions ranging from program directors to janitors. Other federally sponsored programs which operate in the county, such as Operation Service, Employment and Redevelopment, the Home Improvement Program, the Manpower Development Training Program, the Concentrated Employment Program, the Home Education Livelihood Program, and the two Neighborhood Youth Corps Programs, have employed less than four of the many qualified Negroes who have made application. Their cumulative staff positions total over one hundred and fifty.

The economy of New Mexico and particularly Albuquerque is one which depends overwhelmingly on federal appropriations. The U.S. Government, directly and indirectly through subcontracts, provides and supports the livelihood of approximately 90,000 of the county's population. City, county, and state institutions provide the economic means for about another 20,000. The total number of Negroes employed by these institutions is less than 1 per cent. The median number of school years completed for the Negro is 10.9 years. For the Spanish-American the median is 8.7. Viewing these statistics one would think that the Negro's opportunity for employment would be enhanced because of his comparatively higher level of education. This unfortunately is not the case, because, as previously indicated, the economy of Albuquerque has a political base. It is overwhelmingly dependent on federal, state, and local government appropriations. Congressional representatives support certain measures like the War on Poverty which bring additional jobs into a given area. They refer and recommend job candidates for the openings in the supported programs. The majority of these referrals are individuals who have supported the Congressional representative previously either by providing a bloc of votes or an endorsement. The Negro in Albuquerque and elsewhere in New Mexico being unorganized, inexperienced, and essentially uninvolved in politics would be hard pressed to pay the price for this type of ticket of admission. In order to procure employment under this system, involvement in politics has become a prerequisite. Because the Negro is not involved in politics, his chances for procuring employment are relatively slim.

The government policy of issuing funds to impoverished ethnic groups was expedient and necessary in 1965, but has become outmoded. Federal programs with the goal of providing equal opportunity for the poor, regardless of race, now have led to the revitalization of the separate but equal doctrine, especially in the area of opportunity. It has increased the conflict between the Negro and the Spanish-American communities. And it has decreased the opportunity for the Negro in Albuquerque to achieve equality.

Within the past year a movement has started in the Spanish-American community, particularly among the League of United Latin-American Citizens, a newly formed civil rights organization, directed towards social change and developing an ethnic economic base. As Spanish-Americans, they already had a political base, 26 per cent of the total population of the Albuquerque area and 28.3 per cent of the state population. LULAC has become involved to the point of controlling some of the federally sponsored programs in this area. The hiring practices of these various programs clearly reflect the perspective of those who are in control. There has been wholesale hiring of Spanish-Americans, not because they seem to meet the established hiring criteria, but because they are Spanish-Americans and such a practice is politically desirable. This quiet Brown Power middle-class movement has had the sanction and support of the established political machine. It has led to the strengthening of the already formed coalition between the whites and the Spanish-Americans. It has also been done at the expense of the Negro.

The potential danger to the Negro in the LULAC movement is not its goals, because the development of an economic base preceded by the establishment of a sound political base is exactly what should be considered as the prime objective of the Negro. The main danger, however, lies in the fact that LULAC's successes or failures will have a great impact on the Negro and on his aspirations and opportunities to develop an economic and political structure which will assist him in assimilating into the mainstream of American culture. If LULAC is to succeed it must suceed not only in procuring employment for its membership but must also take every possible step to insure that the War on Poverty and other federally and locally sponsored programs, where LULAC members hold key positions, also succeed. Also LULAC's success should not be accomplished at the expense of the Negro. The involvement and hiring of Negroes in the various programs, particularly in the Community Action Programs, should be considered and expanded. It is in these programs that the black will be able to develop the political and social leadership which his community so badly needs.

Ethnic equality in Albuquerque seems to depend on political strength. Opportunity seems to be achieved not because it is right or moral, but because of organized voting power. The framework and rules for operating in this highly political system have been established. The Negro must respond in a political manner. But the Negro, the minority of minorities in Albuquerque, has traditionally used the existing political machinery to attempt to achieve his goals and solve his problems.

The Negro in New Mexico is concerned about meaningful employment, adequate housing and equal educational opportunity. This concern can take one of three directions. It can explode because the majorities are reluctant to make the necessary concessions; it can result in the Negro becoming more involved in the established political structure; or it can lead toward the development of a separate black political organization.

The Negroes' frustration in New Mexico has not reached a point which would give rise to a Molotov Cocktail party. But their frustrations are increasing at an alarming rate. Unless the necessary solutions to these conditions are developed, black militants might just persuade the local poor Negroes to face reality. Such a movement would have to depend on outsiders, for the most part, because the local Negro leadership is middle class and is not equipped to rally the black masses.

The Negro in New Mexico could and should involve himself in local and state politics. But whether this involvement would improve the total Negro situation is doubtful. Using the past as an indication, involvement in the present coalition between the white and Spanish-American, unless the Negroes are well organized, would undoubtedly reflect the goals of the majorities and not the goals of the Negro. A Negro participating in such a coalition without an organized constituency would primarily represent himself and not the Negro community.

Responsibility to a Negro constituency is a prerequisite for the Negro politician if he is committed to representing, working for, and achieving political goals which will benefit the total Negro population and not just himself. But the task of representing the Negro community is difficult if not impossible if the Negro community is not organized.

The change in the civil rights struggle from a moralistic to an essentially political level has not been felt by the Negro New Mexican. The energies which have been spent in search of a new ethnic identity across the nation lie untapped, dormant and isolated, like most of New Mexico's resources. At a time when Negroes in most other areas of this nation are declaring that they are

Negro, Black or Afro-Americans, desirous of creating their own ethnic image, the Negro in Albuquerque is breaking mirrors.

The problems of assimilation facing the lower-class Negro in Albuquerque are certainly problems created by the white community. But they are problems that will never be solved until the Negro and the majority communities take the initiative. Apathy is the major problem, but what lies at the root of this condition? What can explain the fact that, in light of the black activity and accomplishment elsewhere in America over the past fifteen years, the Negro's position in Albuquerque has remained static?

The answer to both of these questions is identity—self identity and ethnic identity. The Negro in Albuquerque wants to be everything but himself. He wants to be white because he doesn't know what being a Negro really is like. Not only has the "white" system robbed the Negro of his African heritage through the institution of slavery, it has also denied him any recognition concerning the great contributions the Negro has given to the making of American society. The Negro has not only been invisible to the white community but to himself as well. The small size of the Negro population has made this rather easy. As a consequence, the Negro in Albuquerque does not know how to be or have pride in the fact that he is a Negro. Until he realizes a positive rather than a transparent ethnic image, his position will remain static and apathy will continue to muffle his aspirations and goals. A positive ethnic awareness is one where the Negro believes that he is a man and assumes the knowledge and responsibility of being a Negro and thinking Negro—and likes it. Whether he assumes a militant, an African-oriented, or Black Nationalist position is of little importance. This awareness will eliminate the apathy, and muted resentments. The Negroes' parochial existence, and dormant hostilities will be replaced by a desire to articulate and participate in actions which will benefit and strengthen their identity and achieve for them human dignity and acceptance.

If progress and equal opportunity are to become a reality, the Albuquerque Negro must realize a positive ethnic identity and channel this awareness and its energies into a unit, thus creating a source of power. Such an organization, a pressure group, could demand solutions to grievances, attract allies and eventually develop a strong coalition which will adequately reflect and incorporate the Negroes' aspirations and problems. The Albuquerque Negro must develop a politically-oriented organization. But the Negro's involvement in politics must include more than merely exercising his franchise. It must include the capability to initiate and influence the political, social, and economic structures that surround him. He can only do this if he has power. In Albuquerque he does not have economic power, so he can only achieve power through organizing. And the Negro can become organized only when he positively accepts the fact that he is a Negro and acts in his own behalf. By doing this the Negro will destroy the invisible image held by himself and the white system and, thus, force a much needed reappraisal of his position in Albuquerque and produce solutions to his problems.

To some, the development of a Negro political organization would seem contrary to the principles of integration and would increase racial strife. But such an endeavor would essentially provide an acceptable means of releasing the accumulated and future frustrations and provide an approach which would insure economic, social, and political equality and dignity and acceptance for the Negro in New Mexico.

Part 5

PROGRAMS OF REFORM

Introduction

From one point of view, American schools have been in a state of reform since colonial times. From another, little has changed. But both of these things could be said about any national school system. Schools have a national character, a character that is consistent with the culture and national interests of that society. And, of course, as societies change in some economic, social, or political way, the schools must be adjusted to conform. Historically, these reformations have been the business of national leaders or educational experts. Rarely have students or the people had much to say about the reforming of their schools.

For our purposes, there are two periods of reform that need to be examined. The first set of reforms occurred just before the turn of this century—any good history of American education can supply the details. But the point is that virtually the entire structure of education, as we know it today, was established by several committees of experts. Curiously enough, these experts were not experts in the needs of American society, but experts in limited subject matter areas. They were held together, however, by one deep commitment: they knew that their private academic interest in congress with the interests of one another was what the American people needed. We say *needed,* not wanted. No effort, at any level, was made to determine what the American people wanted. No research was done. No questions asked.

The second reform movement followed the Sputnik launching in 1957, when Americans, brave Americans, perhaps for the first time lost their nerve. The Soviet Union was ahead of us and someone was to blame. Why not blame the schools? Why not indeed! They were without political or economic power, unprepared to answer an organized attack, and their most powerful and inspiring voices from the days before World War II were either dead or in retirement. Anyway, a reform might eliminate some of the unnecessary "frills and fads" and save the middle class something in tax money.

Again the experts jumped into the vanguard of educational reform with advanced physics courses guaranteeing to provide an uninterrupted flow of scientific manpower for the defense and space industries. When someone discovered that the scientists thus provided were illiterate, the experts went back up on the mountain and came down with new programs for the good of people—or some of the people, some of the time.

But this time the experts didn't get away with it. Little by little, Americans noticed that things weren't getting better. Cities were not better places to live, but worse. The dream of the American farm or rural community was becoming a nightmare of poverty and hopelessness—unless one had substantial farm subsidies. Wars continued overseas, and men still hated one another at home. And the environment began to stink.

But most importantly, in spite of a trickle of Blacks and Browns who made it into the middle class, education still left millions precisely where their parents had been. Education was not the key to success in America. Cultural annihilation was. It wasn't what a man could learn, it was what he must give up that separated the haves from the have-nots. But in spite of the trickle, social mobility was not available to everyone, and some people could not get an education in an American school. The gap between their social style and the school was just too great. The role of the school as a middle-class institution was not the issue. What it did for middle-class children was not the issue. The issue was what it did *not do* for millions of good people living in this country.

It is axiomatic that there were educators who recognized this dysfunctionalism and who spoke out against it. But the public was not prepared to take them or their research seriously. First the fires had to be set and the inequality of American civilization had to be etched into the thinking of middle-class America by blind rebellion and destruction.

If middle-class America did not owe the Black man enough already, it owes him a debt now for the new message of education he has sent. And all the while the message was so simple: Whatever you do in your school, America, it isn't enough and it isn't done well. Your successes come not because of your schools but in spite of them. Our failures come because you have not permitted us an alternative. We demand that alternative. Whatever it is, we are going to do something different and it will be our thing.

The experts had their hands in this, but at least some of them were educational experts, not defense or military or academic experts. Nevertheless the power comes from below. The President and his Commissioner of Education fought Head Start and the other legislation through Congress, but it is difficult to believe they would have dreamed these programs up if they hadn't read accurately the anger of all the American disadvantaged.

We do not have space here to begin to discuss the plethora of educational experiments going on in America today, both inside and outside the educational apparatus. There is legislation and there are some governmental funds, but more importantly there are store-front schools, there are parent-operated schools, there are schools to restore the human image of people, there are efforts to give back to the people the control of their schools; even the Government has acknowledged that the social mix of a school is worthy of a pedagogical attention, and people are taking a long, hard look at the curriculum and methodology of the school to determine, for themselves, whether it is what they want after all.

30

Compensatory Education Programs*

WILLIAM B. LEVENSON

It is more than a coincidence that when the push was mounted for school desegregation in the North, the concept of compensatory services gained acceptance. Centered at first in New York City, the notion spread that special measures are needed to correct socially induced learning disabilities. Genuine equality of educational opportunity requires that educational services be decidedly unequal.

This principle is not new. Dedicated teachers have long utilized it. The pupil in need of special help has received additional attention, special assignments, tutoring, and a number of other aids. In most states, special services for handicapped pupils are provided by increased financial assistance; class size is kept small, special equipment is used, paraprofessionals are employed. The new element is the recognition that handicaps are due not alone to physical, mental, and emotional factors but also to environmental deprivation, and that society has a stake in alleviating these handicaps.

One of the earliest approaches to this more recent concept developed from a recommendation made by the New York City Board of Education's Commission on Integration. It proposed a special program to identify and stimulate able children from poor neighborhoods. As an outgrowth of this recommendation, a Demonstration Guidance Project was set up at two schools, Junior High School 43 (86 percent nonwhite) and George Washington High School (38 percent nonwhite). Starting in September, 1956, the project began in the three junior high school grades and continued until the initial seventh grade class left in June, 1959. The project was then shifted to the senior high when these students entered and continued until June, 1962. Slightly over half the pupils were placed in experimental groups by a process of interviews, tests, and teacher recommendations. Any pupil who seemed to have potential was included, though the groups were kept flexible for the six-year experiment. Most of the pupils included were from culturally disadvantaged neighborhoods.

The compensatory or special services were furnished in a number of ways: classes were kept small, two periods of English were scheduled daily, small-group

*Copyright 1968 by Rand McNally & Co. Reprinted by permission of the publisher from William B. Levenson, *The Spiral Pendulum: The Urban School in Transition,* pp. 143-67.

tutoring as well as intensive counseling was provided. Part-time psychologists and social workers were added to the junior high staff. The goal was improved scholastic achievement.

After the pupils entered the high school they were involved in a wide range of enrichment activities: concerts, theaters, museums, out-of-town trips. Special guidance materials were developed, and the program was interpreted to parents.

The Progress Report issued by the New York City schools listed these five results after three and one-half years:

Out of 105 students who took before-and-after intelligence tests, 78 showed an increase in I.Q.; 25 showed a drop; and 2 were identical. Sixty-four students (61.0%) gained more than 10 points; 11 students (10.5%) lost more than 5 points; and 6 students (5.7%) lost more than 10 points. "In 1956 the median I.Q. . . . was 92.9; in 1959 . . . the median I.Q. was 102.2. The changes in I.Q. in the project pupils are more significant, perhaps, in view of previous findings that the I.Q. of students with a community background of educational limitations goes down as the students grow older."

"64% of the group graduated, compared to an average of 47% for the four previous classes" coming from Junior High School 43 and graduating from George Washington High School.

"39% more pupils finished high school than before; 2½ times as many completed the academic course of study; 3½ times as many went on to some form of higher education."

Eleven of these students "obtained honors on one or more subjects. Four won New York State Regents scholarships. Three won seven medals or certificates for academic accomplishments. Three received four awards for outstanding citizenship records. One had the distinction of being a Commencement speaker. Three of the project students ranked first, fourth and sixth in a graduating class of over 900. Some of these students did work far beyond anything that could have been anticipated."

"There were also many intangible results that were directly due to the project. . . . As their high school course drew to a close, it was apparent that many of them had developed poise, maturity, and a sense of self-worth. Most important of all their attributes was this new image of themselves, which enabled them to achieve in many areas and face the future with hope and confidence."

In 1959 the Demonstration Guidance Project was extended to other schools in New York City under the name Higher Horizons Program. Whereas in the Demonstration Guidance Project only children with potential were included, it was now decided to provide additional services for all the children in the schools selected—the academically disabled as well as the able. The program was first introduced in the third grade of 31 elementary schools and in the seventh grade of 13 junior high schools. It was extended to other schools in the following years. By 1963, 64,000 pupils in grades three to ten were involved. In 1964 a detailed evaluation was made in cooperation with the U.S. Office of Education.

The results were less encouraging than those submitted following the Demonstration Guidance Project.

As compared with pupils not in the program, changes in I.Q. levels were similar, arithmetic gains were below expectancy but behavior improved as did attendance. Most teachers favored the program while all principals did; but in general, academic growth did not justify great enthusiasm.

An interpretation of the seeming disparity in the results of the two programs should include consideration of several factors: different types of pupils were involved, per capita costs were greater in the Demonstration Guidance Project, and thus supportive services were not comparable. The difference in administering the two programs limits comparison. The Demonstration Guidance Project was centrally controlled, while Higher Horizons was administered at the local school level, and rigid controls, as between schools, were difficult to maintain.

Experiments with compensatory education spread through other large northern cities, often with the support of the Ford Foundation's Gray Areas Project. Various approaches were used, though in all of these "Great Cities" the purpose of the compensatory education experiment was to raise the levels of aspiration and achievement among pupils in the disadvantaged areas. In Buffalo the emphasis was on the teaching of reading. Beginning in one predominantly Negro elementary school, additional services were provided to reduce the retardation in reading among pupils. In Chicago the program concentrated on children between the ages of 14 and 16 and sought to accelerate the promotion of low achievers to the high schools. There was also an attempt to begin early vocational preparation for slow learners. To assist them, cultural activities, special trips, and additional guidance programs were utilized. A part-time work program was established which emphasized vocational counseling and short-term training courses leading to placement as nurses' aides in hospitals and in various jobs in the needle trades, as well as in food service. Pittsburgh made use of a team-teaching approach with emphasis on reading and language arts. In both Oakland and Milwaukee the emphasis was on special school community services for migrant and transient children. In Oakland also a child-care center was established, which serviced the preschool children of working parents.

Beginning in 1961, San Francisco established a five-year project in two elementary schools, one junior high school, and three senior high schools, largely in Negro neighborhoods. The program was designed with emphasis on three areas of development: academic, community involvement, and the world of work for youth. Special curriculum materials were developed. The Cleveland project, centered at Addison Junior High School in the predominantly Negro Hough area, made special use of ten home visitors to work with parents in an effort to bridge the home-school gap. Detroit's project included curriculum revision, the reorganization of instructional schedules, the use of school-community agents, after school and evening classes for youths and adults, special trips to cultural centers, tutorial assistance. Perhaps more than in other cities, Detroit placed special emphasis on helping the teachers to work with children with limited backgrounds.

Philadelphia made use of interschool and intraschool teams composed of the principals, teachers, counselors, and the school nurse, working with a school-community coordinator and a language laboratory teacher. Special emphasis was placed on the orientation and the extensive involvement of parents. Other cities in the North, such as South Bend, Indiana, and Grand Rapids, Michigan, also developed special compensatory programs, and in several northern states the concept was endorsed and, to some extent, financed on a statewide basis. Such developments took place in New York, California, Maine, Rhode Island, and Pennsylvania.

In the fall of 1961 Project ABLE was begun in New York State, financed by a special appropriation of $200,000. The project was designed to help local systems develop educational programs to meet the needs of disadvantaged children. Project ABLE grants were made in 16 communities in 1961-62. "These sixteen programs embraced city, village, and rural schools at the elementary, junior high, and senior high levels. Their general emphases are primarily on intensified identification of potentially able students from these socially disadvantaged groups and the provision of enriched and extended educational opportunities and activities for them."

The spread of compensatory education programs occurred at the same time that postwar school enrollments continued to climb. The urban population was undergoing a drastic ethnic change. The civil rights movement was a strong influence, though cultural deprivation should not be equated with race, for one-third of the Negro children equal or exceed the educational norms of white pupils. A climate of acceptance for compensatory programs was created by economic, social, and political forces that rallied in the cause of "The Great Society."

When the Great Cities undertook the expansion of compensatory programs, particularly in the central areas, there was some suspicion expressed in civil rights circles. They feared such efforts were to be a northern version of "separate but equal"; that these programs were contrived to forestall integration. In the view of some, such as Doxey A. Wilkerson, this was a justifiable attitude. "Their skepticism was warranted, because the response of some school systems to early desegregation demands was to offer compensatory education instead." On the other hand, as Wilkerson also notes, ". . . merely to enroll white and Negro pupils in common schools by no means constitutes an adequate approach to equality."

Problems remain even after desegregation. The cause may be understandable, but the fact is that the academic achievement of many, though not all, Negro children is considerably below that of their new classmates. As noted earlier, ability grouping practices need analysis, and improved teacher insights are essential, along with revised instructional materials. Even these will not suffice, however. If cultural deprivation is to be minimized, and in fact if white pupils are to remain in the school and resegregation is to be avoided, an infusion of supportive services is also necessary.

Thus neither one, integration or compensatory education, can stand alone. Both must be undertaken concurrently if the goal of quality integrated education is to be attained. Let us turn now to a consideration of those compensatory projects which have been launched in various cities. The emphasis will be on those projects which have been developed since the Great Cities experiments of the early sixties.

It is significant to note that Project Head Start, the largest program for young children ever sponsored by the federal government, was introduced not by the U.S. Office of Education but by the Office of Economic Opportunity. This fact gives substance to the notion that essentially the great increase in recent federal allocations to education had an economic, political, and social orientation. This does not denigrate the objective, but it suggests again the shifting of power away from traditional educational auspices.

In the summer of 1965, 560,000 children participated in 2,500 summer centers involving the help of over 100,000 adults (teachers, parents, physicians, psychologists, volunteers). In 1966 a full-year program was launched. Subsequent congressional endorsement indicates that Head Start may well become an on-going feature of the urban educational scene.

The antecedents of Project Head Start were a growing body of psychological and psychiatric research data, as well as demonstration projects like the Baltimore Early School Admissions Project, the Akron Pre-kindergarten Classes, and the Early Training Project in Tennessee. The Child Development Centers, formally known as Project Head Start, with a budget of 112 million dollars in 1965, were conceived as more than educational programs. The goal was to marshal all resources which could contribute to the child's total development: health, nutrition, education, social services. Centers were operated by public, parochial, and private schools, as well as child-care centers. Pupil-teacher ratios were kept low; for every 15 pupils in class there were one teacher and two assistants.

The initial follow-up reports as represented in February, 1966, by the sponsoring agency, the Office of Economic Opportunity, indicated that the I.Q.'s of the youngsters participating in the summer program rose an average of eight to ten points. Dramatic as these findings are, officials stated that the major value of the project was in calling attention to the health needs of small children.

Observers have praised the Head Start classes because of the personal relationships and individual attention that were evident (one adult to every five children). Others believe that the biggest dividend has been the effect on teachers: they were alerted to the needs of the poor; they saw that progress could be made even in eight short weeks; they were committed to follow through in the fall. Many proponents believe a major gain was the involvement of ghetto parents who, though they want the best education for their children, often do not know how to stimulate the desire in their children. By direct involvement in Head Start, many parents were helped in this regard.

There is a widespread belief that the program was hastily conceived and perhaps too quickly launched. However, the turnout of sheer numbers—over half a million children—clearly demonstrated both the national interest and the long delayed need.

It was perhaps inevitable that a "crash program" would leave some criticism in its wake. The need for better preparation and evaluation is often mentioned. There is general agreement that the program will have little lasting value without follow-up and a continuing commitment to quality education as these children pass through the grades. Compensatory education cannot be effective unless the efforts are sustained. Fred Hechinger's comment concerning Project Head Start represents realistic caution:

"The inherent danger of any pilot project is that it may deceive the public into believing that an early success can easily be translated into routine—without the same investment of money, time, and people on a regular, massive scale. It is a lesson painfully taught many times over—most recently by the initial success and long-term failure of New York City's 'Higher Horizons' program, a special enrichment effort for children in slum neighborhoods. It worked like magic—but only as long as the extra teachers, extra funds, and extra care were forthcoming. Once institutionalized and watered down, the program faded into ineffective routine."

Aside from the compensatory values of Operation Head Start's aim to provide "environmental intervention," it placed the national spotlight on the importance of preschool education, particularly for children of disadvantaged areas. Early childhood schooling is being increasingly recommended, not as a frill to be undertaken only if budgets can warrant it, but rather as a powerful molding force if the cycle is to be broken whereby lower-class children grow into lower-class adults.

Recognizing that the potential values of Head Start can be attained only if the compensatory effort is sustained, President Johnson's request for the fiscal 1968 budget included project "Follow Through." Disadvantaged children, mostly "graduates" of Head Start, in grades 1-3 would be served by special programs similar to those of Head Start: health and nutritional aid, individualized instruction, enrichment activities. The program would get under way in the 1968-69 school year, with about 150,000 youngsters eligible for enrollment in several pilot cities.

One approach to the provision of special services for children already in school but in need of additional help has been to make use of so-called free time: after-school hours, Saturday mornings, and the summer vacation. Many school systems, large and small, have undertaken compensatory programs during these periods when middle- and upper-class children have traditionally learned music, dancing, skating, and so forth. The projects that will be mentioned here are a limited but representative sample selected from among cities with a population of over 300,000, though there are, of course, disadvantaged pupils and compensatory programs needed in smaller communities and certainly in many rural areas. No attempt at a judgment of quality is presumed in this listing. The aim is to suggest a variety of approaches that may be considered. The following plans illustrate the use of after-school hours:

Inner-city children in the upper elementary grades of Oklahoma City were involved in The Emerson Project. They volunteered, with parental consent, to participate in the program. "Big Brothers and Sisters" from Harding High School volunteered to supervise after-school activities at Emerson School twice a week. These Harding students were members of the Key Club, the Future Teachers of America, and the chorus. In addition to the staff at Emerson, lay volunteers, the PTA, and the Superintendent's Advisory Committee on School Dropouts gave assistance and advice. The project offered cultural enrichment through a variety of activities: music and dance, arts and crafts, physical education and games, library and reading, or storytelling and drama. Participating pupils stayed at school until their parents returned home from work. This activity replaced a portion of the unsupervised time the students had had before. For the first time, some of these lower-class youngsters had the opportunity to identify with middle-class exemplars. Students from Harding High School had the experience of interacting with children from a social class other than their own. (The child of all-white middle-class suburbia is also culturally deprived.)

The Human Development Project of Richmond, Virginia, led to the creation of six school centers in which a variety of compensatory services were offered. The after-school programs in two of the centers are illustrative. On Monday, Tuesday, Wednesday, and Thursday afternoons the library was kept open with a teacher in charge to give whatever assistance might be needed. Because many of these children had no place to study at home and no one capable of helping them, this study hour was well patronized and did much to help pupils improve their academic achievement. Also on Monday afternoons, children went bowling under the supervision of a teacher. The bowling alley provided a bus which picked up the children at 3:15 p.m. and returned them around 5 p.m. Arts and crafts were offered in one center on Wednesday afternoons and on Thursday afternoons at the other. In each instance, teachers provided the leadership for pupil activities. From October through May groups of girls from fourth, fifth, and sixth grades walked from the school to the YWCA for an afternoon of swimming, ballet dancing, and other activities. The greatest difficulty was in securing adults to accompany girls to and from the "Y."

In Washington, D.C., inner-city schools designated as Twilight Schools permit boys who create discipline problems to attend small all-male classes from 3:30 to 7:30 p.m. One hundred and eighty boys were enrolled in two pilot schools.

The Elementary School Community Opportunity Program of Los Angeles provided 20 hours per week of supplementary teaching time beyond the regular school year in each of six elementary schools located in culturally disadvantaged areas. The additional periods of instruction were held after the regular school day, the length of the class period generally being 60 minutes in length and scheduled from 3:30 to 4:30 p.m. These six schools included student bodies whose backgrounds were predominantly Mexican-American, Mexican-American-Oriental-Negro, and predominantly Negro. Student Achievement Centers were established in the high schools of the inner city where reading and arithmetic were stressed.

After the Watts riots several state-financed projects emphasizing vocational skills were established, but the school system's policy, at least as related by one official, was to spread special programs throughout all poverty areas and not only in the Watts area; "otherwise we support the notion that violence is needed to get results."

Most metropolitan school systems have used after-school periods for remedial and enrichment activities. An extension of this concept has been the establishment of afternoon and evening study centers, where tutoring services have been available. Here are a few examples:

After-school study centers have been in use in Milwaukee since 1963. Volunteer tutors from colleges in the region assist high school pupils in the academic areas in which they need help. Students of Providence, Rhode Island, were tutored on a one-to-one basis twice weekly after school. The activity was undertaken in cooperation with a social service agency and the use of part-time volunteers. In this instance the pupils were at the elementary grade level. The VEAPS (Volunteer Educational Assistants' Project of the Greater Portland, Oregon, Council of Churches) provided tutoring for children from kindergarten through high school. In addition to academic subjects, assistance was provided in home economics. In a Cleveland program, conducted during the summer, outstanding high school students assisted elementary school pupils from both public and private schools. Help was provided in arithmetic and the language arts. The tutoring sessions were held in 60 locations throughout the inner city: libraries, recreation centers, settlement houses, and schools. The high school tutors came from public and private schools throughout the Greater Cleveland area. In 1964 and 1965, 4,000 elementary school pupils were tutored by 1,600 high school pupils who were supervised by 20 volunteer supervisors, most of them teachers in the area. In Seattle, Washington, volunteer tutors from nearby colleges assisted disadvantaged elementary school children in two ways: academic improvement and the guidance of Adventure Tours to college campuses, science laboratories, museums, the zoo, cultural centers, and nearby dairy farms. The use of a longer school day quite naturally led to the consideration of a longer school week, and, increasingly, Saturday morning activites were planned for both enrichment and remedial purposes.

St. Louis has had long experience with Saturday reading clinics. It has conducted remedial instruction on Saturdays for primary grade pupils from public and parochial schools. In Long Beach, California, the use of Saturday mornings was planned for supportive services, such as health and counseling, cultural enrichment, tutoring, and extended use of junior and senior high school libraries. The plan in Cincinnati was to conduct Saturday enrichment classes for able but disadvantaged pupils in grades five and six. Small classes and individualized instruction were planned for pupils in the top 10 percent of their schools. The Boston Program AID (Ability Identification and Development) had as its purpose the motivation of interests and hobbies. Elementary grade pupils met in small groups with specially oriented teachers after school and on Saturdays.

The operation of summer schools is nothing new. Camping education for the disadvantaged also has a long history. The former, however, has usually been conducted in the traditional classroom manner, while the latter, with some exceptions, has not been a school enterprise. Changes are evident in both directions, and it is a rare system that does not now operate an expanded program of summer activities. A longer school year is a realistic projection during the next decade.

In Akron, Ohio, a mansion was the setting for three "creative learning classes," in which experimental programs in writing, art, and music were conducted. Other centers have since been established. By having talented pupils from various parts of the city study together, opportunity was provided for intercultural association.

A number of large school systems, starting with the Ford-supported Gray Areas projects, for the first time participated in camp programs.

Perhaps the outstanding example of a school-system camp, one that is operated all year, was conducted by the Toronto, Canada, school system. On an island in Lake Erie, several miles off the Toronto shore, a school and dormitory were constructed. Students participated in one- to two-week periods of academic instruction with an emphasis on science, utilizing the natural environment of their school setting.

A significant use of the summer period for compensatory education has developed through the interest of many collegiate institutions as well as a number of independent schools. The Oberlin summer project, the Junior Scholar Program at Case Western Reserve, the Connecticut College program for 40 disadvantaged high school girls, the summer remedial program aimed at college entrance which was conducted by Columbia University—these illustrate the kinds of enterprises which have spread throughout the nation. One of the better known activities of this type was Project ABC (A Better Chance) at Dartmouth College. Teen-agers selected by the Independent Schools Talent Search Program, many of them Negroes, were enrolled for eight weeks of summer school at Dartmouth as a transition to their entrance as scholarship students in various preparatory schools.

Independent schools have offered summer enrichment programs for able students for several years. One of the earliest was the Advanced Studies Program at St. Paul's School in Concord, New Hampshire, in the mid-1950's. Project SPUR, conducted by Phillips Exeter Academy in cooperation with six large city school systems, represented a comprehensive approach to the elevation of student aspirations. Pupils from the inner cities lived in dormitories and studied in small classes with youths from favored homes. The association, it was hoped, would spur the ghetto youngsters to raise their goals and pursue them.

The foregoing programs conducted by public schools, collegiate institutions, and independent schools suggest the types of special services that have been offered through the extension of school time after school, Saturdays, or during the summer. Compensatory approaches and supportive services have been used even more during the regular school hours. As noted earlier, most of the larger school systems conducted special help programs before the passage of major federal legislation.

Some of the government proposals derived from earlier foundation-assisted activity. When Title I funds were made available to school systems wherever children of low-income families attended, additional services were offered, such as: remedial work in communication skills; special programs for the handicapped; use of social workers and home visitors; more medical, dental, and psychological care; enrichment through field trips, more music and art; employment of teacher aides; and special library programs.

Occasionally, as in San Francisco, special themes were employed because of unusual community resources. The Drama Demonstration Project, conducted both in and out of school, was based on the assumption that the drama would be a most useful means of providing instruction and cultural enrichment for the child of the deprived areas. Community talent was utilized, plays were prepared and presented, dances offered, field trips to theaters were conducted, stage sets constructed after visits to furniture factories, costumes made following trips to decorators—varied student abilities were employed.

Special types of compensatory education are determined by the nature of the population. In cities with a large Puerto Rican population the value of the New York program is readily apparent. To provide better communication between teachers and parents, several Spanish-English pamphlets were prepared. Classes in Spanish were offered to teachers of Puerto Rican children. Tours to Puerto Rico were arranged for school personnel to help them gain a better understanding of the background from which these pupils come. An extensive program of classes in English for Spanish-speaking adults was conducted.

Most urban school systems have for some time used teachers in special assignments for enrichment, upgrading, home liaison, and supportive purposes.

Numerous designations are employed for their roles: adjustment teachers, master teachers, in-service teachers, enrichment teachers, team-teaching leaders, and others. Use of enrichment teachers is illustrated in the following program.

The "enrichment unit program" of Columbus, Ohio, entailed the assignment of an enrichment teacher for every three or four primary classes in the disadvantaged districts. Special help was provided in the language arts. Part of the time was also used to relieve the regular classroom teacher so he could attend in-service sessions at school headquarters. A similar approach was employed in the Long Beach, California, schools, where "in six schools of greatest educational deprivation" one assisting teacher was assigned for every two regular teachers. This in-service training is consistent with the general awareness among urban systems that the compensatory approach demands the improvement of pre-service and in-service teacher education. Some of the techniques used were described in Chapter 4.

The Atlanta school system undertook a novel program of retraining teachers to become school social workers. In cooperation with two local universities, the problem of securing trained social workers is being overcome. Trainees were first used as visiting teachers and then assigned as professional social workers to improve home-school rapport.

Although Title I has had the greatest effect on the spread of compensatory efforts, other legislation also has helped. Funds made available under PACE (Title III of ESEA) stimulated a wide variety of "creative" approaches, many of which are compensatory in nature. In addition, the Economic Opportunity Act of 1964, Title II, Part A, allowed for expanding health services for underprivileged children.

The More Effective Schools Program, which was advocated by the New York City teachers' union, is still one of the most heavily financed compensatory projects. Special services and smaller classes were provided in 21 elementary schools supported by two and one-half times the usual budget. Among the schools selected were those with superior programs equivalent to those in the better suburbs.

The New York Center for Urban Education made a detailed analysis of the results. These are the salient findings: school principals are happy with the progress; parents think well of the schools; teachers like the program as do the pupils; morale is high. Three types of observers, including private school headmasters, university professors, and school practioners, made essentially the same ratings. They stated they would be delighted to send their own children to these schools. But—and here is the basic reservation—according to the study, in two and one-half years of the program there were no unusual gains in reading and arithmetic. The growth was identical with that in 21 matched schools not provided with special help. The teachers' union disputes this, stating there has been some gain in addition to the usual program.

The key, says Robert Dentler, Director of the New York Center for Urban

Education, is the teacher. If with smaller classes and more materials the teacher does not change her traditional teaching methods, then few gains result. Teachers need help to capitalize on a new setting. Dr. Dentler contends that tenure and uniform salary schedules stifle initiative and reduce incentive. If more money were spent on modifying teacher behavior than is spent on school buildings, then greater returns, he claims, would be achieved.

This listing of compensatory activities is only suggestive. A description of the wide array of services offered by the New York City schools alone would be extensive.

Furthermore, there. is widespread recognition that special services in the inner-city classroom should be accompanied by special help to parents. For example, an encouraging development in several cities has been the continuance of meetings by parents of Head Start children. More directly, in many cities, among them Houston, Texas, large projects were funded to reduce adult illiteracy. In fact, the essence of many compensatory programs for both young and old is the improvement of communication skills. Since these are at the heart of the educational process, this aspect of the urban school's effort will be considered in the next chapter. A discussion of compensatory and special programs would be incomplete, however, without mention of the increasing contributions being made by volunteers.

In a number of compensatory programs which increase supportive services to the classroom teacher, reference has been made to teacher aides, assistant teachers, and others. In most instances such personnel are paid, but in many large systems the use of volunteers is expanding.

The history of lay participation in American education is of course a long one, from the early visiting committees to the present-day school board. These bodies have functioned largely in the development of school policy. Lay interest has also been expressed through parent-teacher associations which have served to reinforce and interpret school efforts. Some have been effective in improving local schools, but, in many instances, regrettably, the PTA has served largely as a spectator of the educational scene and has dealt with trivia, thus alienating some of the potentially most productive citizens.

More recently, volunteers have become active participants in the educational process. One of the earliest efforts, dating from 1955, was the New York City School Volunteer Program. The San Francisco schools also pioneered in this activity. The success of such participation has led to the National School Volunteer Program of the Public Education Association. Financed by the Ford Foundation, experience and materials are shared among 20 large school systems.

School volunteers relieve professional staff of nonteaching duties and provide needed services for individual children to supplement the work of the teacher. Their programs enrich the experience of children beyond what is otherwise available in school. In the community, volunteers build better understanding of school needs and stimulate widespread citizen support for public education.

To borrow a metaphor from hospital adminstration, many school systems are still using doctors to make the beds. Teachers, often in short supply, are still used to operate bookstores, arrange bulletin boards, show movies, and so on. Continuing the admitted strained analogy, whereas a structured hierarchy of skills is employed in hospitals, from orderly to medical specialist, supported by many volunteers, by and large the schools have not fully learned to conserve special skills for certain tasks. Certification requirements need to be met or altered; however, the continuing shortage of quality teachers underlines the importance of effective manpower utilization. Team-teaching, the increasing use of teacher aides, assistant teachers, and lay readers—these are steps that have been taken in the right direction. But volunteers have been helpful in providing a wide variety of nonprofessional services.

The use of college students and even capable high school pupils as tutors and study center guides has been mentioned. However, many cities are drawing upon adults, usually housewives, to help in various ways. For example, a number of Philadelphia parents were trained by a library supervisor to establish libraries in individual schools with books supplied by the board of education. The goal in Cleveland was to set up a library in each of 135 elementary schools. Funds for books and equipment were contributed by local industry and supplemented by the board. The staff came from volunteers provided by the National Council of Jewish Women, the Junior League, the Temple Women's Association, and the local PTA groups.

In Detroit, laymen provided actual instruction in cooperation with classroom teachers. Thirty members of the United Auto Workers Retired Workers Center helped children learn at three elementary schools. Their skills ranged from auto mechanics and carpentry to accounting. It would be hard to say who gained more, the children or the aging adults who found new uses for their wealth of experience. When greater state reimbursement for local schools was needed to "help evaluate learning in Pittsburgh," a group of women volunteers studied finance, and through their efforts 20,000 letters and telegrams were directed to the governor and legislative representatives, resulting in an improvement of state support for Pennsylvania city school districts.

It is difficult to list any form of volunteer participation which has not or is not being tried in the nation's largest city. One of many interesting projects in New York was the use of mothers as teacher volunteers at P.S. 89 in The Bronx, where seriously emotionally disturbed pupils receive help so that they can attend regular classes. Using daily lesson plans prepared by regular members of the faculty, the "teacher moms" were able to work with individual pupils.

The Exchange Club of Minneapolis assisted inner-city schools. Two-man teams visited classes "to provide students with an opportunity for contact with persons from the community-at-large. The visitors also became more aware of the problems facing teachers and youth in the downtown elementary schools." Eighteen members visited nine classes once a week.

The program conducted by the San Francisco Education Auxiliary, with 70 volunteers, was based on three premises. First, that a teacher in a public school can use a dependable, intelligent volunteer once or twice a week to relieve him of the many nonprofessional chores. Second, well-educated volunteers can assist the teacher as part of a classroom team, i.e., testing a small group on vocabulary, giving drills in number combinations, listening to a child read. The third premise is that talented school volunteers, such as artists, musicians, writers, actors, and other professionals, can provide cultural enrichment on a regular basis.

It would be a mistake to assume that public participation is always eagerly sought by the school staff. The point at which interest may become interference is not fixed. Mutual understanding and coordination are essential. Most large systems have either created a department of school volunteers, as in Detroit, or a staff member has been designated to work closely with the volunteers. Organizations such as the National Council of Jewish Women, which participates in school projects in 33 communities, have recognized the merit of conducting prior training programs for their volunteers. At the same time there is growing recognition that different levels of volunteer services range from simple housekeeping duties to paraprofessional activity. Though many if not most volunteers come from fringe and suburban areas, the involvement of inner-city parents in the Head Start Project has emphasized the fact that in the heart of every slum there are adults who, in spite of many handicaps, possess skills and common sense which should be enlisted at their level of competence in the aid of their own neighborhood schools.

If attractive compensatory program titles were an assurance of educational gains, then the time for cheering would be here. Clever acronyms and impressive proposals are more expressions of hope than evidence of achievement. Yet how realistic is it to assume that the school can in a short time compensate for the deficiencies of a childhood in the slums? Referring specifically to Negro pupils, the U.S. Commission on Civil Rights stated in 1967 that it had serious doubts whether the ghetto schools can be improved through investments in compensatory education. Their investigation showed that of the programs studied "None has had a lasting effect in improving the achievement of Negroes in segregated schools."

The effects of school programs on children need further analysis. "Everybody is trying something different and nobody seems sure what is effective," notes M. W. Kirst of the National Advisory Council on the Education of Disadvantaged Children. A U.S. Office of Education Survey, often referred to as the Coleman Report after its senior author, concluded that the number of pupils per teacher, the size of the school, the number of library books per student, the grouping of pupils by ability, the number of counselors, a special curriculum, have very little effect on the achievement of pupils. Although some authorities reject such negative findings, nevertheless the conclusions are of particular concern since so many compensatory programs rest on the assumption that these factors are crucial.

If the traditionally accepted factors make little difference to educational outcomes, particularly to disadvantaged children, what does matter? Research evidence suggests that an important element is the kind of people in the school environment; that is, the other pupils and the teachers. It is the social class makeup and not alone the racial composition which makes the difference. An all-white school of a lower class will have little, if any, positive effect on the previously segregated Negro child. It is generally true that disadvantaged children are more sensitive to outside-family influences than are middle-class children. Thus, the Office of Education Coleman Report, "Equality of Educational Opportunity," found that teachers who have strong educational backgrounds and who themselves have had rich cultural experience will benefit their students most. Unfortunately, the pattern which often prevails is that the teachers of the poor are usually less well trained and have had more limited cultural backgrounds than the teachers of middle- and upper-class pupils.

Exceptions can be debated, but few will argue that the contributions of the school can be separated from the total social setting. In the long run, schooling for most will be improved only if home environment is improved. This can be done if opportunities for economic mobility are increased. In the meantime many would agree, as stressed before, that both social integration and instruction compensation are needed.

Even if one accepts such programs as these described here largely on faith, there is manifestly a massive stirring in the big school systems. When a willingness to try permeates a traditional institution, then a major step has been taken. In that sense some optimism is warranted.

In the context of experimentation one factor requires attention, particularly in view of what has been learned about the crucial importance of the child's early education. In the urban school system, generally the higher the grade, the smaller the class size—that is, class size resembles a pyramid with the largest academic classes at the lowest levels. In few of the programs listed earlier, aside from Head Start, were attempts made to reduce class size. In fact, in many instances the class became larger because superior teachers were removed to work on special projects. The use of supportive services and specialists is of course helpful, but many teachers would gladly forego this help if their classes could be reduced. The usual reply is that there is little or no research evidence to support the merits of a smaller class. It would be difficult to convince an experienced teacher of that notion. The larger class in the city means that each student in the city school has a smaller share of the teacher's time than the student in the suburbs. The ratio is particularly damaging because often the child of the slums has only the teacher to turn to for help, while most suburban children can also be helped by their parents.

What would happen educationally if the pyramid could be inverted, with smallest classes in the lowest grades and largest classes in the highest? The torrent of objections can already be heard: accrediting associations use traditional criteria; state payments are based on different formulas; there would be staff, space, and equipment requirements. Yes, the complaints would be loud, clear, and probably stifling to initiative. But the question must still be asked: Have we not learned that a head start, even a fair start, is vital to future educational success? And what good does this knowledge do unless traditional patterns can be changed, at least experimentally?

Historically the school curriculum in the city has been essentially the same for all in a smiliar grade. In some instances, where modifications have been attempted on the grounds of varying pupil needs, the school board has received charges of discrimination. It has been alleged that pupil aspirations were downgraded and a caste system perpetuated. In isolated instances these allegations may have been justified, but as a general rule such contentions were not valid. The community, its minority groups included, must face up to the fact that children of different environments need different school experiences, at least until they can catch up. It is ridiculous to demand French as a symbol of "culture" when the fundamentals of English need yet to be acquired. The urban curriculum is not to be a diluted one; rather it should be full of unusual materials. As Abraham Bernstein remarks:

"We cannot do so simply by putting Dick and Jane into blackface, or applying burnt cork to American history. Instead, we must build a curriculum that transforms lack into possession, not only by showing a recognizably dirty neighborhood, but how to change it to a clean one, or why some people prefer it dirty; not only by showing conniving and honest merchants, but how to count change and read package labels; not only by phonics, but how teeth, lips, tongue and throat make *man* distinguishable from *mad.* We must show how the rote drill of multiplication and spelling makes you more at peace with yourself; how society means conflict, and how force is used and controlled; how democracy is not always a sweet-running, placid flow, but lobbies, pressure groups, filibustering, and people who hate you; how poets and novelists know more about you than you know about yourself; how algebra and geometry don't train your mind but train your imagination, and why they hurt and are hard."

A promising development in tomorrow's city schools will be not the use of new labels for old practices, but a refreshing and frank recognition of what the slum kid needs to know and how he can best learn it.

In this connection, the aid of the urban university should be enlisted to a larger degree. Thus far the contribution to the local systems has been largely through departments of education and psychology. Since the influences of the child's total environment must be considered, the resources of the university in other fields, such as sociology, law, economics, political science, as well as the health sciences, will need to be utilized. Those involved in higher education need to be reminded that education is a continuum. The formal training of the graduate student starts in the kindergarten, and the whole university, not only the education department, has an obligation to contribute to the total process.

Another resource in school program planning will be private industry. Several projects involving such cooperation are underway or will soon be launched. An example of such joint efforts is Project PLAN in which twelve school systems in five states will join with the Westinghouse Learning Corporation. A system is being developed which uses the computer as an aid to the teacher in providing each student with an individual program of study. Detailed information about each student will be fed into a computer in Palo Alto, California, which will then prescribe a course of study. The student thereby proceeds at his own pace.

It is, of course, much too early to make any judgment about the effectiveness of this or any other school-industry program. It is evident, however, that in the future development of school materials, planning will not be confined to the school system itself, but rather will involve both the profit and nonprofit institutions of the community.

31

Compensatory Education by Community Action*

PAUL STREET

For its centennial in 1957, the NEA produced the film, "A Desk for Billie," to interpret the historical role of the school in effecting identification of a pupil with the larger society. Assigned her own desk on the first day of school, the "Hobo Kid" observed that hers was "just as good as anybody else's" and took her place among the "smooth people." Whatever school she attended, she found "they" had a desk for her and that she "belonged" with "them."

What the schools did for Billie, the OEO proposed to do for the poor with its community action program. "Community action" is an attempt to provide a place for people of poverty in the councils where the poor, the powerful, and the in-between are brought together. It is to make them a part of the "smooth people," to involve them in the value patterns of the greater society, to give them identity with the various issues and perspectives which concern the group, on the assumption that only as one can perceive himself in new and multiple roles can he become the adaptive, change-accepting person modern technological society requires of those who "belong" to it.

Basic to the theory of community action is the doctrine that poverty is, at base, a problem of the people themseves, of their attitudes and viewpoints, their perceptions of self and of others. Also fundamental is the recognition that participation in the making of value choices supports *implementation* of those choices. Kurt Lewin's experiments with group process, demonstrating the difference between group discussion and lecture as means of generating changes in attitudes and consequently in behavior, illustrate that personal involvement makes the difference.[1] Daniel Lerner's work in development implies that only to the extent that people are able to project themselves "outside their own skins," to become vicariously *other people,* and to see themselves in other roles, can change essential to social and economic development take place.[2] Such studies provided the basic model for the OEO's Community Action Program.

Community action, therefore, represents a kind of conspiracy against the more intangible elements of poverty, a subtle attempt to poison the roots of it, by insidious persuasion to incline the poor to seek their own salvation. It is an attempt to resolve the perennial dilemma faced by those who would help the poor: How to help them without generating more dependency. It recognizes that while there is also a concomitant, poverty of the spirit.

THE KNOX COUNTY PROGRAM

In spring, 1965, OEO funds generated action by a county-wide council (on which the poor had representation) in Knox County, Kentucky, to establish 14 community centers, mostly in rather remote mountain hollows. Each center, in a rehabilitated old schoolhouse or former residence, was headquarters for a local council which elected delegates to a county-wide group. It housed a wide range of social, political, and economic activities—including a kind of kindergarten program for pre-school youngsters. Out of it worked home economics, home improvement, and health advisers—usually indigenous people under "outside" supervisors. The centers were located, as their first director put it, "far enough up the hollows to reach the isolated people and far enough down to pull them out of their little neighborhoods"—the intent being to widen their socio-polit-ical-economic horizons and to entangle them in the complexities of the bigger world. By their involvement they were expected to take new roles: to have their opinions asked, for instance; to take committee or other leadership assignments; to discuss, argue, and vote on issues relevant to their own doings as well as those of the larger world—to rub shoulders and minds with the "smooth people."

While the study which is the basis of this report included evaluation of various special projects undertaken by the community action group in Knox County—the early childhood program, for instance—the focus of the study was upon appraisal of "community action" itself as a weapon in the anti-poverty arsenal.

DID THE PROGRAM CHANGE PEOPLE?

A fundamental part of the study was done by Lewis Donohew and B. K. Singh, who, by interviews with householders of the hollows, gathered measures of a wide range of variables related to degrees of "modernity."[3] Such attitude variables as *empathy, alienation, sociability, communicativeness,* and *openness to innovations* characteristic of modern living were measured. Measures of adoption of innovations, particularly those promoted in the specific programs of OEO, such as health practices, home improvement, and higher education and employment aspirations, were included. They found statistically significant tendencies for those living in areas served by centers, compared with similar populations in areas not served by centers, to move (in the two years between inter-viewing) toward more modern attitudes. Also, they found that those who had participated more actively in the community center program, as reported by the center directors, moved more than those who had not.

Herbert Hirsch[4] and Morris Caudill,[5] who measured attitudes and learnings of youth, obtained results that were less clear but somewhat similar. Hirsch found that the child who participated in center activities was more inclined to participate in such other activities as 4-H or athletics. Caudill likewise found youth participating in a wider range of activities in the county—presumably a "modernity" tendency—but did not link their doing so to participation in the OEO program. He found that their vocational and educational aspiration levels, however, declined—suggesting that perhaps they were a bit more realistic—while, surprisingly, both empathy and alienation levels climbed.

Now empathy, which rose for both householders and youth, is a measure of adaptability. It goes with modernity, which requires mobility and openness to change. Alienation, conversely, is a measure of one's separateness from others, of defensiveness, suspiciousness, wariness toward society generally. In some respects it seems paradoxical that the levels of both of these measures should rise in youth. The implication is that with modernity comes a higher level of aspiration, a broadening of community horizons, an openness to change—but also a loss of naivete, a more sophiticated guardedness, and some frustration, consequent to the insight that portends disillusionment—when a higher standard of life is perceived but left beyond reach.[6]

DID THE POOR IDENTIFY?

Willis Sutton, one sociologist member of the team, studied the effect of the program on leadership and people's perceptions of leadership.[7] He found that in a two-year interval during the program the people living in the hollows in areas served by the community centers became more conscious of the leadership. Also, they took part in more meetings dealing with more decision issues. On the average, each could name more persons as county leaders. Fewer leaders in all were named, but they were named more times—suggesting that people in the areas served by the program had become involved to some degree, either directly or through diffusion of the program, and had become more sophisticated with respect to who were actually the top leaders of the county.

Interviews with leaders supported the observation that, although the program had not basically changed the leadership structure of the county, it had enlarged and clarified perceptions of who were the leaders. Also, leaders themselves reported observing that the feelings and wishes of people of poverty were considered and perhaps respected more than ever before. Furthermore, there was a shift from the naming of branch-office or agency executive people as leaders toward mention of more persons from stable but relatively low-income groups, as well as more poor people.

This is to suggest that measurable impact was generated, that the people involved in community action did move more toward a stronger identity with the larger society than did those not involved, and that in a sense people of poverty not only were "educated" a bit regarding the realities of the decision process of the county but actually became, at least in small measure, a force for consideration by the leadership and at least a small part of that leadership.

WAS THE PROGRAM ON TARGET?

Nevertheless, though the impact may have reached the target generally, it did not touch the bull's-eye. Ottis Murphy and I found that almost one-third of those living in the areas that community center directors had defined as those whom their programs were expected to serve reported, after more than two years of the program, that they had never heard of it and could not identify it even when suggestions of personality, event, and location connections were offered.[8] Members of this group, by comparison with those who did know of the program, were significantly different statistically—living a bit farther from the centers; being older; and having lower levels of education, employment, and income—in most respects the very people the program was meant to involve, but also obviously those most difficult to reach.

WAS THEIR LOT IMPROVED?

Lowndes Stevens took measures of changes in living standards, by such indicators as use of telephone, mass media, appliances, running water, and so on, and of income.[9] He found all these up; but, paradoxically, he found employment levels down, with more dependence upon transfer payments (welfare and pension types of income). He concluded that there was a movement, more long-run than immediate, which portends ultimate economic growth.

A striking improvement did appear, however, in the rise in new low-cost housing of the type promoted by the community action program. Thomas Field, in a comparison between Knox and Clay counties (Clay having no comparable community action program and being a comparable neighbor in many respects), found Knox having built 60 new FHA type C and D homes since 1965, with Clay having built none of these—suggesting a significant impact upon the living standards of the lower-income group particularly.[10]

WERE THEY MORE SELF-SUFFICIENT?

Stevens' observation about slight unemployment increase, decline in employment levels, and rise in transfer payments is discouraging. It is worth considering, of course, that until people want a change in their way of life they cannot be expected to change it by their own efforts—that community action is not especially aimed at immediate economic improvement. Perhaps Stevens is right in concluding that a foundation has been laid for economic improvement by the program.

Murphy and I approached the question directly, asking people: "Do you feel the OEO community action program has made poor people better able to take care of themselves—or has it made them more dependent upon government? Or has it made any difference on this point?"

Of those who knew of the program, 42 percent said community action made people more independent. On the other hand, 26 percent held that more dependency had been created, the remainder either offering no opinion or saying that it had made no difference.

Certainly no definite answer is possible, especially considering the short terms of the study. (Indeed, it was a gratifying surprise to some of the study team themselves that several statistically significant measures of change emerged out of such a short-term study, considering its nature.) The launching of a job-training program and construction of an arts and crafts center for training and for sale of handicrafts produced by poverty people were in promising stages as the study ended. Such obstacles as the indigenous factionalism with perenially deep-rooted alignments, and the alienating provincialism which characterized the culture, must be weighed against the gains substantiated in the study, if one is to judge the eventual outcome.

IS COMMUNITY ACTION THE WAY?

Perhaps it is a biased hope on my part that the experiment may not be abandoned, at least not yet. The Knox County community action program, still in operation, has not so far been a glowing success. It has succeeded partly; it has failed partly. It should not be overlooked that its task is a most difficult one, that the people it is meant to reach are those whom existing institutions and forces—the school, the church, the agencies of reform, the enticements of technology with its high-powered advertising, and the still enduring tradition of self-sufficiency—have been unable to rescue from poverty.

There is some inclination for the study team to feel that a large proportion of the Appalachian middle-aged and older are not likely to find places in modern society outside, where either they or society will profit, whatever success community action may have. A program that will make life for them, where they are, more tolerable, or indeed richer, by attention to good things at hand in the area, is certainly a luxury the greater society can afford. But the largest concern must be for the children and youth, and for those in the middle years who are still adaptable and potentially self-sufficient.

Perhaps the easiest course would be for society to be reconciled simply to perpetuating dependency by almost indiscriminately—as some feel is already done—distributing the "dole" to the "needy." By so doing society would commit itself to maintaining an unbridged chasm between classes so long as it should endure, with millions living out their lives as "parasites," while others who scorn them pay for their "keep."

Such programs as community action are expensive, and so far they do not show very gratifying results. But at least they are an attempt. They are something—as opposed to nothing! At least they are a denial that the future of this society shall be the kept on the one side and the keeper on the other. They are an attempt to provide the counterpart of a desk for Billie, that the poor may come to belong among the "smooth people."

Therefore, let the critics of community action or of other attempts to unravel the tragic snarl of poverty reflect upon the choices: whether we shall hide from the reality of poverty in a land of plenty, or continue our general self-righteous system of voting corn to the mob, or keep on trying by such means as community action to encourage people to help themselves.

31. NOTES

1. Kurt Lewin, "Conduct, Knowledge, and Acceptance of New Values," in *Resolving Social Conflict* (New York: Harper, 1948), pp. 103-24.

2. Daniel Lerner, *The Passing of Traditional Society* (New York: The Free Press, 1958).

3. Lewis Donohew and B. K. Singh, "Modernization of Life Styles," Unit 7 of *Community Action in Appalachia* (a report under Contract No. 693 to the Office of Economic Opportunity by a University of Kentucky study team; Paul Street, principal investigator).

4. Herbert Hirsch, "Poverty, Participation, and Political Socialization," Unit 5, *Community Action in Appalachia.*

5. Morris K. Caudill, "The Youth Development Program," Unit 6, *Community Action in Appalachia.*

6. Lewin, *op. cit.,* pp. 103-24.

7. Willis A. Sutton, Jr., "Leadership and Community Relations," Unit 8, *Community Action in Appalachia.*

8. Ottis Murphy and Paul Street, "The 'Image' of the Knox County Community Action Program," Unit 9, *Community Action in Appalachia.*

9. Lowndes F. Stevens, "Economic Progress in an Appalacian County," Unit 2, *Community Action in Appalachia.*

10. Thomas P. Field, Wilford Bladen, and Burtis Webb, "Recent Home Construction in Two Appalachian Counties," Unit 13, *Community Action in Appalachia.*

32

One Step Off the Sidewalk*

JONATHAN BLACK

Like so many large cities, New York is in the midst of educational ferment. The bitter teachers' strike of last year only underlined the terrible failure of formal education to reach the children of the ghetto. Those ghetto students who do persist through the indignities and irrelevancies of the public school system generally end up with a fairly worthless scrap of paper—the general diploma. Those who graduate with an academic diploma may be scarred in subtler ways, with their imaginations blunted, their enthusiasm cauterized, and their hostilities toward the system aggravated beyond repair.

The imposition of decentralization from above has proved a decisive political failure in New York, and it may be some time before the experiment of community control can regain its momentum. But there is a dynamic decentralized school system sprouting from below, a string of storefront schools in three boroughs, that threatens to restructure the roots of education.

The idea of storefront schools is derived partially from economic and physical necessity, but more significantly from a belief in the critical relevance of education. Schools *should* be only a step off the sidewalk. Where the step between a community and its schools has widened into a chasm, it is crucial that that intimacy be restored. The ghetto school has only a fragile hold on its children, and if the realities of ghetto life are ignored, even that tenuous communication is lost.

Street academies are storefront schools. They are schools for high school dropouts. Each academy has from fifteen to thirty students, three teachers, and usually one street worker. The academy program envisions a three-step process: several months at a local street academy, additional time at a more formalized Academy of Transition, and finally "graduation" to either Newark or Harlem Prep (privately funded high schools, the latter a recent outgrowth of the academy system). But college education, although it may be the ultimate goal, is only one of the levels on which academy staffs operate. The genesis of the academy idea is in street work, putting together a dropout so he *wants* to get his high school diploma. The academies are built up from the kids, shaped by their needs. The street worker is not a seven-hour-a-day caseworker. He lives in the dropout's world, shares his sidewalk and his problems, and not infrequently ends up in night court with bail money. Eventually, if he is good, he may succeed in coaxing the kid to an academy where he can start picking up the pieces of his education.

There are now fourteen operating academies, eight in Harlem, the others elsewhere in Manhattan and Brooklyn. The style of one academy may differ substantially from the style of another. Sometimes this is dictated by the demands of the neighborhood, sometimes by financial expediency, and frequently by the individual preferences of the head teacher who still retains a high degree of autonomy in the academy system. At one of the Harlem storefronts, the teacher explains his line: "How do you get these kids to college? I tell 'em, dig me. You want money, you want to talk black power, you want to make it in the system? You gotta have that degree. These kids have to be hipped to a lot of stuff: the Jews, the Mafia, basketballs. Every cat bouncing a basketball around Harlem thinks he's gonna be a pro. Forget it!" Educational philosophy? "These cats are bored. Everyone's bored. You gotta excite 'em. You give them pride. You make them think black is worth something."

A typical social studies lesson in this academy was an informal rambling brew that slid over Vietnam, Biafra, the French Foreign Legion, the concept of civil war, capitalists in Texas, Indians in Mexico, drugs in Mexico, academy students in Mexico (a summer trip organized by this teacher), American imperialism, white imperialism, etc. When asked who sponsored this academy—each school is funded separately by a sponsoring corporation—the black teacher leaned over sheepishly and whispered under his mustache, "Chase Manhattan." Obviously, this teacher has a friend at Chase, but the freedom within this academy is apparently typical of a non-interference policy of all sponsoring corporations. And a little illogic is a small price to pay.

The tone of a Lower East Side academy is quite different. The school is housed temporarily in a church while its old building undergoes renovation. There is not much talk of black power, and the twenty students enrolled for the spring term are as mixed as the neighborhood. The head teacher here is white (about one-fifth of the forty-two academy teachers are white), and he puts great emphasis on revitalizing a formal curriculum. His style is more teacher than revolutionary. He believes in a deep personal involvement with his kids, but is skeptical about the practicality of the academy functioning as a full-time family surrogate. As in many individual academies, the effectiveness of this academy's program is difficult to evaluate. This is a transitional phase, and the academy as a fully funded, fully staffed unit is only beginning to gel. The entire academy program is still an experiment, still relatively small, still groping. Its potential is only beginning to be explored.

A Brooklyn academy, located in Bedford-Stuyvesant and sponsored by Union

Carbide, exemplifies the program at its best. As in all the academies, the four or five rooms are a pleasant eyeful, crisply renovated by an imaginative group of young architects called Urban Deadline, sportily furnished and brightly painted —in pale lavender, sky blue, and lemon—with little resemblance to the fermented green of most school buildings. Posters clutter the walls, and partitioning creates a varied and exciting use of limited space. As in all the academies, there are people just lounging around. And there is a charge of excitement here. "It's just beautiful," says the street worker from the area. "These kids would be lost. Now they're working; they're back in school. They're worth something." Perhaps the most unlikely smile is spread all over a white face, an attorney from Union Carbide now working at the academy. Initially sent for a limited three-week training period, he now stops in at Carbide about once a week and spends most of his time teaching English at the school, taking kids to ball games, and bailing students out of jail.

Carbide has been more than cooperative. Beyond their basic contribution of $50,000, they have donated three cars, furniture, movie equipment, and an elaborate "wine and dine" affair with Carbide executives when students graduate from the academy. Carbide is considering setting up a completely black-owned factory in the area. And from Carbide's point of view, the association has been equally fruitful. They have a handy information laboratory to test out ideas and familiarize themselves with expansion into ghetto communities and a direct tap on a vast employment pool. IBM, which also sponsors a Harlem school, is as deeply involved with the operation of its academy, and other corporations, notably banks, are taking advantage of the job link for recruiting ghetto employees.

The history of the academy program has been brief, hectic, and explosive. It started seven years ago with a white street worker, Harv Oostdyk—himself a college dropout—and a suburban Christian movement called Young Life. The initial organizers simply picked up kids off the streets and organized a tutorial center for dropouts at the Church of the Master on Morningside Avenue, where the Reverend Eugene Callender was an enthusiastic sponsor. Ford Foundation money—$700,000 in grants—kept the program alive and growing. The academy was a going thing when Callender, appointed executive director of the Urban League of Greater New York in 1966, took the program under the aegis of the Urban League. Since then, the Union Coalition has become involved, and through its contacts corporations now provide the lifeblood of funding—about $50,000 a year to operate each academy; Calender has left the Urban League; Oostdyk has left the academy; and the academy idea, boosted by the enthusiasm of New York Urban League Director Livingston Wingate, is being carried nationwide by the National Urban League.

In New York, a variety of expansion plans are under way. There is an informal goal of at least one academy in each of the city's five boroughs, and the possibility of twenty schools by the end of 1969. The role of the street worker is being explored, and an institute to train street workers may be set up soon. There is talk of either expanding Harlem Prep—seventy students graduated this year—or of developing an additional prep school fed by satellite street academies. A committee of sponsoring corporations has been formed and meets once a month to pool resources and evolve new strategies. And finally there are broad plans for meeting the continuing needs of academy students, in school and out, during studies and after graduation. "We're just beginning to look at the total needs of our kids," says Wingate. "We've guaranteed that they'll not only be picked out of the street, but sent through college."

One of the success signals of academy work has been a growing cooperation between storefront schools and the New York City Board of Education. Ordinarily, there is an informal relationship between academy staff and the high schools. Street workers may talk to students outside school, during lunch hours, in their homes, around the neighborhood. There is an obvious advantage, however, in establishing some liaison directly with the high school to facilitate contacting dropouts, present or future. A Rockefeller Foundation grant permitted the Urban League to set up a cadre of eighteen salaried street workers, assigned to be physically present in three high schools. Haaren, Brandeis, and Charles Evan Hughes. In Haaren, where the dropout rate averages 60 per cent, the principal, Bernard V. Deutchman, has been particularly pleased with the relation between his school and the McGraw-Hill Street Academy a few blocks away. Deutchman views the academy not only as a second chance for kids who are having trouble, but also as an invaluable laboratory, a training ground for "sensitizing" teachers to dropouts' problems. As the relation between Haaren and the academy develops, Deutchman envisions the academy being physically located within the school, offering credit courses, and serving as an alternative to those who for some reason or other cannot make it in the public school system.

This program touches a shared ideal among a number of disparate academy staff and consultants. The thought is that as the academy reaches it maximum utility as an educational model, and, as its methods are deemed successful, it will be incorporated into the city board of education. "You can't just tell the system what's wrong," explains Robert Rogers, acting head of the academy system. "You've got to show them."

There is no question that the academy can serve a vital role as a teacher-training ground. The first teacher to "return" to Haaren under Deutchman's program was bubbling with enthusiasm, and exchanges between the school and the academy will increase. The academy can serve as a school for both dropouts and teachers. There are problems, however. For one thing, although the teachers in the academy program are highly qualified in their work, some are not college graduates, few meet certification requirements, and probably only a handful have any interest in teaching in city schools. The methods of a number of academy staff probably would not be palatable to the board of education, and it is unlikely that the United Federation of Teachers would welcome the new-comers with much enthusiasm.

More fundamentally, however, the orientation of the academy program from its inception has been socio-psychological, demanding a twenty-four-hour-a-day commitment to its students. Much of the academy's success is undoubtedly attributable to its image as an *alternative* to public school education. It functions personally, tutorially, remedially. It has the leisure and the dedication to explore education in the broadest of contexts—the total life of its students. Ideally, this should be the function of a public school education as well, but the danger of the academy's doubling back into the school system is that this uniqueness and intense personal involvement may be lost.

A similar challenge faces the Urban League. One of the rare qualities of the academy has been the extraordinary richness and diversity of persons attracted to its programs, from black militants to white seminarians, from corporate attorneys to ghetto junkies. Much of the energy and vitality comes from this dialectic. Teachers learn and learners teach. The Urban League provides an attractive umbrella organization to manage the academy program and facilitate smooth and controlled expansion. But street academies have always sprung from grass-roots concerns. Much of their success is due to this "building up" process, institutions shaped by human needs, the very opposite of a formal public school education. Academies have remained diffuse, flexible, and relatively autonomous in operation. Conceptually, the Urban League is not opposed to this orientation, but control from above threatens the decentralized richness of any such program. The very success of the academy has undoubtedly made such an institutionalization inevitable, but established organizations, wary of a public image, have a sluggish dynamic of their own and sometimes a gluttonous politic. So far, frictions have been minor, but there are pitfalls to be aware of. Similarly, the growing involvement of the sponsoring corporations must be continually probed, lest the academies become just another item in a corporate publicity brochure.

As the academies develop, these questions must be faced. And they must be faced with a courage and a confidence in the concept of storefront schools, because the educational system needs the academy desperately.

33

Project 100,000:
The Training of Former Rejectees*

I. M. GREENBERG

During the 1960's there was growing concern in government, in the educational community, and among public leaders over the fact that one-third of our nation's youth were being declared unfit for military service under standards established by the armed forces. We are all aware of numerous programs which were initiated in the past decade to upgrade the educational and skill level of disadvantaged youth and assist them in finding jobs and a future in our society. Project 100,000 is a Department of Defense effort to make a contribution toward helping solve this most pressing problem by accepting for military service large numbers of young men who would have been previously rejected for military service.

In this article I shall describe our experience with Project 100,000 men and then discuss the factors which contributed to the success of the program.

The program was announced in August 1966 by Secretary Robert McNamara in a speech which stressed the relationship between poverty, poor education, and social unrest. In October 1966 the armed forces lowered the entrance requirements for military service. We began accepting thousands of young men who were previously being rejected because they failed the standard entrance tests or the educational requirements for service. Provision was also made for accepting some men with easily correctable physical defects.

The goal was to accept 40,000 such men the first year and 100,000 each year thereafter. Project 100,000 derived its name from this annual goal. We have been meeting our input goal. By the end of March 1969, thirty months after the program began, we had enrolled 190,000 men. More than half were volunteers; the remainder were draftees. Some 93 percent were accepted by lowering the test standards and educational requirements. The other 7 percent were volunteers for medically remedial surgery or physical conditioning.

The Department of Defense is not a social welfare institution; its primary responsibility is to provide the combat capability needed for national security. We do feel, however, that the DOD, along with all other major institutions,

*Copyright 1969 by Phi Delta Kappa. Reprinted by permission of the publisher from *Phi Delta Kappan*, June 1969, pp. 570-74.

should be concerned with the broader aspects of national security. Our well-being as a nation suffers when we lose the potential contribution of a sizable proportion of our young men because of low academic achievement, undeveloped talent, and despair. Project 100,000 recognizes the opportunity of the armed forces to contribute their unique capabilities toward improving the competence of a portion of our nation's youth.

Most of the statistics quoted in this article come from a computerized name-by-name tracking system which was set up to manage the program. The file also contains comparable information on "control groups" of men who entered service with higher scores on the Armed Forces Qualification Test. Results from this tracking system are compiled and published periodically.

CHARACTERISTICS AND PERFORMANCE

Project 100,000 men come primarily from poor families and disproportionately from geographic areas and localities which have high rejection rates for military service. Nearly 40 percent are Negro, compared with a 9 percent Negro input for the control group; 47 percent of the Project 100,000 men come from the South, while only 28 percent of the control group entered from that region.

The educational profile highlights the gap between their school attendance and their achievement level.

The educational deprivation of these men is also reflected in their scores on the Armed Forces Qualification Test. The average percentile score for Project 100,000 men is 14, compared with 54 for the control group.

Project men are not "mentally retarded" as the term is generally used in education and psychology. Although entry standards were lowered, about 10.5 percent are still being rejected for failure to pass the written tests. This means that about 200,000 young men who reach military age each year still cannot pass the "mental standards" for military service.

When we started the program we were confident that the vast majority of men would be able to qualify as satisfactory servicemen when exposed to our instructional and motivational techniques. The results exceeded our expectations:

	Project 100,000 Men	Control Group
Percent high school graduates	43.3	75.8
Number school grades completed (ave.)	10.6	11.9
Reading ability— median grade	6.1	10.9
Percent reading below fourth-grade level	14.4	1.1
Percent who failed or repeated school grades	47.0	unknown

● In basic training 95 percent graduated, compared with 98 percent of all other men.

● In formal skill training courses only 10 percent failed to graduate, compared with a 4 percent attrition rate for the control group attending the same kinds of courses. Those who fail usually succeed in another type of course or are given on-the-job training.

● Some 60 percent of the Project 100,000 men are being given noncombat-skills assignments. Most of the assignments have direct or related counterparts in the civilian economy. After combat training, the most common assignments for Project 100,000 men are in the fields of food service, supply, wire communications, motor transportation, equipment repair, construction, and military police. The men have been assigned to more than 200 different occupational specialties.

● Their promotion record has been excellent. The enlisted grade structure has nine levels, starting with grade E-1. After 20 months of service, 52 percent were in grade E-4 or above, compared with 59 percent for the control group. Many are entering leadership positions.

● The annual court-martial rate for these men has been less than 3 percent. This figure is heartening because we did expect more severe disciplinary problems.

● Men with severe reading limitations are given full-time remedial education for three to eight weeks during basic training. More than 80 percent complete the course and show gains averaging 1 3/4 grades.

● The attrition from service—for all causes—has been modest. For example, a cohort with twenty months' service had a 12 percent separation rate compared with a 6 percent rate for all other men. This includes men separated for unsuitability, misconduct, medical conditions, family hardship, and also battle casualties.

Our records show that project men do not perform as well as a cross-section of men with higher educational levels. The differences in performance are, however, not very large. Most of the project men have become highly satisfactory servicemen. Although they all scored low on the service entrance test, they are not a homogeneous group. Given the opportunity, many of the former rejectees do a better job than men who had higher test scores.

What are the factors which have led to the high rate of success these men have had in military service?

THE MILITARY ENVIRONMENT

The young man who enters military service is separated from his previous environment. He enters a form of residential training. A conscious effort is made to build self-confidence, pride, and good work habits. The environment is highly structured and disciplined. The system acts rapidly to reinforce satisfactory performance and correct deviant behavior. Group competition is used to foster teamwork and motivate men to succeed and help their buddies succeed. The early months of military life are hard for all recruits, but they know there are penalties for not trying or quitting.

Military life opens a new chance, often viewed as the last chance by many who have tasted only failure and poverty. The typical drill sergeant announces on the first day: "I don't care whether your daddy is rich or poor, whether you went to college or just grade school—you're all the same to me. Right now you are a miserable-looking bunch, but eight weeks from now this platoon is going to be the best damn platoon in the battalion." As the weeks go by the recruit gains confidence as he masters the simple skills in basic training and is ready to learn more complex skills.

Training instructors and unit commanders report that Project 100,000 men, on the whole, have greater difficulty in coping with personal problems—debts, family crises, girl friends—but the machinery exists to counsel and help them. The environment is demanding but at the same time supportive. The individual does not feel alone or adrift.

The recruit knows there is a place for him after he finishes training. The job may be quite basic, but it is a man's job because of the organizational setting. Being a cook in a tank battalion or on an aircraft carrier provides more status than working in a hometown restaurant. In the service the man is a member of a military unit, such as an aircraft wing, a ship, or a regiment, which has its own heritage and traditions. His uniform announces his full-fledged membership in one of the military services, and this membership bestows upon him the grandeur acquired in past wars and battles—events recorded in the history books he has seen in school. The same organizational loyalties that lead men to sacrifice in combat also provide some of the motivation that helps them to learn to read better, study harder, and strive for promotions.

Men coming from deprived backgrounds and black ghettos find that the military doesn't hold them back because of their race or previous social status. What counts most now is their performance. Their inadequate education does keep most of them out of the more complex jobs initially, but they do have a chance to become supervisors and improve their education if they work hard enough.

INSTRUCTOR ATTITUDES

The majority of the instructional staff used to train enlisted men is military. We do employ some civilian teachers in technical schools and educational development courses. The military instructors are carefully selected and are given instructor training before they assume their duties in training centers or technical schools. They are competent in the limited subject matter they are required to teach and are given well-developed lesson plans to follow. Although they are not professional educators, they have qualities which help them perform well in their teaching tasks.

The instructors are optimists; they assume that the young man's personality can be modified and his ability level improved regardless of the deficiencies in prior background. The personnel planners in the Pentagon set the standards for entry into military service and operate the computerized assignment systems which deliver men into different training courses. These operations are not governed by the training centers and schools. When the recruit or student arrives for training, the instructor assumes he is educable.

Of course some men do fail in training. In most cases the instructor feels that the student's failure occurred because somehow he, as an instructor, was unable to motivate the student to try harder. The instructor rarely attributes the student's failure to cultural deprivation or genetic limitations. This attitude is certainly unsophisticated, but is perhaps the best approach for helping Project 100,000 men reach their full potential.

Military instructors work very hard. Those involved in basic training work about seventy hours a week during the training cycle. In schools, the instructors spend evenings tutoring men who are having difficulty in keeping up with the class. Project 100,000 has put a considerable strain on the military instructor. We feel that he has been the single most important reason for the success of the program.

ASSISTANCE DURING TRAINING

Project 100,000 men are trained along with all other men in our regular training centers and schools. There are provisions for helping them, if necessary, at all stages of their training. They are not stigmatized as slow learners on the basis of their entrance test scores. They—and all other men—are given extra help only if they need it.

A variety of methods is used to provide assistance to those who cannot keep pace during training:

   ● *Tutoring and Counseling*—This technique has proven to be very effective with Project 100,000 men. Schools usually schedule two-hour study periods three evenings per week. While most students study on their own, those who are having difficulty in the course are tutored by an instructor or another student.

   ● *Recycling*—Men repeat portions of their training by being set back to a training company or class which is in an earlier stage of training. Some men are recycled because they missed several weeks of training due to illness or emergency leave.

   ● *Special Training Companies*—Each basic training center has a unit which is organized to provide concentrated attention for men requiring physical conditioning, slow learners, or those who have serious motivational or adjustment problems. About half of the trainee population in these companies are Project 100,000 men. The stay in these special training companies averages two weeks, with a range of from one to thirty days. Men are returned to a regular training unit as quickly as possible.

   ● *Remedial Education*—Project 100,000 men and others who have severe reading limitations are sent to a remedial reading course before or during the basic training cycle. The Army course, called Army Preparatory Training, is six weeks in length, although some men leave after three weeks. The men get six hours of academic instruction each day, four in reading, one in arithmetic, and one in citizenship studies. Introductory military training is also provided at the end of each week day and on Saturday morning. The students are encouraged to read in the evening. The Air Force and Navy courses are somewhat similar.

Results have been excellent. About 80 percent of the men who enter the remedial education courses make progress. The gains in reading ability average 1 3/4 grades. The typical student enters with a 4.0 grade reading ability and is reading close to 6.0 when he graduates. The improvement is substantial, although it is recognized that some of the measured gains are achieved by refreshing dormant reading skills. The remedial education courses are improving the men's chances for success in military training and providing the foundation for future educational growth. The technical schools continue to improve the reading ability of these men during tutoring sessions. Programmed instruction materials in arithmetic are in use in various technical courses to provide the mathematical skills associated with the occupation.

Opportunities for continued educational upgrading are available after the men complete training and are assigned to units. The military General Educational Development (GED) programs award eighth-grade and high school equivalency certificates. Although the GED program is usually conducted during off-duty times, commanders try to make duty time available for those who do not have a high school education.

HETEROGENEOUS GROUPING

Educators have shown interest in our experience in training Project 100,000 men along with all others in our regular training centers and schools. This is why we adopted this policy:

First, we wanted to avoid stigmatizing the men as a sub-par group. Our goal is to improve their confidence and self-esteem. Segregation on the basis of entry scores would defeat this objective. Men who come into service with a history of failure in civilian life take enormous pride in graduating from a regular class. Their grades may be below the class average, but they now feel they can compete and survive.

Second, although we use achievement and aptitude tests in qualifying men for service and as assignment tools, we recognize that these instruments have limitations. While the men accepted in Project 100,000 are a relatively homogeneous group in terms of entrance test scores, their actual performance varies widely. As we anticipated, the aptitude test scores underestimate the potential ability of many Project 100,000 men.

Third, we feel that Project 100,000 men learn more by associating with a cross-section of American youth. Learning, in the fullest sense, doesn't stop when the training day is ended; it continues informally in the barracks, the dining room, and the enlisted men's club where the men drink beer. The mixing of ability levels also enables us to use the "buddy system" during training. Bright students are given responsibility for helping those who are making slow progress.

I do not mean to criticize ability grouping as an educational technique. We have been able to operate under a policy of mixed grouping in Project 100,000 because our total setting made it feasible. We are fortunate in having a wide spectrum of skill training courses that Project 100,000 men can master. We assign very few of them to complex courses such as computer programming, electronic maintenance, or meteorology. In the main, they are trained in the simpler skills at the beginning. However, in any course they take, the student body contains a cross-section of ability levels. Each occupation needs men who will be able to fill supervisory ranks and later take more advanced training in the occupational field. Therefore, even in the simplest courses attended by the Project 100,000 man, he will be grouped with others of greater educational achievement. To help sustain the system of homogeneous grouping, we have procedures for helping the man who cannot keep pace; or, if necessary, we assign him to another type of training.

IMPROVED TRAINING METHODS

When we started Project 100,000 we were confident that the curriculum and training methods used in recruit training centers were satisfactory. The only changes we made were to expand the capacity of the special training companies and, later on, add the capability of providing remedial reading instruction. Fortunately, the big improvement in basic training occurred prior to Project 100,000. The armed forces had taken steps to raise the selection standards, training, and prestige of the drill sergeants.

The military services have for many years been leaders in the field of technical education. Their vocational-type courses are job-oriented, stress practical exercises, and utilize modern training devices. We did feel that we should make changes in some of these courses to enhance the success rate of Project 100,000 students. The military services have made revisions in more than fifty courses and the process is continuing. The changes fall into these main categories:

- Eliminating subject matter and theory found to be unrelated to the job.
- Simplifying the reading levels of the materials. We used simpler words, shorter sentences, and added pictures, diagrams, and cartoons to increase comprehension.
- "Hands-on" training was increased to allow more by doing, and lecture time was reduced.
- More audio-visual aids were added and many of the training aids were improved. For example, in an eight-week automotive maintenance course we added twenty-one kinescopes, fifty new slides and charts, and five new simulators to better demonstrate the vehicle components.
- Instructors were added to some courses to permit training in smaller groups.

• Tests used in the courses were revised to make them relevant to the job the man would be required to perform. In some cases pencil and paper tests were replaced with performance type tests.

Not every change we made proved to be effective. For example, some programmed texts proved to be too boring; others were too difficult for men with low reading ability and poor study habits. Some material which was rewritten in cartoon format flopped because the same unintelligible language was transferred from paragraph form to cartoons. We also found that there are limits to the simplification process. Some courses do require the learning of theory, the reading of complicated technical manuals, and the use of high school level mathematics. We did not choose to dilute the quality of training in the process of simplifying a course.

On the whole, we are pleased with the results of our course modification effort. Most of the changes we made proved to be of benefit to all men attending the course. Project 100,000 served as a catalyst, triggering the reexamination of the way we were preparing men for jobs. The military services are developing new procedures for redesigning a technical course in a systematic way.

Many Project 100,000 men, especially in the Navy and Air Force, receive their skill training on the job instead of attending a resident course. On-the-job training is not left to chance. The training objectives, study guides, and tests for each skill are prepared centrally by training agencies in the services. The man's supervisor in the supply depot, maintenance shop, or hospital also serves as a teacher.

COSTS OF THE PROGRAM

The cost of Project 100,000 is estimated to be $19 million a year, or about $200 per man.

These costs are low because they are "added" rather than total. The strength of the armed forces was not increased for Project 100,000. We are accepting these men in lieu of other men with higher educational or physical qualifications. Most Project 100,000 men complete their training on schedule and become satisfactory servicemen. There are only minor costs for this group. The added costs are primarily for:

• Remedial education for those who need reading improvement.
• Higher attrition rates in training and longer training time for some.
• Hospitalization, physical conditioning, and convalescence for men with correctable physical defects.
• Data processing, research, and administration.

THE FUTURE

The program is expected to continue operating at the current rate during this year. The numerical objective is subject to change if the armed forces are reduced in size.

We are seeking ways to improve the program by investing in research. The ongoing research effort includes work on: 1) culture-fair or nonverbal tests of mental ability; 2) new methods for teaching men with low verbal abilities; 3) determining the minimum literacy requirements of certain military jobs.

Some of the first Project 100,000 men who entered service have now returned to civilian life. We plan to conduct follow-up studies on how well they adjusted to civilian life, compared with like men who were not in the military. Most of these men need some assistance in gaining a foothold in the civilian economy. The armed forces have established Project Transition to help smooth the way for these men who are returning to civilian life. Men can volunteer to spend the last few months of their military service working toward a high school degree or acquiring a civilian type occupation.

LIMITATIONS

Project 100,000 is reaching only a portion of the young men who suffer from educational and skill deficiencies. About 200,000 men each year are still being disqualified for military service because they cannot pass the tests of mental ability. The young men who are being rejected have even more severe educational problems than the enrollees for Project 100,000.

It is not practical to expand Project 100,000. The men who are accepted on the basis of lowered entrance standards are being used to fill jobs in the military services. The overall size of the armed forces was not increased to accommodate this program. Last year one out of every nine men accepted for the enlisted ranks was a Project 100,000 man. The job composition of the military services and the need for men who can progress to the higher ranks limit the number of poorly educated men who can be accepted each year. Military service is providing rehabilitation to only a portion of the men who need a new chance to succeed. The number who are assisted by military service may even drop in the future. If the armed forces are reduced to their pre-Vietnam level, we can expect a proportionate curtailment of annual input of Project 100,000 men. The main task of remedial education and job training still rests with our civilian institutions.

The military approach to training provides no blueprint that can be followed by civilian institutions. A major part of the success of Project 100,000 is due to the total environment of military life. This setting cannot and should not be introduced into our civilian school system and rehabilitative agencies. I do believe that the military experience in training Project 100,000 men may provide others with some helpful ideas and encouragement.

34

The Integration-Compensatory
Education Controversy*

DANIEL U. LEVINE

During the past few years the most important thrust in American education has centered in the need to provide better education for the hundreds of thousands of Negro youngsters who attend segregated schools in low-income neighborhoods in our large cities. First catapulted to national attention by James B. Conant's reference to the "social dynamite" which was accumulating in the urban centers in the early 1960's, disadvantaged youth who participated in widespread disorders in Watts, Chicago, Hough, and elsewhere have since proven that Conant's descriptive phrase was too mild: rather than "social dynamite", the urban centers are facing the equivalent of social "atom bombs". Educators and lay leaders cognizant of the urgency of the situation have responded by pushing to eliminate the segregated patterns of schooling and by organizing special remedial programs that might compensate for the learning handicaps associated with a background of deprivation and poverty.

As both these drives gained momentum in the sixties, it became clear that in some respects they embodied contradictory plans of action which inevitably would create a good deal of controversy. This has happened, and unless we somehow resolve the controversy by placing the whole problem in the perspective of a larger synthesis, the heat generated will limit effectiveness in working to achieve either integration or compensatory education.

To understand why this is so, it is only necessary to review the arguments and examine the implications for action of each position. Many vigorous advocates of integration, on the one hand, begin with the Supreme Court's 1954 generalization that separate schools can never provide equal educational opportunities for minority group students, if only because the very lack of choice involved in a minority student's *de jure* or *de facto* attendance at a segregated school teaches him that he is not considered "fit" or good enough to participate fully in society. Relying on a solid body of knowledge in psychology and sociology, this position emphasizes the likelihood that an individual whom society has taught to doubt his own worth will not perform as efficiently as the individual with self

*Copyright 1968 by Kappa Delta Pi. Reprinted by permission of the publisher from *Educational Forum* 32, No. 3 (March 1968), pp. 323-31.

confidence. The overriding importance of the student's assessment of his own capabilities in nourishing or crippling his performance in the classroom has been explicated as follows:

> Of all the forces operating in a school the energy of the learner is the greatest. If it is 'turned on' at full voltage—and directed straight into the task at hand—it is almost irresistible. Even if teaching is mediocre and material resources are meager, the youngster will somehow move ahead. But if it is 'turned off'—or diverted from the task or opposed to it—nothing else matters very much.
>
> That flow of energy is controlled by the learner's perceptions. . . . If a full charge of energy is to be delivered to any learning task, two conditions must prevail: The learner must see the task with clear eyes and sense that it is relevant to his private goals; and he must have faith that he is worthy to tackle it, that he is the kind of person who ought to do this sort of thing and who can do it if he stretches.[1]

If the disadvantaged Negro child is to overcome the debilitating mental effects of nonvoluntary segregation, concludes the strong advocate of integration, it is necessary to end the exclusion which implicitly calls into question his worthiness to claim an equal chance in life. In its implications for practical action, this position suggests that the primary effort in helping the disadvantaged Negro child must be to place him in an integrated school, even though doing so might put him in classes composed mostly of children without serious learning handicaps and would thereby make it very difficult or even impossible to provide special instructional experiences designed to overcome his particular academic deficiencies.

Advocates of compensatory education, conversely, tend to concern themselves not so much with the disadvantaged Negro child's possible sense of exclusion and alienation from the wider society as with the probability that his mental development has been inhibited, if not crippled, by the environment in which he grows up. Recognizing the undeniable fact that our educational system generally has had neither the will nor the knowledge to work effectively with the slow-learning youngster, who does not respond very well to standard techniques and programs, they believe that steps must be taken to overcome the pupil's learning handicaps before he is placed in a more or less standard educational environment where he could only be made to feel more inadequate and inferior. The obvious conclusion is that integration could or should be de-emphasized, if not actually postponed, until the pupil has been prepared to function satisfactorily in competition with youngsters who are not handicapped by a disadvantaged background.

Despite the clarity of the difference between the two positions, a number of complications in the argument have emerged. Many advocates of both positions, after all, are sincerely desirous of supporting the program which will be most advantageous for the child, and this means that they cannot completely ignore the apparent logic of opposing points of view. In addition, the logic of each position, if pushed far enough, begins to work against itself in a most curious way. For example, the advocate of integration who argues that quality education is seldom, if ever, attained in an all-Negro school is interpreted as implying that this means there really is something "wrong" or inferior about Negroes. To counteract this conclusion, he may search out examples where educators such as Dr. Samuel Shephard in St. Louis appear to have made great strides in raising the performance of disadvantaged Negro pupils, in order to show that his line of reasoning assumes no inherent inferiority among Negro students. But in so doing he greatly weakens his case. Even if he then argues that integrated education is prerequisite as much or more for social and moral development as for academic understanding (an argument which has much to commend it), his general posture is still much weaker than it would be if he continued to insist on the unequivocal necessity of integration for improved academic achievement.

The advocate of compensatory education, if he is open-minded, is also forced eventually to acknowledge an element of validity in the central position of his opponent. His commitment to the welfare of the disadvantaged Negro child, for one thing, should predispose him to lend at least some credence to the arguments of many of those leaders in the Negro community who push vigorously for integration. Even more important, however, is the fact that as he starts to wrestle with the classroom aspects of a program of compensatory education, he immediately confronts the fact that the self-concept does play an exceedingly important role in determining how a student responds to a particular set of learning experiences. Once he does so, it is but a short step to recognizing some validity in his opponent's insistence that a Negro child can hardly have an adequate self-concept unless given an opportunity to participate in the affairs of the larger society.

Without a fully developed set of priorities to order the convolutions of these two positions, the situation—to say the least—is confused, and it becomes still more confused as one reviews the small amount of research that bears on the outcomes of integrated and of compensatory education. In essence this research confounds the critics on each side by suggesting that either compensatory programs or racially integrated school settings *can* result in academic gains among disadvantaged Negro youth.

With regard to compensatory education, most technically acceptable studies dealing with compensatory programs have failed to find significant and lasting improvements in experimental groups as compared with comparable non-experimental groups in regular instructional programs (e.g. the final report on the Higher Horizons Project). The results, in fact, have been discouraging so often as to justify Ivor Kraft's recent capsule history of the typical compensatory program for an inner-city Negro school as one which ". . . begins with a fanfare of slogans, proceeds to a bustle of committees, advances to a much publicized and photographed new school and smartened-up curriculum, blossoms into a series of weekly newspaper testimonials, and culminates after two or three years in a typical inner-city slum school which has been sucked back into the inner-city slum environment and forgotten."[2] Emphasizing the failure of so many compensatory programs, Kraft goes on to conclude that

> We are going to have to integrate the schools. There is no other solution. We are going to have to bring rich and poor, black and white together under the same roof. . . . Given the contemporary political and social reality of urban American life . . . there is no compensatory device, no neighborhood concept, no idealistic notions of community centers that will keep those schools from being centers of inferiority and backwardness.[3]

Despite the failure of most compensatory projects, however, the available evidence supports an interpretation which is more sanguine than Kraft's. Here and there, that is to say, studies can be found which show compensatory interventions yielding results better than would be predicted on the basis of the previous performance of a group of disadvantaged youth or the performance of similar pupils in a control group, particularly when the students involved have been in the upper 50 percent of their classes (on measures of achievement or motivation) and/or have been in the primary grades or in preschool classes. Even though they prove the exception rather than the rule, such studies do support the conclusion that compensatory programs can have positive results providing that sufficient attention and resources are devoted to making them effective.

There are a few studies dealing with the achievement of Negro pupils in integrated as compared with segregated schools, but the small amount of data which are available tend to indicate that pupils in the former situation do better in school than do comparable pupils in the latter setting. Despite the admittedly incomplete nature of this research, the results are consistent enough to justify the conclusion that integration is more likely to result in improved academic performance on the part of the disadvantaged Negro child than is a compensatory education program, though either approach can have some positive effect, providing it is well implemented.

As regards the relative merits of the two approaches, by far the most important and relevant findings are described in the section on "Comparative Effects of Compensatory Programs and Desegregation" in the invaluable study on *Racial Isolation in the Public Schools,* which the United States Commission on Civil Rights released on February 20, 1967. After first reviewing the results of large-scale compensatory programs in St. Louis, New York, and elsewhere, the commission emphasized the failure of most such programs in pointing out that

> Because the data often were incomplete and the period in which the programs had been in operation was too short, it is not possible to draw absolute conclusions about the relative success or failure of these programs. In most cases, however, the data did not show significant gains in achievement.[4]

In order to assess the relative potency of compensatory as against integrated education, the commission then proceeded to review programs in four cities (Syracuse, Berkeley, Seattle, and Philadelphia) in which sufficient data had been collected on comparable groups of pupils in each condition to allow for valid comparison. The results were clear cut, and the commission concluded that while the data do not ". . . suggest that compensatory education is incapable of remedying the effects of poverty on . . . academic achievement . . . [the fact remains] that none of the compensatory programs appear to have raised significantly the achievement of participating pupils. . . . " Disadvantaged Negro youth in the integrated schools in these four cities, on the other hand, appeared to have progressed more rapidly in academic achievement than did comparable pupils in *de facto* segregated schools in each city.[5]

What, then, are we to conclude about the claims of those who primarily favor integrated education or compensatory education? On the one hand, the failure of so many compensatory education projects indicates that it is inordinately difficult to implement such a program successfully, probably because, as the Civil Rights Commission went on to point out, compensatory programs do not in themselves ". . . wholly compensate for the depressing effect which racial and social class isolation have upon the aspirations and self-esteem of Negro students . . . the evidence reviewed here suggests that efforts to improve a child's self-esteem cannot be wholly productive in a student environment which seems to deny his worth."[6] The success of a few compensatory programs such as those referred to above, however, does suggest that the disadvantaged child's particular learning deficits can be remedied sufficiently well to lead to significant gains. When this happens, it must be assumed that even in segregated situations, disadvantaged youth somehow gained greater confidence in their own capabilities, and that strengthened self-image played an important mediating role in making it possible for them to do better in school. Nevertheless, no one has yet succeeded in delineating in any significant detail the particular components or dynamics which are responsible for the success of those compensatory programs which apparently have had some positive impact.

Although our understanding of the dynamic forces at work in the integrated school is hardly more satisfactory than our understanding of the compensatory classroom, the study of equal opportunity conducted and published by the U.S. Office of Education shed much light on the factors that operate to make integrated education a potentially effective means to improve the performance of the disadvantaged Negro child.[7] In brief, the evidence showed that Negro youngsters who had experienced integration tended to have a slightly less positive *academic* self-image than did comparable students receiving their education in all-Negro schools, which apparently push students less hard and are less competitive than the integrated school. The effects of this small difference, however, were more than overbalanced by the fact that the Negro youngsters in integrated schools appeared to possess a stronger *general* self-image in terms of feeling more power over their future and the world around them than did the sample who had experienced only the sense of powerlessness seemingly generated from non-voluntary segregation. In addition to clarifying the psychological effects of integration, moreoever, the study of equal opportunity reported relatively direct evidence supporting the conclusion that integrated education can be a potent force in improving the academic performance of disadvantaged Negro youth. Summarizing this part of their study, the authors conclude that in the many cases in which integration involves the placement of some low-income youth in schools with less disadvantaged students, the achievement of the former group improves with no detriment to the achievement of the latter:

> If a minority pupil from a home without much educational strength is put with schoolmates with strong educational backgrounds, his achievement is likely to increase . . . the principal way in which school environments of Negroes and whites differ is in the composition of their student bodies, and it turns out that the composition of the student bodies has a strong relationship to the achievement of Negro and other minority pupils.[8]

These findings of the equal opportunity study, incidentally, call attention to an important problem which has not been much discussed and which may become a matter of controversy as educators refine their thinking about integrated and compensatory approaches and begin to identify the best tactics for achieving one or the other or both. As indicated in the preceding paragraph, one reason why integrated education can be a promising way to help disadvantaged Negro youth is that integration *per se* appears to exercise a salubrious effect in counteracting a student's sense of exclusion from society. At the same time, however, the equal opportunity study as well as other studies indicate that it is the opportunity to watch and learn from more privileged pupils that is responsible for much of the improved performance often noted among disadvantaged Negro youth placed in integrated classrooms. Thus the evidence presently available suggests that the socioeconomic mixing which usually accompanies integration as well as the racial mixing itself both can exert a positive effect on the performance of the low-income minority child. If so, the possibility immediately suggests itself that disadvantaged Negro youth whom it proved impossible to place in integrated classrooms might be helped by a calculated effort to place them in schools with appreciable numbers of middle-income Negro pupils. It is perhaps unlikely that middle-income Negro parents could be persuaded to agree to such a plan, especially since many such parents already are enrolling their youngsters in private and parochial schools precisely in order to remove them from the influence of their disadvantaged peers. It may be confidently predicted, moreover, that few middle-class Negro parents will even listen to such a proposal unless they are convinced that it is part of a sincere and massive effort to desegregate white schools serving pupils of all income levels.

Although the general implications of the varied research studies dealing with integrated education and with compensatory education projects should now be evident, it is important to spell them out as forcefully as possible in order to minimize the possibility that unnecessary energy will be consumed in continuing what now appears to be a spurious and wasteful argument between schools of thought that turn out to complement each other as much as they contradict or detract from one another. Perhaps the best way to summarize the situation is to call attention to some preliminary findings in one school district which is making a vigorous effort to reduce *de facto* segregation at the same time that it is providing intensive remedial and developmental services for those disadvantaged Negro students who remain in segregated school settings. Describing the initial results of both the newly-integrated arrangements brought about by redrawing of school boundaries and other desegregation efforts in White Plains, New York, and of the Project Able Compensatory Program, Superintendent Carroll F. Johnson recently stated that the academic performance of disadvantaged Negro students had improved over previous rates of growth in each situation. Noting that it cost considerably less money to bring about more integration than to conduct expensive compensatory programs, Dr. Johnson regretted the fact that it had not been possible to assign every Negro child to an integrated school. The fact that both approaches were proving beneficial for the disadvantaged minority child, however, is most encouraging, and is in line with the conclusions argued in the preceding pages.

The study of equal opportunity provided massive evidence which convincingly supported a proposition perceptive educators had long recognized, namely, that family and neighborhood generally have been much more influential than the school in determining how well students perform there. Aries, in his scholarly history of the family in Western society since the Middle Ages, has explained how it came about that the school and the inward-looking, nuclear middle-class family begin to reinforce each other's work in developing a child's intellectual potential, but the school never succeeded very well in finding ways to counteract the depressing influence of the low-income environment in which family life remained disorganized.[9] When we add to the weight of family and neighborhood influence the psychological effects of exclusion in a *de facto* segregated setting, it is not hard to understand why most projects to improve the education of the disadvantaged Negro child have not succeeded.

More particularly, it would be a tragic mistake to interpret the considerable evidence that most compensatory programs do not work as indicating that compensatory education cannot work. For one thing, it is unlikely that all or even most disadvantaged Negro youngsters now in school can be placed in integrated classrooms, no matter how vigorously federal and state officials and local educators might work together to end *de facto* segregation; to reject the possibility that we can learn to conduct more adequate compensatory programs, without complete certainty that such a development is impossible, might be tantamount to giving up on the future of hundreds of thousands of young people. Second, the philosophy underlying compensatory education often makes a good deal of sense, as can be seen, for example, in a program which brings the severely disadvantaged together and keeps them together in classes of ten or twelve in which they receive help from professional speech therapists or other highly specialized personnel. Third, and equally important, just as compensatory programs are severely handicapped when conducted in a largely segregated school system which implicitly teaches Negro youth that there must be something inferior about themselves that will forever cause them to be "kept in their place," so the potency of integrated education in improving their performance may be severely limited by a social context which also subverts their self-concept because it is based on the explicit belief that they can never learn unless exposed to the influence of other racial groups in an integrated school. On the one hand, it can hardly be expected that youngsters severely handicapped by a disadvantaged, segregated background will live up to their inborn potential unless they have concrete reason to believe that the social barriers which signify their exclusion are really beginning to give way. By the same token, demonstrations that education can be significantly improved in the segregated slum school—that "black power", so to speak, can be a concept denoting pride and not defensiveness—will prove invaluable in dissolving the psychological bonds which keep many disadvantaged Negro youth mired in a state of bitter hopelessness. What we need to do, then, is to demonstrate—and seek out demonstrations—that both integrated education and compensatory education can be effective in improving the achievement of disadvantaged Negro youth.

If for ideological or other reasons we look for examples where either integration or compensatory programs have failed to result in improved academic performance among low-income Negro youth, such examples will be easy enough to find. But if we truly wish to help these children of poverty and despair, we will rather mark those instances which credit than discredit either approach. For, given the almost unimaginably difficult task we thereby set for ourselves, progress must be made simultaneously along each front.

It would be easy to misinterpret the implications of the equal opportunity report, or of any other report that highlights how ineffective our schools still are in overcoming the deleterious effects of environments which are not conducive to good performance in the classroom. Soon after the report was issued, for example, Joseph Alsop argued in a syndicated column that if even those inner city schools which now have the best facilities and most expensive programs are not very effective in overcoming the influence of the slums, it is more constructive to conclude that we need still better and more massive compensatory projects than to conclude, as some have, that education can make no difference. Even Alsop's conclusion, however, is still inadequate, for it ignores the complementary potential of integrated education as a key factor in the battle to defuse the social dynamite resulting from the failures of educational and other social institutions in the big cities.

Keeping in mind the evidence that integrated education benefits the disadvantaged Negro student academically by reducing his feeling of powerlessness and isolation, vigorous initiative to implement plans to reduce *de facto* segregation is indeed a legitimate professional response to the *educational* problems associated with disadvantaged and minority status. Even those who work primarily in the area of compensatory education should lend every effort to reducing segregation whenever and wherever practicable. While it may be unrealistic to expect that most Negro students in the big cities can be placed in integrated schools during the next few years, it would be a serious mistake to do other than redouble our efforts to provide integrated education for as many disadvantaged Negro youth as possible. If this can be done for at least enough Negro students so that integrated education is a visible fact of community life, it may then be possible to convince even those students still in segregated schools that equal opportunity for themselves and eventually for their children is indeed becoming a reality rather than an empty slogan. Let us not underestimate the perceptivity of disadvantaged Negro youth, for their intuitive understanding of the attitudinal and behavioral orientations which underly American society is often far superior to that of sophisticated adults. Provided that educators and concerned laymen really make a dedicated effort, despite intense obstacles, to pursue every possible path toward desegregated education and are successful in significantly reversing the continuing trends toward *de facto* segregation, we may counteract much of the sense of powerlessness, exclusion, despair, and inferiority that militates against all our most profound efforts to implement meaningful compensatory programs. If and when this happens, integrated education and compensatory education will no longer be seen as embodying mutually exclusive answers to the challenge of improving the education of disadvantaged minority youth with all the means at our command in American education.

34. NOTES

1. Fred T. Wilhelms and Paul B. Diederich, "The Fruits of Freedom," in Fred Wilhelms (ed.), *Evaluation as Feedback and Guide* (Washington, D.C.: Association for Supervision and Curriculum Development, 1967), pp. 234-35.

2. Ivor Kraft, "Integration, Not 'Compensation,' " *Educational Forum* 31, No. 2 (January 1967), p. 212.

3. *Ibid.,* p. 213.

4. *Racial Isolation in the Public Schools,* Vol. I (Washington, D.C.: U.S. Government Printing Office, 1967), p. 127.

5. *Ibid.,* pp. 128-38.

6. *Ibid.,* p. 138.

7. James S. Coleman et al., *Equality of Educational Opportunity* (Washington, D.C.: U.S. Government Printing Office, 1966).

8. *Ibid.,* p. 22.

9. Phillipe Aries, *Centuries of Childhood: A Social History of Family Life* (New York: Knopf, 1965).

35

Methods and Materials in Intergroup Education*

JEAN D. GRAMBS

WHAT IS INTERGROUP EDUCATION?

Education assumes change. The person who has learned something acts in a
different fashion from the person who has not learned this same thing: the first
person has been "educated;" the second person has not. Intergroup education
similarly assumes that, as a result of selected materials and methods, individuals
will be changed, that their attitudes and behaviors toward persons of other
groups, and toward members of whatever group they themselves belong to, will
be changed.

Change is not always for the better. Attitudes may change as a result of
deliberate educative efforts, but not necessarily or not always in the direction we
desire. In intergroup education, the selection of methods and materials is
directed specifically toward the development of attitudes—or the change of attitudes which may already have been formed—which make for *more* acceptance of
persons who differ and *more* acceptance of one's own difference from others.

Intergroup hostility has marred the history of mankind. Wars have been
fought and lost because of irrational hates and fears of a "different" people. We
can look ruefully through the bloodstained pages of history finding incident
after incident in which group prejudice against group resulted in widespread
unhappiness, destruction, death.

*If persons can be educated to hate and distrust others, then they can be
educated to like and trust others.* This is the basic assumption of intergroup
education.

Intergroup understanding and acceptance do not "just happen." Children, like
anyone else, do not just naturally like other children. Children can and do learn a
great deal about other people, and much of it does not necessarily lead to liking
and trust. The deliberate education of the child about himself and others is the
province of the educator and cannot be left to chance.

In education, we talk about the "teachable moment." When my little boy
puts his finger on the hot stove and yowls, is a teachable moment. I say
promptly, "Peter, hot stoves burn. Don't put your fingers on hot stoves." And

*Copyright 1967 by Allyn and Bacon, Inc. Reprinted by permission of the publisher from
William C. Kvaraceus et al. (eds.), *Poverty, Education and Race Relations,* pp. 139-59.

Peter has learned to approach stoves with caution and find out whether they are hot before he explores them further.

In intergroup education, we can wait for the teachable moment or we can, to use the analogy above, create our own "hot stoves." In intergroup education there are literally thousands of teachable moments in any classroom or group of children. Unfortunately, many teachers do not notice the moments when they occur, or there is no opportunity to exploit them for educational ends. Some aspects of intergroup understanding may not occur within the teacher's purview at all. Or if one waits until the right moment comes along, it may well be too late. Intergroup feelings and attitudes are learned very early. If we wait for the teachable moment to conduct our lesson in intergroup relations, we may wait forever. Thus we create out own teachable moments, or light our own "hot stoves." What kinds of devices, situations, materials, methods are the ones most useful in intergroup education? The answer to this question is our major concern in this chapter.

SOME MAJOR ASSUMPTIONS

1. As has already been stated, one assumption basic to intergroup education is that changes in attitudes toward others can be achieved through educational means. That is, children's feelings and attitudes *can* be affected by deliberate education.

2. All persons are affected by the social valuations of groups: who is good, who is not so good, who rates, and who does not rate. In the culture of the United States today, it is almost impossible for a child to grow up without an awareness of group differences and of social valuations accorded to these differences.

3. Learning to like and trust persons in one situation is not necessarily transferable to other situations with other people. A child who is comfortable and at ease with persons whom he has been taught are trustworthy may not transfer this sense of trust to other persons who differ from him and whose differences have been pointed out to him by his culture. *Transfer* of feelings of trust and acceptance *must be made explicit.*

4. Learning new attitudes and new feelings and gaining understanding of familiar attitudes and feelings about others and oneself occur through the *intellectual exploration of experience.* It is not sufficient to have a child burn his finger on a hot stove; he must see some connection between the hot stove and the burned finger. Similarly, in intergroup education, merely experiencing a congenial interracial situation will not necessarily produce lasting or visible changes in feelings and behaviors in other settings unless the experience has been explored intellectually: discussed, identified, labeled, argued about, researched, and tried again and again, vicariously and in actuality.

METHODS AND MATERIALS

General Comments

Discussion regarding the differentiation between materials and methods in education is futile. Any given type of material makes a particular method or spectrum of methods necessary or inevitable. In the intergroup area, methods and materials are inextricable. Some methods may depend on specially prepared materials or materials utilized in a special manner. There are some methods whose only "material" will be the imagination of the teacher and the interactions of children.

Many of the methods and materials we will discuss have been available for some time. The pioneer research and study in the field of intergroup relations, undertaken under the direction of Hilda Taba in the 1940's, included most of what we would consider relevant methodology in intergroup relations today.[1] We have relatively little "hard" research on the ways in which intergroup or intercultural attitudes are changed and can be changed. Although there are many studies of attitudes and of conditions whereby attitudes have been affected, long-range reports are not available, nor are there studies contrasting and evaluating different kinds of intervention. The complicating factors of age, sex, socioeconomic status, family relationships, school and community climate, make the research task almost insuperable. Thus we have to rely primarily on hunch and personal experience.

Just as children and schools vary, so do teachers. A method which one teacher finds congenial may be difficult or impossible for another to use or adapt. Materials which some teachers find valuable may seem inadequate or limited in another situation when viewed by other teachers. We can offer, then, primarily a "cafeteria" of methods and materials for teachers, school systems, and children to explore and try out, to find what seems to accomplish the task best within any particular setting for any particular group of children.

The best guidelines for utilization of instructional methods and materials in intergroup education appear to be the following:

Teachers will tend to use materials which:

- are intellectually sound and stimulating.
- are authentic.
- support creative use.
- are not overdemanding on teacher out-of-class time.
- are easy to utilize with groups of children and youth of 25-30 in a standard school situation.

Children are most apt to respond to and to be engaged by methods and materials which:

- enable them to become participants.
- are honest and unsentimental.
- report the real world as children already know it.

It is clear that the criteria above limit us to those methods and materials which are most easily used within the classroom. We have not included in our discussion such readily identifiable resources as classroom visitors, visits to the community, interviews with selected persons, and other such community-based activities. Such resources are extremely valuable and, in some instances, may speak more loudly to the student than all of the audio and visual materials we may provide in the classroom. Few things can substitute for the "live" person who exemplifies what it is we are talking about. For many teachers, however, the right person or the right community agency or neighborhood are not easily available or are difficult, if not impossible to find. The logistics of a field trip are enough to make any teacher choose another path to wisdom. And how many resource visitors have failed to show up, or have ignored all instructions as to topic and audience! Despite these handicaps, however, we would indeed strongly urge the teacher to use the alive, immediate environment *before* any of the materials suggested here. And if the environment is used in conjunction with those teaching materials and methods we have described, the effective education achieved will be measurably greater.

It is important to point out that no one particular group of children has a greater need for intergroup education than any other group of children. The approach taken to intergroup education may vary because of the group the child belongs to or the place in which he has been reared. Certainly we would say that the Negro child, the Puerto Rican, the Jewish child may respond differently to different kinds of materials and the emphases may differ. But it is also just as true that an Anglo-Saxon Protestant child raised in the homogeneous climate of a middle-class suburb is desperately in need of intergroup education, though this need may not be readily accepted or recognized by his parents or his teachers.

There is ample evidence that prejudice against others is widespread throughout the United States and does not depend on whether a child does or does not have any actual contact with a given group. The mass media have been instrumental in spreading stereotypes about certain ethnic and racial groups in the United States. Only now is one beginning to see movies which provide a respected role for Negroes as Negroes, and also as part of the general social and cultural scene. Advertisements also show Negroes as well as whites in group pictures.

Cultural blindness, however, is still with us. In a report of a social studies project, for instance, one finds the following passage:

> All classes listened to many Christmas stories and poems and told many stories. The story of the first Christmas was used in all classes and the story of Hanukkah was used in classes where there were Jewish children.

Evidently only Jewish children needed the extra dose of religious understanding. In the same course of study, in the fifth grade, a study is to be made of persons from foreign countries who came to the United States, yet no mention is made of Negroes—only "other" immigrant groups—although "In early days, many people settled in the north to avoid competing with the slave labor of the south." Listed under "activities" to develop a better understanding of race, the following is suggested:

> See a movie, "The Pussycat That Ran Away." Children of our race live in other countries. This is an adventure of children in Norway.[2]

One wonders what definition of "race" is being provided here.

A rather different approach to intergroup education is the human relations program of the Wilmington Schools.[3] The project was one aspect of the school's efforts to ease the desegregation process in the schools of the city and emphasized the broader interpretation of intergroup education. One can agree with the premise of this project that adequate human relationships underlie adequate intergroup understanding; but one searches in vain for examples of specific discussions with children about race and the meanings of race. Did race and problems of race fail to come to the attention of children? Or does the report merely omit them? Certainly, as is pointed out on page 245, desegregation caused many fears, yet the specific *intergroup* content which underlay these fears is not reported.

Without our even knowing it, we may be expressing attitudes and stereotyped feelings toward groups. A teacher who used a pair of book ends which depicted Mexican peasants reclining under a cactus, with serapes draped over their shoulders and hats over their faces, was providing an education in intergroup relations daily to all her students—the wrong education.

Recent outcries against all-white textbooks have resulted in production of many new texts which "color them brown" in order to indicate that the books are "integrated." It is interesting to note that the brown color produces merely "tan Nordics," rather than realistic pictures of Negro-Americans. Some texts are moving farther than this in utilizing actual photographs of children from various racial and ethnic backgrounds.

The interest in providing integrated text material is hardly new. The biased discussion of population groups and the history of various ethnic and racial groups have been presented in the literature of education for many decades. Only recently, with Negroes sitting in large numbers on the selection committees of major urban school districts (which incidentally enroll most of the children, too) have book publishers and educators responded to the critics of the lily-white text and the exclusion of the Negro from American history books after the Civil War.

Miseducation of generations of people about the role of minority groups is, however, not easily overcome. It takes more than brown-colored pictures or stories in an urban setting to provide depth to our efforts in intergroup education.

We have some clues as to the kinds of materials which may make most sense to the child of a minority group. He will, we are fairly sure, respond most readily to those materials and situations which have most relevance to himself. He will pay attention to a movie in which, if he is a Negro, he sees Negroes as part of the scene. He will further be moved to develop more positive feelings about himself if this portrayal of Negroes makes it clear that they have a respected social and cultural role.[4] One study showed that handicapped children tended to write more voluminously about pictures showing handicapped children than about normal children. It would be reasonable to conclude that this would also be true of children of any particular group identification. Boys respond far better to material in which boys play a major role, or in which male or masculine traits are exemplified.[5]

How to prepare a child for acceptance of prejudice against himself as a member of a discriminated group is not easily answered. In fact, there is considerable controversy not as yet resolved by any research findings. In a celebrated exchange of views, Bettelheim and Lewin took opposite sides of the debate as to what preparation helps the Jewish child cope best with expected discrimination. Bettelheim feels that the child is best prepared who is loved and helped to feel secure within his group, without necessarily so labeling it. Lewin, on the other hand, feels that it is imperative to provide the child with a sense of his group so that he can gain feelings of pride and security. Later discriminatory acts or attacks are then deflected against his armor of self-respect.[6]

There is little agreement among educators as to the way in which the concept of "race" shall be presented to the Negro child. Parents as well as teachers may feel that it is a taboo subject better left undiscussed. Although most Negro parents may report that they try to explain to their children that differences in color are hereditary accidents which really don't make a difference, at the same time there is considerable evidence that there is extreme color conflict in most Negro homes which induces conflict in children about what color means to them.[7]

Interestingly enough, in our search of the literature of intergroup education, practically nothing of recent publication was found on the question of race or skin color for young children to read outside the primary-grade materials prepared by the Black Muslims.[8]

Some Promising Practices

In the following few pages we shall try to introduce the major ideas of some promising practices in intergroup education. None of what we are saying here is new. These approaches have been in the education literature for years and in the repertoire of good teachers. The need now is to help more teachers to use more such methods and materials in many more classrooms.

1. *Role Playing.* Role playing (or dramatic play) provides a chance to try out the ways in which people feel and the ways in which others respond to them. The technique is relatively simple: a dramatic situation or confrontation is identified by the teacher or the class. The persons involved in the situation are described, and the action is outlined or the outcome is suggested. The role

players "try out" the situation. The class may offer comments regarding the reality of the action or the authenticity of the role taking. The scene may be played again with new actors, or with the first ones trying to follow the instructions of the class. Following one or two enactments, the class discusses the problem raised by the role play and their response to it. The emphasis is on spontaneity of response: no lines are written, no script is memorized, the "solution" comes from the enactment itself.

Role play is essentially designed to induce reflection and discussion. Its aim is not to produce or train great actors nor is the acting itself the primary interest. Role playing is utilized to provide an immediate, common experience for a group which involves the group at an emotional as well as an intellectual level. The persons who play a role are typically very much affected by the emotional demands the role playing makes upon them, and this is turn influences their feelings and attitudes and learnings.

> *When exposed to persuasive messages, persons who are required to play a role that entails putting the content of the message in their own words to others will be more influenced than those who are more passively exposed.* This tendency toward "saying is believing" has been found to occur even when role playing is artificially induced, as in experiments dealing with the effects of communications designed to modify. . . *evaluations* of previously disliked tasks, policies, or ethnic groups. . . . The tendency to accept personally the content of a message that one is required to verbalize to others has been found to increase as the amount of *improvisation* increases. . . .
>
> The success of improved role play might be attributed to several psychological processes. Festinger suggests that the main gain from role playing comes about from efforts to reduce dissonance between what one is saying and what one actually believes. . . . An alternative explanation is in terms of self-persuasion: When attempting to put the message across to others, the role player is likely to think up new formulations of the arguments, illustrations, and appeals that are tailor-made to be convincing to himself. . . . Role playing under acceptable, benevolent sponsorship produces more attitude change than role playing under seemingly manipulative or exploitative sponsorship.[9]

Role play also has a significant effect upon the audience viewing the enactment, not just through subsequent discussion, but while the situation is being developed and throughout the process of selecting actors and the ensuing dramatic development.

Role playing may be introduced by way of incompleted stories, as described by the Shaftels, by Nichols and Williams, and in the Citizenship Education Project materials.[10]

A rather unusual type of role playing is described by Lippitt[11], who showed how the use of empty chairs could provide a substitute for "live" actors in a role-playing situation. This device, although not widely used in school settings, could be of great value particularly for the teacher who is not too sure of role-playing technique. The chairs can represent people, and the class can help to describe how someone sitting in each chair might feel, what he might do, how he might react. The chairs can be shifted at will and can represent many kinds of situations and persons. With a large group in which role playing might be difficult, the empty-chair technique can be quite successful. The audience is drawn into dramatic imagining of what might be the feelings of the "persons" sitting in the empty chairs. In one such demonstration with an audience of more than 150 teenage girls, remarkably free and spontaneous remarks and questions about the sensitive problems of race in a southern region were elicited, facilitating later small-group discussion of feelings among Negro and white girls.

Another variation of role playing may be the use of hand puppets, either constructed by the children or purchased. The children, protected by the puppets, may feel more able to express their real feelings and emotions in an area in which there may be tension. Similarly, doll play with family dolls which are both Negro and white (available from Creative Playthings) permits children to manipulate the dolls in scenes which they have devised for gaining insight into intergroup relationships.

2. *Open-ended Situations.* The stories developed by the Shaftels and others are designed specifically for role playing. They are "open-ended." They do not solve a problem, but present a dramatic confrontation in which several possible alternatives are available for resolution through role playing. Other open-ended material may be used either for role playing or for class discussion. With older children, written endings may be developed by groups or by individuals. A class may then discuss various endings and judge which seem to be most feasible. Essential to the use of any open-ended type of material is the recognition that *there is no single right answer.* There may be *many* answers, depending on the way in which students choose to define the situation, the aspects of it which make most sense to them, and what they know about their own world. A teacher who uses role playing or any open-ended device must be fully able to accept many answers, and many of these may be far from what she might consider "right" or "proper." To invoke teacher judgment of what is the right or proper response is to destroy the value of these techniques.

The teacher may find the answers students give highly revealing, however, and therefore useful in a diagnostic sense. She may note that students reject solutions which, in terms of the world they live in, would be appropriate. This may suggest to her the need for further discussion and wider experiences. Take, for instance, a group of Negro students presented with an open-ended story about a youngster who is hunting a job, but is undecided whether to go into a store with the sign up "Messenger wanted" because he is afraid he would be refused on account of his color. The class may agree that he should not try for the job. In the teacher's eyes, this might not be a "good" answer, though in reality the class is saying to her that they fear rebuff for themselves, have experienced it too often, and therefore will not test the situation. Exploration of the reality of job discrimination should certainly become an important lesson for future classes. The *NEA Journal* has carried short open-ended stories for student completion, as have *Scope and Read* and some of the commercial children's magazines. Noteworthy, in most instances, however, is the fact that problems of ethnic or religious or social-class differences are absent.

Teachers, with the help of their students, can devise their own open-ended stories from the real life around them. Using stories already prepared will help children to see a pattern which they can adapt to their own experiences. Open-ended scripts can be developed by the teacher by tape-recording role-play situations. These are then transcribed, are somewhat modified, and the endings are removed. The reading of the script sets the stage for the problem, establishes the roles and the characters, and then, by leaving the "cast" in midstream, forces them to act out their own solutions. Or if the class prefers, the group can discuss the possible alternatives for the problem.

Another useful open-ended device is the film. Few open-ended films are available. It is unfortunate that more such films have not been made, since they provide a dramatic springboard for either role play or discussion.

Other open-ended situations are provided by problem pictures. These are pictures suggesting a situation which is familiar to children or youth, but which leaves the analysis quite open. The teacher could ask: "Would your answer to the problem be any different if this child, or this child, were of another race?" "Why might it make a difference?" And the discussion can roll from there.

Another open-ended situation is created by the asking of "open questions," or incomplete sentences. Examples of these are:

How I felt when . . .
I felt left out when . . .
Others like (or dislike) me because . . .
Things I don't like about people are . . .
I'd like to move because . . .

It has been stated that the uncompleted task is likely to be the one which is remembered longest. There is a human urge to finish something, to get it completed, to know the ending. Thus an open-ended device, whichever one may choose to use, draws the class into involvement because of this very urge and need to find a satisfying and satisfactory solution. The fact that there may be many solutions, and that these may be debated, tends to increase the level of involvement as well as the level of remembering.

3. Flat Pictures. Ours is a pictorial culture. Illustrations are used everywhere. A book without pictures would strike a young child as something not for him! Only adults read books without pictures, and even for adults there is a wide (and expensive) market for the lavishly illustrated history or art or "culture" book.

Currently there is a renewed interest in the value of flat pictures and photographs for intergroup education. A large folio series published by the John Day Company is one example.[12] These folios include a series of groups of large photographs around such themes as:

Growing Is . . .
A Neighborhood Is . . .
Recreation Is . . .
A Family Is . . .

The materials have been arranged in the sequence developed for each folio on the basis of the underlying theory and organization of the editors. It is possible that a teacher may, however, wish to separate the folios, using pictures in another sequence, or several from different ones, or encourage children to organize their own sequence. The pictures in this group are designed to be particularly evocative of children's responses because of their photographic reality.

Although not designed specifically for classroom use, some recent, and some not so recent, volumes of photographs are to be highly recommended.[13] It would be the height of educational luxury if several copies of each of these books were available so that teachers could cut them up and mount the pictures, thus allowing children to develop their own sequences, to use pictures for class or individual work, and in innumerable other creative ways.

There are, in addition, books which focus particularly on the intergroup problem, use pictorial material to increase the impact of the problem presented, are sources of pictorial material of particular value for upper-grade children and secondary school youth.[14]

The teacher, however, can very well make her own collection of pictures. The pictures found in *Look, Life, Ebony,* and *Photographic Annual* are often very closely related to the many ideas and themes teachers will want to discuss with children. The students may write or tell stories about the pictures; may arrange their own "picture book" from a selection the teacher makes available; may discuss a group of pictures in terms of how "near" or "far" the content of the picture feels to them. It goes without saying that children should at all times be encouraged to make their own pictures, write and illustrate their own stories, feelings, and ideas.

Though not traditionally utilized in this fashion, the pictures in a standard text could be examined to see how true to life they are. Do they portray people as we know them? Who is in the picture? Who is left out? What difference would it make? What difference should it make?

Finally, older children may do their own documentary picture taking. The ever-present camera could be tool of student study and evaluation. It is possible that some of the least verbally minded youngsters would respond to the challenge of finding situations to photograph which illustrate a theme or idea developed out of a discussion of intergroup relations. A photographic contest could inspire them to making an extra effort.

4. Affective Materials. Some of the materials we use in teaching have more power to move us emotionally than others. These we can group under a general label of "affective materials," since they produce an impact over and beyond mere intellectual recognition. Many of the items and methods listed previously, such as open-ended situations, role playing, selected photographs, have an intrinsic affective impact.

There are numerous reports of teachers using many kinds of books to evoke similar responses. The deliberate use of books to "educate" emotions is called *bibliotherapy.* For this purpose, our books are selected which aid the individual in gaining insight into his own personal situation, whatever it might be.

In the intergroup area, we have a large resource to draw upon. One source, autobiography, is particularly effective with adolescents in providing an immediate sense of the world of the Negro.[15] Biographies depicting the personal struggles of members of other ethnic groups are likewise useful sources.[16] Currently, few books for children deal directly with the intergroup area through fiction without glossing over the pain and hurt and providing a "nice" ending.

Drama has always been a source of emotional education. The plays of the American Theater Wing require minimal production needs and focus on the recurrent problems of human relationships. High school drama groups could produce the plays for presentation in elementary schools and at PTA's. The University of Maryland Drama Department has for a number of years successfully toured the area around the university putting on one of these plays each season. No doubt other college or university drama departments and local little theater groups could also co-operate. Recent on- and off-Broadway plays, such as *Blues for Mister Charlie, In White America,* and *A Raisin in the Sun,* can be read and/or produced by high school groups.

Although an increasing number of films illustrate the dilemma of the minority-group individual, these may not be available for school use or may distort more than they assist. The UNESCO listing of documentaries from many parts of the world suggests an unused source for authentic materials, though the problem of procurement is a major barrier.[17] Educational use of such a film as *Twelve Angry Men* can demonstrate the power of influence, as well as the power of prejudice. The film made from the TV program, *The Eye of the Beholder,* is also a valuable educational device to illustrate the perceptual distortions that we unconsciously practice. A publication of the National Council of Teachers of English is of value in showing how teachers may utilize this medium creatively.[18]

Other media, such as recordings of plays or music, are also avenues for affective education. The scripts of *The Ways of Mankind,* available on records, are a valuable introduction not only to the field of anthropology but to the "feel" of social data.[19] One recording company has specialized in authentic music of cultures here and abroad, and contemporary and historical material as well.[20] The recording of *In White America*[21] can be effectively used with or without the reading of the script itself. Often the spoken word comes through more clearly than through reading. Teachers of primary grades know the value of reading aloud; this technique should also be utilized by teachers at other grade levels. The major pitfall is that training and practice are required for effective oral reading. A teacher might be well advised to tape a reading, play it back, and "hear" herself before inflicting a reading upon children or youth. Short anecdotal stories that are designed for reading aloud and followed by group discussion are available.[22]

Novels, like fictional movies, are the teacher's great resource for affective material. A few of the many that a teacher could use are *To Kill a Mockingbird* by Harper Lee, *A Different Drummer* by William M. Kelley, *The Invisible Man* by Ralph Ellison (winner of the National Book Award). Since most of these are in paperback, the teacher may well find that many students in secondary classes have already read them. What is essential is intellectual reflection upon the content and meaning of the material, and this the school can add.

Just as a documentary film has a special kind of impact, so does documentary history have an effect unlike paraphrased history. The past and the present can be brought vividly to life for the child or the adolescent by means of a several-volume anthology *In Their Own Words* and a collection of the reminiscences of slaves which was sponsored by the Federal Writers Project.[23]

History provides ample source material. Much of it, however, is beyond the intellectual grasp of young people unless carefully selected and in some cases translated into contemporary English.[24] The problems to be encountered in utilizing such source material have been discussed in connection with the development of the junior high school program of Educational Services Incorporated.[25] The dangers of unexamined history based wholly on textbooks or secondary sources are everywhere apparent and in no other instance have they been quite so damaging as in disseminating the mythology surrounding the American Negro. In attempting to undo past damage and produce more authentic history, there may be a temptation to err in the opposite direction. Although Crispus Attucks is accepted as being the first person to be "killed" in the Revolutionary War (and he was a Negro), there is substantial evidence that he was part of a drunken mob and was no hero in the sense in which we generally revere heroes. To turn him into a hero is as much mythmaking as to deny the role of Negroes their rightful places in the story of this country.

It would be vaulable for the teacher to turn to accepted sources of authentic reporting, such as the issues of *Hi Neighbor,*[26] describing the member nations of the United Nations, for contemporary material. Journals such as the *UNESCO Courier,* or *Atlas,* the world press in translation,[27] are valuable for comparative studies. Often the foreign bias will be as apparent as that of the United States, and this is a useful perspective for young people to gain.

Intergroup education is not, however, the exclusive domain of history or literature. Stendler and Martin provide an interesting commentary in relation to arithmetic:

> When the children studied Roman numerals, she saw to it that both the numerals and the people who originated and used them were appreciated. We think this is a particularly significant example because arithmetic does not seem to be an area of the curriculum in which we could accomplish much in intergroup education. Yet this third grade teacher succeeded in identifying for her children the part that each of the many groups of people played in the development of our number system.[28]

CONCLUSION

Intergroup education can permeate every sector of the educational scene. Indeed, through the interactions between children, through the education of children via nonschool influences, intergroup education is taking place all of the time for all of us. The educational task is to recognize contemporary needs and to develop deliberate programs of education and re-education about the many groups that make up America, their parts in its history, and their share in the world in which we live.

35. NOTES

1. Hilda Taba et al., *With Focus on Human Relations; Elementary Curriculum in Intergroup Relations; Curriculum in Intergroup Relations: Secondary School; Reading Ladders for Human Relations; Sociometry in Group Relations; Literature for Human Understanding; With Perspective on Human Relations; Leadership Training in Intergroup Education; School Culture; Intergroup Education in Public Schools* (Washington, D.C.: American Council on Education, 1947-1955). There is material of considerable current interest in this series, despite the dates.

2. Clyde I. Martin, *An Elementary Social Studies Program* (Austin: University of Texas Press, 1963).

3. Muriel Crosby, *An Adventure in Human Relations* (Chicago: Follett, 1965).

4. Charles F. Hoban, *Focus on Learning* (Washington, D.C.: American Council on Education, 1942); "The Usable Residue of Educational Film Research," in *New Teaching Aids for the American Classroom* (Washington, D.C.: U.S. Office of Education, OE-34020, 1960), pp. 95-113.

5. E. E. Maccoby and W. C. Wilson, "Identification and Observational Learnings from Films," *Journal of Abnormal and Social Psychology* LV (July 1957), pp. 76-87.

6. Bruno Bettelheim and Kurt Lewin, *Securing our Children Against Prejudice* (New York: Community Relations Service, 386 Fourth Avenue, n. d., paper).

7. Carl T. Rowan, "We Tell Our Children. . .," *Saturday Evening Post*, August 22, 1959, pp. 18 ff.; Eugene B. Brody, "Color and Identity Conflict in Young Boys," *Psychiatry* XXVI, No. 2 (May 1963), pp. 188-201; J. Saunders Redding, *On Being Negro in America* (Indianapolis: Bobbs-Merrill, 1951, paper).

8. Christine X. Johnson, *Muhammad's Children* (Chicago: University of Islam, 1963), a first-grade reader.

9. M. Brewster Smith and Irving L. Janis, "Effects of Education and Persuasion on National and International Images," in N. C. Kelman (ed.), *International Behavior: A Social Psychological Analysis* (New York: Holt, Rinehart & Winston, 1965). Italics are those of the authors; footnotes have been deleted.

10. Fannie and George Shaftel, *Role-Playing the Problem Story* (New York: National Conference of Christians and Jews, 1952); Hildred Nichols and Lois Williams, *Learning About Role-Playing for Children and Teachers* (Washington, D.C.: Association for Childhood Education International, 1960); *Experiences in Citizenship for Elementary School Children:* "Caring for Public Property"; "Choosing Good Leaders"; "Taking Responsibility"; "Understanding the Disabled" (New York: Bureau of Publications, Teachers College, Columbia University, 1956).

11. Rosemary Lippitt, "The Auxiliary Chair Technique," *Group Psychotherapy* XI, No. 1 (March, 1958), pp. 8-23.

12. *Urban Education Studies* (New York: John Day, 1965); Teachers' Guide by Betty Atwell Wright, 1965.

13. Edward Steichen, *The Family of Man* (New York: Simon and Schuster, 1955); Hubert Bermont and Shelley Langston, *The Child* (New York: Pocket Books, 1965, paper); Wayne Miller, *The World is Young* (New York: The Ridge Press, 1958, distributed by Simon and Schuster); Ken Heyman, *Willie* (New York: The Ridge Press, 1963, distributed by Atheneum); Margaret Mead and Ken Heyman, *Family* (New York: Macmillan, 1965); *Feelings and Learning* (Washington, D.C.: Association for Childhood Education International, 1965); Rachel Carson, *The Sense of Wonder* (New York: Harper & Row, 1965).

14. Philip M. Stern and George de Vincent, *The Shame of a Nation* (New York: Ivan Obolensky, 1965); Shirley Tucker, *MIssissippi from Within* (New York: Arco, 1965, paper), Lorraine Hansberry, *The Movement* (New York: Simon and Schuster, 1964); Lillian Smith, *Our Faces, Our Words* (New York: W. W. Norton, 1964, paper); Shirley Burden, *I Wonder Why . . .* (Garden City: Doubleday, 1963; also available as a film from the Anti-Defamation League of B'nai B'rith); Langston Hughes and Milton Melzer, *A Pictorial History of the Negro in America,* revised edition (New York: Crown Publishers, 1963); Dick Gregory, *From the Back of the Bus* (New York: Avon Books, 1965, paper); David Potter, J. Joel Moss, and Herbert F. A. Smith, *Photosituations: A Technique for Teaching* (Minneapolis: Burgess, 1963).

15. Suggestions are Richard Wright, *Black Boy* (New York: New American Library of World Literature, 1945, paper); Sammy Davis, Jr., *Yes, I Can* (New York: Farrar, Straus & Giroux, 1965); Althea Gibson, *I Always Wanted to be Somebody* (New York: Harper & Row, 1958); Dick Gregory, *Nigger* (New York: E. P. Dutton, 1964); Malcolm X, *The Autobiography of Malcolm X* (New York: Grove Press, 1965); Ethel Waters, *His Eye is On the Sparrow,* ed. Charles Samuel (Garden City: Doubleday, 1951); John H. Griffin, *Black Like Me* (Boston: Houghton Mifflin, 1961, paper); Claude Brown, *Manchild in the Promised Land* (New York: Macmillan, 1965).

16. Oscar Handlin, *Immigration as a Factor in American History* (Englewood Cliffs, Prentice-Hall, 1959) and *The Uprooted: The Epic Story of the Great Migration that Made the American People* (New York: Grosset & Dunlap, Universal Library, 1951); Emma G. Sterne, *I Have a Dream* (New York: Knopf, 1965); Alice B. Spalding, *"Eating Low on the Hog," Harper's Magazine,* March 1965.

17. *The UNESCO Courier* (New York: UNESCO Publications Center, USA, 317 East 34th Street).

18. Marion C. Sheridan *et al., The Motion Picture and the Teaching of English* (New York: Appleton-Century-Crofts, 1965).

19. Walter Goldschmidt, *The Ways of Mankind* (Boston: Beacon Press, 1953).

20. Folkways Records, Inc., 117 West 47th Street, New York, N.Y.

21. Martin B. Duberman, *In White America* (Boston: Houghton Mifflin, 1964, paper); recorded by Columbia Records.

22. Dorothy T. Sproel (ed.), *Tensions Our Children Live With* (Boston: Beacon Press, 1959).

23. Milton Meltzer (ed.), *In Their Own Words: A History of the American Negro, 1619-1865* (New York: Crowell, 1964); *In Their Own Words: A History of the American Negro, 1865-1916* (the same, 1965); B. A. Botkin (ed.), *Lay My Burden Down: A Folk History of American Slavery* (Chicago: University of Chicago Press, 1945, paper).

24. *Call Them Heroes* (Morristown, New Jersey: Silver Burdett, 1965, a series of booklets); Bobbi Cieciorka and Frank Cieciorka, *Negroes in American History: A Freedom Primer* (The Student Voice, n.d., designed for use in the Freedom Schools); Larry Cuban, *The Negro in America* (Chicago: Scott, Foresman, 1964, written for high school youth).

25. Franklin K. Patterson, *Man and Politics,* The Social Studies Curriculum Program, Occasional Paper No. 4 (Cambridge, Mass., Educational Services Incorporated, 15 Mifflin Place, 1965).

26. *Hi Neighbor* (New York: Hastings House, 1960-65), showing the work of UNICEF for elementary school children.

27. *Atlas,* The Magazine of the World Press (31 West 57th Street, New York, N.Y.).

28. Celia B. Stendler and William E. Martin, *Intergroup Education in Kindergarten-Primary Grades* (New York: Macmillan, 1953), p. 116.

36

Blueprint for an Educational Revolution*

FRANK RIESSMAN

Many ways of educating disadvantaged youngsters have been developed around the country. For example, in Detroit, they have developed new readers with which low-income youngsters' reading improves considerably; and as a matter of fact, not only their reading improves, but the reading of the middle class improves also, because the readers are peppier or lively—just pleasanter to read. In Washington, Arthur Pearl has developed an exciting program for delinquent dropouts—as they weren't late in dropping out, they were both delinquents and dropouts—who in a very short period of time have developed excellent reading skills through employment as nonprofessionals: working as child-care aides, settlement-house aides, research aides. Involving them in this work and teaching them through the work has helped them remarkably.

Nongraded classes have been used in other parts of the country. Multiple periods have been used at different places. In New York, Mobilization for Youth employed homework helpers or tutors who worked with elementary school youngsters and improved their reading and general work in school. In St. Louis, Sam Shepard, through a program of motivating the youngsters, involving their parents, and giving teachers considerable freedom, was able to improve the work of elementary school and junior high school youngsters all the way up—brought them up to grade level in no time flat. In Alabama, criminals, who also were illiterate, through programed learning were taught poetry after a period of one year. Programed learning has been used with dropouts quite effectively in New York. Role playing has been used in various parts of the country—in Syracuse, in Chicago, and in Washington.

After reviewing all of these different techniques and approaches, you might ask, "Why don't we have an extremely optimistic view about the education of these youngsters?" I think we do not have this view. I think what has occurred is that people have become quite pessimistic and have retreated instead to emphasis on the preschool period: you have to get them very young or else you cannot be effective. To my mind, this notion that the preschool is the only

*Copyright 1967 by Allyn and Bacon, Inc. Reprinted by permission of the publisher from William C. Kvaraceus et al. (eds.), *Poverty, Education and Race Relations*, pp. 128-38.

approach is really a very dangerous one, because for the most part, the gains that have been achieved in the preschool do not remain if the school is not changed to back up the new motivations or improvements in the children. A number of researchers have pointed out that youngsters who improved in the preschool period dropped back in the regular school.

SHOOTING FOR THE MOON

My goal, therefore, is to see how we can combine these techniques and approaches in the school to produce a revolution in education—shooting for the moon in the school itself. We have to think about combining these different approaches and techniques, rather than keeping them separate as we have previously. In the Great Cities projects and other programs around the country, different kinds of things were tried: team teaching, ungraded classes, all kinds of new methods, new readers, and so on. Each city tried a single element, a different approach, and they had small successes in varying degrees. Now is the time for us to think about putting these things together, really integrating them, packaging them in some kind of coherent, meaningful way. This is the task I would like to put before you in our discussion. I think it is also a good way to bring out some of these techniques and approaches.

The Need for Leadership

In developing such a moon shot in education, we aim for far more than bringing youngsters up to grade level. The first thing that is required is some kind of school system which is willing to experiment, is willing to accept Federal monies to do this on a large scale, and in which we can find some leader who thoroughly believes that these youngsters are educable, not just improvable up to a certain point, but able to be deeply, drastically improved. Such an educator would be somebody like Dan Schreiber, who originally developed the Higher Horizons program before it was watered down in more recent years. Another illustration is Sam Shepard in the St. Louis Banneker District. I think you have to recognize that it is extremely important to have a completely dedicated leadership which believes thoroughly that this improvement can take place.

Teaching Personnel

A second crucial element that is needed is personnel. You have to have teachers who are willing to work at this program of improvement. You might say, "Well, let's pick all the good teachers that we can find in various parts of the country and bring them together." You have heard programs such as this actually being suggested. It would rob other schools of teachers who are working very effectively in their systems and would be a mistake. By contrast, I would be quite willing to take young teachers, new teachers, teachers in training, and involve them in this type of program.

Selective Approaches

What are the kinds of elements that we can put into this program? We could think, for example, of combining all the different things that have worked all over the country. We could have a potpourri of twenty or thirty different techniques, approaches, methods, and so on. This would be an eclectic thing to do, and I think it would be a mistake. A much more meaningful thing would be to pick three or four or five approaches that apparently have been effective and to develop some kind of coherent theory as to why they have worked and how we could package them together.

A NEW KIND OF SCHOOL MANPOWER

I would like to begin with the idea of introducing a new kind of manpower into the schools. This new manpower we call nowadays nonprofessionals, *indigenous nonprofessionals*. These are people who are drawn from the poor themselves and are brought into the school to function as teacher aides, teacher assistants, homework helpers, tutors, communicators between the school and the parents. This has been done quite effectively in Philadelphia, Pittsburgh, and Washington. It has a number of very valuable purposes.

First of all, the use of this new kind of personnel frees the teacher to do what he is really intended to do; namely, teach, and teach creatively. Too much of teaching time is spent with taking attendance, tying kids' shoelaces, putting up a moving-picture projector, taking youngsters on trips, correcting homework, and various odd jobs of this kind which do not fully require the professional training that teachers can bring to the situation. In other words, teachers have been prevented from really teaching, particularly in crowded classrooms. So what I am suggesting, first of all, is that we bring in this new, rather inexpensive personnel. Nonprofessionals where they have worked have been paid anywhere between $3,500 and $4,500 a year, and they functioned to assist in these various tasks: taking youngsters on trips, helping them to put on their clothes, going over their homework with them, checking on their attendance.

Not only do these nonprofessionals relieve the teacher; they satisfy another very valuable purpose in the school, and that is to provide a role model for the youngsters. Children in the disadvantaged areas have never seen people from their own neighborhoods employed in a professional setting. Now, for the first time, they can see people from their own background, who live around the corner, working in the school, relating to the teachers, functioning as monitors in the halls, taking attendance, taking care of so-called troublesome children in various rooms. They can see that these people are like themselves. The youngsters do not have to have the faraway model of the teacher.

In addition, these nonprofessionals serve another very valuable function. They are very close to the youngsters and their families and they talk the same language; they can communicate very easily, then. They can be understood and can understand the child in turn, and this is extremely valuable. For example, in the use of paid tutor adolescents at Mobilization for Youth, the youngsters learned very well from these people, who are really their peers. There is a good deal of evidence that people learn from other people who are their peers in the same age level or near the same age level and the same background, and that they learn in very different ways from what has been expected of them in school. These helpers in the classroom can play a decisive role in bringing educational material to the disadvantaged youngster by finding the right idiom, the right example, and in general, serving as a buffer and a communicator between the teacher and the child.

The teachers badly need assistance. I do not think we should put our money into extra services outside of the teaching situation, psychological assistance and the like. What we need is teaching and direct assistance to the teachers in the classroom.

TECHNIQUES AND GOALS

What is the next plank in this program that I would like to consider? It relates very much to the question of teaching technology, techniques, and approaches. I think it is extremely important to find techniques that are useful with disadvantaged youngsters in classrooms which consist of both disadvantaged and nondisadvantaged youngsters. It is important to find these techniques, because this is fundamentally what teachers want. They do not want to be told a lot of sociology and other things that have no direct relevance to the classroom. They want immediate, specific kinds of help. It is important that they be given this kind of help, but it may be useful to give these techniques in a meaningful context. So I would like to suggest that the context be the goals that we are looking for with these youngsters.

There are two very different goals that are generally considered. The first goal relates to the idea of having these youngsters become middle-class citizens exactly like us; to become, in a sense, carbon copies of us; to be people just like us in their goals, in their methods, in their learning, in their academic motivation, and the like. I submit that this is a very difficult thing to achieve and we are not going to be successful in doing it most of the time. We can be very successful in having these youngsters learn and become part of the mainstream of our society in the schools provided we want to get something from them as well as give something to them. Let me explain what I mean by this.

The great concern for the role of the Negro and the civil rights movement has demonstrated to us rather beautifully that we have not given something to the Negro in terms of the civil rights achievements, but we have gained an enormous morality from the Negro demands that we start to be truly American, that we institute the basic civil rights which belong to the Negro and thus begin to be able to hold our heads up high and fundamentally feel democratic. The Negro has given us this in our national life, but we have not fully reached the goal, though we are moving in this direction.

Similarly, I think these youngsters and their parents can give us something very fundamental in the school. They can enliven the school program and procedures. Most of the criticisms of school by these youngsters and by other types of critics have emphasized over and over again that the school is a dull, boring place, with no pep, with no relationship to life. These youngsters demand, more than our outside critics, that the school system have these kinds of qualities. The kinds of techniques that we are going to talk about—the use of hiptionaries, the use of slang dictionaries, the use of role play—these kinds of things which these youngsters in a sense want and through which they learn will be extremely beneficial to the school as a whole and to the middle-class children in the school. But in order to get these values from the disadvantaged youngster, we have to listen to him, we have to respect him, and we have to look for his strengths and begin with them. We cannot simply impose upon him what we believe to be good and right.

GAME TECHNIQUES

A beautiful way to illustrate this is to take one of these techniques. It is called the dialect game. (Games are extremely useful with these youngsters.) This game arose, as most of the techniques that I talk about have, from actual use by teachers. The teacher that told me about this discovered it from the very, very old joke about the youngster who would say, "Look at the *boid* outside the window." The teacher would say to him, "No, that is not a *boid,* it is a *bird.*" And the youngster would say, "Funny, it *choips* like a *boid.*" This results in typical intellectual confusion; in trying to give him an education in language, the teacher is confusing him about the object.

The teacher learned something very important from this old joke. She decided that there is really no reason why the child has to learn that one word is right and another way of saying it is wrong. He could learn that his dialect is accepted; that under certain circumstances it is perfectly all right to say *cah* in Boston, and that under other circumstances, it is more appropriate to say *car*. Similarly, with this child, he could say *boid* under certain circumstances with his peers, his mates on the street, and with his family, and so on; but under other circumstances he ought to know that the standard way of saying it was *bird*. It is just like one's practice with a foreign language. You learn the English way of saying something and the foreign way of saying it, and for two different situations you use the two different ways. Actually, what she did was to make this little example into an interesting game for the class so that they took all the words they could think of down one side of a list and saw the pronunciations in their tongue—in the street tongue, in the hip language—and the kinds of ways you could say these things in other kinds of language.

The same idea was used recently with hip words. Let me give you an illustration of this. Take the word *bug,* which is the hip word that means to bother, disturb, annoy. *Cop out* means to avoid conflict by running away. *Cool it* means to be quiet, peaceful, tranquil. You simply put part of the words down one side of the blackboard or of a paper and have the youngsters define them on the other side. You can do it either way. You can have the youngsters define an English word in the hip language or give a hip word the appropriate English definition.

This is an extremely interesting game. It not only teaches the youngsters both sets of words and shows respect, you see, for two cultures, but it does something else which is very interesting. It draws attention to language. It interests the child in language, and this is, you recall, one of the basic things we want to do with disadvantaged youngsters whose language skills are presumed to be deficient. We want to get them interested, to have them focus toward language; and this kind of game does this.

The same method can be used in the teaching of English to Puerto Rican children in New York schools or to Mexican children in California schools. Instead of telling the Spanish children not to say a word of Spanish in the class, because that would be terrible, you can have the Spanish children teach Spanish to the English-speaking children and vice versa. In this way, you respect the language and the culture of the person, the Spanish person. You give him a task to do in which he plays a leadership role, in which he is helping somebody else; and he has to learn some English incidentally in doing this.

There are many other kinds of techniques and games which illustrate again the respect and use of the youngsters' culture and background. Take another brief example. In Syracuse, they used a simple little poem by Langston Hughes:

> I play it cool and dig all jive
> That's the reason I stay alive
> My motto, as I live and learn,
> Is: Dig and Be Dug in Return.[1]

They used this poem to start discussing poetry and language in the class, and the first question the teacher raised was, "What is the meaning of the word *cool?*" because this is a word from the youngster's own language. The students were inarticulate, and if they had stopped at this point, the teacher would have said "Oh, it is typical; these youngsters are even inarticulate in their own language."

They decided instead to act out what it means to be cool. What would they have as a cool situation? One of the youngsters suggested, "Why don't you have me walk down the hall, and you tell me to get over on the other side of the building, I don't belong there?" The teacher said, "Let's do it." So the youngster walked down the hall, kind of shuffling along, and the teacher said to him, "You get over there where you belong; you are on the wrong side." And the youngster, without changing his expression, looked at the teacher very calmly and simply walked to the other side and did what he was told to do. That was playing it cool.

Next the class was asked, "What are some other ways of playing it cool? What are some of what we call *synonyms?*" Now the class was able to discuss this. They talked about being calm and collected, and the teacher introduced a new word, *nonchalant.* Then they got into a discussion about whether the word *cool* was exactly identical with *calm* and *collected.* They began to realize that it was not, which is one of the reasons why the word *cool* has actually been adopted, because there is no way of simply substituting the words *calm* or *collected.* We had to get a new word, and we borrowed it from the hip world. The word *cool* has become a part of our basic language because it does something which other words have not been able to do so easily. The youngsters, in discussing this, got interested in language and the nuance of language and how different words—for example, from a foreign language, such as *coup d'etat*—cannot be simply reproduced in the English language, which is why we use the foreign word or the hip word.

What other kinds of approaches and techniques might we use in this kind of situation in working with the disadvantaged? I would suggest that we look at the Montessori kinds of methods, because they emphasize the sensory-motor dimensions of learning, which are likely to appeal to the action style, to the physical way of learning, of these youngsters. They learn by doing, by acting upon, by taking trips, by seeing, by touching. The use of programed learning and teaching machines and visual materials, movies, and so on, will be extremely helpful in this situation. So will the use of games, like acting out the meaning of an adverb, which is a kind of a role-playing approach. These youngsters learn things also through dance. A lady in Washington, Claire Schmays, has used dance forms, motion, to help these youngsters develop concepts of roundness, of smoothness, of numbers, and so on. As a matter of fact, she has them dance out some of the rhythms and stories of the street, again using in doing this their own experience.

INVOLVING THE PARENTS

So far, we have talked about the idea of using techniques and of using nonprofessionals, a new kind of personnel. Let's talk about some other levels that we might use. How about the role of parents? How can we utilize parents in our moon-shot program? I think it is extremely important to involve the parents, as Sam Shepard has done in St. Louis, in motivating the children, checking on their homework, telling the children it is important to go to school, and so on. I do not think it is useful, however, to have the parents read to the children. Many people have suggested that it would be wonderful if these parents would do this, but the plain fact of it is either they cannot read or do not like to read or are too tired to read. It is not a good idea to ask parents to do something they are not easily able to do.

READERS FOR THE DISADVANTAGED

Another means that we could add to our moon-shot repertoire is the use of school readers—bringing in the readers that have been developed by Bank Street and the Macmillan Company in New York, by Follett in Chicago, and by the Chandler Company in San Francisco. These readers have been developed especially for the disadvantaged youngster. I think they can be added to the resources that we are thinking of here in this integrated, rounded, moon-shot type of program.

PEERS AS HELPERS

Another thing we can do is to develop helpers in the school itself, not only tutors and homework helpers from the outside. Lippett in Detroit used sixth-grade youngsters who were not doing terribly well, who were potential dropouts, to help for a half hour a week fourth-grade youngsters who were doing poorly. The phenomenal thing about this little study is that both groups improved as a result of it, not just the fourth graders receiving the help; the givers of help—the sixth-grade youngsters—improved in their work and their motivation as a result of playing the helper role. It is quite similar, you see, to Alcoholics Anonymous, where the alcoholic who is helping the other alcoholic may be getting better from giving the help; it is not only the receiver of help who benefits.

The need, as I see it, is for a very different kind of program in the school system. We are calling for new kinds of personnel, for new kinds of techniques, and for use of hiptionaries, for the use of role playing, games, Montessori kinds of approaches, dance techniques. *Scope Magazine* suggests a number of excellent ways of working with these youngsters. We must pull all of this together under the leadership of somebody who believes we can really aim for the moon, utilizing teachers who also believe this, but who are not necessarily long-experienced in the school system.

36. NOTES

1. From *Selected Poems by Langston Hughes* (New York: Knopf, 1959). Copyright 1959 by Langston Hughes.

37

Bonnie and Clyde Tactics in English Teaching*

ROGER W. SHUY

The decade of the 1930's will long be remembered for the Depression, the rise of the New Deal, and a mood which produced some of the more exciting gangsters of all time, including Bonnie and Clyde. Few need to be told that Bonnie and Clyde were noted for their fast eradication of those who stood between them and their various coveted goals. Although it may strain the analogy to refer to the Bonnie and Clyde syndrome in relationship to English teaching past or present, such a metaphor seems appropriate. One may argue, for example, that English teachers wipe out evil while Bonnie and Clyde eradicated without discrimination. Those who so argue either point bear the burden of proof. It is the eradication *per se* that concerns us here.

English teachers have long borne the secret guilt of overly negative evaluation. Most of the marks and comments on any given composition will support the assertion that English teachers are overly concerned about what is wrong with the universe, the student and the student's ability to write and think. We set about to note the negative aspects of a written composition, we correct oral language lapses, and we search for weaknesses in the formal properties of the debates and interpretations of our speech courses. The paucity of positive criticism is carried on even through graduate seminars in Shakespeare where term papers have been known to return with a lone grade and a number of corrections concerning style, mechanics, and punctuation.

Although it is customary for such long-nourished pedagogical traditions to be given frozen immortality, recently the English teacher's accent on the negative has been reexamined in connection with the description, analysis, and application of data about nonstandard English. In this paper I will describe several current approaches to the problem, suggest the motivations for and effects of changing the current system, and note some of the materials currently available.

CURRENT APPROACHES TO THE PROBLEM OF NONSTANDARD ENGLISH

1. Eradication

In an editorial in the *San Diego Union* (September 10, 1967), Dr. Max

Rafferty, Superintendent of Public Instruction for the State of California, strongly urged the return to a pedagogical strategy of teaching that right is right and wrong is wrong with regard to social varieties of American English:

"It is precisely education's job to deal in rights and wrongs. Because a child may count on his fingers and toes at home is no reason for his arithmetic teachers to let him keep doing it at school. And because a bigoted neighborhood may revel in racism doesn't make it okay for the civics instructor to neglect teaching the Bill of Rights to youngsters who call that neighborhood home.

"Neither does the fact that mom and pop say 'De cat ha just split' when they mean 'The man has just gone' make it right, any more than my Irish great-grand-father was permitted by his American teachers to go around voicing such Old Sod barbarisms as 'Shure and begorra, 'tis a foine spaleen ye are, bad cess to ye.'

"After his teachers had finished with him, great-granddad spoke good English, and he was thankful for it all his life. His parents went to their graves speaking brogue."

Although justifiable criticism may be made for selecting this particular representation of the position of those who possess what might be called the Bonnie and Clyde syndrome, it nonetheless establishes the position with pristine clarity.

A more scholarly position statement in support of eradication was made by Robert Green in reference to the more generally held sympathy toward biloquialism noted at the 1964 Conference on Social Dialects and Language Learning:

"It was further indicated that if a person has a dialect that is peculiar to a given area and moves to another area, we should not attempt to change the dialect since it is acceptable in other parts of the United States. I would say that this point of view is not necessarily a defensible one, and I would again present the argument stressed previously—that area dialects which allow one to be identified and discriminated against perhaps should be restructured . . . The very inadequate speech that is used in the home is also used in the neighborhood, in the play group, and in the classroom. Since these poor English language patterns are reconstructed constantly by the associations that these young people have, the school has to play a strong role in bringing about a change in order that these young people can communicate more adequately in our society."[1]

It is not surprising that two leading educators such as these men would adopt the Bonnie and Clyde syndrome with respect to the teaching of standard English to nonstandard speakers. The English teaching profession has long nourished such a position. Children are corrected in speech and writing from their earliest days in the classroom to the last rites of graduation. The anomaly of the situation is perhaps best seen in the report of Murray Wax in his observations of how English was being taught to the Pine Ridge Sioux Indians:

"Teachers are trained to criticize [the local dialect] as 'bad English,' and so, no sooner does the Indian child open his mouth to speak English, than he is branded publicly as speaking incorrectly."[2]

If it seems undesirable to produce predictable regional features such as those found among the Pine Ridge Sioux Indians, how much more undesirable it must be to produce socially identifiable features such as those found in ghetto communities. The great American assumption, it then follows, is to rid oneself of the stigma of those features by simply eradicating the features, a time-honored tradition in the English Departments of our country.

2. Biloquialism

A second position is easier to describe than to name. The term *functional bidialectalism* was suggested at the Conference on Social Dialects and Language Learning as a way of identifying a person's right to continue speaking the dialect of his home (which may be nonstandard) even after he has learned a school dialect (which may be standard). Since the term *dialect* seems to carry such a heavy pejorative connotation these days, other terms have been suggested in place of bidialectalism, including the recently coined term *biloquialism* and the term borrowed from the field of bilingual studies, *diglossia*. It is relatively safe to assume that both of the latter terms are more neutral than any term which involves the word *dialect*. Whatever it is called, most linguists will agree that a speaker of any language will make linguistic adjustments to specific social situations. These adjustments in phonology, grammar, and lexicon will range anywhere from the obvious adjustments between adults and small children to the more complicated sociolinguistic switching between school, home and playground talk. Those who encourage the adoption of biloquialism feel that the teacher's job is not to eradicate playground English—or any other kind. Instead, teachers should help children to make the switch comfortably from one setting to another.

3. Nonstandard for Standard Speakers

Recently a third position has received considerable attention. Although the topic has been discussed for several years now, I know few linguists who have publicly advocated that instead of offering standard English to nonstandard speakers, we should do exactly the opposite—present nonstandard to standard speakers. However, in his review of the *Roberts English Series,* Wayne A. O'Neil observes:

"Instead of 'enriching' the lives of urban children by plugging them into a 'second' dialect (if that enterprise is too 'enriching' (sic): why don't we let everyone in for the fun and games; 'enrich' the suburban kid with an urban dialect), we should be working to eradicate the language prejudice, the language mythology, that people grew into holding and believing. For there is clear evidence that the privileged use their false beliefs about language to the disadvantage of the deprived. One way to stop this is to change nonstandard dialect speakers at least for some of the time, i.e. when the nonstandards are in the presence of the standards, currying favor of them, jobs of them, etc. This seems to me intolerable if not impossible. Another response to language differences would be to educate (especially the people in power) for tolerance of differences, for an understanding of differences. This could be naturally done, easily done in elementary schools, but only by teachers who are themselves free of language prejudice. In many ways this is the more important kind of language study that needs to be accomplished in the schools."[3]

Those who share O'Neil's position will argue that a brutal frontal attack on the problem, such as the one advocated by those who encourage the development of biloquialism, will be fruitless. They argue that this is not simply another case of bonehead English, that a frontal attack will alienate nonstandard speakers from us and from education, and that indirection is likely to work better than a head-on attack since their language will change of itself as they are introduced to a wider and wider world. Furthermore, advocates of this position feel that it is as morally defensible to change the rest of the world as it is to change the linguistic behavior of the nonstandard speaker. These three positions, then, characterize current thought on the question of what to do about nonstandard English. A further position might be added in order to account for an even larger portion of the teachers of America—that of historic lethargy. One might opt for continuing to ignore the problem.

MOTIVATIONS FOR CHANGING THE CURRENT SITUATION

Before delving too deeply into the techniques of the approaches of eradication, biloquialism, or nonstandard for standard speakers, it may be wise to examine briefly the reasons most frequently listed for engaging in such behavior.

The eradicators, of course, carry the flag of unquestionable morality. Standard is better because it's nicer, but why it is nicer is never really explained. To accuse the people who hold this notion of ethnocentrism would be to involve the fierce wrath of the Mortimer Smiths of America on one's head. Smith, in fact, has recently observed:

"We can only hope that teachers of English, especially of the deprived, can resist the notion of linguistic equality. We hope, as we have said before in these pages, that teachers will continue to operate on the theory that education must seek to enlarge the horizon of the student, to improve and change and refine him, and to move him on to something better than he now knows."[4]

The eradicating Bonnies and Clydes of Smith's persuasion apparently feel that "enlarging the horizon of the student" means that he should forsake his old ways, his old culture for something vaguely represented as "refinement" and "something better than he now knows." That this runs counter to the natural flow of education and life experience in general seems not to have occurred to the editor of the *Bulletin* of the Council for Basic Education. At least it seems reasonable to assume that learning one thing does not necessarily require the eradication of another thing, even if they are diametrically opposed to each other. One can only hypothesize how eradication can be conceived as enlarging one's horizon, particularly in a free society.

The motivations of the advocates of the biloquial position are considerably more complicated and deserving of attention. I will mention two motivations relating to social goals and two relating to intellectual goals.

Social Goals

1. Upward Mobility. By far the most commonly stated reasons for teaching children to be biloquial is to enable them to ascend the social ladder. Whether this is viewed crassly or altruistically, it must be listed as the goal most frequently cited. Those who are critical of upward mobility as a goal of American education feel that our concern should be not with economic achievement but, instead, with expanding one's intellectual potential. It is difficult, of course, to disagree with this reasoning and there may be, in fact, no real reason to disagree with it. At least some of those who favor biloquialism do not consider upward mobility as mere social climbing. Instead, they mean to provide the learner with the linguistic tools with which he can operate synchronically on a number of social levels at one time. He can identify with and communicate comfortably to a wide spectrum of people. He can refrain from both talking down to and talking over the heads of his audiences. If such teaching is accompanied by condescension toward the lower socioeconomic groups and fawning toward the uppers, it is the practice which errs, not necessarily the philosophy. And this, of course, can be a serious problem. If the practitioners of biloquialism hold only a hollow regard for nonstandard and do not view it as a legitimate form of language which, like other legitimate forms, has boundaries of propriety and ludicrousness, they are not really advocates of biloquialism anyway. They are only masquerading Bonnies and Clydes.

2. Manipulation. With the healthy advent of black self-awareness and ethnocentrism comes a different possible goal for learning standard English—that of increasing one's ability to manipulate Whitey. The overtones of such a development range from the most extreme form of hatred of whites to the less excitable need for establishing an economic base within the black population. In some ways this goal is subject to the same criticism which we noted for those whose goal is upward social mobility. One can reasonably wonder whether the aim of English teaching is to help people become powerful every bit as much as we can wonder if it is to help people become financially secure. Yet certainly many teachers would agree that the black community needs to develop this power and ability to manipulate its environment. If biloquialism helps contribute to this goal, well and good. If it is used to foster hatred, however justifiable this may seem, again it is the practice, not necessarily the philosophy which needs to be repaired.

Intellectual Goals

1. Understanding the Language System. A relatively untapped but perfectly legitimate reason for encouraging biloquialism is that it can provide a convenient and interesting way to observe the systematic nature of language. Those who feel that learning can take place effectively by the use of contrast will want to seriously consider aspects of the contrast of systems between standard and nonstandard language. We can make no claim, in this case, for the use of such contrast merely to teach standard English, however much this might be true. A more likely outcome could be that students will learn something important about the systematicity of language, a fact which may be very helpful in building important understandings across social classes in both directions. And they just might learn something about how languages operate too. It seems reasonable to assume that studying the system of nonstandard English can lead to an appreciation of its speakers.

2. Observing Language Dynamics. If English teachers seriously believe that their subject matter is one of the most dynamic in the curriculum, they can be strengthened in their belief by observing language variation in process. It seems to be totally relevant to study the varieties of our contemporary language in relation to the current social scene. This can be done poorly—and probably will be by some. But if linguistic variety is approached as a means of developing self-awareness—what it is like, linguistically, to be thirteen years old rather than thirty-five or what it is like linguistically to be black rather than white, we may be on the verge of presenting the English language in its most meaningful and dynamic dimension.

The motivation for changing current pedagogy, then, differs considerably for the eradicators and the biloquial advocates. The former lean heavily on time-honored notions of rightness, giving little concern to cultural relativism or social pluralism. The advocates of biloquial education feel that it is their duty as educators to provide the learner with the alternatives to make his life what he wants it to be. If he chooses to cut cleanly with his past, he can do so by learning standard and eradicating nonstandard forever and ever. If he chooses to become fluent in both standard and nonstandard, he is given this option also. If the student's motives are selfish, the educator may be sorry about this, but he can do more about it than my former college literature teacher who worried herself sick over what might happen to us if our reading D. H. Lawrence would lead us to sexual promiscuity. Her worries were real and well motivated. But the decision of whether or not to offer D. H. Lawrence was really never hers. The course demanded it. Our education required it. Her duty as an educator was to offer the material and let us decide what to do with that knowledge. She had to provide us with that option. Our application of it, whether altruistic or selfish, whether we remembered it or forgot it immediately, was, in one sense, none of her business.

The motives of those who advocate presenting nonstandard to standard speakers are undoubtedly good. The reasons for the low esteem in which nonstandard English is held derive from mankind's lowest points. Snobbery, hatred, inequality, racism and jealousy are all likely candidates. There can be no question about the need for removing these aspects from human life, and there can be no doubt that we will continue to fail to do this. But there is no reason why we shouldn't try and I hold very great sympathy with the advocates of nonstandard for standard speakers in this respect. To be sure, we need to engage in a massive attack on the legitimacy of nonstandard English for and by itself. This might be done through the study of Black English grammar (once one is written) in the high schools, through the study of language variety and change (noted earlier) and, more likely for now, through an enlightened social studies program.

In order to do any of these things, however, linguists need to tell us a great deal more than we now know about nonstandard English—particularly that variety used by Negroes. If we are going to use English as a Second Language techniques for teaching standard to nonstandard speakers, educators need to tell us why we should use this method and exactly how to delineate the differences between learning a second dialect. From psychology we need to learn adult norms of standard English along with other aspects of the problem of motivation. From many disciplines (or perhaps from none) we need to learn how to direct men's hearts away from hatred, jealousy and greed.

CURRENT MATERIALS

A majority of the materials currently available for teaching standard English to nonstandard speakers rest on the uneasy assumption that TESOL techniques are valid for learning a second dialect. They do this without any solid proof. We do not have a viable evaluation tool at this time nor are we likely to get one until the linguists complete their analysis of the language system of nonstandard speakers. Most current materials deal with pronunciations although it has long been accepted that grammatical differences count more heavily toward social judgments than phonological or lexical differences.

It stands to reason that there is a hierarchy of importance in matters of teaching standard to nonstandard speakers, whether from the stance of biloquialism or Bonnie-and-Clydery. If grammatical matters count more heavily in social judgments, it seems reasonable to assume that grammatical matters should receive high priority in materials development. I know of only one set of oral language materials which has done this so far.[5] Most focus on pronunciations and few specify the nature of the problem beyond the usual list of aberrant features, Until a clear hierarchy of importance with respect to nonstandard features is established, however, it will be difficult to decide when a learner has reached the point at which no negative social judgment is made of his oral language (or to decide the point at which pursuit of standard forms buys him so little that it is not worth the effort).

An even more perplexing problem has to do with distinguishing between those features which black speakers wish to retain in order to be identified as black and those features which give them low social status. Contributing to our difficulty here is the unsettled state of things in general at this time. Ron Karenga, for example, has argued that black people need to become socially distinct as a basis on which to function politically and economically with unity. In order to do this he advocates a cultural revolution which involves developing a mythology, a historical tradition (with new heroes and new holidays), the restoration of emasculated black males, the development of new political and economic organizations, and an education, art, literature, and music which will create and support a black ethos. At his center for instruction in Los Angeles, Karenga also encourages black people to learn an African language, Swahili, to tie language to the cultural revolution. Although it is quite perceptive to recognize that language is an extremely important part of developing black ethnocentrism, three things might be said of Karenga's choice of Swahili. First, it is quite unlikely that Swahili was an ancestral language of very many of the black people of America. It is an East African langauge and most slaves were uprooted from West Africa where other languages, such as Hausa and Yoruba, were spoken. Second, one may legitimately wonder whether Karenga is not making his job harder than it need be by going back to Africa to resolve the language question. Third, it is unlikely that blacks will be any more successful in teaching Afro-Americans to speak Swahili than are our high schools in teaching Euro-Americans to speak French, German or Spanish.

Certain distinctive characteristics of contemporary Negro speech may well suffice to serve the same purpose. At this point, this is only a hypothesis, of course, but could it be that two or three phonological features such as the final consonant cluster reduction and the devoicing of the final voiced stop consonants /b/, /d/, and /g/, will suffice to provide this black identity? A major difficulty with such a suggestion is that phonological features are not very high in the threshold of speaker awareness. These features, for example, are often the last remnants of nonstandard Negro speech primarily because the speaker is not aware that they so identify him. Indeed, it might be easier to select grammatical features which Negroes can use to satisfy their black consciousness since it would be easier to restructure conscious indices than to make unconscious ones conscious. At this point, one can most sensibly observe that the topic bears further investigation.

It would appear that the three positions described in this paper (the Bonnies and Clydes, the biloquialists, and the advocates of nonstandard for standard speakers) are not necessarily in mutual opposition. As in politics, it is frequently difficult to tell the Republicans from the Democrats. There are eradicators who claim to be biloquialists and biloquialists who sympathize to standard speakers. The latter two positions have more in common, however, than either of them with the eradicators.

It is difficult to tell exactly what the most efficient procedure will be from here on, but it seems clear that all English teachers should concern themselves with the following questions:

1. Is what I am teaching about the English language the most important thing that my students can study at this time?

2. Is my English language teaching completely unbigoted?

3. Am I honoring my obligation as an English language teacher to provide the most useful alternatives or options for my students' self-fulfillment (not just job opportunities)?

4. Is my English language teaching utilizing the most dynamic and timely principles and data for undertaking the system of language?

5. Am I taking every advantage of the opportunities in my English language class to develop healthy attitudes toward social justice, brotherhood, and human rights?

If the answers to any one of these questions is no, we had better reexamine our motives for being where we are and for doing what we are doing.

37 NOTES

1. Robert Green, "Dialect Sampling and Language Values," in R. Shuy (ed.), *Social Dialects and Language Learning* (NCTE, 1965), pp. 122-23.

2. Murray Wax, Rosalie Wax, and Robert Dumont, "Formal Education in an American Indian Community," *Social Problems,* Spring 1969, p. 82.

3. Wayne A. O'Neil, "Paul Roberts' Rules of Order: The Misuses of Linguistics in the Classroom," *The Urban Review* II, No. 7.

4. Mortimer Smith, "The New English," *Bulletin of the Council for Basic Education* 13, No. 1 (September 1968), p. 4.

5. These materials were developed as part of the Sociolinguistics Program at the Center For Applied Linguistics under funding from the Carnegie Corporation of New York. The author, Irwin Feigenbaum, developed these materials in the Washington, D.C., schools over a period of two years. They will be published under the title *English Now.*

38

Upward Bound Accomplishments*

THOMAS A. BILLINGS

Upward Bound came into existence as a national program for disadvantaged high school youth in the summer of 1965. Pilot programs were funded on eighteen college and university campuses, involving approximately 2,000 high school students from America's rural and urban slums. The assumption undergirding the programs was this: There are many bright youngsters born into America's poor families. These youngsters, though generally underachievers in high schools, are bright and promising nonetheless and, if given hope and a program of enrichment and remediation, will demonstrate that promise in academic motivation and achievement. Upward Bound was one of many experimental programs designed to test the effectiveness of "higher education" as a way out of poverty for American youth. Before launching there were questions:

1. Could the youngsters be recruited? Would they be interested in the program?

2. Would American colleges and universities open their great resources to poor youngsters in America?

3. If the programs were successful in preparing disadvantaged youngsters for college, would college and university admissions officers, trustees, and faculties admit them when they knocked at the college gate?

4. Would a poor youngster find financial support for his college education after Upward Bound left him in the registrar's office?

5. Could poor youngsters survive the academic firing-line, once removed from the protective cover of a national program of support and enrichment?

A dramatic "yes" to the first two questions came from the eighteen pilot projects: the kids could be recruited and the colleges would open their rusty old treasure chests. Sufficiently encouraged by the pilot projects, Sargent Shriver, then director of OEO, decided to fund Upward Bound as a national emphasis program in the summer of 1966, increasing the number of programs from eighteen to 220 and the number of students from 2,000 to 20,000. (A conservative estimate of the pool of such youngsters is 600,000, of whom less than 8 percent normally go to college.) College professors, perhaps for the first time in the history of American education, worked closely with high school teachers at a task that both colleges and high schools had generally ignored or avoided.

Though Upward Bound's first large graduating class entered college as regular freshmen in September 1967, early returns from the few who entered in fall 1965 and fall 1966 are encouraging. The data are these:

Pilot Programs–1965, 80 percent admitted; 1966, 78 percent admitted; 1967, 83.1 percent admitted.

Casualty Rate–1965, 12 percent dropout, freshman year; 21 percent, sophomore year. (Overall, 67 percent retention.) 1966, 13 percent dropout, freshman year; 18 percent dropout, sophomore year. (Overall, 69 percent retention). 1967, 8 percent dropout after first semester (based on 40 percent sample).

These data suggest that Upward Bound graduates remain in college at about the same rate as all other college students. They answer the third question affirmatively: College and university admissions officers will admit the kids. There are now approximately 10,000 Upward Bound graduates enrolled in colleges and universities. In almost every case the institution has waived its traditional entrance requirements to "take a chance" with a youngster whose performance record prior to Upward Bound would automatically have denied him admission.

Not only have colleges been willing to admit youngsters, they have developed financial packages which provide for at least minimal support for the youngsters admitted to their institutions. Many colleges have taken an important additional step: they have developed a system of tutoring and counseling supports for the Upward Bound freshman, cushioning as best they can his transition from the ghetto and the protection of the Upward Bound program into the often cold, impersonal academic world. These support systems are as varied as the campuses which develop them. But they all serve the same purpose: they would maximize the poor kids' likelihood of "success" as success is historically measured on college campuses.

In gross terms, all five of our original questions have been answered affirmatively. And the assumption regarding the potential of poor kids seems to be valid. The youngsters are there, they are bright, and given a modest stake in the nation's mental, spiritual, and financial bounty, they will demonstrate their potential both academically and socially.

So much for the record of numerical achievement. Though many of us don't want to believe it, such a record may be irrelevant. If the alienation of American youth is as pervasive as it sometimes seems, a program for the preparation of youth for college may be an exercise in futility. If the establishment is as corrupt as the New Left and the flower children tell us it is, the college, as an integral part of that establishment, is the last place we should encourage our young to enter. But as a product of the American system of education, I am neither convinced by the system nor by the critics of the system that it is in need of anything more than openness—to be made honestly open and responsive to every American youngster who wants to enter. That it has not been open, that it has been the exclusive property of the well-off and the advantaged, that it denies its resources and its concern to poor families, is simply a fact. Our system of education, i.e. our schools, even at the lower levels, has been the property and the birthright of the American white middle class. Only rarely did that system of education, those schools, become available to the nation's poor—paradoxically, the very segment of our population in greatest need of sound education. Our colleges and universities have, to quote my predecessor, "made a name for themselves by the number of people they reject."

Beyond getting x number of poor kids out of poverty by way of higher education, Upward Bound has set for itself two other goals: (1) opening American colleges and universities to bright poor youngsters, and (2) making the American high school more responsive to the needs of the child of the inner city, the child of the reservation, the child of white Appalachia, the black child of rural Alabama and Mississippi and Georgia and Southern Ohio and Florida.

That we have been successful in opening the colleges and universities to a modest but significant number of poor youngsters is a matter of record. Given a yearly increase in the number of youngsters graduating from Upward Bound, and given a reasonable retention rate among our early graduates, I am confident that the unrealistic admissions requirements of American colleges and universities will change markedly in the next decade, followed by marked changes in course offerings, teaching methods, and academic purposes. We just might get ourselves a democracy yet!

Whether the presence of Upward Bound students and teachers in American high schools has caused any significant changes at that level is difficult to assess. Our strategy to accomplish change in the high school has been to require that one-third of our Upward Bound staff be drawn from the service high schools, and that youngsters who are recruited be drawn as a "cluster" rather than as singles from service high schools. This is consistent with the ancient maxim that there is safety, hence power, in numbers.

Whether our strategy has inched us toward our goals, whether the vast system of secondary education is even aware of our presence, except in isolated cases, is a moot question. Twenty-six thousand youngsters may not cause much of a ripple in a sea of millions. It may be that the secondary schools are so inundated by the incredible demands placed upon them by state legislatures that they simply cannot respond any more effectively than they do to poor youngsters. As a former high school teacher, I recall all too clearly how staggering were the tasks assigned to me by the Board of Education. Had somebody come around to ask my why I wasn't more sensitive to the needs of poor youngsters, I would have belted him one. I am confident that American high schools do not suffer a lack of sensitivity but a lack of resources—political, financial, and (perhaps) intellectual.

If the recommended escalation of Upward Bound to 100,000 students is honored by Congress, the ripple effect of that number on American high schools might well be significant. I can foresee a few of these effects.

(1) The most effective young teachers might compete for assignments in the schools serving hard-core poverty youth.

(2) The textbooks which have been generally irrelevant for the past fifty years might be abandoned for more productive approaches to learning.

(3) Communities might rearrange the deployment of their resources and give the education of all children top priority.

(4) Schools might become general community resources open to rich and poor alike.

(5) The apprentice and journeyman systems of American business and labor might be pervasively rooted in the high school so that job training would commence early in the high school years, with a supporting curriculum developed accordingly.

(6) Employment offices might become one of the major components of the high school operation and the excellence of the high school might be determined by its job or college preparation and placement. Just as Upward Bound project directors are expected to negotiate their graduates into colleges and universities, why can't we hold high schools responsible for "brokering" their youngsters into appropriate employment or higher education after graduation?

If OEO survives the overwhelming conservatism of the 90th Congress, and Upward Bound is allowed to grow with reasonable speed, it may serve as a catalyst for a dozen long-due changes in our system of education. In two years we have made a good beginning, but it is only a beginning. And we are not without our critics. So far the program has survived and has been strengthened by the criticism.

I am asked repeatedly if this big national laboratory has yielded any insights or generalizations which might be helpful to educators at all levels. I am asked if all projects are equally good or if they vary in quality, and if so, what accounts for the variation; in short, I am asked what makes a "good" project—meaning high student morale, vigorous academic thrust, close and open staff-student relationships, a low attrition rate, a high college placement rate. Those are the external signs of a "good" project. In attempting to identify the factors which define a "good" program, the staff has generally agreed that it has:

1: An intense emotional center, usually the project director, which develops around itself a program warmth and involvement that enlists and nurtures the emotional life of staff and students alike. Programs which lack an intense emotional center are "flat" programs, generally unable to involve the youngsters more than superficially, hence unable to accomplish any of the other academic and social goals of the program. If poor youngsters have anything they have acute emotional radar, an acute sensitivity to sham, pretense, phoniness, hypocrisy. For one reason or another, our best programs have at their center a person or persons who have passed the emotional inspection of 50 to 100 kids and have not been found wanting.

Our best programs have this intense emotional center, however else they differ. The emotional center is primary.

2. A second necessary characteristic of a good program is involvement of the youngster's family and neighborhood in the project. Programs which remain aloof and remote from the families of their students are consistently less successful than those programs in which families and neighborhoods are pervasively involved.

3. Novel approaches to a subject are more important to a project's success than novel subjects. Certainly all subjects should stand the test of relevance, but the pedagogical approach may determine a subject's relevance. My favorite example of traditional subject matter approached uniquely is the teaching of United States history with folk ballad and twelve-string guitar rather than with chalk and textbook. The youngsters were taught history episodically via the ballad rather than chronologically via textbook. They seized upon an episode in history in which they were interested, "researched" it, wrote the lyrics for a ballad about the episode, and their instructor put those lyrics to music. The folk have always approached history this way; it's just that we pedants won't recognize the mode in which folk history is written. And shame on us! It may well be a more valid record of human events and achievements and agonies that the generally color-blind, deaf and dumb stick-horse accounts which fill our dusty libraries.

I recall watching an amazing Upward Bound class at the University of California in Berkeley in which the instructor was teaching twenty black kids from Oakland "probability theory" by converting his classroom into a simulated Las Vegas gambling casino. The subject matter was traditional but the approach was novel—and relevant. The kids learned more about mathematics in that class in six weeks than they had learned in the seventeen years which preceeded it.

4. A last (though really the first) characteristic of a good program is structure and purpose. A program may be as casually structured as the Mississippi River, but who will argue that the Mississippi is unstructured or that it lacks purpose? A good Upward Bound program has something of the same casualness, some of the same twists and turns, some of the same artless grace as the Mississippi River. And just as the river knows its limits and knows its destiny, so a good project knows its limits and its destiny. The little stream that emptied into the great river in Missouri is not the same stream when it moves past the delta and hurries on toward the sea.